D1269449

CONTEMPORARY HARMONY

CONTEMPORARY HARMONY

Romanticism through the Twelve-Tone Row

By LUDMILA ULEHLA

THE FREE PRESS, NEW YORK
Collier-Macmillan Limited, London

A DIVISION OF THE MACMILLAN COMPANY

Printed in the United States of America

Collier-Macmillan Canada, Ltd., Toronto, Ontario

Library of Congress Catalog Card Number: 66-10391

FIRST PRINTING

CONTENTS

Preface

The understanding of the musical techniques of composition can not be reduced to a handbook of simplified rules. Music is complex and ever changing. Combinations of sound that are undesirable to one period become an idiomatic expression of another, spearheaded by the writings of a new group of composers.

It is the purpose of this book to trace the path of musical growth from the late Romantic period to the serial techniques of the contemporary composer. This is not a review of musical history however. Through the detailed analysis of the musical characteristics that dominate a specific style of writing, a graduated plan is organized and presented here in the form of explanations and exercises.

The exercises within each chapter pertain specifically to the material presented and do not demand a talent in creative composition. The theoretical practice of building chords and applying them to given bass and melodic lines is a familiar procedure, here adapted to the Impressionistic and Modern periods. A new analytical method substitutes for the diatonic figured bass and makes exercises and the analysis of non-diatonic literature more manageable.

The explanations describing each technique are thorough. They are designed to help the teacher and the student see the many extenuating circumstances that affect a particular analytical decision. Complex situations are deliberately brought forth so as to provide a background for the necessary reasoning that must be applied to all modern analysis. Conclusions, in many cases, must remain flexible. Composers do not write stereotyped compositions. More important than a dogmatic decision on a particular key center or a root tone, for example, is the understanding of why such an undeterminate condition may exist. In this respect, the given exercises may seem easier than the explanations. The student must receive a solid firsthand experience with each technique to appreciate the subtlety and artistry with which the composer molds his ideas.

In using the book, the teacher may find it helpful to work with the examples that are used for the explanations. The direct contact of playing or hearing the music simultaneously with the explanation is worth two dozen words and an equal number of lengthy sentences. With such classroom explanations, the student may then review the material. The numerous assignments in analysis always contain a complete musical thought of two or more phrases in order to provide a more meaningful application of the specific material for discussion. Direct questions pertaining to each composition pinpoint the areas of musical interest. For further reference, and supplementary discussion, a list of compositions using appropriate materials is included in each chapter.

This book may be of value to all musicians or to persons with a musical background who wish to have at hand an organized approach to the specific practices which link chromatic harmony to the present-day techniques. It is necessary to be familiar with some basic diatonic and chromatic terminology, but it is not necessary to remember or worry about the "rules" that formerly seemed to occupy theoretical texts. Through the explanations in this book, enough review material is presented to start a plan of study from the Romantic period to the present. Assignments in analysis contain direct questions so that the essential areas of the composition are focused upon, and the student does not aimlessly miss the point. The exercises can be fun to do, as their mission is to complete the given materials into a musical result. They offer many good solutions. You can be the judge as to whether your result sounds well, or sounds appropriate to the particular lesson.

In the listing of examples from literature, and in references for further study, the author has considered the availability of the compositions, both in the form of recordings and in printed music. The examples illustrate a particular point of study and do not reflect any judgement or preference on the author's part. It would be impossible to mention the hundreds of fine compositions that are performed and established. It is my hope that students will seek new literature, and in their research will find useful some of the subject matter set forth within these pages.

In conclusion, I would like to extend my warmest thanks to all of my colleagues at the Manhattan School of Music who have encouraged me in writing this book.

PART I

Musical influences present in 1900

The techniques of contemporary harmony have evolved gradually from the musical expansion of the late nineteenth century. Chromaticism influenced melody, expanded the scope of tonal modulation and kept stretching the harmonic boundaries until they exploded with *Le Sacre du Printemps* by Stravinsky. The writing of today is not divorced from the nineteenth century; in fact, it carries on the growth which started at the beginning of musical time. It is a cumulative result of varying influences, affecting each composer in a slightly different way. The individual characteristics of a composer do not remain his sole property, but become absorbed by the next generation. Each musical step forward is accompanied by a renewal of some traditional forces. Romanticism provided the composers of the early twentieth century with a knowledge of chordal growth, but it was left up to them to use this knowledge in new creative ways. One of those changes affected the motive and phrase structure of melodies. It is with this regard that the contemporary techniques of phrasing will first be linked to practices that were developing through the Romantic period.

1 Rhythmic and melodic structure

Decline of symmetrical motives

A new attitude of rhythmical design began to take shape in the melodies of Brahms and Wagner. Today's concept of elastic, irregular rhythmic lengths is strongly influenced by the subtle departure from the powerful symmetrical shapes found in these composers' works. One could find, in the sixteenth century, the same irregular rhythmic interest. However, the Classical period intervened. The gradual breakdown of the symmetrical melody and the rise of increased rhythmical complexity can be approached through the writings of some late Romanticists.

The symmetrical design of Classical melodies is felt in rhythmic units divisible by two. Most phrases are of a four-bar length. This breaks down in the middle, to a motive of two bars, and a two-bar continuation. Or, the phrase may start with a one-bar motive, followed by some form of repetition or modification and the customary two-bar development to a cadence, complete or incomplete. This can be seen graphically in the following way:

Motivic divisions within a four-bar phrase:

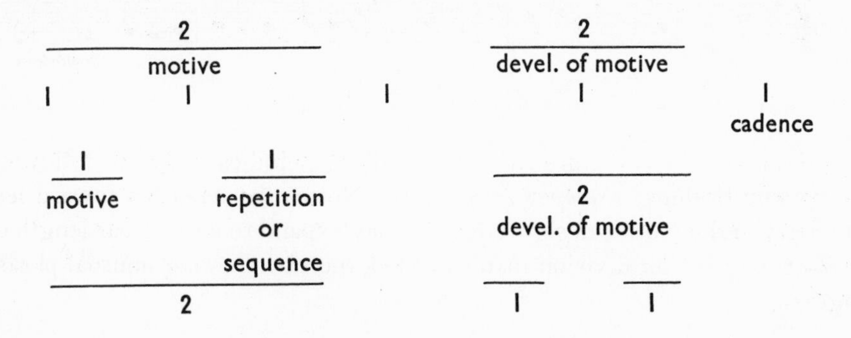

Neither the phrase nor the motive length is confined to a notational setting of one or two bars. Various tempi can prompt a composer to set the phrase into eight or more measures. Even a two-measure phrase is possible in a very slow tempo. In hearing a phrase, the listener is guided by the recognition of a motive and its continuation toward the cadential pause. The visible shape is only a matter of convenience to the composer and performer. The symmetrical motivic divisions within the four-bar phrase can therefore be expanded or reduced in equal ratio. Extensions to the Classical phrase are also generally of two-bar length.

The following melodies, taken at random from both the Classical and Romantic periods, illustrate the above common phrase constructions. See *examples 1a, b,* and *c.*

Compare the structure of the preceding melodies with the following excerpts by Brahms: *examples 2a, b,* and *c.* Notice the tendency toward less symmetry in the motive design. Motives may expand to a three-bar length or contract to a shorter division than expected, thereby creating unusual phrase lengths.

The irregular motivic lengths can be frequently traced to an extension of a rhythmic figure within the motive. (The term, figure, is defined as the smallest succession of tones grouped rhythmically together, which form a nucleus for further expansion.) In *example 2a*, an excerpt from the "Andante" of Brahms' *Third Symphony*, the irregular motivic result is caused by the repetition and sequence of the triplet figure in measure four. This development of the triplet figure lengthens the second half of the phrase and is heard as the irregular response to the singular use of the triplet figure in the first motive.

An expansion caused by an active harmonic progression is recognized in *example 2b*. The unexpected E chord in the fourth measure propels the motive onward to rest on the subdominant F. It gives the effect of an evaded progression, but is not intended as a candential phrase extension. It provides irregular motive treatment within the phrase.

In the third measure of *example 2c*, Brahms begins the second half of the phrase by modifying rhythmically the previous motive. The essential descending pitches of F♯ to B are maintained but disguised within neighbouring eighth notes. As this measure unfolds within the theme, the listener is aware of the expansion given to the first motive, as well as to the new rhythmic design which carries the melody on toward another motive, in measure four. Such overlapping of motives creates an elasticity within the phrase which removes the strong rhythmic symmetry common to the early Classical period.

The following melodies of more recent vintage develop the small figures into irregular divisions within the phrase. The opening motive of the Prokofiev *Fifth Symphony*, *example 3a*, is also aided by a prolonged tonic background within the three-bar division.

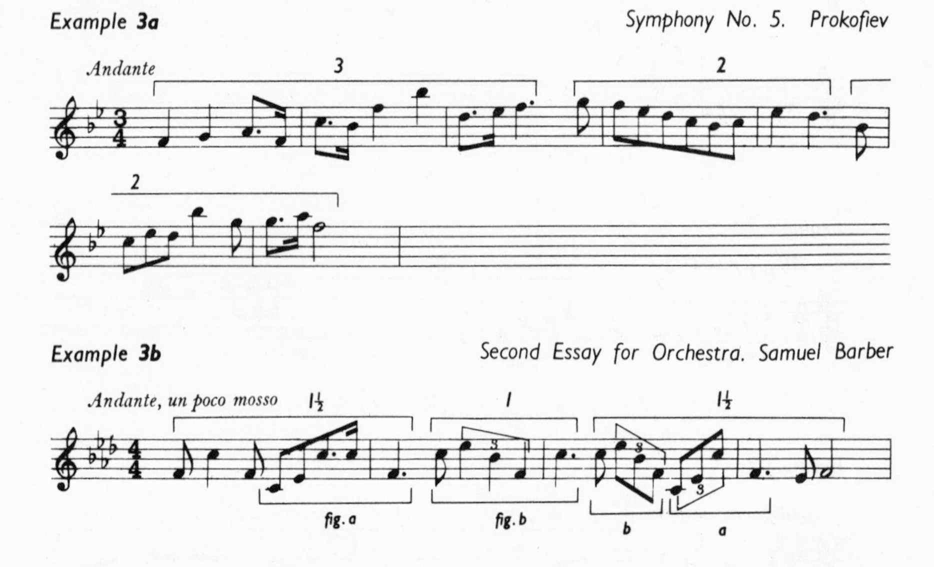

In *example 3b*, Samuel Barber begins with a theme which consists of very few tones, expanded by many different rhythmical groups. From the first motive, one may extract the group of tones called Figure a, so as to identify their return in the latter part of the third measure. Likewise, Figure b is extracted from the continuing second motive. These melodic fragments are combined at the conclusion of the phrase, having spun an interesting irregular motivic design within a normal four-bar phrase.

Shostakovich, in his Symphony No. 10, gave the clarinet a broad, lyrical theme, against which the violins play a counter melody (see *example 3c*). The smooth continuity of both melodies is enhanced by an overlapping of motives and phrases. As the clarinet reaches the end of the motive in the fourth measure, the violins move forward giving a subtle emphasis to their melodic contour.

Notice how the normal pause, expected in the eighth measure, is avoided. The clarinet phrasing clearly shows the desire for an unbroken line. Given a tonic tone at that point, the phrase might very easily come to a close, merely by a poor interpretation! As it stands, the violin counterpoint aids the fluency of the phrase by sounding a new harmonic tone. Together, both melodies develop

the simple rhythms, and conclude this long phrase by a simultaneous start of the beginning motive, this time given to the strings. The melodic expansions, sometimes created by sequential figures, as in measures ten and eleven and at other times, by the rhythmically expanded tones, form an uninterrupted phrase. Even as it concludes, the harmonic material does not forecast the cadence. Only the cessation of the clarinet on the tonic chord, and the recognized return of the main motive in measure 16 indicates that the next phrase is in progress.

Meter changes

So far, we have discussed motive development within an unchanging meter. Again, one can go back to Brahms' melodies and find the beginnings of the modern use of the flexible bar line. Brahms used two methods of notating the irregular melodic groupings that characterize so much of his music. The same choice of notation applies today, described as follows:

If a motive no longer fits the rhythmic stresses of the predominant meter of a composition, (1) the meter might nevertheless be retained, providing the new irregular motivic length is so clearly phrased as to negate the normal stress given to the unwanted downbeat; or (2) the measures may be lengthened or shortened by metric change so as to accommodate the differing stressed pulses.

The first method is more appropriate if within the next few measures there is a return to the original form of rhythmic stress. However, if an irregular grouping of downbeats persists, it is simpler to change the meter as necessary.

In selecting the proper method of notation, consideration must also be given to the effect of syncopation. Syncopation is the result of accenting the weaker beats in a measure while not entirely eliminating the stress demanded by the downbeats. This effect can be desirable or undesirable depending on the composer's intentions. Compare *example* 4a and 4b. The $\frac{4}{4}$ meter with its inherent stress on the first beat is maintained in *example* 4a, notwithstanding the irregular and varying length of the motive. The feeling of syncopation is present as the accented fourth beats are followed by the normal weight of the first beats. *Example* 4b contains no syncopation. The irregularly placed downbeats are the sole source of rhythmic accent.

Example 4a

Example 4b

The harmonic background of a melody plays an important role in both methods of notation. *Example* 4c illustrates an appropriate harmonization for the melody as notated in *example* 4a. The syncopation is emphasized by the fourth beat accent in the first measure, and by the return to the tonic chord on the next downbeat. The normal pulse of a $\frac{4}{4}$ meter is retained within the entire phrase. If meter changes are used, the harmonic rhythm* must accurately

* rhythm resulting from the movement of chords

support the meters involved. *Example* 4d illustrates a modern approach in which the selected dissonances of the left hand strengthen all of the accented downbeats, thereby showing a convincing need for the metric changes. This harmonic background is so thoroughly allied to the motives of the melody that it also may be notated as seen in *example* 4e, without causing any unwanted syncopation. This latter method is generally employed only when the background rhythm is steady, so that accents can completely control the desired metric feeling. Notation via meter changes is so explicit that accents are not necessary, and if indicated, they merely reinforce the changing downbeats.

In *example* 5, the codetta to the *Capriccio*, Op. 76, No. 5 by Brahms, the meter is felt in $\frac{5}{8}$ but not labeled that way because it evens itself out at the ending. Brahms chose to indicate his irregular feeling by notating the eighth note groupings over the bar line, thus avoiding syncopation. For a better understanding of these particular motives, analyze and listen to the entire piece, so that the effectiveness of the rhythmic contraction from the opening meter of $\frac{6}{8}$ to the implied $\frac{5}{8}$ of the *codetta* can really be felt. It is a sudden burst of movement, rushing toward a tumultuous end.

In the song entitled *Sapphische Ode*, *example* 6, Brahms develops motives and figures into an interesting blend of irregular length phrases in which meter changes play an important role. After one measure of introduction, the phrase begins with the song's melody, and cadences quite completely in the third bar of the phrase (measure four). This phrase does not divide readily into motives or figures because the continuous movement of quarter notes provides no pause or break in the pattern until the cadence is reached. It can be explained as an extended use of a motive, forming nevertheless, an abbreviated phrase. A prolongation of the tonic chord helps to expand the melodic material within the phrase, thus preventing a rhythmic demand for symmetrical harmonic changes. (This is similar to the Prokofiev theme, *example 3a.*)

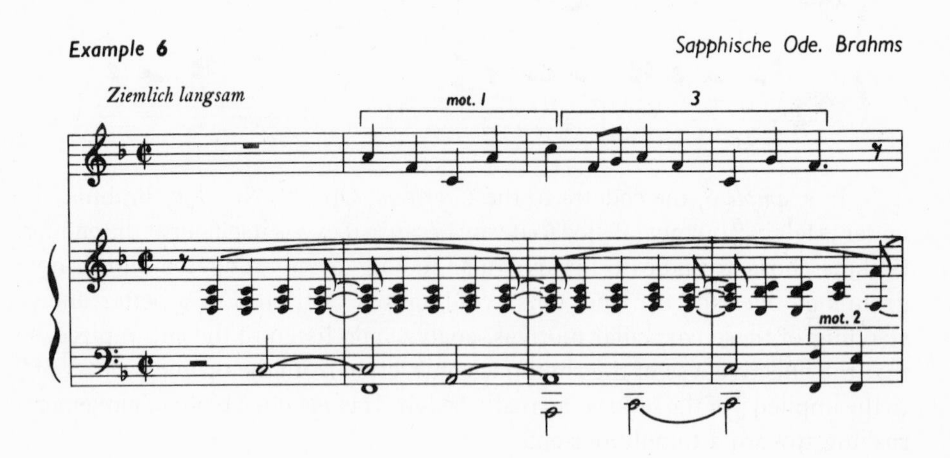

The second phrase, beginning in measure five, announces two distinct melodic ideas which can be separately identified with the terms Motive and Figure. Again, the total three-bar length of the phrase suggests the hearing of an expanded motive. The melodic material that begins the second phrase contains the rhythmical continuity drawn from the first phrase. The descending scale contrasts the earlier arpeggio motive, and with that in mind, may be called Motive 2 although it is an outgrowth of the first motive. While the phrase begins with Motive 2 in the melody, it is actually anticipated at the cadence in the bass part. Within its normal melodic development, Motive 2 discloses an eighth-note pattern which will become significant as the song continues. This eighth-note group, occurring on the second and fourth beats of measure six, is linked with a neighbouring quarter beat, together occupying one-half of the bar. The term Figure applies to this portion of the Motive. It is incomplete as a thought, but can be identified because of its rhythmic individuality in this composition. It is the repetition of this Figure that extends the Motive into the three-bar phrase length. Positive reference to motives and figures is only worthwhile if their continued participation in the theme's structure is evident. Many rhythmical patterns come and go which do not contain a meaningful individuality, but merely connect the more essential thematic material. Looking back to the first phrase, this would be true of the eighth notes present in the second measure of the melody. These do not symbolize any particular characteristic of the theme, and although, technically, they may be termed a Figure, it would be foolhardy to enumerate such groups, which only bind a melody's shape.

From the beginning of the third phrase (measure eight), the elasticity of this melody becomes most apparent, as metric changes occur with each bar line up to the cadence. The first differing bar line setting is seen in the eighth bar itself. The accompaniment starts the sequence of Motive 2 on the downbeat, which is contrasting to the elision that took place at the cadence to the first phrase. Compare measures eight and four. Due to this imitation between the piano accompaniment and the voice, the rhythm of the phrase has shifted and necessitated the $\frac{3}{2}$ meter so that the figure of eighth notes would not be metrically distorted. After a return to the duple meter, which corresponds to the previous cadences, measure eleven portrays the flexible lyricism that expands phrases and nullifies the symmetrical demand of a beat. Specifically, the chromatic unrest of the accompaniment prevents a cadence in the tenth measure, and by continuing forth with the same rhythmical design, is able to delay a downbeat stress until desired. Against this chromatic extension, the melody tone, common to all three chords of the eleventh measure, swells as the pull of the harmony stretches it beyond its expected duration. It merges into Figure a (drawn from the second phrase) and gradually descends to close the phrase, and the theme of the song.

As seen in the above phrase, the harmonic rhythm is frequently responsible for the changing meters. The downbeat stresses can be controlled by spacing active harmonies within the measure, and selecting the more stable triads to supply the firmness demanded of the first beat of the measure. The rhythm formed by the contrasting selection of sounds may be as irregular (or as symmetrical) as the composer wishes, providing that some unity of motive and design is also present. The melody may provide the initial source for the metric changes, yet unless the harmonies are suitably combined, the result may sound all right but may look like an incorrectly notated score. The stronger and weaker stresses inherent in the harmonic movement dictate the placement of the bar lines, not the reverse.

Some composers have experimented in removing the bar line entirely, except for designating phrases. For the solo performer, it may present no obstacles as the music is first studied and then performed. For any kind of ensemble playing, this type of notation is impractical; not so much because of the problem of counting and maintaining a "togetherness", but because of the absence of clarity as to the points of stress in a phrase. A player, involved in an alto or inner part, would first have to hear and comprehend the movement of the outer voices before he could play his part intelligently. Musical pulse is affected by the correlated melodic and harmonic design, which provides a changing degree of stress to the pulsating beats. Not like the mechanics of a clock which is devoid of harmony, the pulse of a composition depends upon other forces which do not disappear with the omission of bar lines.

The melody in *example* 7a is contained within one phrase. The division of strong and weak beats is open to many solutions. Play the phrase several times and select different possible downbeats. To be convincing, each downbeat should contain a suggestion of harmonic change. Two solutions are given in *example* 7b and 7c. Both are different in their harmonic backgrounds as well as in the metric divisions, and yet, each sounds equally plausible. The actual composition is illustrated in *example* 7d, with no predetermined metric flexibility. The composer uses meter changes in order to accurately convey the stresses that he hears, and not as a gamble or as the result of the toss of a coin. The integral result is a union of melody, harmony and rhythm in a predestined course, creatively inspired.

Example 7d — *Song Without Words. Ludmila Ulehla*

EXERCISES

A *Analysis*

1] In *Example 8a*, *8b* and *Example 9* observe the metric changes. Discuss the reasons for the particular bar line placement. Are there any alternate bar line possibilities that would not sacrifice the rhythmic intent?

In these excerpts, trace the expansion of the first figure, and its growth into the phrase.

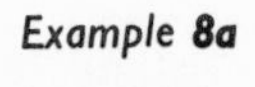

Example 8a — *Microkosmos No. 140. Béla Bartók*

sempre f
Example 8b
Béla Bartók
sf dim.
sf
etc.
Example 9
Concerto for Orchestra. Béla Bartók
p

2] Using brackets, mark motives in *Example 10* and trace their expansion or contraction. Observe the accompanying bass motive and discuss its rhythmic interplay with the flute solo.

Example 10 *Symphony No. 9, 2nd Movement. Shostakovich*

3] *Examples 11* and *12* were written by the composers without the inclusion of bar lines. Play and listen to each composition, selecting appropriate locations for each bar line. Give reasons for your choice. Indicate the necessary metric changes.

Example 11 *Concord Sonata. Charles Ives*

Example 12 *Danses de travers. Erik Satie*

Provide rhythm and a flexible meter for the following melody lines. Retain the motives as marked. Accompaniment is optional.

Example 13a

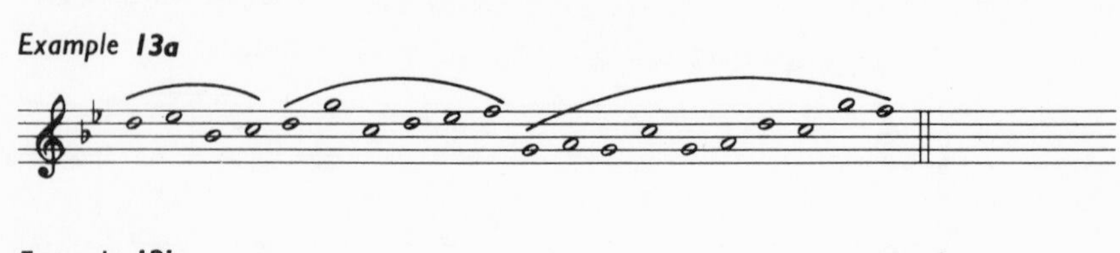

Example 13b

Example 13c

C Provide rhythm and meter to the following harmonic progressions. Add a melody. Complete the exercise by continuing the same idea in an original second phrase. See model.

Example 14a

Model:

Example 14b

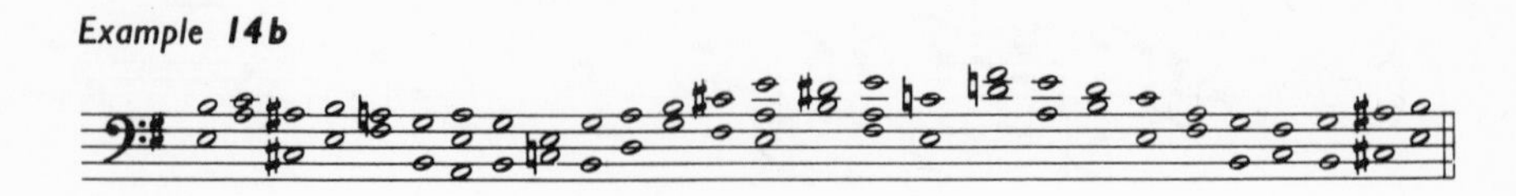

D Mark motives and figures in each of the following phrases. Rewrite the first measure of each phrase and continue by expanding the figures and motives into a longer, irregularly constructed phrase. Use repetition, sequence, and any rhythmical alteration to the motive that you find desirable.

Select some phrases for harmonization. A single bass line, as a contrapuntal melody, may be used to gain an overlapping effect of the motives, while a chordal idiom may provide some interesting harmonic extensions.

E Working with meter changes, expand the following motives into period forms or small ABA forms. Be free to use the melody in any way which seems appropriate to you for this more modern idiom.

Example 16c

For further listening with reference to meter changes and development of motives and figures, the following are cited:

Moussorgsky: "Promenade", from *Pictures at an Exposition*
Stravinsky: Music to Scene II and Scene III from *Histoire du Soldat*
Copland: *El Salon Mexico*

2 Intervallic unity

The study of Brahms' compositions is valuable from still another point of view. He gave increasing importance to the concept of motivic development through an adherence to the specific intervals that make up a motive. This results in an intervallic relationship as a means of unity and expansion for a composition. The Classical period, and most of the Romantic period also, relied on a rhythmic pulsation, or momentum within which the motives of the themes were developed. Rhythmic coherence was the backbone of the developmental material. The actual intervals of a motive changed, preserving enough of the contour and most of the original rhythm for a unifying recognition. Today, the intervals may completely bind the composition, as in a twelve-tone serial piece. In these instances, the rhythm is frequently disjointed, abandoning the traditional movement of basic pulsations. In its place is a thematic unity, made entirely of intervallic relationships.

Brahms retained a rhythmic continuity, but his preoccupation with an intervallic control is most notable. This is illustrated throughout the *Intermezzo* Op. 119, No. 3, excerpts from which are quoted in *examples 17a, b, c* and *d*. The motive of two and one-half bars is made up of a figure of four tones. Through rhythmic shifting, these tones grow, by repetition, into the irregular length motive. Following the initial statement of the main motive, a secondary motive begins in the latter part of the third measure. It retains the rhythmical patterns of Motive 1 but varies the intervals as in the normal Classical procedure. This may be called Motive 2, a one-bar pattern which extends sequentially. In measure six, a repetition of the last two tones of Motive 2 occurs and this gives rise to the thought that a separation of the motive into smaller figures will aid the analysis. The fragmentation of Motive 2 is seen first. One figure is contained in the three stepwise tones and another in the descending scalewise unit of the quarter and the eighth. The first motive may also be divided into two figures. The descending drop of a third, from G to E, receives a more independent role during the second part of the composition. In the beginning, however, it is entirely the result of the four-note nucleus, moving as if in a circle, eliding the fourth tone with the first of the figure. As illustrated, Motive 1 contains the four tones as Figure a, and Motive 2 will be separated into Figures b and c.

Example 17a *Brahms*

The first phrase expands by the sequential use applied to the figures. For example, Motive 2 is followed by two more direct sequences, but in measures six and eight, only Figure c is involved; first by repetition and in measure eight by a sequential change to the first tone. Measures seven and nine contain Motive 2, now rhythmically shifted to the downbeat. In the second half of the motive, the skip of the perfect fourth illustrates the Classical retention of rhythm but a change of interval in the motive. This particular treatment is utilized toward the end of the *Intermezzo,* but it does not demand another special analytical identity.

Rhythmic shifting occurs again in the twelfth measure when Figure c is altered to an eighth note followed by a quarter note. The accents are also syncopated. Notice that the phrase has finally come to a cadence in the middle of the eleventh bar; all of its material grew out of Motive 1.

Rhythmic alterations

Before discussing more of the analytical and musical interest crowded into this simple composition, the following specific methods of rhythmic alteration of a motive are listed:

1] Augmentation is the rhythmic lengthening of note values as applied to specific tones of a motive. If the tones C, D and E are first stated as quarter notes, and in an ensuing part of the composition are used as half notes, the process is one of augmentation.

2] Diminution is the rhythmic shortening of note values of specific tones. If the quarter notes C, D and E are later stated as eighth notes, the process is called diminution.

Both augmentation and diminution can be applied to a single tone of a motive, or to an entire phrase. Observe that in Motive 1 of the *Intermezzo* (*example 17a*), diminution occurred in the second measure as the original group of four tones ended with a quarter note, G. With the rhythmically displaced motive, the fourth tone, G, is given only an eighth note value, on the third eighth beat of measure two.

3] Expansion or extension applies to a free increase of motivic material and does not directly involve any specific rhythm. A motive, a phrase, a cadence or a chord may be extended by any melodic means convenient to the composer.

4] Contraction or fragmentation applies to a reduction of size of the motive or phrase. Something must be omitted if the material or phrase is to shrink. Again, no specific rhythm is involved.

Melodic alterations

1] Sequential extensions retain a motive's intervallic shape, but transplant the entire unit to another pitch. Slight modifications of rhythm or interval may not impair the basic pattern.

2] Inversion of motives occurs when the melodic contour reverses direction. An ascending group of tones, C, E, F, G, are inverted when their use is converted to a descending group, C, A, G, F. This may also start on sequential tones, as D, B, A, G.

3] Retrograde is the term used for a motive that unfolds its relationship to the first idea by using a right to left movement of pitch, or moving backwards, as it were. The original tones, C, E, F and G are in retrograde when used in the order, G, F, E and C. It is noticed only occassionally in music before the twelve-tone idiom.

The terms just defined are all techniques of the twelve-tone serialism, yet they appear in Brahms also. In fact, it is not fair to many composers of a much earlier date to suggest that Brahms "discovered" these. Not at all—these melodic developments have been used since composers first were conscious of balance in a composition. Brahms' creativity places a spotlight on these techniques as they contain a more deliberate purpose. It is not by accident that an augmentation or diminution is heard. In this way, it approximates the planning of the serial composition. One important difference must be emphasized, however: Brahms used these devices only where inspiration suggested a particular design; a tone-row work relies entirely on the various melodic organizations of the row or "theme" and does not deviate from them.

4] To make the melodic alterations complete, another technique may be mentioned, although it is very rare in works prior to the twelve-tone idiom. "Retrograde inversion" is the use of contrary motion, or the reverse direction of tones established as being in retrograde. This is really an artificial plan. It is not compatible with the free continuity of ideas that prompts the other melodic patterns.

Examples illustrating these techniques can be found in Brahms. In the *Intermezzo, example 17b*, observe the contraction occurring as the initial phrase of twelve bars is now reduced to four. Motive 1 is directly attached to the cadential syncopated Figure c. This is a phrase contraction. The next sequential phrase illustrates a motive contraction. Originally used as a two and one-half bar motive, it now starts normally in the fifth bar, but omits the last quarter- and eighth-note pattern. The motive has been contracted to two bars, and is followed by two additional one-bar sequential contractions. Paradoxically, the technique of contracting a motive may lead to an extension of the phrase. The added sequences lengthen the phrase, and in this case they keep stretching until the complete rise and fall of the melody is accomplished. Notice the return of the drop of the third, found in Motive 1. It is used as the focal point of the crescendo and of the development in this middle section of the piece. Subsiding in intensity, the rhythm of Figure a returns in measure thirteen, followed by a fragment in measure fifteen. Again, paradoxically, a contracted motive contains an augmentation of a tone. The figure is not complete. Instead, the third note, F, receives an exceptionally lengthy augmentation. This slackening of pace is not accidental; it ushers in a complete augmentation of Motive 1. The original eighth notes are now quarter notes. This produces an interesting point of form because the key and pitch of the motive return is symbolic of a Part

Three, or a return to "A". Nevertheless, the retarding feeling is still present, and suggests the rhythmic return four bars later. The augmentation produces a phrase which anticipates the real return and yet strangely is already in the tonic key. Such irregular treatments of form can also be thought of as outgrowths of the irregular phrase and motive concepts.

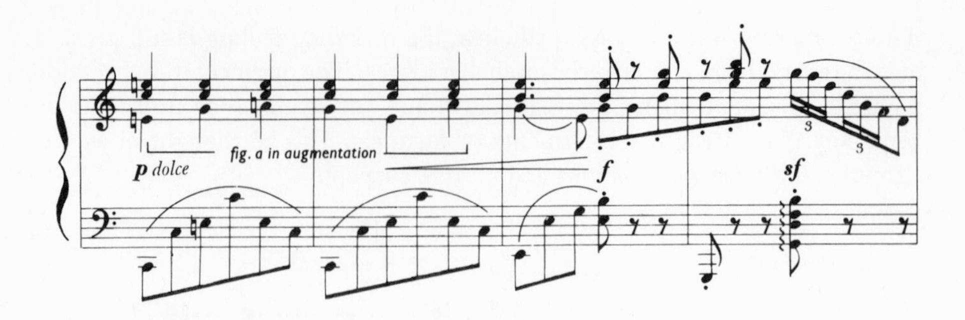

Diminution is seen in *example 17c*, another fragment of the *Intermezzo.* Sequences develop from the original seventh and eighth measures (transposed). In order to provide the final burst to the ascending line, the technique of diminution was applied to Figure c, together with the continuing rise of pitch. The quarter- and eighth-note figure was shortened to a pair of eighth notes and then extended by sequence.

Example 17c

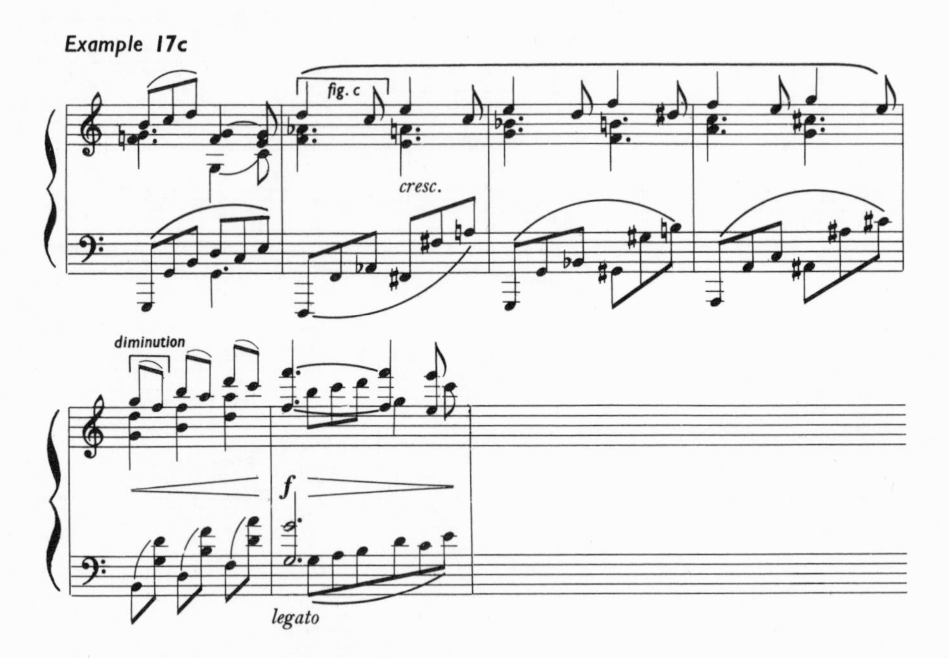

One final motivic reference to Figure a must be pointed out. The cadence, *example 17d*, includes the motive as part of a tonic extension. It retains the eighth note rhythm but augments the pitch. Two motives, which included three figures, and an entire *Intermezzo* was born!

After this type of extensive analysis, the question always arises: did Brahms think about all of this as he wrote it? The answer lies in a somewhat qualifying statement. He did not deliberately set out to invert the motive here,

Example 17d

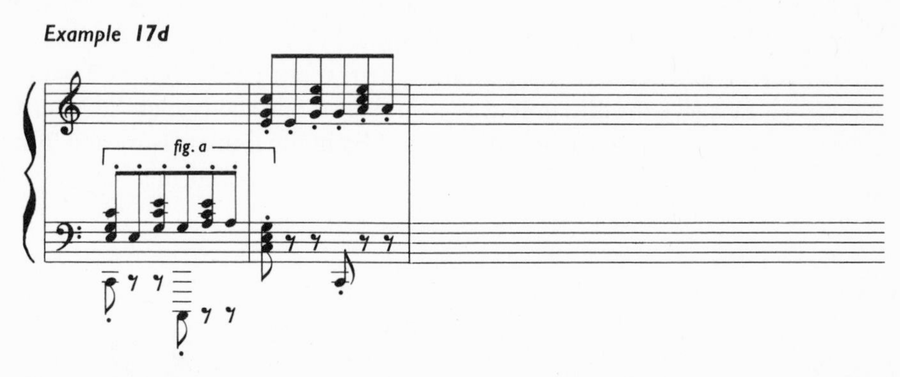

augment it there or incorporate it in a bass line counterpoint elsewhere. Nevertheless, he did think about it. The musical background of a composer subconsciously places all of these possibilities within his grasp. The spontaneous creative urge suggests a certain motivic response, which the composer freely molds to the needs of the composition as a whole, never as an artifice. The student may find it necessary to deliberately extend a motive by augmentation into an irregular phrase, or to experiment with meter changes, but this is the difference between a student's attempt to incorporate these ideas into an inseparable part of his knowledge and the composer's finished results.

The techniques of motive inversion have a long history and frequent implementation in the contrapuntal compositions of the seventeenth century. Bach, in his fugues, often inverted a subject, if that added to the musical interest. *Example 18* from "Fugue 15" of Vol. I of the *Well-Tempered Clavier* illustrates the subject and its inversion. In order to retain a tonic tonality, the diatonic inversion generally substitutes the fifth degree of the scale for the tonic. The change of direction then maintains the first triad relationship.

Example 18 Bach

Brahms pursued this means of motivic unity, within his greater homophonic texture, but did not necessarily retain the limiting harmonic choice of tone. Compare *example 19a* and *example 19b*, excerpts from a different *Intermezzo*, Op. 118, No. 2. An inversion of the main motive occurs in which the melody tone, D, is replaced by the third, F♯. This results in an adherence to the original subdominant harmony. While the exact inversion is used only for the two bars of the main motive, the continuing part of the phrase retains a balance of interval. Observe the alto imitation in measures one and two of the inverted phrase. It includes a diminution of the tone of F♯ in the first measure and forms a vertical, harmonic interval of the seventh in the second measure, as the imitation continues.

An instance of retrograde inversion may be pointed out at the cadence of the original phrase. It must be stressed, however, that this is undoubtedly a subconscious weaving of material. Had it been deliberate, the cadence to the inversion would have probably adhered to the plan. Compare the first figure with the last three melody tones of the first phrase of *example 19a*. Follow the transformations as illustrated in *19c*—(1) Think the sound of the first figure in retrograde; (2) Change the direction and you have a retrograde inversion; (3) Transpose this pattern, starting from F♯; (4) Augment the last two tones, and finally shift the rhythm. It must indeed be obvious that this plan was not concocted first and then made use of! It is merely a cadence that contains an expression of the motive and, by coincidence, can be proven by technical specifications.

Application of motivic contractions

The form of a composition, that is, the molding of the composer's ideas into an integral whole, generally consists of two basic functions: the statement of themes at their initial exposure, or, at a return; and the development or continuation of these ideas. Frequently, a misconception occurs with the premise that a development of themes only occurs in a Development Section of a sonata form. Actually, a development of motives takes place probably in the third measure (if not sooner) in all compositions, whether the final shape is a simple song or an involved rondo. Areas such as the middle parts, or "B" sections of ABA forms all contain motivic development. Some use it within transitions which lead to other themes. Other "B" sections are entirely made up of the development of the first and only theme. The specific devices of intervallic unity are generally apparent in these developing passages.

Specifically, the use of motive contraction, or fragmentation, plays an important role in this structural aspect of form. The reduction of size of either a motive or a phrase quickens the pace of the musical flow of sound. The shorter the size of the unit that we hear, the more of such smaller divisions are needed, thereby causing a fragmentation that can be reduced to a pair of eighth notes, as was noted in the C major *Intermezzo.* This increased motivic action must lead to some focal point. It may emphasize a melodic contour, or an intense harmonic cluster, or it may help to define the shape of the form by making noticeable the appearance of a new theme, or the approach of a cadence.

One of the most frequent occurrences of motivic contractions takes place in a crescendo passage in which the melody rises to a peak in an arch design, and then diminishes in volume as it curves downward. The A♭ major *Intermezzo* from Op. 76 contains this in the Part Two of its form (see *example 20a*).

Observe that the one-measure motive consists of a four-note figure which expands by repetition. After the sequence in the second measure, the contractions appear in measure three. The figure is isolated and is immediately sequenced, creating a melodic division of the measure into two half-bar groups. This is a sufficient acceleration of motive to aid the crescendo. Its peak occurs with an embellishing appoggiatura dominant ninth chord and subsides into the dominant ninth of the key, chromatically altered. The rise and fall of the melody has been accomplished within a five-bar phrase.

Accompanying the motive contractions, an acceleration of harmonic rhythm must also take place. This harmonic movement generally coincides with the divisions of the motive. While the sequences are of a whole bar duration, the harmonic bass movement uses first a root-position dominant seventh, followed by a third inversion in measures one and two. The contracted measure shows the increased movement in the bass pattern. The chord changes from root-position to first inversion of the B♭ minor seventh chord. The chromatic arrival on the embellishing dominant is then lengthened, and followed by the E♭ dominant of equal duration. The harmonic rhythm speeds up as it moves toward its goal, and slackens as it expands the climactic effect, gradually leading to the next section.

Motive contractions are not restricted to an ascending column of notes. They may move downward with an accompanying harmonic pace; they may appear contracted while the harmony remains stationary, and they also may function merely as reminders of a previously heard motive. The latter case is illustrated in the codetta to the same *Intermezzo, example 20b*. The first measure illustrates the cadence to the preceding Part Three. The codetta follows, starting identically with the middle section (Review *example 20a*). The second measure of the codetta expands the harmonic rhythm by a metric change, but this is not done solely for the lengthening harmonic effect. Notice the soprano motive. It is an augmentation of the cadence material, specifically the tenor parallel sixths. This places the triplet motive on to the latter part of the $\frac{3}{2}$ measure. The fragmentation of the motive follows, as the harmony retains its lengthened sound. The next to the last measure contains another such sequence, but the harmonic change resolves on the second beat, forming a cadence at that point. The triplet figure is then heard in a reminiscent role. Throughout the codetta, the harmonic changes grow more infrequent, expanding and retarding the musical pace. The melody incorporated both an augmentation of one motive, and a contraction of another.

A musical phrase is not limited to one focal point, or goal within its course. The melody may rise to a peak which does not coincide with a harmonic acceleration, arriving at the same goal. This may be illustrated by a comparison with *example 20a*. As already mentioned, the contracted motives ascend, and arrive at a melodic peak in the fourth measure, together with the harmonic arrival on an embellishing dominant ninth chord. Suppose the melody

Example 20b

reached its peak prior to the harmonic goal. *Example 20c* alters the Brahms phrase so as to show this overlapping technique. Such a phrase would be analyzed as containing a melodic goal, or peak, on the pitch of the high C, and followed by the harmonic impetus which extends one-half measure beyond this point. The melodic and harmonic focal points are not achieved simultaneously.

A phrase may have as its goal the return of a prior section or any phrase which specifically contributes to the form of the composition. This would

Example 20c

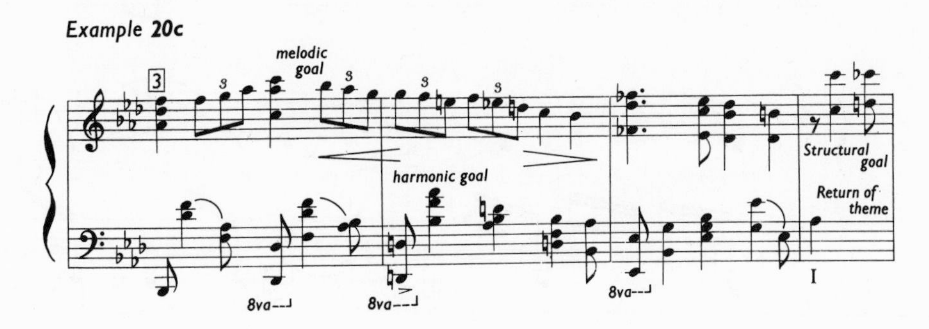

represent the arrival of a "structural goal" which may or may not incorporate the melodic and harmonic techniques mentioned above. Measure four of *example* **20c** represents the return of Part A and is a structural goal.

EXERCISES

A *Analysis*

1] Analyze *Example 21* in the following manner:

a] Mark phrases, motives, and figures.

b] Give reasons for the irregular length of some phrases.

c] Mark two melodic and harmonic goals, and one structural goal.

d] Find instances of augmentation and diminution as well as noting the intervallic unity that occurs through the use of the motives.

e] Do not overlook the imitative counterpoint in the piano part.

Example 21 *Sonata No. 1 for Violin and Piano. Brahms*

cresc.
cresc.
f
f
etc.

2] The melody of *Example 22* starts with a figure of two tones, a perfect-fourth interval. Observe its expansion and its growth into a second motive. Mark extensions and contractions, as they concur with the harmonic rhythm. Note the metric changes. Do not overlook the study of the bass motive, both melodically and rhythmically.

Example **22** *Prelude No. 21. Scriàbine*

3] Compare *Examples 23a* and *23b*. Analyze them accordingly.

4] Mark all instances of intervallic unity occurring in *Examples 24a* and *b*. It is based on a *basso ostinato*.

B Rewrite the following melodic phrases, altering the melody by techniques of augmentation, diminution, inversion, possibly retrograde inversion, as well as sequence and repetition. Mark the figures and your method of alteration. In addition, mark the dynamics, indicating the focal point of your phrase.

Example 25a

Example 25b

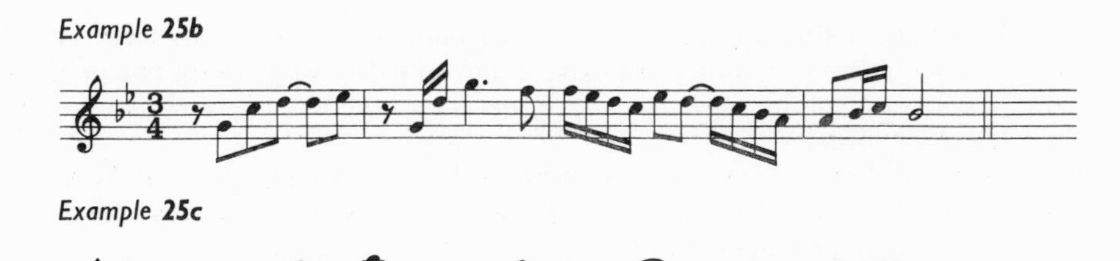

Example 25c

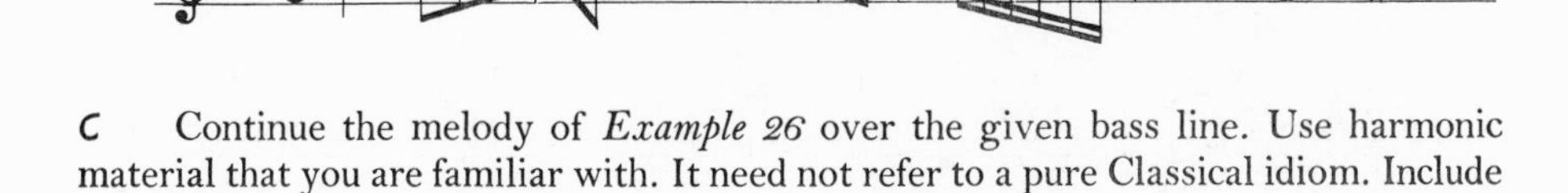

C Continue the melody of *Example 26* over the given bass line. Use harmonic material that you are familiar with. It need not refer to a pure Classical idiom. Include the techniques mentioned above, marking all of the motives.

Example 26a

Example 26b

D Each of the following figures given in a group are related only by their mutual key. Arrange them in any order and expand into an extended group of two or three phrases. Select a meter in which the quarter beat is the unit. Use metric changes where desirable. (See model.)

Harmonize one or more of these phrases. Include dynamics so as to highlight contracted motives used for a mounting increase of tension as opposed to a retarding and diminishing degree of intensity.

Example 27

3 Harmonic growth

Chromatic expansion of tonality

In the Classical period, the chromatic scale functioned primarily as the provider of embellishing tones and embellishing harmonies for the diatonic order of tones. Gradually, as musical growth opened new doors of tonal development, the chromatic scale began to play a more important role in the structure of a composition. Beethoven explored new chromatic paths largely in the development sections of his symphonies, sonatas and the later string quartets. The Romanticists included the new colorful harmonies as an integral part of their lyrical melodies. This growth lead toward new areas of modulation. Key centers were reached which had only a chromatic relationship to the starting tonic tonality. In Wagner's writings, the length and scope of operatic form provided a need for a wandering tonal scheme, which, at times, covers the entire chromatic spectrum.

To illustrate this advance in chromatic usage: Bach inventions or fugues modulate only to keys founded upon the diatonic scale. The first modulation moves to the dominant or the relative major or minor keys. The remaining diatonic key centers may then be used (unaltered in quality) before returning to the tonic. The diminished triads cannot be used as key centers, but in a minor key, the VII may be founded upon the modal degree of the scale, thereby forming a major triad one whole step below the tonic. This chord is actually the dominant of the relative major. Classical composers did not feel entirely bound by these diatonic limitations, and musical progress inevitably lead toward more tonal expansion. In the *Waldstein Sonata* in C major, Opus 53, Beethoven's first modulation to the second theme is to E major, the altered mediant. He approached it through a prolonged passage on the dominant of E minor. Nevertheless, this mediant relationship differs radically from the accepted formula. Similar innovations can be found, all of which herald the greater tonal freedom which the Romantic school then helped to establish. In a sense, one can say that Wagner crystallized this movement. Not only are the modulations free of any diatonic restrictions, but they move so rapidly, and are so impermanent, that cadences may not reflect all of the tonal movement that occurs within a phrase.

Example 28, an excerpt from the beginning of the second scene in the third act of *Tristan and Isolde*, illustrates the tonal movement of key centers. Beginning on a surging D♭ major motive, which utilizes an irregular metric formation, the setting of D♭ is thoroughly established. Seven bars later, the common tone of F connects the D♭ chord to the F dominant seventh. The motive, now transposed, provides a chromatic means through which a brief diminished seventh chord and a momentary A♭ augmented chord lead to the second phrase starting on the A dominant ninth. Notice that the tone G♭ in the ninth measure is really functioning as an F♯, leading toward the seventh, G, in the A dominant ninth chord. The augmented quality arising from the motive is heard via the last eighth note, E♮, which also anticipates the new dominant quality. A series of dominants now follow, all placed against the pedal tone A. Measure eleven contains the E ninth followed by a D V^4_3; which then returns to an incomplete E ninth in measures thirteen and fourteen.

The enharmonic function of the G♯ is evident in the fifteenth measure. Having been used as the third of the E dominant chord (the root is implied), it now changes its role to that of a pedal bass tone of A♭. Appoggiatura tones in the melody form a temporary leading-tone seventh chord, which resolves in measure sixteen to the E♭ dominant seventh chord, placed above the A♭ pedal. The next few measures expand on the A♭ dominant chord and in that respect, the starting tonality of D♭ returns. However, no cadence in D♭ is forthcoming. Instead, the bass tone A♭ rises chromatically to A♮ in measure twenty-seven forming a diminished seventh chord. This triggers a few enharmonic changes. The motive repetitions starting on the high G♭ change to an F♯ in the last two-measure group. The tone E♭, especially prominent in the bass pattern on the last eighth beat is altered in measure thirty. This pitch is now used as a stressed rhythmical tone and notated as a D♯. These enharmonic changes point the way toward the C major resolution. The chromatic function of both the A♭ dominant seventh and of its outgrowth the diminished seventh, is responsible for this climactic progression to C major, in which the fifth is the prominent bass tone. If space permitted a lengthier excerpt it would also be seen that this new dominant extension doesn't cadence to the root of C major, but again is evaded chromatically. This unrestricted use of transient key centers is the first suggestion of the new freedom given to the chromatic scale. The twelve tones of the scale are given equally important functions as temporary key centers surrounding a basic tonic, thus permitting modulation amongst twelve different tonalities and their minor or major modes. With this new unlimited scope, it is just a step closer to the understanding that these same twelve tones can be used as independent melodic tones within a single phrase.

This realization places Wagner as the forerunner of the twelve-tone scale—not to be confused with Schönbergs' twelve-tone row which will be discussed in a later chapter.

Example 28 Wagner

To learn more specifically how these chromatic modulations are created, examine the phrases following the next paragraph and notice:

1] Common tone modulation.
2] Enharmonic function of dominants.
3] Chromatic wandering until diatonic resolutions are made.

Example 29 is a simple illustration from Wagner showing the principle of enharmonic change. The minor ninth of the A dominant chord, the tone B♭, changes to the role of the third of F♯ major as is evident in the enharmonic notation in the fourth measure. This common-tone connection causes a movement of harmony which is not rooted down to the former diatonic progressions.

Example 29 *Wagner*

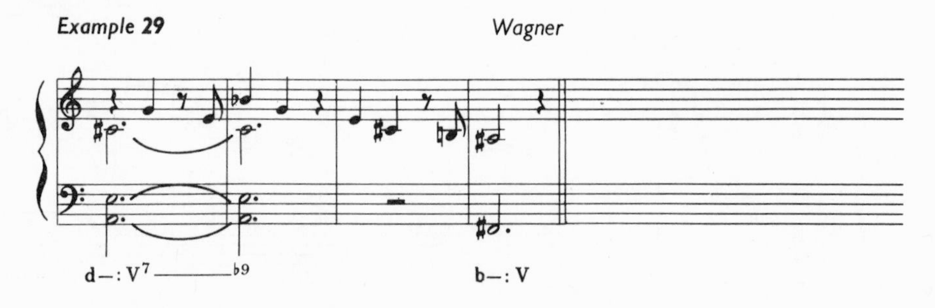

The enharmonic function of dominant chords is frequently recognized in the change from a dominant chord to that of an augmented sixth resolution. This was suggested in the previous *Tristan* excerpt as the A♭ seventh chord altered its tone of the seventh, G♭, to that of the would-be augmented sixth, F♯. (The augmented sixth was not consummated, as the bass changed chromatically in measure twenty-seven.)

The diminished sevenths are exceptionally flexible, being made up of equidistant intervals. *Example 30* from the Verdi *Requiem* illustrates a modulation from D minor to E♭ minor, made possible by the enharmonic changes of a diminished seventh chord. Appearing in the third measure as the leading-tone chord to the subdominant G minor, the resolution then moves to the root of an E♭ minor triad. Verdi did not notate the enharmonic change, but it is heard upon the resolution, as the bass tone A becomes the leading-tone of B♭, the fifth of E♭ minor. Common tones of E♭ and G♭ also provide a connection. The resulting modulation is again a distant one, based upon free chromatic movement.

Example 30 Verdi

Chromaticism also increased in ornamental melodic writing. Typical of this embellishing use of the chromatic scale is the excerpt from Chopin's *Prelude* No. 21, *example 31*. Representing a harmonic cadence built only on the dominant, and leading toward the tonic, this passage uses almost every chromatic tone, not as a direct scale, but in a sequential pattern. During this descent, the upper motive gives a temporary harmonic stress to a few chords which receive some of the embellishing movement. But these do not gain any

Example 31 Chopin

rhythmic stress and are not recognized as harmonic progressions. For example, the subdominant is prominent in the second measure. By sequence, A major follows and has a leading-tone function as it then progresses to the real cadence on B♭. Nevertheless, the entire chromatic passage is heard above a dominant extension.

Appoggiatura chords

In a harmonic analysis, have you ever puzzled over a melody tone, wondering whether it is or isn't part of the chord? A Bach chorale, for example, will contain suspensions and passing tones which also turn out to be sevenths. A good analysis would include recognition of the contrapuntal writing as well as a figured bass which shows the harmonic result. Difficulties occur when analytical terms drawn from one stylistic period are mistakenly applied to a style in which they may be incongruous. For instance, Mozart frequently cadences with a melodic pattern, similar to the closing theme from the *Jupiter Symphony, example 32a*. Students who have become familiar with dominant thirteenth chords may mistakenly see the melody tone, B, in measure two, as a

Example 32a *Mozart*

Example 32b

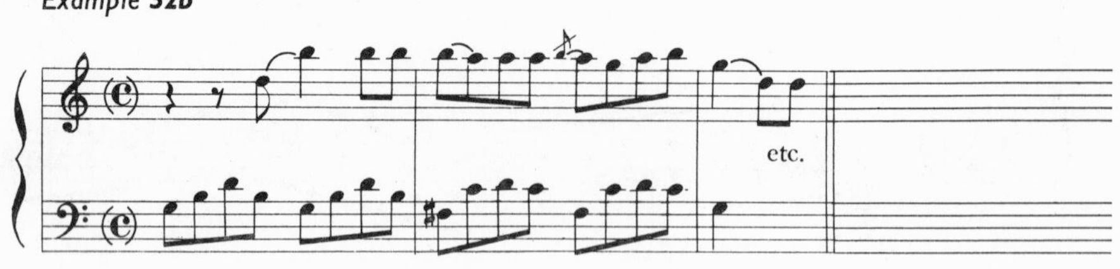

harmonic tone of the thirteenth instead of a contrapuntal tone. In *example 32b*, the second measure includes first a suspension and then an échappée. We know that Mozart did not build harmonic structures such as raised elevenths or thirteenth chords. If tones which add up to these higher intervals are present in his melody, they can only be represented as non-harmonic tones, all leading toward a resolution within a triad or seventh chord.

At some point, however, the recognition of the presence of these higher-numbered tones in a melody must be made. Factors which help determine a melody tones' status in a harmonic structure are:

1] Manner of resolution—

a] All tones which resolve stepwise into the existing triad or seventh chord do not have a harmonic identity. The ear differentiates between the greater dissonances of such non-harmonic tones and recognizes the more consonant resolutions as harmonic. In *example 33a*, compare the sound of the non-harmonic tones on beats one and three with the sound of their resolutions on the weak beats.

b] Some non-harmonic tones do resolve by a skip. They are the échappée, the cambiata, the double auxiliary (or double neighboring tones), all belonging to the general family of "changing tones"; and tones occurring in a compound melody which temporarily appear to skip, but actually resolve stepwise after hitting one or more tones in a different range level. See *examples 33b* and *33c*. (The motion to the ornamental tone in an échappée is contrary to the direct line of motion between the harmonic tones; while in the cambiata, the motion is in the same direction.)

2] Rhythmical duration—Most non-harmonic tones are equal in time value or shorter than their tones of resolution. The exception may be the appoggiatura. This tone, resolved stepwise, sometimes merges as a chord note, giving rise to the term "appoggiatura chord." Such a designation would apply only to an appoggiatura receiving rhythmic stress and duration that is fully supported by the lower chord members, thereby sounding complete by itself and not requiring a resolution. *Examples 34a* and *34b*, extracts from the beginning of the *Jupiter Symphony*, show several tones of the suspension and appoggiatura which, although qualifying rhythmically, can not become appoggiatura chords because the resolution is needed to fulfill their harmonic status. However, a true appoggiatura chord exists in the form of a IV $^6_4$ in the second measure of *example 34b*. The tones forming both the F and A are contrapuntal appoggiaturas resulting in the subdominant harmony which merely embellishes the tonic chord.

3] Resolution accompanied by a harmonic change—Any well built potential chord tone, which resolves stepwise or by skip into a different chord, will be heard also as a chord member in the first harmonic structure. This is how sevenths gained their status as chord members. Originating out of the contrapuntal 7–6 suspension, they became chord members in the Baroque period when heard as part of the V7–I progression. See *example 35*.

Similar to the incorporation of sevenths into the harmonic vocabulary, ninths and thirteenths follow a gradual change in status from contrapuntal tone to harmonic tone. Wagner's melodic style brought this chordal growth a notch closer toward the eventual unrestricted use of higher-numbered tones. His melodies abound with accented, lengthy non-harmonic tones. As these melody tones become harmonized, perhaps with a highly chromatic background, their entire vertical grouping may merge into a passing chord or an appoggiatura chord. What could slip by as a collection of non-harmonic tones may also supply a newer order of chord members. Appoggiatura chords such as the "appoggiatura ninth" or "appoggiatura thirteenth" are those in which the melody tone of the ninth or thirteenth originates as an appoggiatura, suspension, or accented passing tone. The duration of this tone within the vertical sound must be long enough for the listener to identify the complete upward tertial ladder of chord members. Upon hearing this complete chord, all members deserve recognition, even though a resolution to a simpler chord may also take place, on a comparatively short rhythmic value.

The detailed use of all ninths, elevenths and thirteenths will follow, but their growth from melody tones is observed here. A ninth adds an additional third, major or minor, to a seventh chord and is generally in the melody in this style. As an appoggiatura, it receives rhythmic stress and resolves downward (9–8), or upward (2–3).

An appoggiatura eleventh adds another third above the ninth. Rather than counting on the fingers, remember the eleventh as forming a distance of an octave and a fourth, or an augmented fourth, above the root. Most commonly the eleventh is treated as a suspension, resolving down to the third in the 4–3 figuration.

The thirteenth is remembered by its forming a major or minor sixth above the root, expanded then by octave widening. As an appoggiatura, it falls downward to the fifth of a seventh chord.

Example 36 includes three different melodic approaches, each forming an appoggiatura ninth chord. In the first instance, the ninth is approached by a skip and is held until the fourth beat resolution. This duration permits the appoggiatura tone to be identified with the lower chord members. In the third measure, the suspended F becomes the minor ninth of the E dominant chord. Here too, the tone resolves into the dominant seventh chord, but in such a delayed manner that the resolution is more apt to be heard as the passing tone. Harmonically the eighth note E is expected, but rhythmically the weight of the sound is on the ninth chord. The fifth measure produces a ninth by means of a syncopated passing-tone, this time resolving up to the third of the chord.

Contrasting with the preceding instances, the appoggiatura in measure six (the melody tone G) does not form an appoggiatura chord. Harmonized by a B♭ major triad, the chord does not include the seventh, necessary for the recognition of the higher harmonic extensions. The high G is an appoggiatura tone, not merging as a chord member.

The seventh measure contains a melodic sequence, but this time is

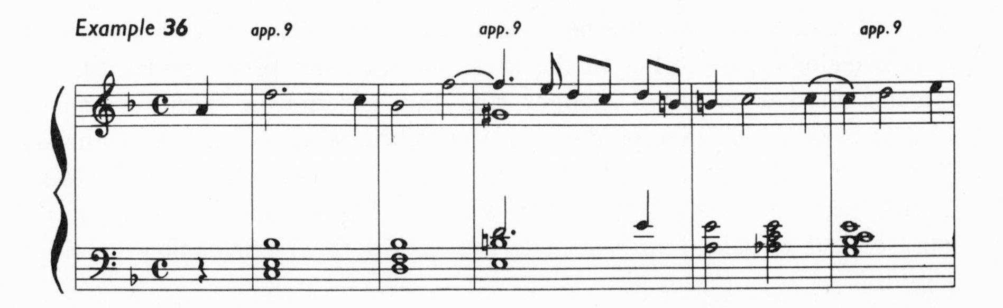

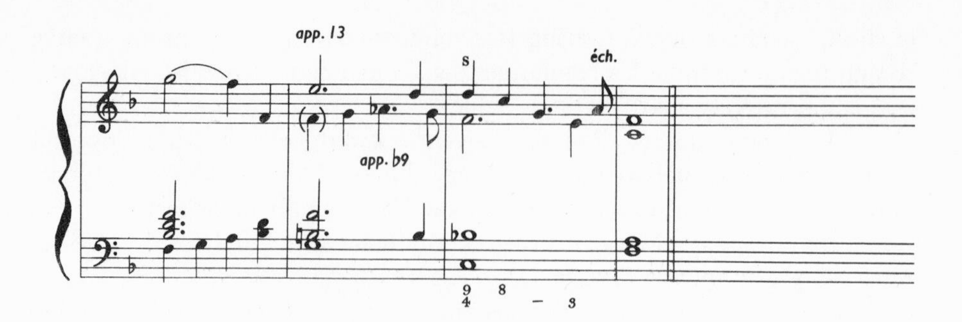

harmonized by a very complete thirteenth chord. The alto imitates the preceding bass line, and rises to form an appoggiatura minor ninth, adding much color to the soprano thirteenth. A thirteenth chord, however, does not require the support of the ninth; a seventh is sufficient. Preparation for the cadence is made by non-harmonic tones. The soprano places a stress on the suspended ninth, but its duration is equal to the resolving tone, and is much shorter in ratio to the complete measure. Such tones show the merger of melodic and harmonic recognition without creating a demand for either single analysis. In the alto, the Classical 4–3 progression is evident. Treated as an accented, passing appoggiatura, it also shows the merger with a potential eleventh. Resolved properly, a preferred analysis retains the non-harmonic connotation. as illustrated.

In the Romantic period, the appoggiatura chords are frequently found at melodic points of tension. By involving a greater number of harmonic tones, the appoggiatura chords emphasize the rising tension generally found in the upward melodic curve of a phrase. With the resolution and downward tendency of most appoggiaturas, the arc design of the phrase is completed. This is illustrated in the following examples from the preludes by Chopin. *Prelude* No. 13 in F♯ major, *example 37*, starts slowly with very little melodic and harmonic movement. The ornamentation contained in the accompaniment pattern receives the chief interest. Observe the phrase pattern. A normal two-bar motive, continued by a modified repetition, is then followed by a three-bar group. This is unusual for Chopin, as most of his writing retains a Classical symmetry. In this example, the bass extension that follows the cadence in the short three-bar motive fulfills this rhythmical need. After a parallel phrase, omitted in this excerpt, the next phrase, *example 37b*, develops the motive, not in melodic height, but in the harmonic intensity produced both by the greater number of chord changes, and the selection of dominant quality chords in contrast to the predominantly triadic quality in the former phrases. The focal point of this phrase occurs with the appoggiatura thirteenth in the second measure. It occurs with the highest melodic tone of this phrase, and enriches the chromatic quality of the embellishing dominant chord.

The cadence is interesting in that it uses the échappée in an exaggerated rhythmic pose. The duration permits the ear to also accept it as a thirteenth, as a harmonic continuation of the dominant seventh on the downbeat.

The first phrase of the D♭ major *Prelude, example 38,* rises melodically toward the peak in the third measure. The inner voice, moving in parallel sixths with the soprano, fulfills the harmonic rise by arriving on the ninth of the dominant chord. Its resolution downward is accompanied by a harmonic change to the tonic, thereby fulfilling the requirement of chord tones and resulting in a complete V^9, as opposed to the appoggiatura resolution. Of course, one can still feel the kinship with the appoggiatura. Nevertheless, the ninth quality is maintained for the duration of that root. By contrast, measure four depicts an appoggiatura thirteenth, which resolves to the fifth, a tone one-quarter of the rhythmic value of the appoggiatura.

Example 38 Chopin

Example 39, the *Prelude* in B♭ minor, starts with a burst of excitement. The appoggiatura technique is used as an immediate bold pronouncement commanding your attention to "sit up and listen!" A *Presto con fuoco* follows this one-measure directive and, if brilliantly played, can be most rewarding.

EXERCISES

A *Analysis*

1] In *Example 40*, mark all harmony; identify appoggiatura tones. Mark the non-harmonic tones by the symbol X above the tone, and indicate the merging chord members (app. 9, etc.). Observe the shifting tonalities. Find one particular melody tone which is harmonized by a minimum of six different ways within an eight bar extract.

2] Mark harmony and appoggiatura analysis in *Examples* **41a–d** as indicated before. Observe the melodic contour and its relationship with the harmonization. If possible, listen to the entire song for this structural connection between melody, harmony and form.

Example 41a *Traüme. Wagner*

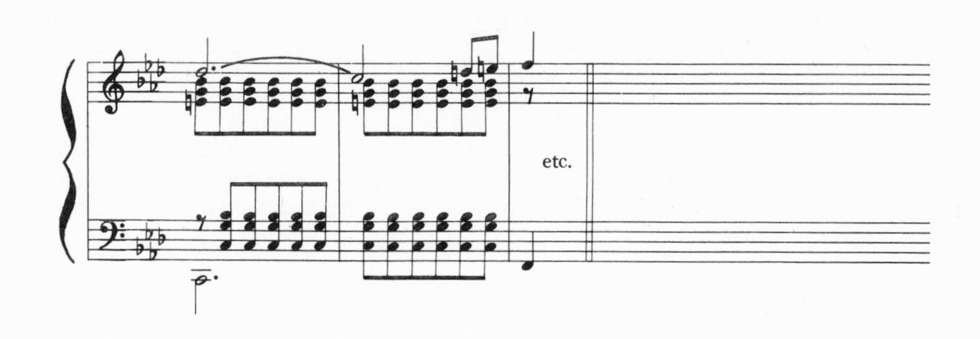

Example 41c

Example 41d

3] Analyze *Example* **42a**, and **b**, in the same manner but think in a slower tempo; be aware of the contrast in style noting the chromaticism of Chopin and that of Wagner. Compare the opening motive with its cadential use in *Example* **42b**.

Example 42a Chopin

Example 42b

4] In *Example* **43** mark motives, figures, and observe the phrase construction. Mark the quality of all seventh chords; their key relationship (roman numerals), and the appoggiatura tones.

Example 43 *The Infinite Shining Heavens. R. Vaughan Williams*

5] Analyze *Example* **44** in the same manner, giving special attention to the motive of the accompaniment and its rhythmic development throughout.

Example 44 *Waiting. Vittorio Giannini*

B A common-tone modulation drill is contained within the short phrases of *Example* **45**. Find the tone that connects the two keys of each example and harmonize it by using an appropriate dominant, diminished chord, or an augmented sixth chord.

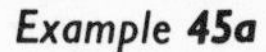

C Harmonize the following melodies. Select an appoggiatura chord for each melody tone marked by the X symbol. *Example* **46a** is suitable for a basic "piano-style" bass part. In *Example* **46b**, try a two voice, imitative idiom, as illustrated at the beginning.

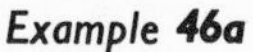

C Above the given harmonic bass line, add a melody which includes appoggiatura tones. Mark all chords.

Example 47

For further reference in constant chromatic modulation, see *Auf einer Wanderung* and *Die ihr schwebet*, songs by Hugo Wolf.

4 Details concerning the ninth chord

Location in the overtone series

The natural overtone series, *example 48*, helps to explain many processes of the growth of chords. Notice that the pure intervals of the octave, the perfect fifth and perfect fourth, occur between the first four partials. Then the "impure" interval of the third enters as the fifth partial and forms the major triad. The seventh partial produces the dominant seventh quality, and a third above that a ninth is added, a major ninth, to be specific. The overtone series makes it evident that the ninth exists above a dominant seventh, not just a triad. When the tones of this diagram are played on the piano, the partials are not exactly equivalent to the sound we hear because of the tempered tuning. The seventh, B♭, sounds lower than the exact vibrations of the partial indicate. However, these impurities do not affect the growth of chords, as arising from the overtone series, and combined with the tempered scale.

Example 48

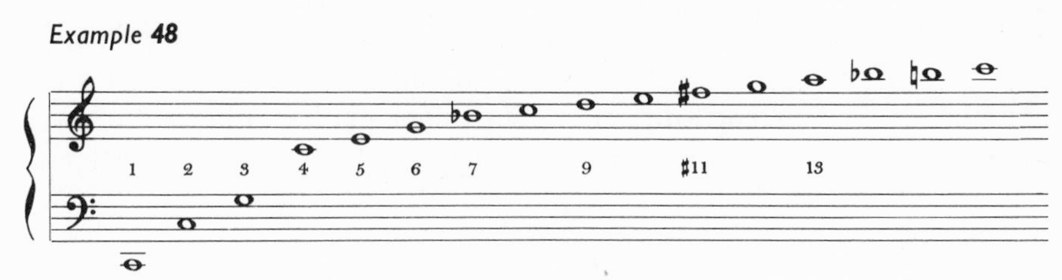

Dominant ninths in the major and minor scales

While the dominant seventh chord is built upon the same tones in both the major and minor keys (the minor scale always uses the raised leading tone for the V^7 chord), the addition of the ninth reflects precisely the scale from which it is derived. The V^9 of the key of C major has the A, the sixth degree of the scale, forming an interval of a major ninth with the root. In C minor, the V9 has the A♭ forming a minor ninth with the root of the chord. This "dominant minor ninth" chord, as it is correctly named, resolves of course, to its tonic minor triad, but may also resolve to the major triad (V♭9 to I, major). See *example* **49**. This privilege of change of mode is only possible when moving from the minor implication into a major resolution, and not the reverse, major to minor. This is exactly the same principle which governs seventh chords built upon the leading tone of a key. The diminished seventh chord, founded in the minor key, may resolve to either the major or minor tonic triad, but the half-diminished seventh chord, reflecting the major scale, cannot resolve to a minor triad. Perhaps these musical practices retain the suggestion reflected by the *tierce de Picardie*—the use of a major triad at a cadence of a minor composition. This was undoubtedly felt to be a more pure ending. To attempt the reverse, whether dealing with a simple melody or with ninth chords, would imply that the pure sounds of the major scale would be forced into the impure, artificially altered tones of the tonic chord of the parallel minor scale. Only for an extremely dramatic portrayal, usually associated with a text, would a composer deliberately use this technique of "going backwards," and even then, never at an ending.

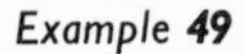

Example **49**

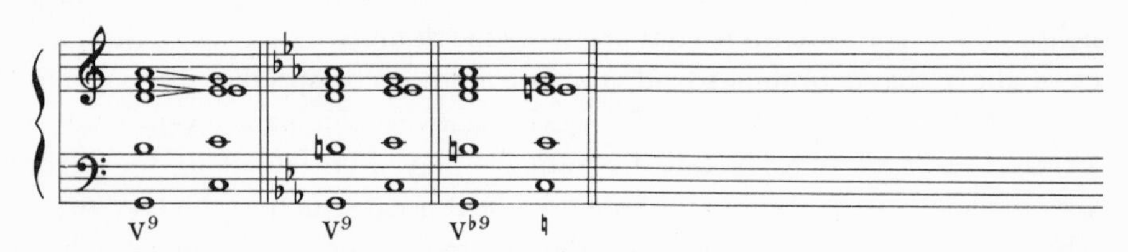

Although the overtone series produces the dominant ninth which is a part of the major scale, the interval of the ninth may be chromatically lowered to produce the dominant minor ninth chord or chromatically raised by one half step forming an augmented ninth. Resolutions of these altered tones must continue in their intended direction. The minor ninth continues downward, while an augmented ninth must resolve up, usually with the half step. See *example* **50**.

Example **50**

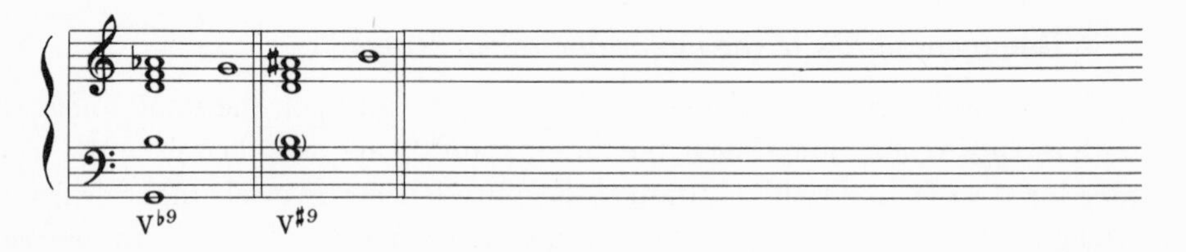

Other quality ninth chords

Ninths may be added to major or minor seventh chords, thereby adding members to chords founded upon any degree of the scale. (Chords built upon leading-tone harmonies are discussed separately—see "Leading-tone Chords.") The tone forming the ninth is usually the one derived from the scale of the phrase involved. The quality of the seventh chord serves as the foundation for all of the higher extensions, and forms the following diatonically conceived ninth chords.

In the major scale, the II9 and VI9 are frequently used. Arising out of the scale, the ninth involved is a major ninth interval which is added to a minor seventh chord. See *example 51a*. The same quality ninth chord is found in the minor scale on the subdominant (IV9) and on the tonic (I9) if used without the raised leading-tone. *Example 51b* illustrates this in the key of D minor.

Example **51a** **51b**

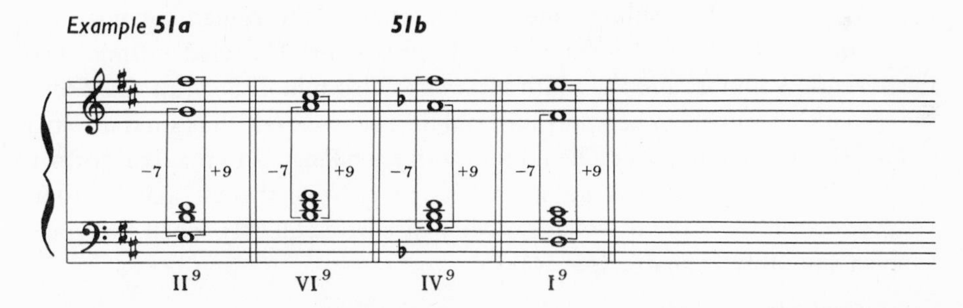

Equally useful are the ninth chords which grow out of the diatonic major seventh chords. The I9 and IV9 of the major scale contain the major seventh chord and add the interval of the major ninth. In the minor scale, this major quality ninth chord is located upon the VI9 and III9. (The leading-tone is not raised.) See *examples* **52a** and **b**.

Example **52a** **52b**

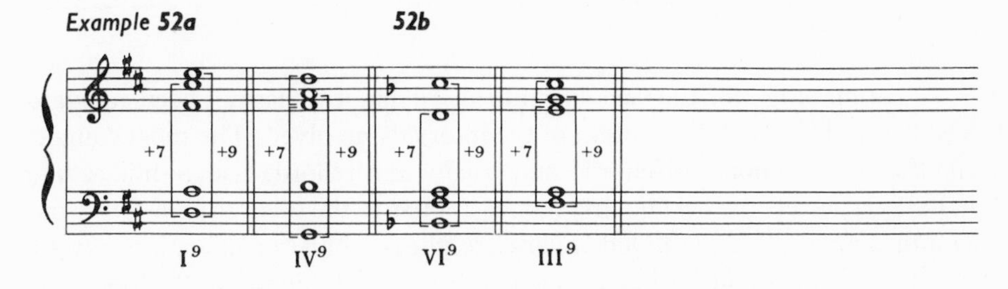

A minor ninth interval added to a minor seventh chord is harsh. It exists as a III9 of a major key but that does not give it much merit. See *example 53*. The conflict arises out of the strong dominant reference that is part of four out of five of the chord members. If you omit the root of the mediant chord, you are left with the dominant seventh structure. If the mediant root is included, it tends to sound as if it is there by mistake, because the dominant quality above, overpowers the mediant tone. It is not the minor ninth interval that causes the disagreeable quality, but rather the scale associations upon which these tones occur. The mediant root is also the third of the tonic chord and, as such, tends to partially represent the tonic while the rest of the chord members of the III^9 belong to the opposite sound of the dominant. The chord suggests the clash of a dominant seventh sounding simultaneously with its tone of resolution.

Example 53

−7 −9

III^9

Aside from the leading-tone seventh chords, the remaining unaltered diatonic ninth chord is the II^9 founded in the minor key. The triad is diminished, the seventh is minor, and the ninth interval is also minor. See *example 54a.* A tonal conflict occurs between the ninth and the root tone which is similar to that of the III^9 described above. The minor ninth's tendency is to resolve down to the tone already present in the chord, its root. Nevertheless, the II^9 to V^9 progresses well and the dissonant quality dissipates quickly when the voices connect smoothly as in *example 54b.*

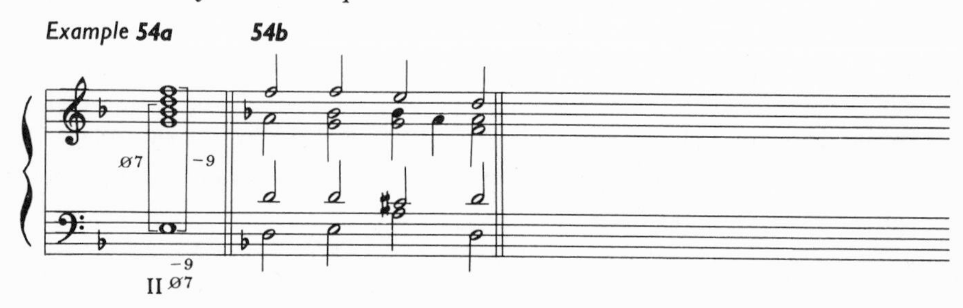

Terminology for the various ninth chord qualities has not been standardized except by actual description of the intervals involved. The most common labels, that is "minor ninth chord" and "major ninth chord," can be misleading. In both instances, the first quality named applies to the seventh chord, to which a ninth, a major ninth, is added. Therefore, the combination of a minor seventh chord and a major ninth has frequently been called simply a "minor ninth chord," but the actual ninth is not minor. A less confusing term is one which separates the seventh chord quality from the ninth interval, such as "minor seventh-ninth chord." The quality of the ninth (and of a thirteenth) is understood as major unless specifically noted. This is the same practice that distinguishes between the terms "dominant minor ninth" and "dominant ninth" in which the major is contained in the latter designation.

All alterations are listed in order of their numerical ascendancy. A chord built upon an augmented triad would be named, for example, an "augmented triad-major seventh-augmented ninth chord," or an "augmented-dominant minor ninth chord." The latter omits the "triad" referring to the augmented quality. The names for these chord qualities may seem long, but they are explicit.

The upper chord extensions are added to the seventh chord quality. Only the highest numbered chord member and any altered chord tones need be listed. A "dominant thirteenth" chord is built upon a dominant seventh; it may include or omit a major ninth and contains the major thirteenth. If the ninth is altered in any way, the label would state the change—for example, a dominant-minor ninth-thirteenth chord.

The symbol b9 or –9 may be used interchangeably to denote the minor ninth interval. In a strict figuration which relates to a key signature, any flat designates the lowering of a tone while a sharp raises a tone. For emphasis, the use of b9 draws attention to an alteration. The sharp symbol applies to an augmented quality in this analytical method, regardless of its effect upon the key signature.

Listed below are different quality ninth chords, built upon various combinations of triads and seventh chords. The diminished triad is included only as indicative of a triad containing a lowered fifth, as symbolic of a super-tonic triad, pending a full discussion of the leading tone chords in Chapter 6.

Example **55a** The minor seventh-ninth chord

b The minor seventh-minor ninth chord

c The same as *example* **55b** but organized to suggest an E♭ V7 over a pedal tone of C.

d The minor seventh-augmented ninth chord duplicates the third enharmonically and is not useful, regardless of the resolution of either tone.

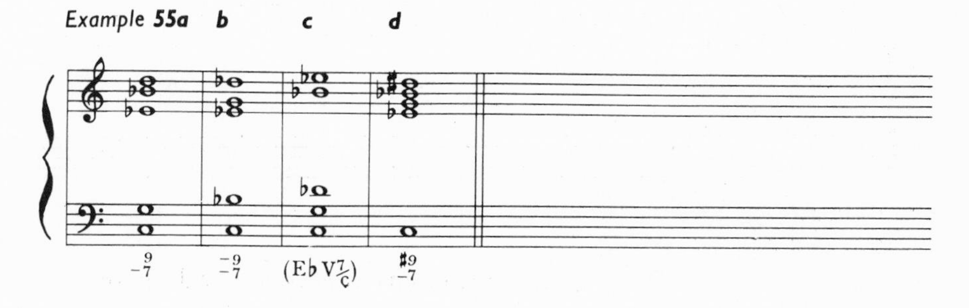

Example **56a** The major seventh-ninth chord

b The major seventh-minor ninth chord

c The major seventh-augmented ninth chord

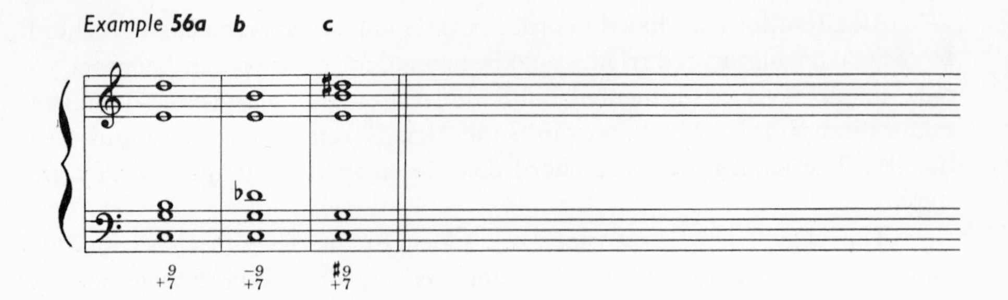

Example 57a The minor triad-major seventh-ninth chord
b The minor triad-major seventh-minor ninth chord

Ninth chords containing triads in which the fifth is raised:

Example 58a The augmented dominant ninth chord
b The augmented dominant-minor ninth chord
c The augmented dominant-augmented ninth chord

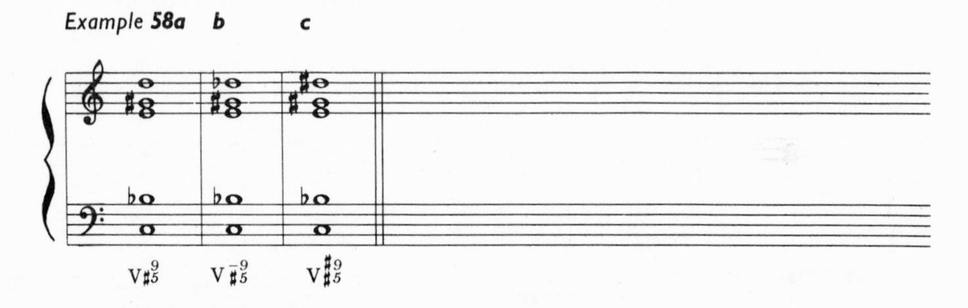

Example 59a The augmented triad-major seventh-ninth chord
b The augmented triad-major seventh-minor ninth chord
c The augmented triad-major seventh-augmented ninth chord

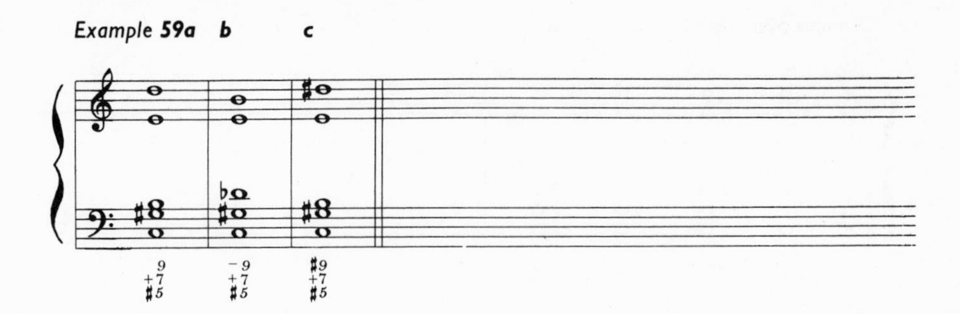

Ninth chords containing triads in which the fifth is chromatically lowered:

Example 60a The lowered fifth-dominant ninth chord
b The lowered fifth-dominant minor ninth chord
c The lowered fifth-dominant-augmented ninth chord

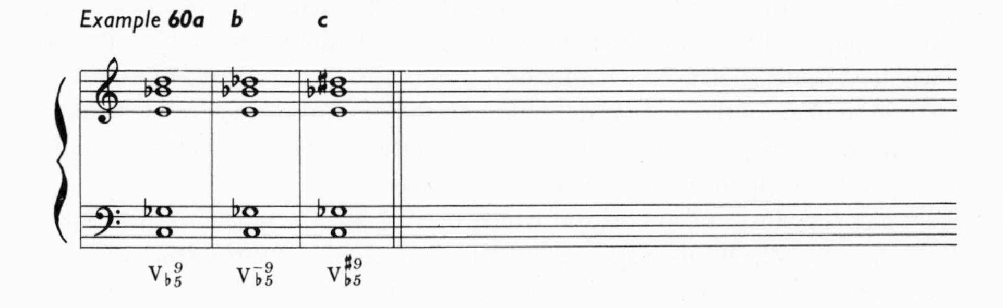

Example 61a The half-diminished seventh-ninth chord
b The half-diminished seventh-minor ninth chord

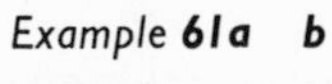

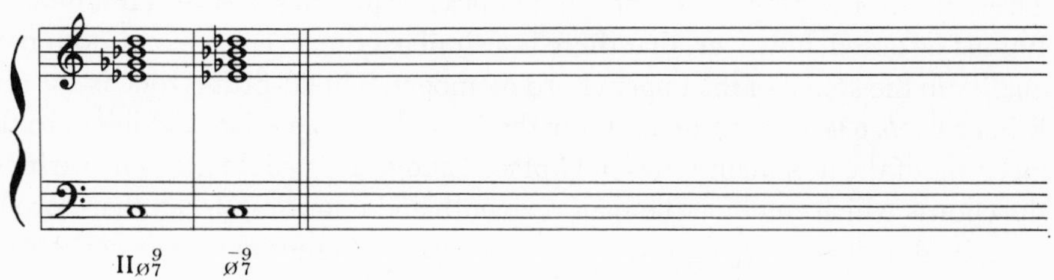

Example 62a The diminished (triad)-major seventh-ninth chord
b The diminished-major seventh-minor ninth chord
c The lowered fifth-major seventh-ninth chord
d The lowered fifth-major seventh-minor ninth chord

Example **62a** **b** **c** **d**

$II^{\circ}{}^{9}_{+7}$ $II^{\circ}{}^{-9}_{+7}$ ${}^{9}_{+7}_{\flat 5}$ ${}^{-9}_{+7}_{\flat 5}$

In *examples 58–62* of the above list, the chords are notated according to their exact specifications. Enharmonic spellings may change the label because of opposing tone resolutions. This will be seen as the study of the upper harmonic extensions continues.

Chromatic alterations to triads, sevenths, and ninths provide a wealth of harmonic color. Some combinations increase a dissonant quality while others function as smooth chromatic substitutes for the expected chord members. All qualities, regardless of their consonant or dissonant make-up, are suitable in a musical phrase if they contribute to the texture and idiom of the composition as a whole. The decision as to whether or not a dominant-augmented ninth should be used in place of the regular dominant ninth does not rest upon the sound of dissonance, nor upon voice leading, but upon the compatibility of that quality sound in the style or manner of the composition.

Nevertheless, a composition which moves about confortably with many varieties of ninth chords may not find all of the above textures desirable. The combination of a minor ninth interval and a major seventh is rarely used. It contains a conflict of purpose in that the lowered ninth is heading downward against the rising tendency of the major seventh. This occurs in *examples* **56b**, **57b**, **59b**, and **62b** and **d**. If the minor ninth is placed below the tone of the major seventh as in *example* **57b**, the widened range aids the distribution of each tone's vibrations and thus lessens the tonal conflict. Compare *examples* **63a** and **63b**. The separation of range and a motivic application justifies the use of this quality. It must be noted, however, that there is a similarity to an enharmonic dominant quality in the sound of the upper chord members. The ill-fitting tone is the alto E in *example* **63b**. Substitute an F for the E, as in *example* **63c**, and listen to the merging of the dominant tones of G placed above a C pedal tone. The rarity of the chords which combine the major seventh and minor ninth can therefore be explained in that they suggest to a composer a different harmonic conception than the one theoretically built in opposition to the basic dominant hierarchy. Any group of tones which between themselves form a dominant quality will sound blended, and will cause to emphasize a tone that is a stranger to their unit. These harmonic combinations that do not comfortably ally all of their chord members are found in compositions in which such an alignment is not expected, or are recognized as chords containing non-harmonic tones in the form of pedal tones or other appropriate melodic designations. *Examples* 55b and 55c of the preceding list illustrate the suggestion of the E♭ dominant seventh over a pedal C rather than a C minor seventh-minor ninth chord.

Example 63a b c

Voicing

All five tones of the ninth chord may be present. Chorale writing permits the *divisi* of sopranos, altos or tenors in order to fulfill the complete chord. A bass divisi weakens the chord's foundation, especially if the root tone is divided. Use it only as a last resort. A notation usually shows the division of a voice or choral part only where necessary. The best division always occurs by contrary motion, both in the separation into more tones as well as in the re-unification to one. Also permissible is an oblique motion in which a common sound is maintained while a divided part moves away or rejoins the existing tone. *Example* 64b illustrates both practices. Avoid, if possible, a division in which a single tone separates by parallel motion as in *example* 64a. In close harmony, this may not always work out, but check the other voice possibilities. *Example* 64b divides the sopranos and, in so doing, removes the awkward alto writing of *example* 64a.

Example 64a b

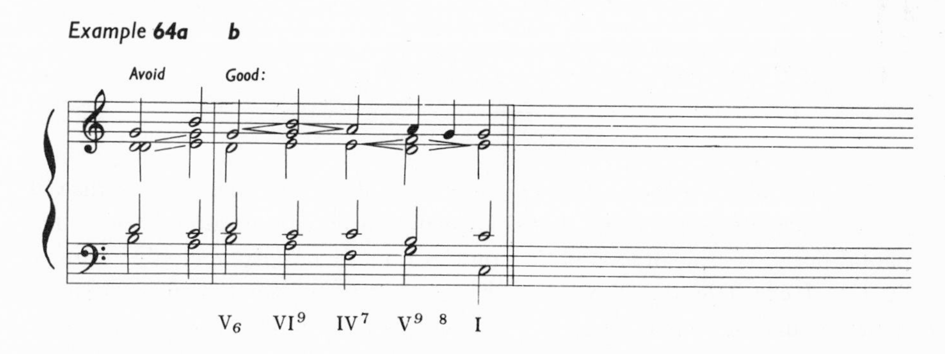

If desired, the fifth of a ninth chord may be omitted. This is a practical way of avoiding certain parallel fifths. A reorganization of voices may sometimes bring about better voice leading in addition to the retention of the complete ninth chord. Compare *examples* 65a and b with *examples* 65c and d. *Examples* 65c divides the tenors, giving that part both the fifth and the seventh of the chord. In this way the seventh resolves normally with the fifth, merging into the same resolution. *Example 65d* illustrates the presence of the fifth and seventh in the alto part, in a dominant ninth chord, first inversion.

Nevertheless, the presence of the fifth can cause unavoidable parallel fifths; and its omission may leave a vertical sound that is too empty. *Example 66a* uses the ninth chord in a well balanced third inversion. The fifths occur between alto and soprano voices. The motion of the fifths, however, is subservient to that of the leading-tone which is located directly below the problematic fifth, in the divided alto part. The contrary motion, produced by the movement of the leading-tone (the major third of the chord) is so essential in this progression that it obscures the upper consecutive fifths. A solution agreeable to the eye is one that doubles the third of the receiving triad, *example 66b*. In major triads, particularly on tonic or dominant triad harmonies, the doubled third is awkward acoustically, as it overpowers the root.

Final judgment as to whether or not a set of visible consecutive fifths will sound poorly depends on the particular progression and the amount of contrapuntal purity which surrounds the composition. Generally, melodic usage, as in *example 66c*, hides the offending fifths which come to view only when stripped of the ornamentation. The omission of the fifth in a dominant minor ninth chord is never necessary because the parallel movement involves a diminished fifth interval and a perfect fifth; see *example 66d*. Further discussion of parallel fifths is contained in the subdivision, "Progressions."

Do not omit the third or the seventh of any quality ninth chord. The sound would be too incomplete for a convincing ninth chord quality. This is not to say that such omissions are bad, however, but merely to state that such sounds do not qualify as full ninth chords. Modern idioms use the ninth as an added tone and may use incomplete combinations, called "intervallic structures" as they are described in a later chapter. At this point, it is advantageous to include all chord members and to divide the voices as necessary.

The location of the ninth in a chord is illustrated in *example* **67a**. As suggested by the overtone series, the ninth sounds best in the highest voice or amongst the upper voices involved in the chord. Appearing in a tenor voice, *example* **67b**, the ninth may sound more like a non-harmonic tone or give the effect of a cluster. This is also true in *example* **67c** where, clustered next to the third, the dominant ninth loses much of its individuality. By keeping the ninth above the third, each chord tone retains its identity, as illustrated. *Example* **67d** illustrates a dominant minor ninth chord in which the minor ninth is placed next to the third. The problem of a cluster does not exist, making this organization a very normal one.

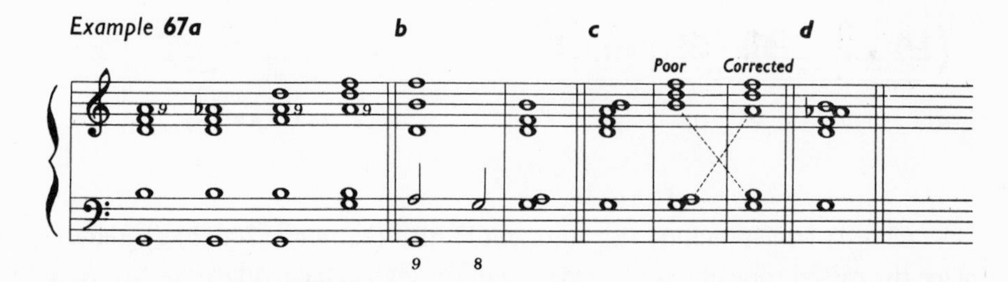

A minor seventh-ninth chord may also benefit by an adjacent ninth and third. The minor second is used deliberately for an added increase of tension. *Example* **68a** starts with such an organization of tones. The progressions which follow mellow the texture gradually up to the G dominant minor chord which precedes the cadence. Here, the tenor is divided and sings the minor ninth and the third. The minor key demands the dominant minor ninth quality. To hear the reverse, substitute an A natural in the tenor part. The cadence becomes very feeble. The entire phrase may be placed in C major, *example* **68b**, for an entirely different and brighter concept.

Tones which are raised, such as augmented ninths and augmented fifths, demand an upper position in the chord. The augmented ninth is chiefly used in the highest voice. Occasionally, a "neutral" perfect fifth may be placed above the augmented ninth, but this is an exception to the basic principle of maintaining the tertiary hierarchy. Compare *example* **69a** and **69b**. A major seventh chord containing an augmented ninth may be used without the major third as in *example* **69c**. This prevents the conflict of the two thirds, and permits the raised ninth to be placed in a lower voice. This omission, however, may suggest a dominant quality augmented triad, heard above a pedal tone.

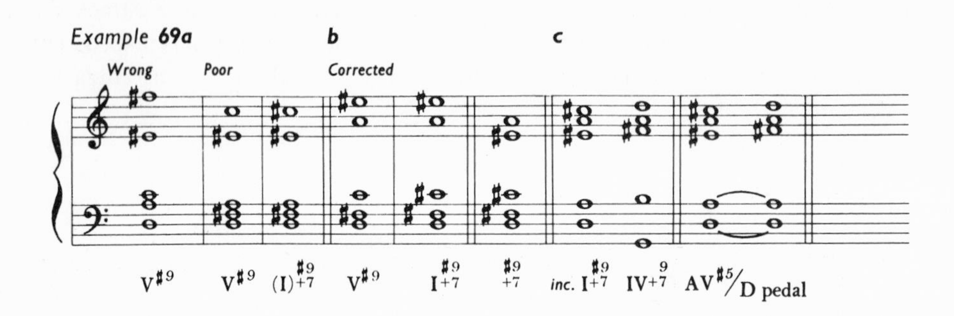

Chords which include the augmented fifth (*examples* **70a**, **b**, **c**) generally place the raised tone above the seventh of the chord, particularly in the dominant quality chords. Exceptions nevertheless do occur, as these chord members are drawn from the whole-tone scale and do not inherit any harmful tonal conflicts between themselves.

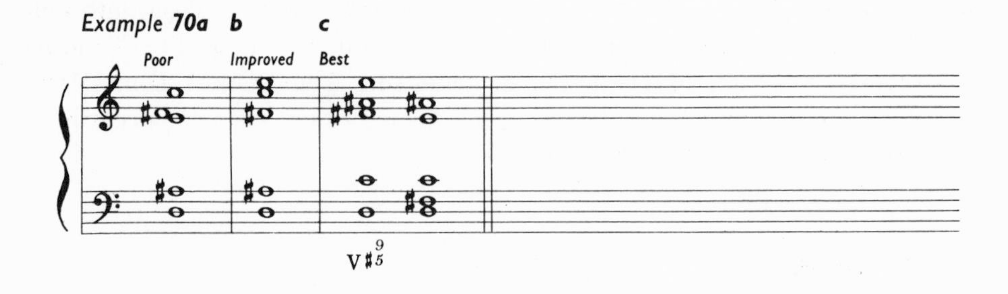

If both the ninth and the fifth are raised (*example* **71a**), the fifth may have an advantage in voice leading if it is the upper tone. Since both tones are raised, their normal resolution moves each tone up one half step. Motion by parallel fourths is preferable to the consecutive fifths that would occur if the voices were reversed, as in *example* **71b**.

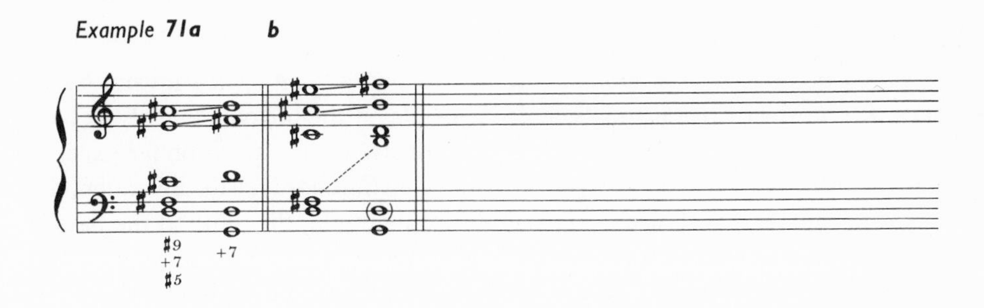

Chords in which the fifth is lowered, generally locate the fifth in a tenor voice, thereby producing the tritone between the bass and tenor. This helps to establish the root and lowered fifth as a base for the remaining chord members. The sound of the lowered fifth, placed in an upper voice, is more apt to function enharmonically as a raised eleventh. The notation and resolution of the tone indicates its intended movement. Compare *examples* 72*a* and *b*.

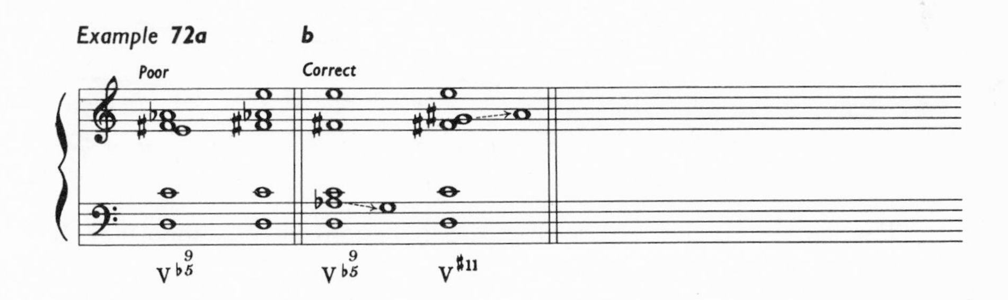

Chords containing both a raised and lowered tone, such as a dominant minor ninth with an augmented fifth (*example* 73) do not present any particular problems. The resolution of each altered tone moves in an opposite direction. If enough intervallic space for this movement is provided, the chord members may be arranged in any suitable organization. Remember to keep the raised fifth above the seventh of a dominant chord and to resolve all altered tones in their intended direction.

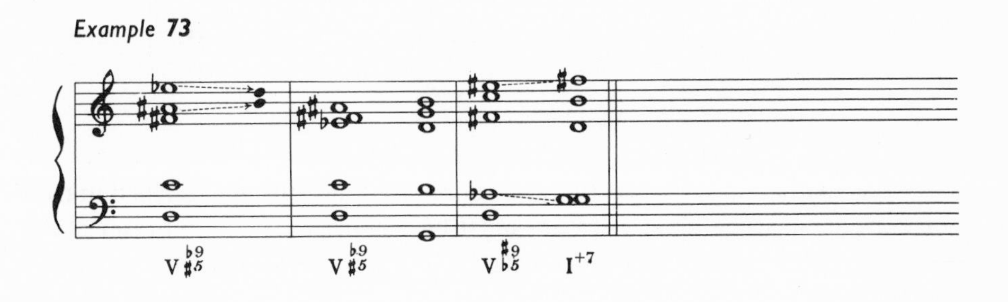

Inversions

All inversions of dominant ninths are possible. As with inversions of seventh chords, or triads, one's choice depends on the melodic line of the bass part, and the degree of strength desired. The use of root position far exceeds that of any inversion and the higher you move up the chord for the inversion, the fewer instances of such usage are found. For example, the ninth in the bass is generally a passing tone in this style of literature. Hugo Wolf, in a song from the *Spanisches Liederbuch I, example 74,* uses the ninth in the bass as a strong melodic factor. Heard as an ostinato, this motive wanders through six different keys and binds the entire composition.

Example **74** *Hugo Wolf*

The location of the root in all of the inversions is very important. If it can't be in the bass itself, then it should appear in the tenor. Generally, keep the ninth above the root and above the third. Space the ninth so that a wide interval separates it from the lower harmonic tones, the root and third.

Play the following illustrations, *example* 75, noticing the sound that results from a different placement of chord tones. Just by exchanging places between the root and ninth, the sound changes from a scrambled set of notes to an orderly harmonic unit.

Example **75**

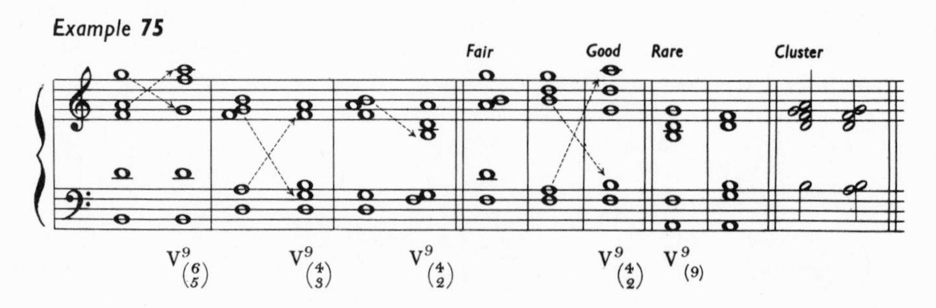

The many different quality ninth chords that have been described in root position may also be inverted. Care must be taken, however, to preserve the original tonal associations that indicate to the listener the particular harmonic make-up of the chord. While the dominant ninth chords assume certain preferred organizations of chord members, they are not destroyed if these chord tones are juggled in other ways. Other quality ninth chords may completely lose their original identity if an indiscriminate mixing of chord members takes place. *Example* 76a illustrates a plain C major ninth chord. An attempted inversion in *example* 76b produces, instead, a conflict of two chord roots. The G major triad stands securely and denotes a root, third and fifth; and not a fifth, seventh and ninth. The tones above simply do not fit the lower organization. Similarly, *example* 77b illustrates an attempted third inversion of a C minor-major seventh-ninth chord. The sound would improve if either the ninth or the root C were to be omitted. By placing the C adjacent to the major seventh (*example* 77c), the remaining chord members build the C minor triad, above which the ninth is related to C and correctly establishes the third inversion. All successful inversions of higher-numbered chords retain the lower triad members in the lower part of the vertical structure, while the ninths and chromatically raised tones are placed in upper positions.

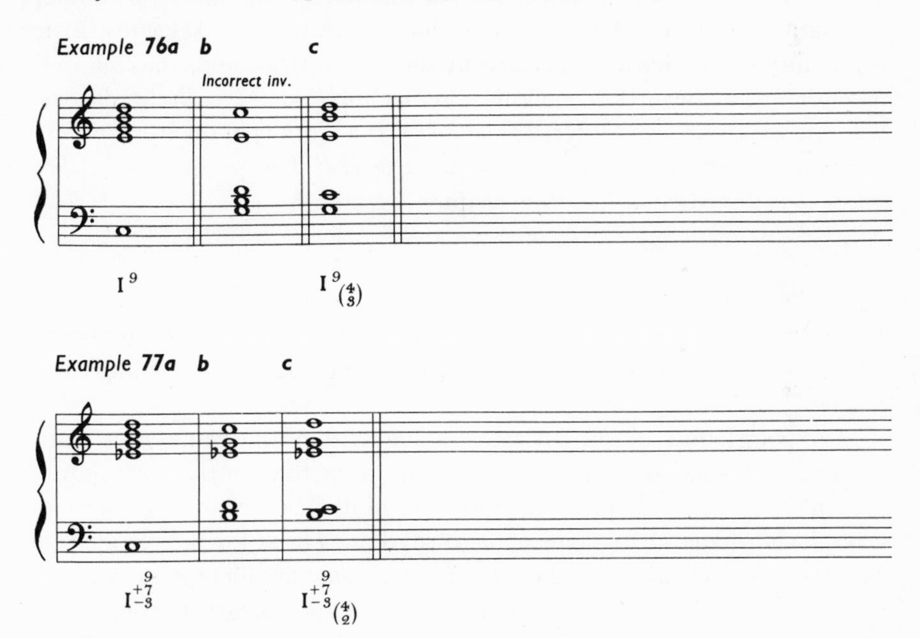

A triad, particularly a major one, which finds itself in a bass position, will create a root tone regardless of the contrary wishes of the student. *Example* 78a is a correctly organized root position F minor seventh-ninth chord. An attempted first inversion took the "bottom" out of this chord. Whether the F is placed in the soprano or in the alto (*example* 78b), it becomes subordinate to the new A♭ major triad which now controls all of the chord. The tone G fits as a major seventh, and F as an added sixth. *Examples* 78c and 78d restore the F minor chord.

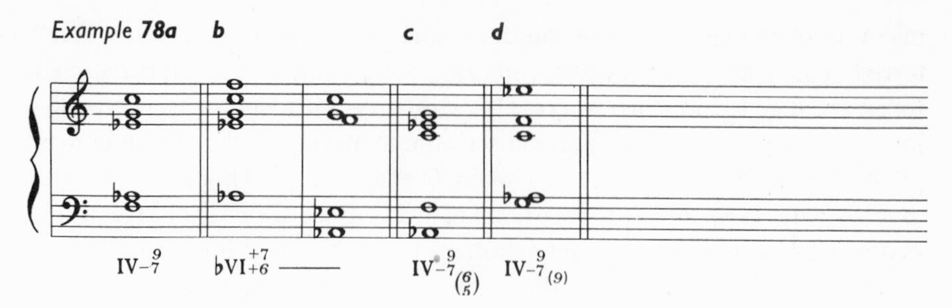

For these exacting demands of chord member placement, inversions of non-dominant chords usually arise from melodic bass movement in which the root is first heard clearly, and then is followed by the inversions. The infrequency of these inversions must not suggest that root positions are better. As with triads, all musical phrases must contain a balance of strong root movement intermingled with the subdued motion of roots in the inner voices, used primarily for contrapuntal effects.

Notation of these inversions is not marked by the figured bass interval association to the bass tone, as is customary with triads or sevenths. Instead, the quality of the chord is indicated by the root relationship, and followed, in parentheses, by the inversion figuration that applies to seventh chords. See the marking given to *example* 77c, 78c, and 78d. If a ninth is in the bass, use (9) in the same lower right corner, as in *example* 78d. The problem of analytical symbols is discussed at length in chapter six.

Progressions

Movement of ninths falls into two categories: (1) resolution of the ninth within the existing harmony and (2) progression of the ninth directly to a new root.

Appoggiatura ninths always resolve within the same root, usually falling as a 9–8 suspension, or resolving up to the third of the same chord. As seen in the previous chapter, appoggiatura ninths (a) occur together with a seventh chord and (b) receive enough rhythmic stress for the recognition of the ninth. A decision as to the naming of a tone, an appoggiatura ninth, is based on a rhythmic judgement and a historical knowledge of style.

There is no hesitancy in the label of a ninth chord if a harmonic root change occurs between the ninth and its resolution or if the ninth skips to another chord tone of the original harmony. No matter what rhythmic value the ninth has (excepting a brief neighboring tone), it will take on the full significance of a chord member. In *example* 79, an excerpt from *Tosca,* Puccini uses ninths in a manner which shows the next stage of the growth of ninth chords, after their use as appoggiaturas. These features are: (1) a predominance of the cadential progression; (2) an almost exclusive use of the dominant quality of ninth chord; (3) a rhythmic equality to the chord tones of the ninth as opposed to the appoggiatura technique; and (4) a surrounding texture of chromaticism that includes other types of appoggiaturas and suggestions of further harmonic growth.

The phrase opens with an active chromatic line in three out of the four voices. The harmony is not established until the chromatic movement ceases in the third measure and a clear G dominant chord is heard. As this goal is reached, the function of the moving lines which precede it can be understood. The bass leads into the root-position by starting on the third, B♮, and descends chromatically. The melody begins on the fifth of the chord, then raises it as an appoggiatura tone, enharmonically notated, and continues upward toward the peak in the third measure. The alto emphasizes the unrest by creating parallel diminished fifths at the outset which then settle and retain the third of the G dominant chord. The tenor for the most part holds the seventh of the chord, the tone F. This chromatic approach contains passing harmonies that briefly form their own identity. The first diminished seventh chord is one, followed by an outer contour which suggests a passing F dominant chord. These roots result from a coincidence of counterpoint, however, not from a harmonic scheme.

With the arrival of the root in the third measure, all voices participate in chord tones of the G dominant ninth. Notice that the ninth in the melody is not a rhythmically exaggerated tone, nor a non-harmonic note. It functions in the melody with the same freedom of movement that might be given to the root or third. It is a chord member resolved only when the entire phrase is heard in sequence six bars later.

Example **79** *Tosca. Puccini*

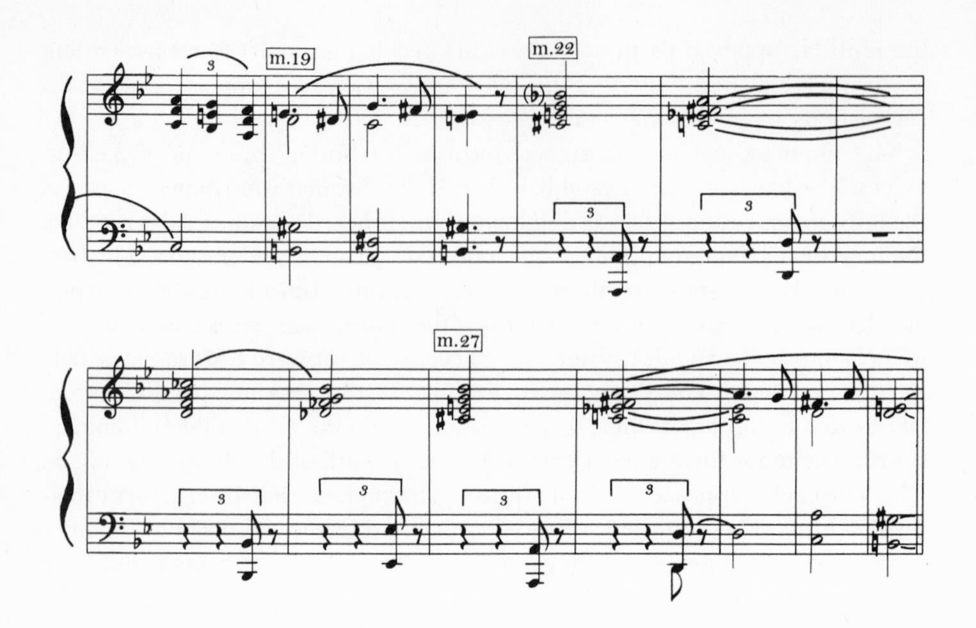

Progressions of the cycle of dominants abound in this excerpt. The opening sequential phrases move from a G dominant to a C dominant. In measure seventeen, the resolution to F is heard. An evaded progression then resolves to an E dominant chord ($\frac{4}{3}$) in the nineteenth measure. Dominant minor ninths use the cadential progression in groups of two, starting in measure twenty-two.

Observe the voice leading in the cadential progressions (measure twenty-two). The seventh and the minor ninth proceed downward—if the ninth had been used as an appoggiatura, it would have landed on the same tone, but in the first harmony.When changing to a new root, the tone to which the ninth progresses is most frequently the fifth. In a continuous progression of dominants, the tone of the ninth (minor or major, not augmented) alternates with the fifth. The seventh of the chord alternates with the third.

Notation for the dominant cycle almost always indicates an accurate vertical harmonic build-up. Most of the voices corroborate this harmonic organization in their resolutions, but one chord member is forced to be a noticeable exception. The chord tone of the third leads to the new root in a dominant to tonic progression. But if another dominant seventh takes the place of the triad, the third must be lowered by one half-step in order to form the new seventh of the next chord. In measure twenty-two (*example 79*) the C♯ cancels to C♮ as the A dominant minor ninth progresses to the D dominant minor ninth chord.

While the ninth and seventh generally descend together in a cadential progression, exceptions occur which derive from the movement of the seventh. *Example 80* illustrates a passage in which all voices move well, but also contain hidden fifths and rising sevenths. The seventh which resolves up is caused by the bass tone (or a soprano tone) taking over the expected note of resolution. For example, the II^9 moves to a first inversion of the dominant chord, sounding the tone of E in the bass. This tone would have been the normal resolution of the alto, which contains the seventh. With this bass substitution, the alto voice moves the seventh up, doubling the fifth of the V$^6_5$ chord. Paralleling the rising seventh is the rising ninth, moving to the tone that would have been the third of the first harmony.

Example 80

By sequence, a I^9 moves to a IV$^6_5$. Again, the bass takes over the alto's resolution, forcing the major seventh, E, up to the tone of F in the chord on B♭. The soprano, with parallel thirds, moves the ninth of the tonic chord up to the major seventh in the subdominant. The tenor at this point, may either stay close to the bass, as in the first two chords, or widen the spacing and move up to the B♭ root. By moving up, a balanced, widely spaced setting is prepared for the cadence. And with this beneficial aspect, parallel fifths arise between the tenor and the upper alto part. These fifths are not objectionable in that—(a) they occur in inner voices partially obscured by a "middle tone," the C in the divided altos, and (b) their harmonic relationship to each root is different. In the F major ninth chord, the fifth interval consists of the third and major seventh. It moves by parallel motion into the root and perfect fifth of the B♭ chord. As the upper harmonic extensions are added in thirds, this type of parallel motion is inevitable. It may be tolerated if it is not abused.

The thickening quality that ninth chords produce also tends to blot out the movement of the individual parts or make it less distinct. The additional chord members contain more common tones between the root progressions. Compare the B♭ major seventh chord (IV$^6_5$) with the following II^9 of *example 80.* All of the upper voices merely change position while the bass skips down to the new G root.

The tenor divides to help create a well spaced II^9 and again, as it does so, parallel fifths occur between the alto and the newly divided tenor. These are not readily detected because (a) the mediant progression containing many common tones effects a chordal blend of sound rather than a polyphonic one, (b) only half of the divided tenors move and form the fifths while the stationary common-tone is the essential feature that permits the large register changes to take place, and (c) the fifths occur between different chord members as described above. To increase the harmonic characteristic of this progression, the alto may also subdivide forming a sixth part temporarily. By holding the F, the inner fifths become more inaudible, and the divided alto line moves nicely into the melodic movement of the cadence. Notice that the alto in the dominant chord avoids consecutive fifths through the use of the suspended tone.

Do not think that the dividing of parts is the simple way of avoiding disciplinary practices. This technique is most valuable for ensemble writing of all kinds. Divisi in the string orchestra is obligatory if a rich sound is desired. In giving the brass or woodwind section of the orchestra a harmonic background of sound, it is likely that there are many more players available than the number of tones in a chord. The skill of expanding and shrinking chordal structures is as important as its counterpart, the polyphonic movement of voices.

All progressions that are effective with triads and sevenths may also be used with ninth chords. A complete departure from diatonic practices occurs in the Impressionistic period, which in later chapters is described in full. The first stage of learning the movement of the harmonic extensions is best accomplished within the familiar root progressions. With this in mind, most of the chromatically altered tones produce some form of dominant quality and progress by the cadential root movement or with an evaded progression.

When using the raised or lowered fifth or ninth, be sure to continue in the direction of the altered tone. An augmented tone must move upwards, usually (but not always), by a half step. A lowered tone is expected to descend. In both instances, a switching of parts may occur, postponing the necessary resolution for the latter voice involved.

In selecting a particular quality of dominant ninth, be consistent with the tonal center of the phrase, and with the quality of triad to which the ninth resolves. For example, in the evaded progression, V^9 to VI^7, the ninth of the dominant chord declares the major or minor tonality of the moment, and dictates the pitch of the submediant root. *Example 81a* illustrates an E dominant minor ninth chord which insists on an evaded progression to an F root, as drawn from the A minor scale. By contrast, a whole step movement from the E to the F♯ minor seventh, *example 81b*, is necessary if the pitch F♯, the major ninth,

Example 81a **b** **c** **d**

Incorrect *Permissible*

anticipates the progression. The incorrect cross relation is shown in *example 81c*, but the reverse form is correct in *example 81d*. The latter progression combines the bass movement of the ascending melodic minor scale with the descending form in the soprano. Each line reaches its intended destination.

The selection of the ninth in a dominant cycle will also reflect the quality of the surrounding key. This may be seen in *examples 82a* and *b* in which the last dominant ninth dictates the quality of the triad to which it is intended to resolve. A surprise switch to the major triad may occur, but this would be heard as an unexpected result. (Review example 49.)

Example **82a** **b**

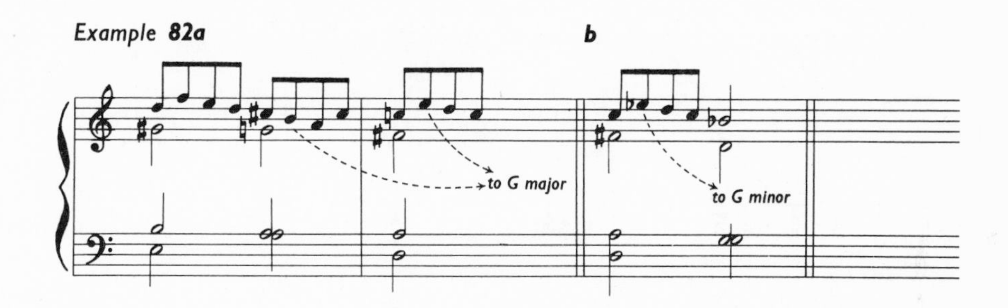

Wagner created such a surprising effect in this passage from *Die Walküre*, reduced in *example 83*. The sound of the minor ninth is chosen as an appoggiatura tone to the regular ninth and spelled accordingly. The accompaniment in the second measure shows the true notation followed by a vocal repetition of the first measure which then reaches its G♭ major destination.

Example **83** Wagner

A chord phrase illustrating the various chromatic alterations that may be given to a substantially diatonic controlled root movement is given in *example 84*. The chromatic texture increases as the modulation to F is realized, and reaches its height in the cadence. A far cry from Wagner, it illustrates a maximum degree of chromaticism that can be achieved with ninths and enharmonic functions. The chords which are altered and become dominant quality chords are marked first by the roman numeral which represents the root relationship of the key. After a semicolon, the dominant quality is symbolized by the familiar roman numeral V, and the inversion indicated in parenthesis in the lower right corner. It is not necessary to switch to this method at this time. The convenience that it will bring to the analysis of Impressionistic and Modern literature will be evident in the future chapters and is discussed accordingly.

Example **84**

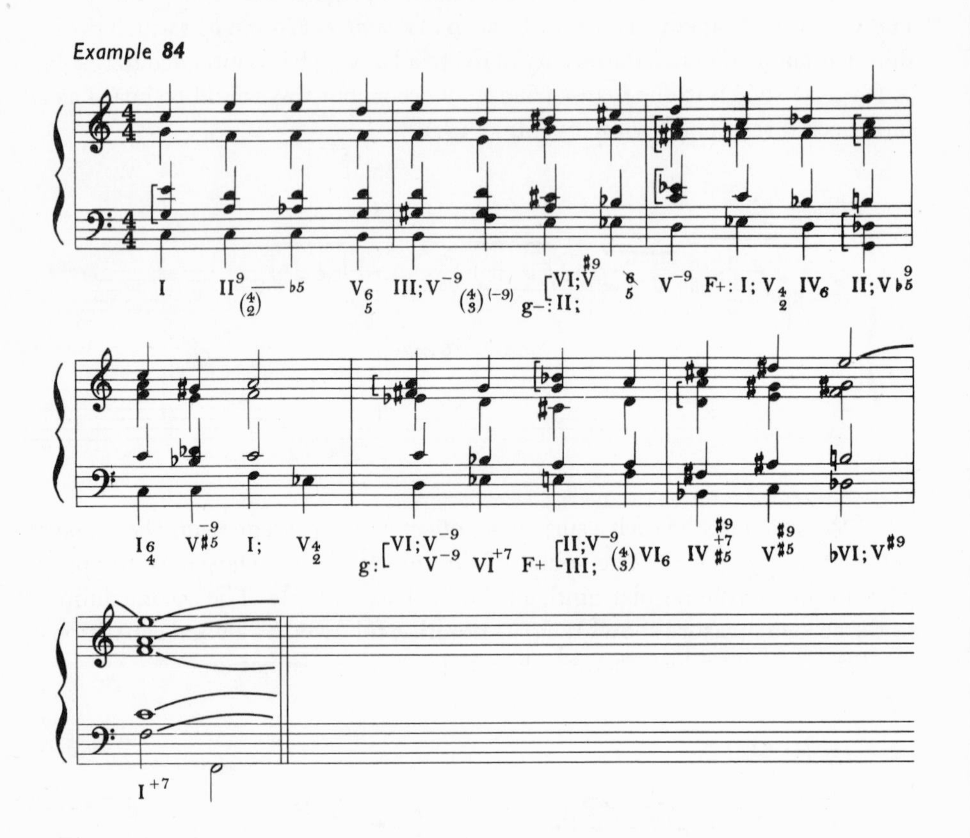

EXERCISES

A *Analysis*

1] In *Example* 85*a*, observe particularly the following features:

a] The individual character of the accompaniment.
The effect of the scale on the harmony of measures one and two.
The quality of the triads in the first phrase.
The unusual voicing of the bass part.

b] Find a ninth in the bass.

c] Find two ninth chords not of the dominant quality.

d] What quality ninth is emphasized in *Example* 85*b*? To which key does this phrase progress? Mark a harmonic analysis for both excerpts.

Example 85a
Nun Wandre, Maria. Hugo Wolf
Langsam und ruhig
p
p
3

Example **85b**

2] a] Examine all chromatic tones in *Examples* **86a** and **b**, noting their raised or lowered functions.

b] Find two ninth chords, one with an unusual voice distribution, and another of a non-dominant quality.

c] Observe the phrase construction in *Example* **86a**.

Example **86a** *Alle gingen, Herz, zur Ruh. Hugo Wolf*

Example **86b**

3] a] Mark a detailed harmonic analysis, with inversions, for *Example* **87a**.

b] Complete the accompaniment in measures 13–16, following an exact sequence of the preceding phrase.

c] In *Example* **87b**, circle the appoggiatura tones and mark the remaining harmony by letter name and quality.

Example **87a** César Franck

Allegretto ben moderato

13
continue accompaniment:
etc.
Example 87b
etc.

B 1] Unscramble the tones of the following ninth chords, *Example* 88, arranging each group in a normal tertiary organization. Retain the given bass tone, as either a root or a chord member of an inversion but change the soprano tone, if desired. Mark the resulting chord quality and inversion.

Example 88a **b** **c** **d** **e**

2] Each group in *Example 89* below begins with a designated ninth chord. Build this chord in the first of each pair of chords and resolve to a chord of your own choice using the given bass tone. If consecutive fifths occur, mark them and include an alternate harmonization or a melodic disguise. Mark all chords.

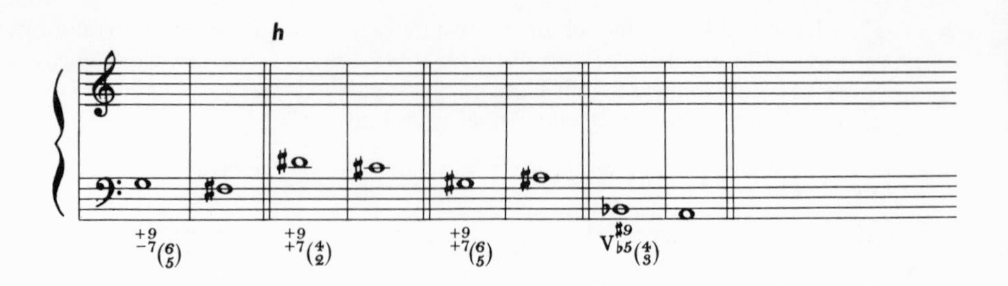

C Complete the indicated harmonizations in *Examples* **90** and **91**. Divide the voices as necessary, chiefly in the alto and tenor parts, forming a maximum of six voices where desired. The plain figuration respects the key signature. The quality is marked only where chromatic alterations are needed. The symbol V refers to the quality of the dominant, not necessarily the key relationship. Mark the quality of all chords and use roman numerals to indicate the relationship of chord to key.

Example 91

D 1] Add the upper voices to the given bass in *Example* **92**. Include simple rhythmic divisions similar to the previous exercises.

Example 92

Andante

2] The unfigured bass in *Example* **93** is suitable for a "piano style" bass part or ideal for a cello part in a string trio or quartet. Write the melody first, either for an ensemble or as a solo piano piece, following the general arpeggio outlines that are suggested. Use a fluent rhythmic style avoiding block chord connections. Include a sprinkling of ninth chords, giving consideration also to chromatically altered tones. If your inspiration prompts a desirable change in the given part, such as a different chromatic tone or an occassional departure from the suggested bass, follow your own idea. Mark dynamics and phrasing, aiming for a successful blend of music and theory.

Example **93**

5 Eleventh and thirteenth chords

Natural elevenths

It would seem logical that if the ninth chord grows out of a 9–8 melodic context, the eleventh chord should emerge out of a 4–3 suspension. Numerically, it does; but in usage the situation is not entirely equivalent. Whereas the ninth of a dominant chord has complete status as a chord tone, having achieved this independence very early, the eleventh chiefly functions as a non-harmonic tone in musical literature up to and even beyond 1900. What are the reasons for this paradox?

Before launching into this discussion, a definition is in order. The natural eleventh is the tone formed by an octave and a perfect fourth above the root of a chord. It is distinguished from the chromatically altered augmented eleventh, existing as an octave and an augmented fourth above a root, generally associated with dominant quality seventh or ninth chords. The natural eleventh, if built upon the dominant chord of a major or minor key, is actually the tonic tone and, as such, has a strong bearing upon the function of eleventh chords, as follows:

Play the V¹¹ (see *example 94a*), by adding the thirds, one by one, above the root, in the key of C major. Listen to the harsh dissonance created by the major third of the chord and the added eleventh. The fact that this interval between

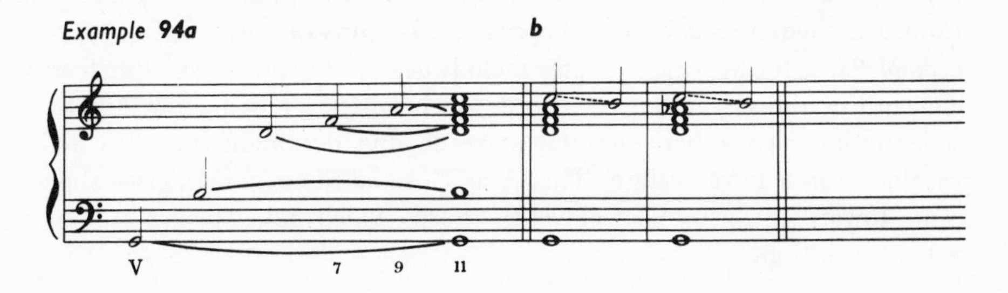

the third and the eleventh is a minor ninth is not the prime cause of the dissonant sound. Rather, it is the presence of the eleventh's tone of resolution, the third, heard simultaneously with the non-harmonic eleventh that causes a functional conflict. This is particularly offensive when occurring, as in this example, on the dominant chord, the 4–3 resolution involving the tonic and leading-tone. Either the third or the eleventh must be omitted.

Play the chord again (*example 94b*), this time omitting the third. Use either the minor or major ninth. This chord now contains no dissonant clash of intervals, but the eleventh will not hold as a chord tone. The resulting emptiness of the lower triad is forcing our eleventh to resolve down and to complete the necessary dominant quality. This melodic insistence of the natural eleventh to descend, in order to fulfill the needed third of the harmonic structure, prevents it from being on equal par with tones of the ninth or thirteenth. The latter may be added to complete dominant seventh chords and does not require a melodic resolution into the existing chord. The natural eleventh becomes a chord tone in Modern styles in which it frequently replaces the third, and in so doing, abandons the former Classical concept of triadic sound.

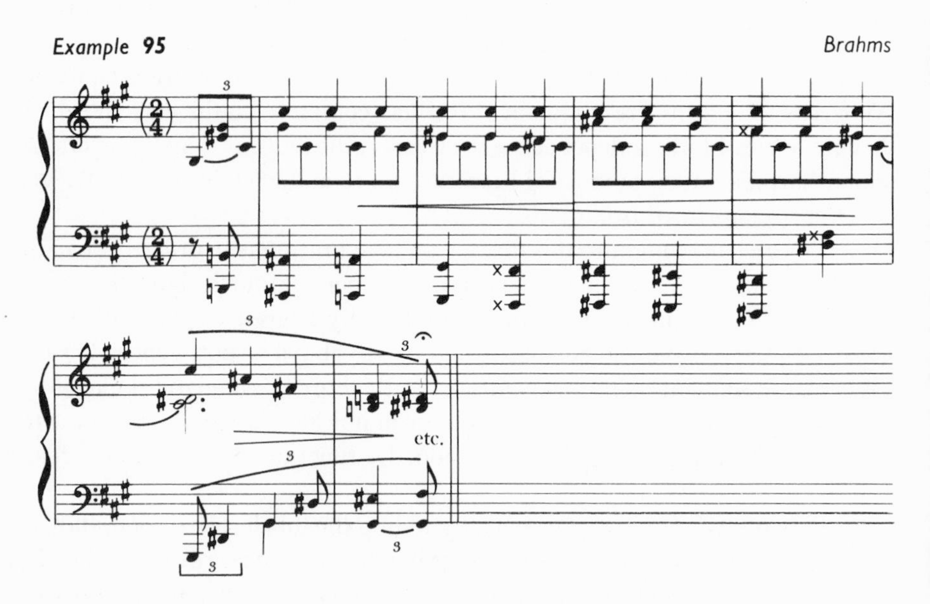

A rare example in which the natural eleventh momentarily frees itself from an immediate resolution is heard in the Brahms *Intermezzo*, Op. 76, No. 6, *example 95*. In the fifth measure, the melody descends in thirds, starting from the eleventh of the G♯ dominant chord. A chromatic embellishing diminished seventh intervenes between the start of this dominant eleventh and its resolution in a lower range. This is as close as the general Classical period came toward the use of an eleventh chord, which nevertheless still fulfills a 4–3 resolution.

A natural eleventh chord may be built upon degrees of the scale other than the dominant. As a II^{11} of a major key (see *example 96a*), the chord of six tones may be complete, including the third of the minor triad. The minor third, if included, must be the lower tone, separating itself from the eleventh by more than an octave. If, however, the 4–3 resolution occurs against the same root, or in a changing progression, it is best to omit the third for reasons of clarity.

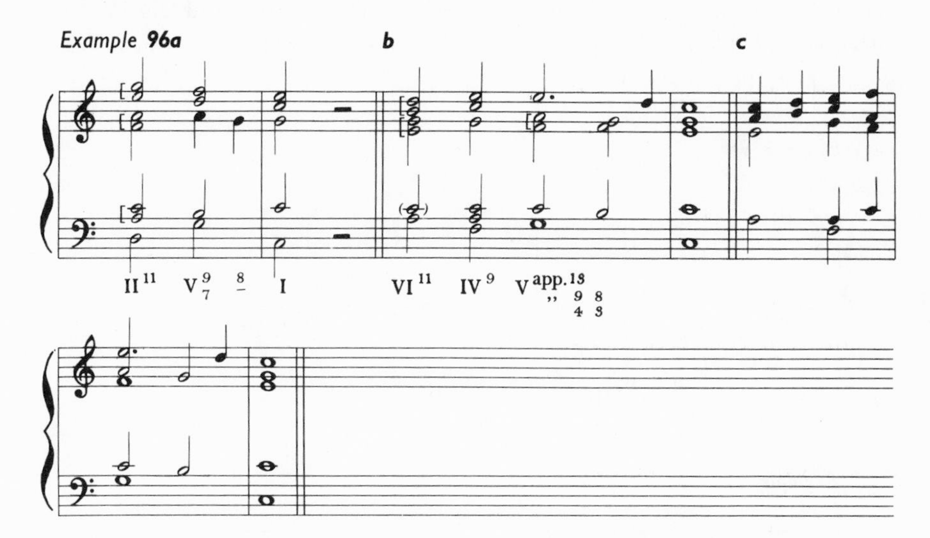

Example 96b, illustrates a VI^{11} proceeding to a IV^9 which then moves into the dominant. This latter chord includes all of the normal Classical melodic demands of the higher numbers: the ninth resolves to the root; the eleventh is part of the 4–3 suspension and the soprano tone is rhythmically elongated as an appoggiatura thirteenth. This dominant to tonic cadence might be part of an appropriate Romantic style, but the VI^{11} and IV^9 are not true to that period. Although not disagreeable, they are forced into resolving against the changing bass root progressions. *Example 96c* shows their allegiance to the basic triad formation, which is in keeping with the style of the cadence.

Adding an eleventh to a tonic major triad does not produce a I^{11} in a major key. The result (see *example 97*), is a V^7 heard over a tonic pedal tone.

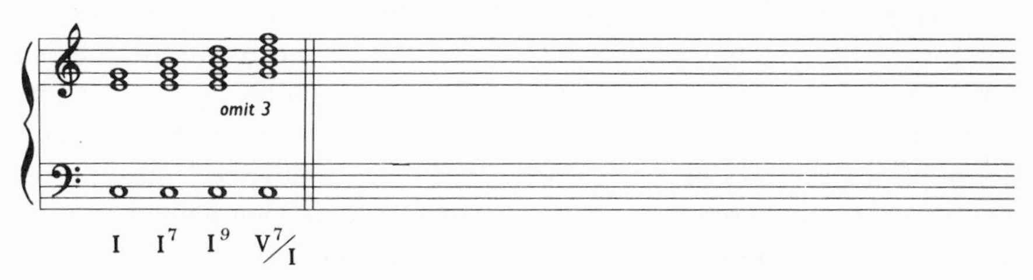

The third of the tonic is omitted, as it is the tone of resolution to the seventh of the dominant. This also applies to other triads of a key, in which the fifth, seventh, ninth and eleventh chord members form a dominant seventh quality in themselves. This occurs as a III^{11} of a minor key, or may happen by chromatic alteration. See *example 98.*

In a minor key, the tonic is represented by a minor seventh chord, and may be expanded into a natural eleventh chord. The I^{11} and the IV^{11} of the minor key are identical in quality to the II^{11} and VI^{11} of the major key. *Example 99* includes the I^{11} and IV^{11}.

Example 98

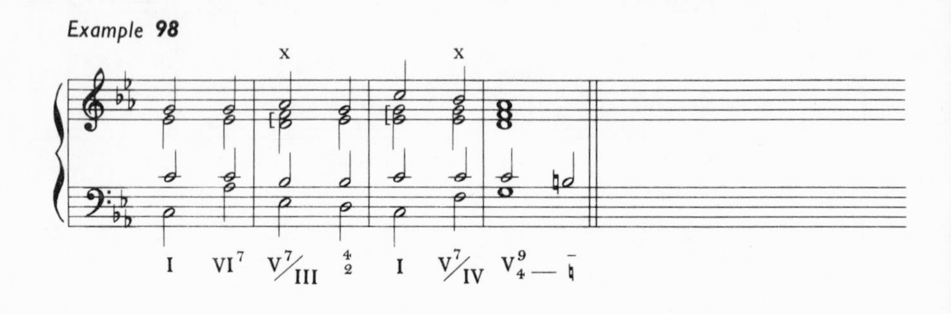

Example 99

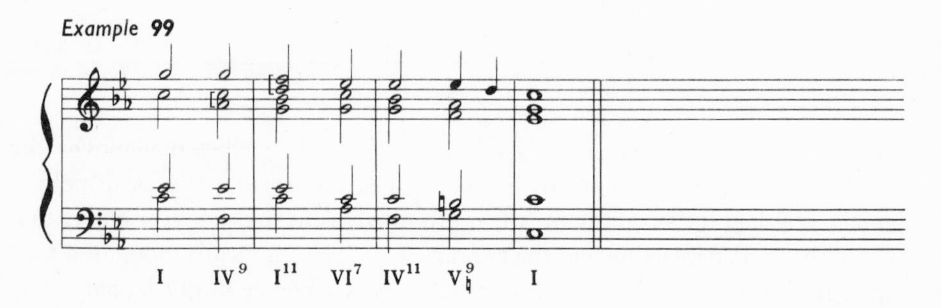

The predominating eleventh chord is, therefore, one built upon the minor triads of the key. Major triads demand the omission of the third and frequently place the status of the tone of the eleventh in doubt. There are two exceptions. The IV^{11} of the major key contains an eleventh which is actually the leading-tone of the scale. The distance from the subdominant root is an octave and an augmented fourth. See *example 100a.* The chord produced by the IV^{11} therefore is a "major seventh-augmented eleventh chord." The presence of the ninth, unaltered, is implied in the term. It may be omitted without any change to the eleventh chord's name. The same augmented eleventh relationship exists as a VI^{11} of a minor key (*example 100b*). The presence of the leading-tone of the key here affects the ninth, which may be raised, or not, depending on the progression. If raised, as in the example, the chord is called a "major seventh-augmented ninth-augmented eleventh chord." (This long name is necessary if a distinction with the dominant augmented eleventh is to be clear.) In both of the above chords the major third is included and, in fact, is an asset to the total quality.

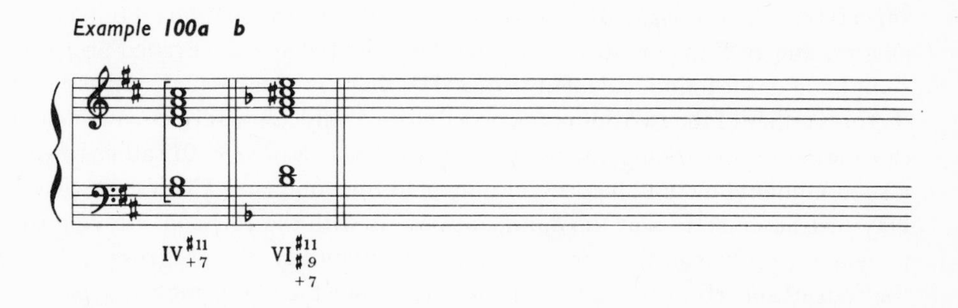

The eleventh, which is added to a half-diminished II⁷ of a minor key, is actually the tone of the dominant. See *example 101*. Most of the chord members, instead of supporting the bass tone of the supertonic, ally themselves with the dominant tone, its widely spaced register and tertiary organization notwithstanding. The lower members of the diminished triad fit the dominant realm as fifth, seventh and ninth. The two chord members, which are distant to both the supertonic root and the dominant, have the basic tendency to resolve down, completing the dominant chord. In this respect, the question arises as to whether the II^{11} can maintain its own identity or whether it merges into the dominant function. *Examples 101a* and *b* are identical except for the analytical conclusion. A justification for the II^{11} may be pursued if the bass voice contains the roots of both the supertonic and the dominant as in *example 101c*. Any inversion of the

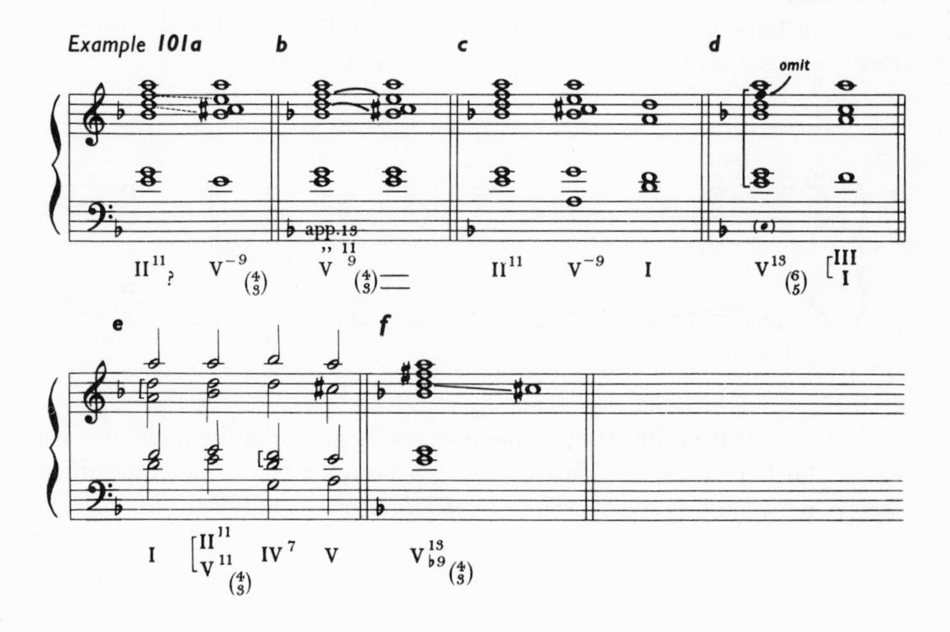

dominant blends with the tone of the super tonic root. In other progressions emanating from this chord, a careful appraisal of its function may reveal leading-tone characteristics that move as a dominant influence rather than as a supertonic one. *Example 101d* illustrates the function of a C dominant thirteenth progressing to F major. Realizing that the cadential and the evaded progressions hamper the individual identity of a II^{11}, that the progression a third down certifies either of the two dominant possibilities, only a few rare circumstances can suggest a II^{11} arising above a diminished triad. *Example 101e* allies it with a subdominant function, before continuing to the dominant. Critics, however, may justifiably state that the dominant begins with the II^{11} and, after a postponement, returns in the pure triad form. Diatonically, the progression from the root of supertonic to subdominant is rare, but the dominant can depart to either of the above roots and then return.

One more point can be presented to support the inclusion of the half-diminished supertonic chord into the dominant quality. If the tone forming the interval of the ninth with the bass tone is major, as in *example 101f*, the suggestion then of the basic major key center offsets the diatonic concept of the half-diminished II^7. The major ninth, F♯, contradicts the D minor tonality as compared with *example 101c*, and inhibits the distinction of a separate supertonic eleventh chord.

Subdominant triads or supertonic seventh chords, placed over a dominant pedal tone, will give an appearance of a dominant eleventh chord. See *example 102a*. The eleventh functions primarily in a non-harmonic role, first as a member of a passing subdominant triad, and secondly as a soprano 4–3 suspension. In the third and fourth measures, the upper harmonic movement contains a complete progression of its own, giving both the subdominant and supertonic chords an independent identity heard above the bass pedal tone. Neither chord is analyzed as a dominant eleventh.

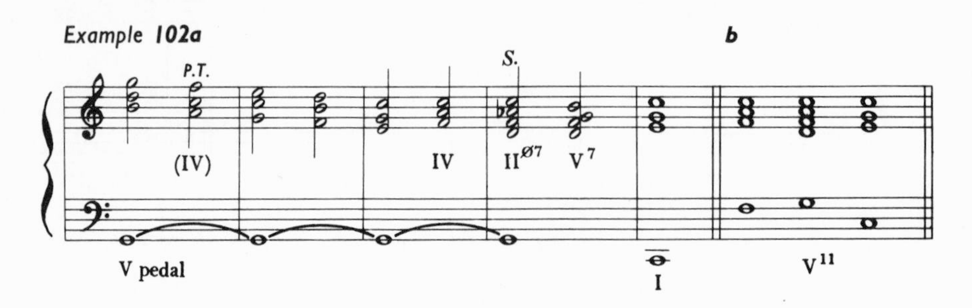

Example 102b, illustrates a melodic prolongation of the tonic tone which momentarily forms a V^{11}. This second chord is not a II^7 over a V; the differing factors between this analysis and *example 102a* are as follows:

1] The progression involves a direct movement of the V^{11} to the tonic, with perhaps a hint of an upper plagal effect, but not via a supertonic seventh;

2] The usual resolution of the highest tone C, the eleventh, to the third B is pointedly lacking;
3] The presence of the chord tone of the fifth binds the upper tones to the root of the dominant, except, (1) if an independant progression takes place among the upper tones, as in example 102a, and (2) if the upper quality itself is a seperate dominant seventh.
4] The dominant chord in this instance is built by the increase of succeeding thirds, placing the eleventh on top. A lower placement of the eleventh indicates a non-harmonic function.

As already mentioned, the omission of the leading-tone is not part of the general Classical harmony, and therefore, this V^{11} cadence represents a pseudo-diatonic idiom in which the progression dominant to tonic still prevails, but includes added tones extending beyond the Classical triads or sevenths. The natural eleventh, in this example, substitutes for the third and does not resolve into it.

These factors of progression, location and melodic independence determine the status of a chord member. Stylistically, minor natural eleventh chords contribute to a modal flavor in a Modern context. Because the third is so frequently omitted, the quality of the total chord may be uncertain.

The minor triad is suggested in the incomplete forms of the eleventh chord, thereby avoiding any dissonant implication with the major third. Such incomplete elevenths are apt to blend smoothly with other chords of similar extraction. Removing the 4–3 Classical heritage, natural elevenths gain much melodic flexibility and are recognized in the Modern idiom.

Augmented elevenths

It is interesting to note that the overtone series (refer to *example 48*) produces the tone that forms the augmented eleventh above the root of a dominant chord rather than that of a natural eleventh. The augmented eleventh, an octave and an augmented fourth above the root, is a chromatically raised tone when built upon the dominant root of a key. The natural eleventh, as already mentioned, is the tonic tone itself when used as a V^{11}. Its omission in the overtone series (at least within the important first sixteen partials) helps to account for the frequency of the cadential progression, root movement of a perfect fourth up. The lack of any anticipation of the next root within the existing harmonic structure creates a desirable motion toward the new forthcoming root.

The augmented eleventh is a smooth addition to the dominant seventh or ninth chord, which may be used in its complete form, or with the fifth omitted. As a chromatically raised tone, the movement of the eleventh must continue upward, generally resolving by a half step—see *example 103a*. If the root changes via the cycle of dominants, the augmented eleventh resolves to the major ninth of the next dominant (*example 103b*). The location of the augmented eleventh in the vertical grouping should be on top or in the upper division. It will not sound as a chord member if the third or especially the fifth is adjacent to it. See *example 103c*. The location of tones approximates the order found in the overtone series. The tones which stretch beyond the lower seventh chord must be separated sufficiently in interval distance with the lower triad in order to convey their role as upper harmonic members.

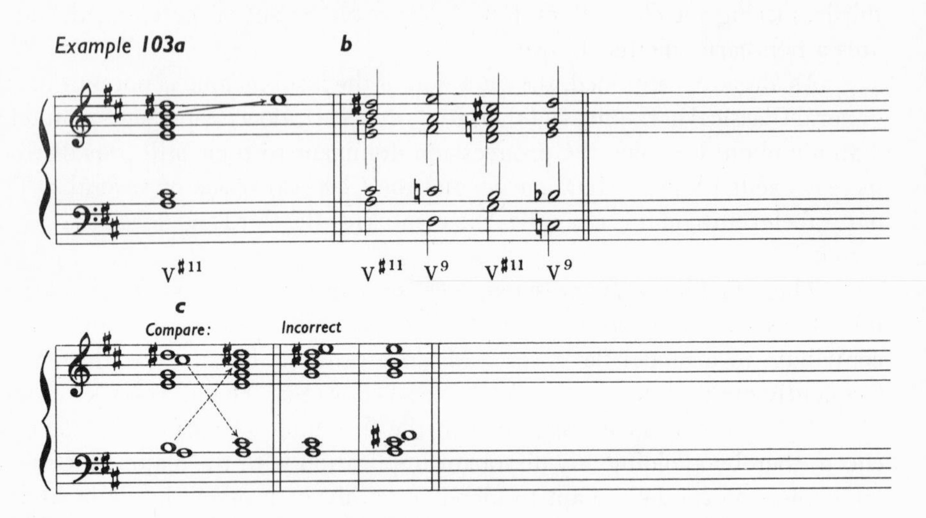

The enharmonic notation of the augmented eleventh results in the spelling of a lowered or diminished fifth to the root. As such, the tone's movement is expected to continue downward, thereby differentiating its function with that of the augmented eleventh. Other distinguishing features resulting from this basic change of direction are: firstly, the diminished fifth is generally not used in conjunction with the perfect fifth, as both have the same directional tendency, and secondly, in substituting for the perfect fifth, the diminished fifth may be located near the bass root, or may be the lowest tone itself, representing an inversion.

Many of the chromatic forms of the ninth chord may include the tone of the augmented eleventh. The dominant augmented eleventh chord may contain the minor ninth or the augmented ninth—see *example 104a*. In addition, the fifth may be raised, as in *example 104b*. The minor seventh-augmented eleventh chord is popular at a cadence. *Example 104c* shows the minor triad with both the minor and major seventh. The major quality seventh chord may contain the raised eleventh (*example 104d*). This combination was noted as occurring diatonically on the IV$^{\sharp 11}$ of a major key and on the VI$^{\sharp 11}_{\sharp 9}$ of a minor key.

Terminology for any of these chords continues in the same manner as for the ninth combinations. The quality of the seventh chord is indicated first. Any chromatic alterations to chord members are marked in numerical ascendancy up to the highest part of the chord. The number eleven, left alone, represents a natural eleventh, or sometimes called a "perfect eleventh" stemming from the perfect fourth interval relationship with the root. If a symbol is desired to call attention to a natural eleventh, either ♮11 or p.11 may be used. Signs representing major or minor are inaccurate. The sharp symbol indicates that the interval is augmented and does not have any association with the key signature. (Do not confuse this with the traditional figured bass indications.)

Example 104a b c d

V♯11 V♯11 ♭9 V♯11 ♯9 V♯11 ♯5 V♯11 ♭9 ♯5 V♯11 ♯9 ♯5 ♯11 −7 ♯11 +7 −3 ♯11 +7 ♯11 ♯9 +7

Inversions

The higher numbered chord members can not be switched into a lower position and remain as "high" extensions to a root. *Example 105a,* illustrates what happens to a natural eleventh when given the lowest bass location. It takes over as a root for the same upper notes.

An augmented eleventh may be seen as a bass inversion, but whether it truly functions as a raised eleventh is questionable. *Example 105b* is well notated as it transfers the melody C♯ into the bass line. The ascending direction demands this notation and the root motion of G to C♯ is fitting. Notice, however, the omission of the perfect fifth in this reorganization of the G chord. This suggests a melodic function for the bass line rather than a harmonic sound of an augmented eleventh followed by a ninth. The symbols for this analysis may nevertheless remain as it is understood that most bass inversions are chosen from a melodic conception, whether dealing with simple triads or involved harmonic structures.

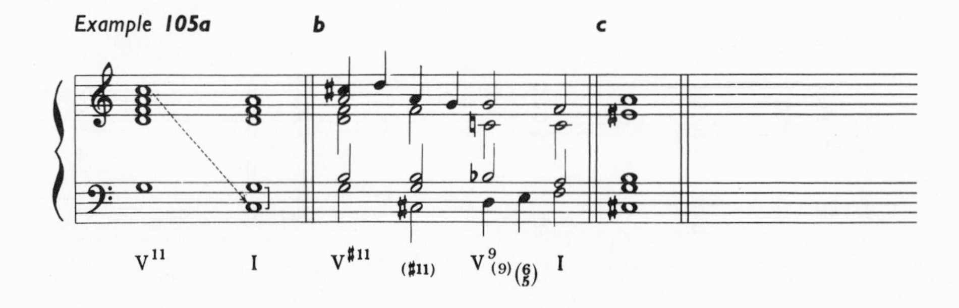

The existing tritone between the two lowest tones also creates an uncertainty as to root distinction. Compare this G chord with *example 105c*, in which C♯ is spelled as root and only the E♯ is enharmonically altered. Although the basic progressions of the G and C♯ roots differ, the tritone prevents the vertical sound from specifying its particular root. Not until the voices move is there a clearer root understanding, and even then certain circumstances may retain a flexibility of purpose. In notation, this tritone is therefore allotted much enharmonic freedom, so that the visual result does not always reflect a decisive harmonic function. (For additional material on tritones, see Chapter eleven entitled *Tritones, The Whole-tone scale* and *Whole-tone dominants.*)

One of the best suited inversions of the augmented eleventh chord is the second inversion. With the widest spread used between the raised eleventh in the soprano and the fifth in the bass, the distribution of chord members is well balanced. *Example 106* illustrates this, as well as the other inversions in their most frequent voice arrangement. The raised eleventh must remain in an upper placement. It can function as a diminished fifth in a lower situation and, presumably, resolve downward.

Example 106

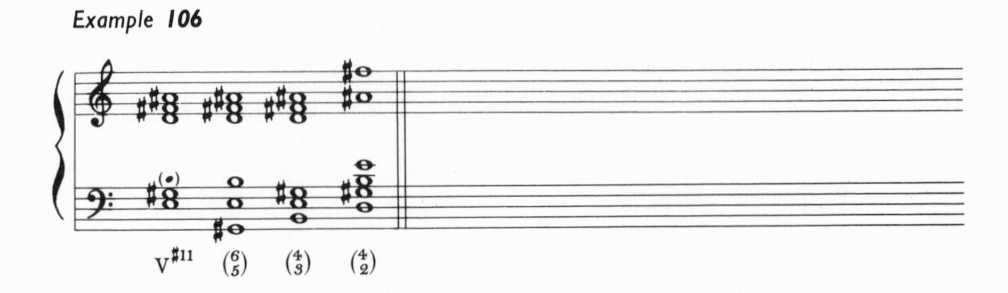

Some inversions of eleventh chords built upon minor seventh chords and major seventh chords are illustrated in *examples 107a* and *107b*. In all cases, the members of the lower triad are used immediately above the tone of the inversion. The inclusion of the third in non-dominant quality chords is helpful in recognizing the root when inversions are used. Therefore the ninth is frequently omitted.

Example 107a

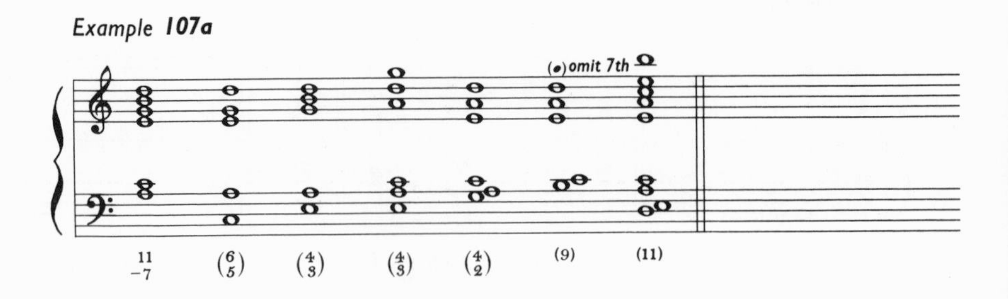

Example 107b

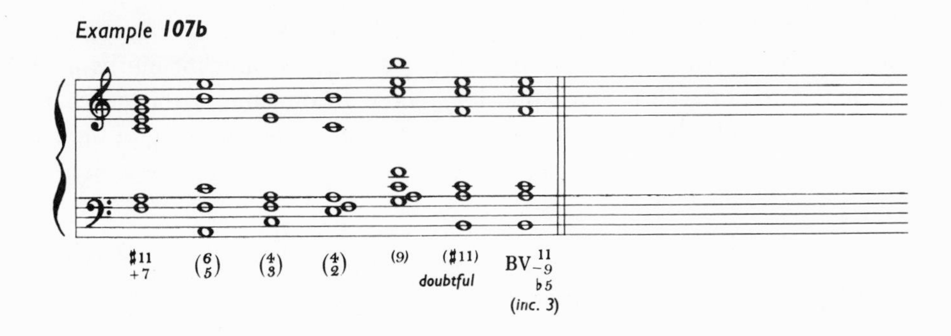

With the ninth in the bass, clustered next to the third, the seventh is omitted. If the seventh should be included in this inversion, it would hamper the root strength by forming other harmonic associations. A ninth in the bass is extremely weak and is heard most frequently as a non-harmonic tone.

In an attempt at the eleventh in the bass, notice the excessive doubling of the root and fifth in the last chord of *example 107a*, intended to detract from the bass tone. Whether it can be heard as an eleventh can only be judged in the context of the composition. There is much harmonic support for the bass tone as root, with an adjacent cluster.

The ninth is most commonly omitted in inversions of the major seventh-augmented eleventh chord, given in *example 107b*. Remember that only the actual counterpoint of the phrase can determine just how the voices should be arranged. Their role as chord tones or non-harmonic tones will be judged automatically when given a motivic understanding.

Thirteenth chords

The dominant thirteenth chord emerges similarly to the ninth chord, both arising out of melodic non-harmonic tones. The tendency of the thirteenth, an octave and a sixth above the root, is to resolve downward to the fifth of the same chord. If the resolution occurs on the same root, the chord will emerge as a ninth. If there is a prolonged rhythmic stress to the thirteenth, and the resolution is short and secondary, then the full harmonic scope will be heard as a V^{13} and may be called an "Appoggiatura thirteenth," similar to the appoggiatura ninth already discussed. If the chord changes upon resolution of the thirteenth, then unquestionably the full stature of the thirteenth has been achieved and the chord may progress in any fashion appropriate to the style of the composition.

Thirteenths, together with ninths, reflect the major or minor scale they are derived from. The G V^{13}, drawn from the scale of C major, has E as the tone of the thirteenth, an octave and a major sixth above the root. In the scale of C minor, the G (V^{13}) would have the E♭ as thirteenth, an octave and a minor sixth above the root. See *example 108a, b*. Being part of a major or minor scale affects their use in a key in the same way that was discussed with relation to ninths. Review paragraph (b) under the heading, "Dominant ninths in the major and minor scales" in chapter four. To indicate a minor thirteenth, use – 13 or ♭13. The latter symbol draws attention to the lowering of the tone by a flat.

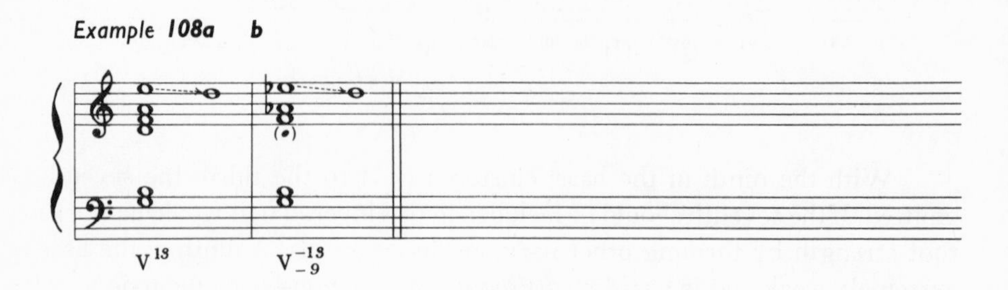

Interesting results can be heard by mixing the minor, major or augmented ninth with the minor or major thirteenth. One can build a dominant minor ninth and add a major thirteenth (*example 109a*). (Remember to omit the eleventh if you use the third.) Reverse the qualities by trying a major ninth with a minor thirteenth (*example 109b*). At first, this may sound very sour! Now omit the fifth, and listen carefully to the top tone we are calling the lowered thirteenth. Its tendency is to resolve upward! It isn't a lowered thirteenth, but an augmented fifth producing a $V^{9}_{\sharp 5}$! (*Example 109b.*) This is caused by the ninth

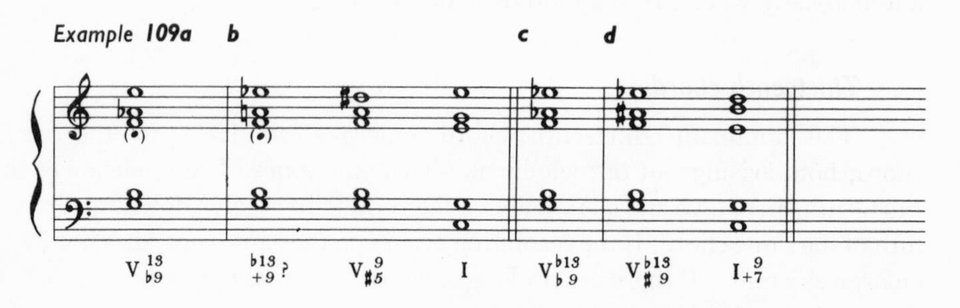

announcing a major tonality, and the raised fifth resolving upward to support that. The dominant with a minor thirteenth generally includes the minor ninth, that is, $V^{\flat 13}_{\flat 9}$ (*example 109c*), or occasionally an augmented ninth (*example 109d*). The major thirteenth can occur with all ninths and with the natural or raised eleventh. Use the raised eleventh with a minor thirteenth only if the distance separating these two tones is large, preferably with the raised eleventh above the thirteenth. See *examples 110a, b, c,* and *d*.

Location of tones in a chord of the thirteenth is twice as important as in the ninth. Due to the upward climb of thirds, the thirteenth rightfully demands the highest position. Occasionally, it will permit the ninth to preside above, with

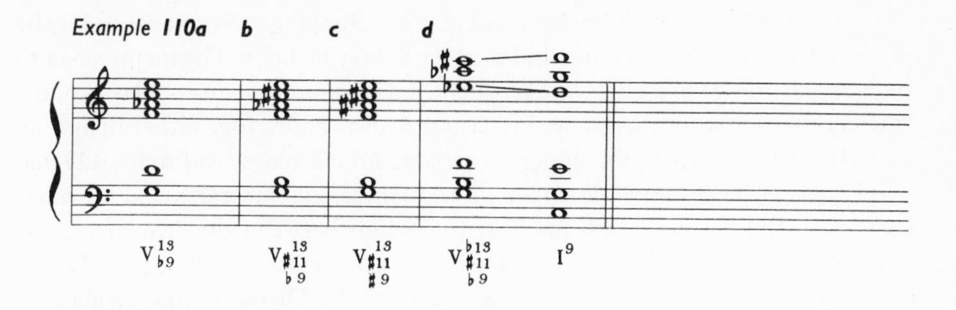

the thirteenth directly beneath. The seventh of the chord must not be placed next to the thirteenth, and the fifth is best omitted. The third and the root belong in the bass or at the bottom of this harmonic ladder. There is one exception to this that is important to remember. With inversions, the root may be placed in the uppermost voice. In this position it merges with the lowest tones, and does not get bottled up inside. First inversions, third inversions, or those with the ninth in the bass, frequently rely on the clarity of the soprano tone to unite the chord members. This is illustrated in *example 111a*. Notice the ninth presiding above the thirteenth in the third inversion, and the root, placed above all chord members in the fourth inversion.

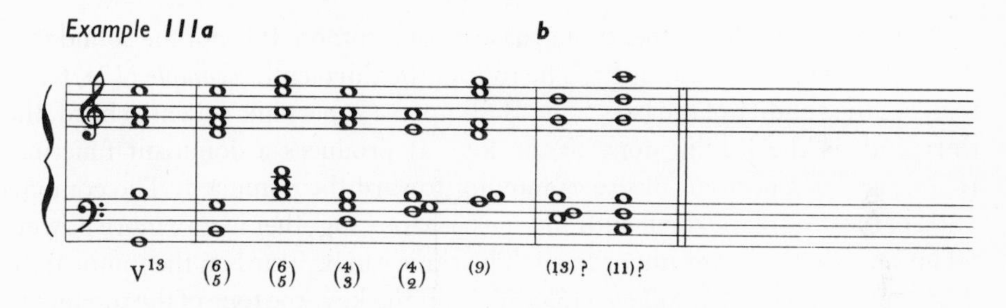

It is most unlikely that a thirteenth or an eleventh could occupy a harmonic bass position. *Example 111b* illustrates an attempt to give the thirteenth a bass position and preserve the G root. Nestled next to the seventh, it becomes unclear and permits the upper tones to predominate. If the seventh were lifted up an octave, the bass tone would become the root for an E minor seventh-minor ninth chord. Completely unsuccessful is the eleventh in the bass. It forms an upper dominant ninth above a bass pedal tone.

These restrictions may seem binding, but consider that the thirteenth chord has seven tones in its full complement. If used without discretion as to the degree of importance of each tone to the root, sounds will emerge that may completely distort the original intention. Any bass tone will have its overtones supporting it as a root, or will combine with the tenor note to create the framework for a different chord than the one planned.

Most thirteenths are of dominant quality. Running a distant second is the major triad upon which a ninth and thirteenth may be built. The major seventh may or may not be present. Used frequently with a tonic quality, the role of the thirteenth, and the ninth, is more in the nature of an added tone rather than as an active chord member of the upper hierarchy. Added tones tend to merely add color to a set function, while upper chord members create a demand for more motion in the harmony. To make a distinction between the two functions; the thirteenth chord is built upon a seventh chord foundation, while added tones are added to triads and do not contain the seventh. Therefore, the symbol I^{13} implies the presence of the seventh and ninth. The triad containing an additional tone is marked I + 6. This is illustrated in *example 112*, and further described within the Impressionistic chapters.

Example ***112***

Minor seventh-thirteenth chords are not common. It is not the sound that is avoided, but the terminology. The tone of the thirteenth, *example 113a*, tends to upset the solidity of the bass tone. Built upon a supertonic seventh chord, the thirteenth is the leading-tone of the key. It produces a dominant function, replacing the supertonic desire of moving toward the dominant. The combination of the tone of the thirteenth and the bass tone together form a more powerful union than the lower minor triad. The same can be heard on the minor triad of the mediant chord (*example 113b*). Within the key, the tone of the thirteenth is the tonic. An E minor seventh-minor thirteenth chord doesn't have a chance! The root is on top, C major.

Examples 114–116, show some useful inversions and progressions, including root movement other than the cadential progression. Notice that

Example ***113a*** ***b***

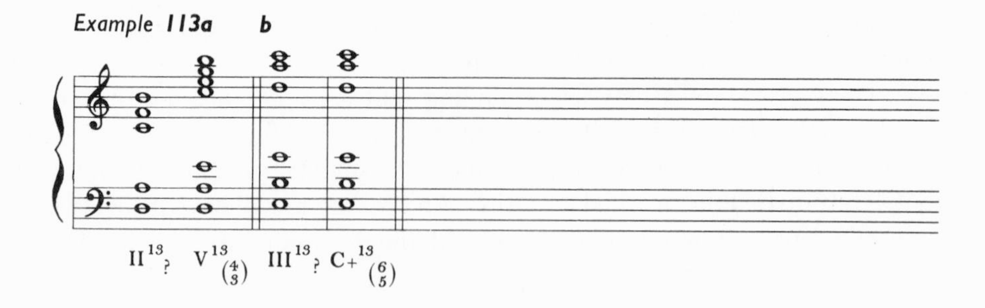

thirteenth chords prefer resolutions to other higher-numbered harmonies. The tone of the thirteenth alternates with the ninth in the cycle of dominant root motion. It may be recalled that the ninth tone alternated with the fifth. It is the fifth that the tone of the thirteenth is replacing. This familiar progression is illustrated in *example 114* of the group below. Notice that the incomplete V^{13} at the cadence produces the effect of an anticipation, or échappée, when resolved into a cadential triad.

The figuration is marked by quality as outlined in the chapter on ninth chords. The symbol V represents the dominant quality and does not necessarily reflect its association to the key center.

The harmonic progressions illustrated in the preceding examples give proof that such sounds were not used at the time when the appoggiatura

Example 116

thirteenth became familiar. In this chapter, the factual organization of these chord tones is important. Their incorporation into good musical phrases will be more meaningful when blended with the Impressionistic style and finally liberated from the hackneyed progressions they are frequently associated with. After the discussion of leading-tone harmonies, the Modern application of these higher-numbered chords is outlined.

EXERCISES

A *Analysis*

1] In *Example 117*, from *Tosca*, observe the following:
a] Treat each accented tone in the introduction measures one to three as an appoggiatura. What chord is being outlined by all of the sixteenth notes?
b] Compare the semi-cadence of the first phrase with that of the second

phrase. How does it differ and what unusual feature is common to both occurrences?

c] Discuss the pros and cons of a possible natural eleventh chord in measure fifteen.

Puccini

2] Mark a complete harmonic analysis in *Example 118.*

a] Mark the letter name roots, qualities and all higher-numbered tones.

b] Find the changing key centers and indicate the subtle effects of modulation that are present.

c] Using brackets, mark the motives and their extensions, observing the irregular phrase construction.

Example 118 *In Dreams. Vaughan Williams*

3] a] Analyze *Example 119* harmonically by marking letter name roots and qualities, including all higher-numbered tones.

b] Many of the dominant quality chords resolve by root movement which differs from the cadential progression. Mark the root movement of dominants as 1. Cad. (cadential, perfect fourth up, or fifth down); 2. Ev. (evaded, step-wise up or down); 3. Pl. (plagal, perfect fourth down) or 4. Med. (mediant, a third up or down).

Example 119 *Moonlight. Vittorio Giannini*

4] *Examples 120a, b* illustrates the gradual merging of the non-harmonic tone and higher-numbered chord tone.

a] Mark these melodic tones by their chord member relationship above the particular note.

b] In the second excerpt (*Example 120b*), note the use of inversions, and their effect upon the similar melodic material of the first excerpt. Mark letter name roots, qualities, and inversions.

c] Rewrite the accompaniment of *Example 120b* so as to gain practice in working with higher-numbered chord tones. In the melody, switch the rhythmic emphasis from the lower seventh chords members to the upper extensions. In the bass, modify the repeated measures by exploring other inversions. Do not hesitate to add chord members which do not appear in the original. Mark your harmonic results.

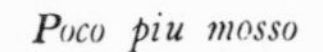

B 1] Unscramble the tones in *Example 121*, reorganizing them in a good tertiary order. Retain the given bass tone and the indicated inversion. Mark the quality that these tones form.

Example 121a **b c d e**

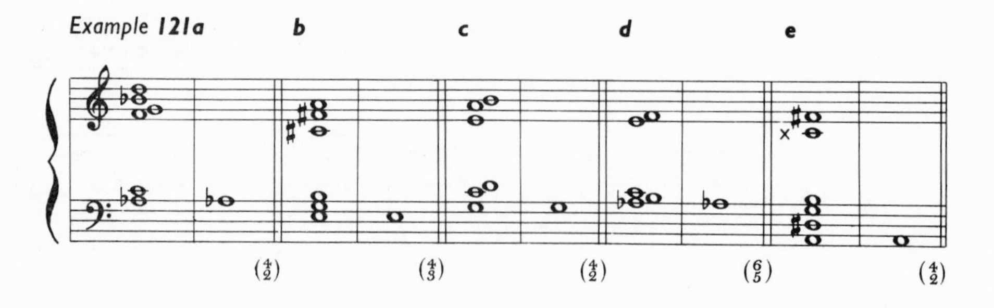

2] In the keys of E major and E minor, build the eleventh chords that are formed by each scale and mark their quality. Indicate any tone that is best omitted.

3] Build five thirteenth chords from the bass root of B, each with a slightly different chord member complement. In addition, select one inversion for each of the above combinations. Resolve the inversion with a cadential progression to either a major or dominant quality chord.

4] Write a melody above the given accompaniment in *Example* 122. Plan it for an instrument such as a flute or violin. Include the indicated higher-numbered chord tones in any rhythmical situation you wish, whether as appoggiatura tones or full chord members.

Example 122

C 1] Analyze *Example* 123 by marking figured bass and quality.

Example 123

2] The figured bass in *Example 124* indicates the harmonization necessary to complete the remaining voices. The dominant symbol represents quality. Add the diatonic roman numerals. A few melodic suggestions are given in the upper voice.

Example 124

3] The given bass in *Example 125* includes suggested figurations. The complete chord make-up is not given. For example, the inversions marked are not intended to represent only seventh chords. The student is urged to try to hear as many higher numbered chords as possible. A rhythmic division of the basic pulse will provide an opportunity for a more lyrical melody as well as the inclusion of more chord members. Use the voices similarly to *Example 123*.

Example **125**

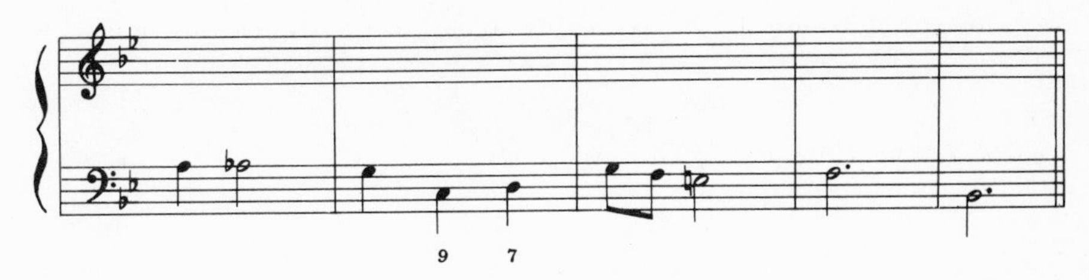

4] Treat *Example* **126** as a Waltz. A suggested melody and bass are given, without figuration. Supply your own harmonization and give the left hand a bouncing accompaniment. Measures nine to twelve require some contrast with the opening style. Try an inner, or soprano contrapuntal motive relinquishing the "beat" for this phrase. After the semi-cadence in measure twelve, repeat part of the first phrase and cadence with your own material.

Example **126**

6 Leading-tone chords

Analytical terminology

There are two theories as to the naming of the leading-tone seventh chord. One theory calls the leading-tone the root, and moves up in thirds respectively to complete the seventh chord, namely VII^7. The other does not acknowledge the possibility of giving the leading-tone status as a root because (a) it has a singular function of moving toward its tonic, and (b) the diminished triad upon which the VII^7 is built cannot accoustically claim to be a root-position chord, according to the theory of overtones and of combination tones.* [Overtones arise from a single sounding tone. A leading-tone would invoke the same proportionate overtone series as any other note, and would therefore include a perfect fifth, rather than a diminished one, as a necessary supporting partial to the root. By the same theory, the diminished fifth does exist as an intervallic formation between the fifth and seventh partials. Combination tones are the product of an interval, or the result of two or more simultaneously sounding tones. The sound of a minor third, struck simultaneously, produces two combination tones both giving the pitch of a major third below the sounding minor third. For example, the minor third, B and D, produces a strong combination tone G two octaves and a third below it, plus another G directly below the original third. This latter one is the result of the first low combination tone and the sounding minor third.] This second theory, therefore, calls the leading-tone seventh chord an incomplete dominant ninth. The chord is described as being built upon the third of the dominant structure with the root omitted. It is marked V_9^0, the symbol "o" meaning incomplete. (Do not confuse this indication with the diminished quality as marked "o7".) There is merit in both of these methods of analysis; each may be applied to its proper situation. Factors contributing to each theory follow.

* For additional reference, see *The Craft of Musical Composition* Book I by Paul Hindemith.

Comparison of intervals between the diminished and half-diminished chords:

A diminished seventh chord has the unique quality of being built with the sound of minor thirds. By adding the dominant tone below it, this distinct color is disrupted by the richness of the major third. The chord VII^{o7} (diminished leading-tone seventh) and the $V^{\flat 9}$ differ in sound. Composers have constantly used the diminished seventh separately with no inclusion of the dominant tone. Enharmonic treatment of the minor thirds provides an excellent means of modulation and of chromatic embellishment. A dominant reference into such passages would certainly cancel the intended subtlety. The symbol for a diminished seventh chord should therefore reflect its individuality and not indicate a dominant framework unless used in that capacity.

The leading-tone seventh chord formed by the major scale is much more conducive toward recognition as part of a dominant ninth chord. (As a seventh chord, the quality is called half-diminished, $VII^{ø7}$, the intervals form the diminished triad but not a diminished seventh.) By not containing equal intervals, the inversions of this leading-tone chord always retain their original functions as dominant chord members. They do not adapt to enharmonic mingling. If the dominant tone (as a bass root) is added to the half-diminished seventh chord, clarity and strength of purpose are gained. The inclusion of the dominant tone enhances the already existing characteristics of the chord members, thereby binding the seventh and ninth chords to a mutual purpose.

Merger of VII^7 and V^7:

The leading-tone and dominant chords become inseparable in their function when they are used in succession, one arising out of the other. The descending melodic resolution of the seventh, intervallically labelled as 7–6 (see *example 127a*), accounts for most of the melodic movement which blends into the V^6_5. Regardless, however, of how these chords merge: in any inversion, or in "reverse," V^7 into VII^7, the total group emerges together as one harmonic entity supporting the dominant.

A re-evaluation of the figured bass

Notice how the numerical figuration, *example 127a*, shows the intervallic distance between the bass tone and the upper melodic movement while *example 127b* illustrates the harmonic recognition inside the dominant structure. In the first example, the figuration accurately denotes the interval relationships present, but does it convey the harmonic function of the chord members? Does the bass tone, B, start as a root and change to a leading-tone? Or, the D and F, do they start as third and fifth in order to become fifth and seventh? Through years of theoretic tradition, $^6_5$, $^4_3$ and $^4_2$ have been translated to represent, respectively, the third, fifth and seventh in the bass. We know how the numbers came about, but are they helpful in a purely harmonic setting? *Example 127c* illustrates an arpeggiated version of the G V^{-9}. All tones are heard with their harmonic reference to the root of the chord, not with an intervallic reference to the bass tones. The rapidly changing bass tones also discourage any particular emphasis on the starting tone, the fifth. All tones merge as one harmonic unit, a dominant minor ninth.

Example 127a **b**

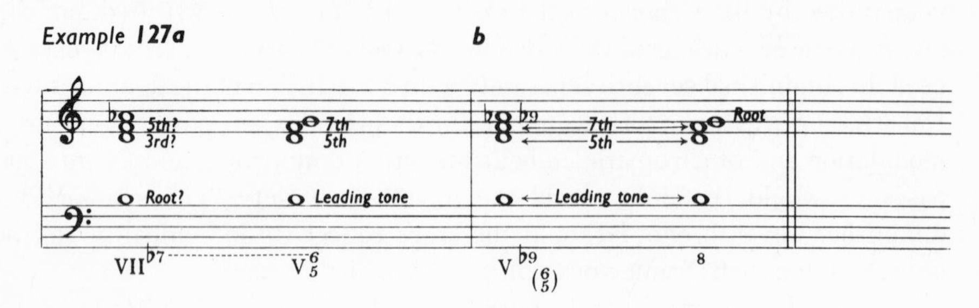

Example 127c

The leading-tone chord, a forerunner amongst the more advanced dominant complexes, suggests the need for analytical terminology which separates the intervallic analysis from the resulting harmonic combinations. The following plan combines the best features from both the aforementioned theories:

Let the marking VII^7 represent the leading-tone chord providing that—

(a) there is no resolution or involvement of the dominant tone, [in which latter case the symbol V would be used];

(b) that the symbol VII represents a quality of sound, either VII^{o7} or VII^{ø7}, resulting from a chord formation built upon a leading-tone—the leading-tone is not a root; and

(c) that no higher-numbered chord member exists beyond the four tones represented by the diminished or half-diminished quality.

This third qualification is necessary because as more chord members are built upon the leading-tone chord, the dominant framework grows stronger. The significant equidistant diminished seventh relationship vanishes as the new intervallic formations are created. This is discussed more fully immediately following this analytical outline.

This plan retains the individuality, particularly of the diminished seventh, when left unresolved to the dominant. It does not imply a five note chord, V$^0_9$, when it doesn't sound that way. On the other hand, if the dominant tone emerges from a VII⁷, or vice versa, it anchors and clarifies the single function of all combined chord members, recognizing the VII⁷ only as a contributing upper part of the dominant hierarchy. In this case, the dominant tone shall be marked as root, and the bass inversions derived from the dominant chord, regardless of the particular rhythmic location that denotes the 7–6 or 9–8 melodic resolution. See *example 128*.

Example 128

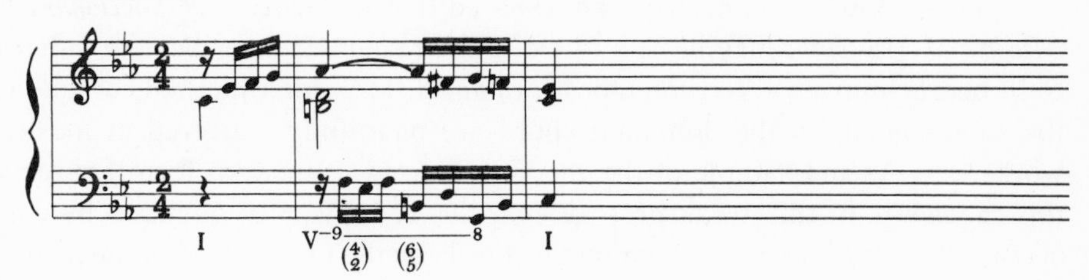

Papillon, by Grieg, *example 129*, illustrates so well the function of each chord member starting in a leading-tone situation. The leading-tone is the G♯, heard by its progression to the tonic, A major. The bass tone, D, is the seventh of the dominant organization; observe its descending motion into the first inversion of the tonic chord. The melody tone begins on the ninth which, at the end of the chromatic sixteenths, resolves down to the dominant tone itself, fulfilling an appoggiatura 9–8 resolution.

Example 129 *Papillon. Grieg*

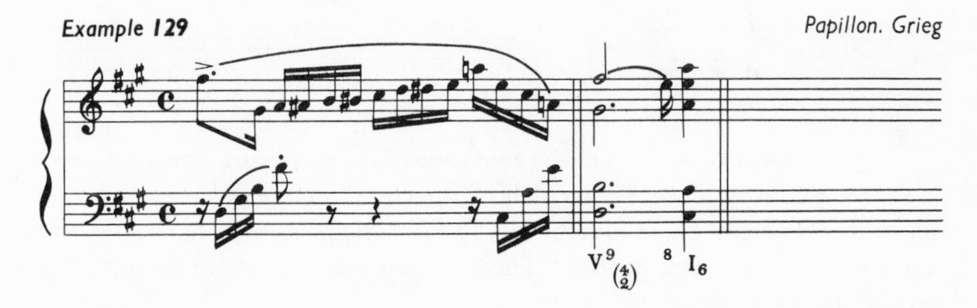

The identification of the chord members results from the selection of a tone which functions as a leading-tone. In many chromatic passages, no single tone of a diminished seventh chord can claim any particular identity. Only upon a resolution can the real leading-tone be detected. If the chord is inverted and the leading-tone is recognized in an upper voice, the bass tone relates to the same tertiary organization that provided the source of the leading-tone. All of the chord members are derived from the dominant organization. A first inversion of the leading-tone chord contains the fifth in the bass, the second inversion is built upon the seventh, and the third inversion arises above the minor ninth. See *example 130*.

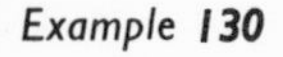

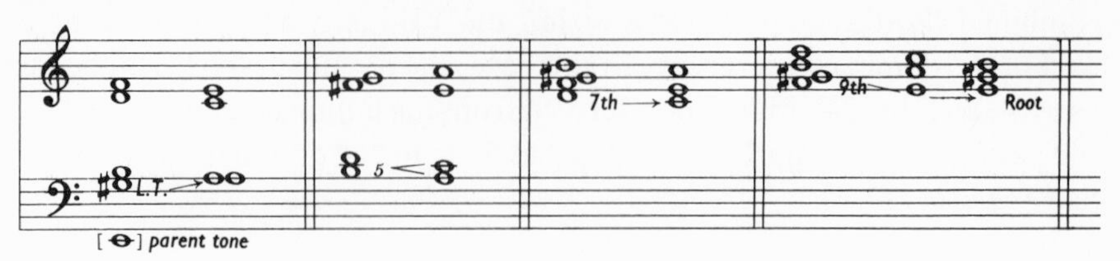

The following quote from an 1889 edition of Grove's *A Dictionary of Music and Musicians* may be of interest to the reader. It describes the cadence to Robert Schumann's *Toccata,* Op. 7, *example 131*: "Other methods of joining the subdominant to the dominant chord are plentifully scattered in musical works. . . . As an example of the theory vitalized in modern form [observe this cadence]. In this weak progression, the I^6_4 is happily obviated by connecting the subdominant and dominant chords by the minor third of the former becoming the minor ninth of the latter; and at the same time the novelty of using this inversion of the dominant minor ninth as the penultimate chord, and its having also a slight flavor of the old plagal cadence, gives an additional vitality and interest to the whole."

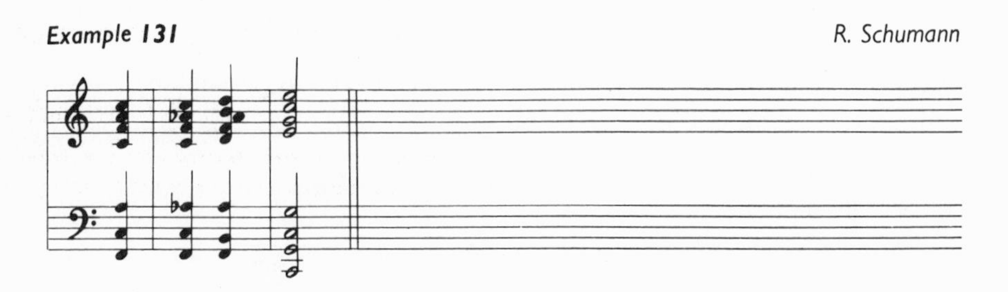

It is noted, of course, that the root tone of the dominant chord referred to is absent in this cadence. Nevertheless, the chord members were drawn from the dominant root. This quote brings to light the process of musical growth. Time can blur facts, or hide them. There was no confusion about the diminished seventh chord in 1889!

The figuration, derived from early contrapuntal principles, and effective for all chords built upon roots, causes misleading implications when applied to

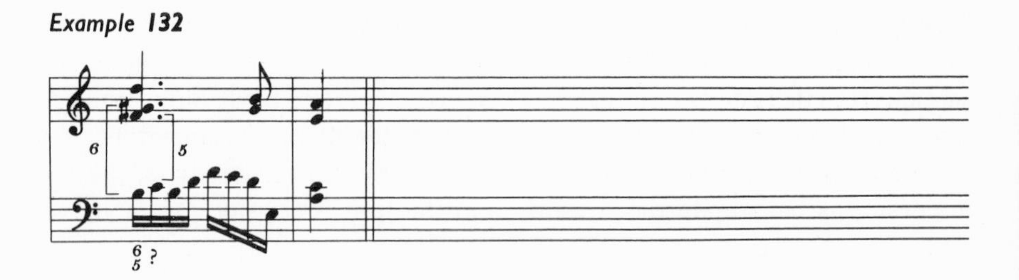

chords built upon leading-tones. As already stated, the numerals denoting inversions have lost their original contrapuntal significance and have been associated with the parts of a chord. Therefore, the two factors relating to the figured bass contradict each other. *Example 132* shows how a first inversion of a leading-tone seventh chord creates a vertical numerical grouping of $^{6}_{5}$ and yet the fifth is in the bass when the total harmonic entity is considered.

In addition to the problem of numerical representation of leading-tone chords, any higher-numbered chord is also awkwardly expressed by the traditional contrapuntal figuration. *Example 133a* illustrates the figuration necessary for a thirteenth chord in root position. Even if the lowest two digits are omitted, do the remaining numbers $\begin{smallmatrix}\flat 9\\ 7\\ 6\end{smallmatrix}$ denote a thirteenth chord, or does the lowest number, 6, imply a first inversion? The figurations for inversions, *Example 133b*, are ludicrous.

Example 133a b

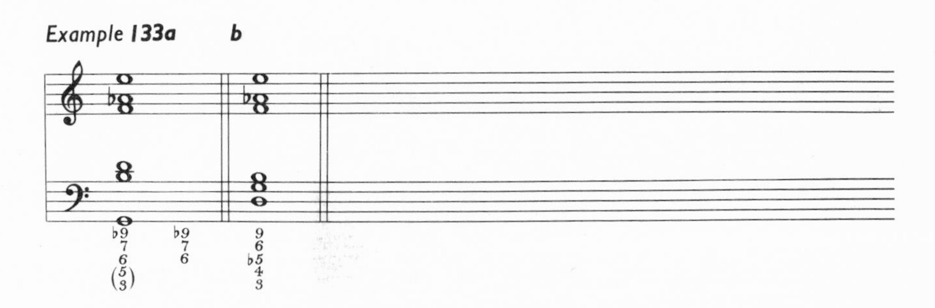

Instrumental compositions, being largely more rhythmic and permissive in the free increase and decrease of parts, tend to present a total harmonic sound which requires less analytical detail for its harmonic understanding. At this point, the figurations $^{6}_{5}$, $^{4}_{3}$ and $^{4}_{2}$ actually signify the first, second and third inversions of a seventh chord, rather than the voices those numbers represent. Other systems have been attempted, such as I_1, I_2 and I_3 intending also to indicate the three inversions in order. The original figurations, however, do not create excessive difficulties as long as the harmony is contained within the boundaries of a representative musical sound.

Higher-numbered chords are awkwardly expressed by the contrapuntal figurations. In order to simplify the problem, the following methods are used in this book:

(a) Place the number of the highest chord member (9, 11 or 13) at the upper right side of the roman numeral or letter name, see *example 134*, and in parenthesis at the lower right side, the traditional figuration, $(^{6}_{5})$ $(^{4}_{3})$ $(^{4}_{2})$ for denoting the inversions.

(b) Since there is no accepted numeral for an inversion in which the ninth or the other upper extensions can be represented in the bass, the simplest plan is to proceed as above and, in the lower parenthesis, add the number which

Example 134

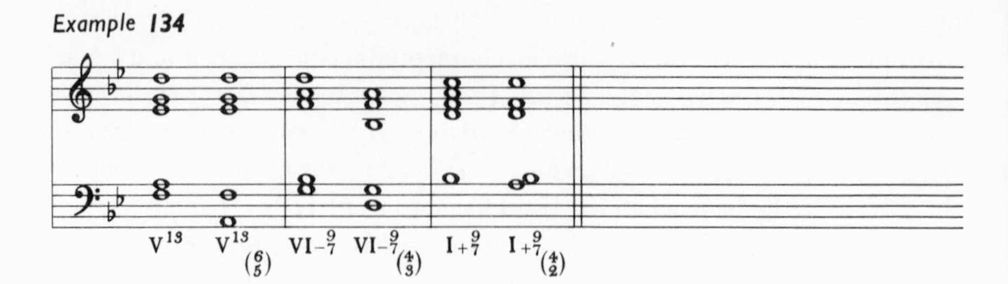

designates the bass tone itself. For example, a dominant thirteenth having a lowered ninth as a bass tone would be marked $V^{13}_{(\flat 9)}$. See *example 135a*. This plan can be extended, logically, to replace the older double set of figurations with the single number representing the bass tone. For example, $V^{13}_{(3)}$ would indicate that the third is the bass tone, or $V^{\sharp 11}_{(5)}$ would designate a second inversion of an augmented eleventh chord. See *examples 135b, c*. With this plan, a uniformity for advanced analysis becomes possible.

Example 135a b c

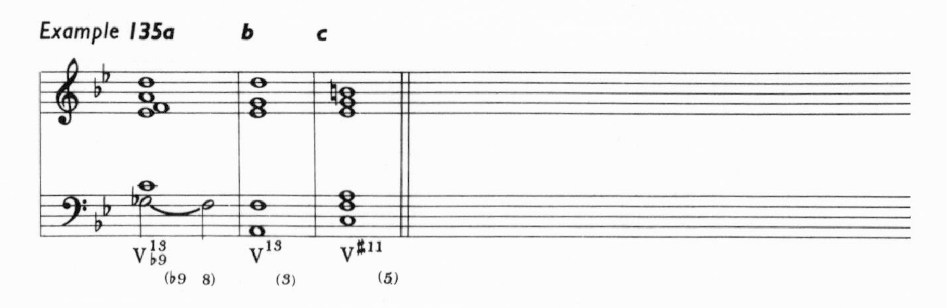

(c) Recognizing that chord members gain their identity through their relationship with the root of the chord, and since this latter plan marks the inversions by the harmonic identity of each chord member, a logical method for marking the movement of chord members can also derive from the root recognition rather than intervallically from the bass tone. For example, a suspended tone, falling into the third of a dominant ninth chord in the third inversion would be marked $V^{9}_{(7)}4\text{–}3$, *example 136*, rather than $V^{6}_{\substack{3\\2}}5\text{–}4$ which denotes the figuration against the bass tone. The latter group of numbers must be

Example 136

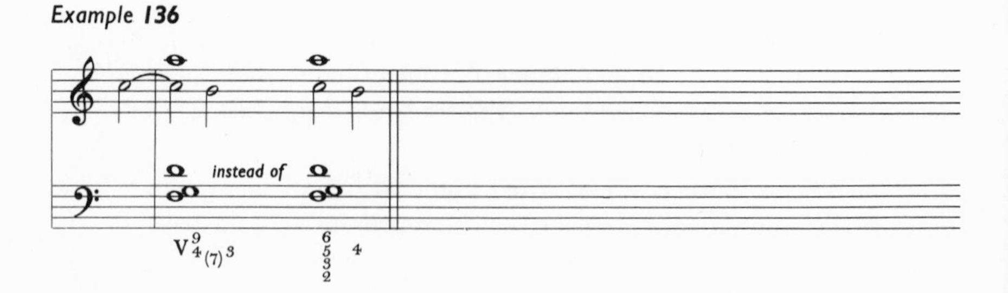

deciphered in terms of tones before an image of what takes place can be understood. The new method immediately indicates the presence of a suspension or appoggiatura delaying the sound of the third regardless of bass movement.

(d) It is within this regard that a solution to the perplexing leading-tone figuration can be offered. The symbol VII07 is still indicative of the four tones that make up the diminished seventh quality. The inversions, however, are not computed by intervallic distance to the bass tone, but by their relationship to the parent tone, the root of a dominant harmony.

To avoid the differing associations that the conventional figuration has conjured, the simplified single number may represent each chord member in its inversion. Since VII automatically represents the third of this chord, the number (3) is not needed. Inversions therefore follow (5), (7), (9) respectively. *Example 137* illustrates this analytical procedure. In order to be consistent, the other quality seventh chords and triads have also changed the inversion symbol. (This book does not abandon the traditional triad or seventh chord figurations, but encourages the aforementioned harmonic indications wherever such use would simplify and clarify the analysis involved.) Observe the two analytical solutions offered in the second measure. It may be desirable to separate the dominant and leading-tone symbols because of a one-bar motivic group in the upper part. Harmonically, however, the first beat substitutes the minor ninth, Eb, for the root D, indicating a continuation of V. A similar pattern of harmonic rhythm then occurs within the sequence, in measures three and four.

Example 137 *Chopin*

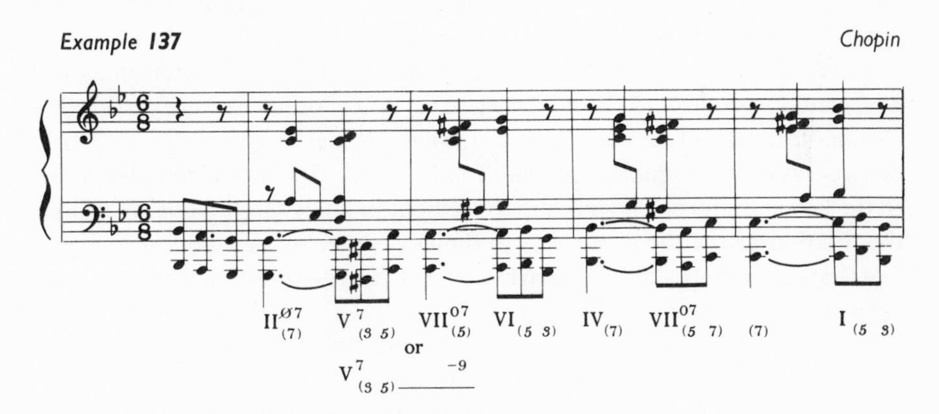

In a passage in which the quality of a diminished seventh chord is recognized, but the sound of a particular leading-tone is thwarted by other chromatic material, the symbol itself is indicative of this quality and inversions need not be emphasized until heard. The quality may be represented by "07" instead of "VII07."

(e) Contrapuntal figuration must not be brushed aside and ignored. There is a need for both types of analysis, depending on the circumstances.

The first phrase of Brahms' *Intermezzo* in E major, *example 138*, shows the convenience of both methods. The first measure utilizes the contrapuntal figuration because that is exactly what is taking place. Against the bass tone, the tenor motive moves chromatically into C♯ minor. The chord of C♯ minor was not planned out of a harmonic scheme; it arose out of a motivic coincidence. The roman numeral VI is not necessary, nor is the augmented triad on the first beat deserving of any further description beyond the simple figuration given.

Example 138 — *Brahms*

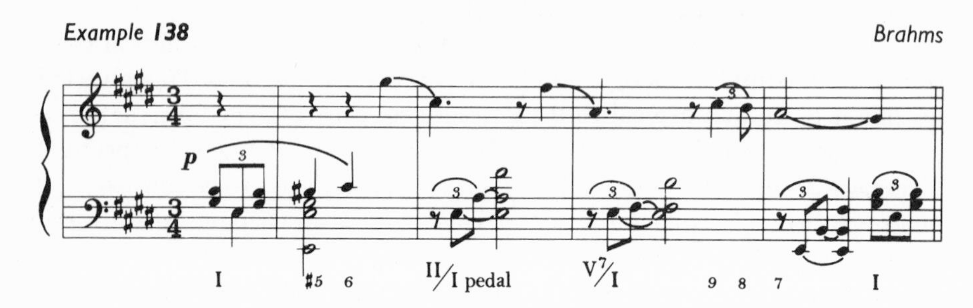

By contrast, notice the ease with which a harmonic figuration may be applied to the third measure. The chord begins as a half-diminished quality over a tonic pedal, but becomes entirely a part of the dominant organization as the dominant tone itself appears in the melody. The indication for the melody, 9–8, is true to the harmonic situation. Had a contrapuntal figuration been marked here, the numbers would read 6–5, measured against the lowest bass tone, and would be completely devoid of any meaning. The contrapuntal sound occurs against a harmonic situation, which relates to the root that we hear.

(f) Figurations have traditionally denoted chromatic alterations to the key center, producing chromatic chords. After the tones are realized, the chromatic nature of the chord is understood. By marking qualities, the analytical process first recognizes the sound, and then adjusts the accidentals necessary to the key signature. The missing ingredient in analyzing by qualities alone is the relationship of the root tones to the key center of the composition. As the diatonic solidity of established harmonies for each degree of the scale weakens, a need arises for a comprehensive analytical plan which will combine the relationship of root tones to the tonic tonality with the differing qualities of the vertical sound.

The seven roman numerals that indicate the degrees of the major and minor scales carry with them the implied quality of the triad and seventh chord that the scale produces. Chromatic procedures have stretched the seven numerals to include all twelve chromatic tones as possible roots. They are indicated by a sharp, flat, or natural sign before the basic diatonic roman numeral. With the appearance of altered dominants and diminished chords on any degree of the scale, various methods have been employed to show how they relate to the scale. In most of the classical literature, the chromatic embellishing chords resolved where they were expected to go. The marking of V/IV as representing a dominant quality belonging to the subdominant chord was explicit. This is now dated and inefficient in terms of Impressionistic or Modern analysis, because the dominant qualities rarely go to their original harmonic destination.

The following method has proved to be efficient in the analysis of the unconventional composition and also brings forth a union of key relationship and quality in the conventional composition:

1. All roman numerals relate to the key center and assume the quality established by the major or minor scale, as is customary. They may be raised or lowered to account for all of the chromatic tones. Such altered root tones are marked by a sharp or flat placed to the left of the roman numeral. Observe the ♭III in the sixth measure of *example 139*. These chromatic root tones, however, do not have an established harmonic quality associated with them.

2. When a root on a particular degree of the scale is part of a chord which does not form the expected diatonic quality, two stages of analysis go into effect. First, mark the roman numeral as usual. Follow this by a semicolon and the symbol for the quality that is involved. For instance, in the first measure of *example 139*, the supertonic root is indicated by II followed by the dominant symbol V. Inversions and upper extensions are included with this latter indication. Other qualities (specifically named in chapters four and five) are similarly represented. Remember that "−7" or "+7" signify the complete seventh chord quality above which any higher chord member is marked. These quality indications are marked as above, following the roman numeral which designates the root tone. Illustrated in measure seven of *example 139* is the lowered supertonic, ♭II, containing a major seventh chord quality. It is indicated "♭II;+7". If only triad qualities are altered, the major or minor

Example 139

symbol (+ or −) is placed to the right of the roman numeral. Observe the minor subdominant chord in the cadence measure of *example 139*.

3. A leading-tone chord whose parent tone is explicit in the phrase, but not actually sounding, is marked:

a] by VII⁰⁷ or VIIø⁷ if it is not chromatic, therefore really located on the leading-tone degree of the scale; or

b] by the roman numeral of the implied dominant root, in brackets, followed by a semicolon after which the diminished or half-diminished symbol VII⁰⁷ or VIIø⁷ is placed. See *examples 140a, b*. The visual recognition of the implied parent tone in diminished seventh chords generally clarifies the basic root progression. Notice the II V I IV motion within *example 140b*.

4. Any chromatic passage which for the moment has no significant tonal orientation, omits the first stage of this analytical method. Only the qualities are then indicated. For the most part, such chords are of a dominant or diminished quality and a visual stream of such symbols makes it evident that the

music is in flux. Upon the return of the basic roman numerals, an association of sound to key is reestablished. When denoting the quality alone, use 07 or ø7 omitting the roman numeral VII. In the case of dominants, however, the one symbol, V, is unavoidable and must function for transient as well as scale degree dominants. To denote the true dominant after a modulatory series, the letter name of the key center may be used in this way: V^9, V^{13}, F + : V^7 I. *Example 141* contains a chromatic passage, anchored to a tonal center only at the start and finish of the passing dominant chords.

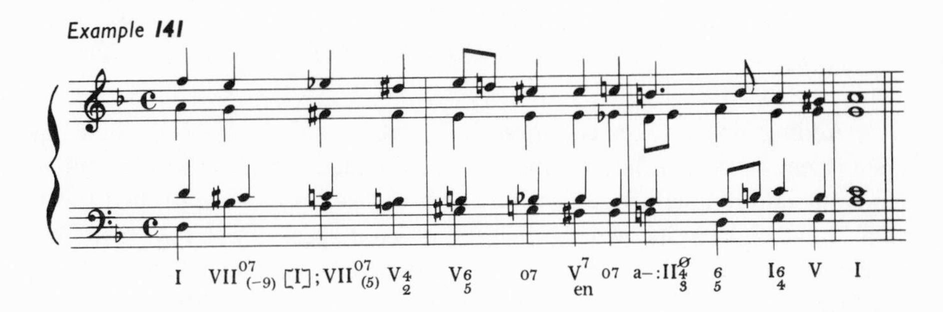

The omission of the first stage of the above method is also convenient in passages in which the counterpoint forms many rapidly changing harmonies, none of which may be important for the appraisal of the harmonic scheme in the phrase. This may apply to any group of chords, whose fleeting rhythmical design does not warrant a constant reference to the parent tonality. The quality may be marked as a representation of the vertical sound alone. The cause of such sounds is a contrapuntal merging of material, rather than part of a harmonic plan that shapes the phrase.

Implied roots

Think of all of the tones of a dominant thirteenth chord and consider that each one has a special tendency, a resolution that it wants to fulfill to the tonic chord. The third (the leading-tone), heads for the tonic; the fifth, if present, doubles the tonic; the seventh moves to the third; the ninth to the fifth; the raised eleventh, if used, to an added ninth, and the thirteenth actually anticipates the entire cadential resolution whether remaining on the same pitch and becoming the third of the tonic chord or moving to other nearby chord members. See *example 142a*.

Play this full chord (*example 142a*), listening to the active role of each tone. Play it again, but omit the bass tone, the root. See *example 142b*. The movement desired by each upper tone is exactly the same. The resolutions are identical, following the course of the original dominant function. The chord is an "implied dominant thirteenth" and is generally used with the leading-tone in the bass but may also occur with the fifth, seventh and ninth as bass tones. See *example 142c.*

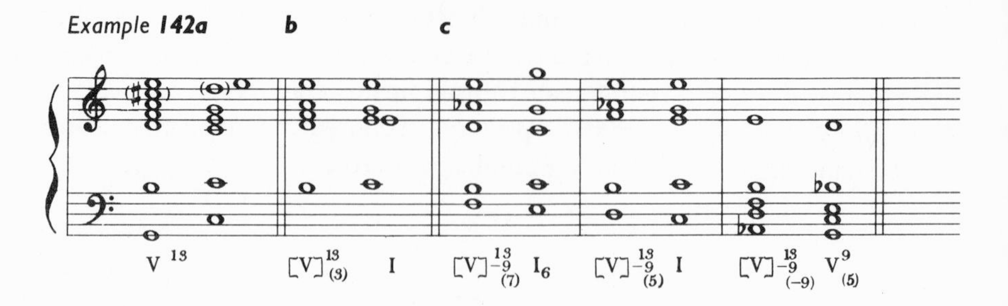

Adding upper tones to diminished seventh chords destroys their equidistant minor-third relationship, and causes them to be absorbed into the fundamental dominant organization. As was described, a diminished seventh chord has a right to its own identity and it is not necessary to always imply its fundamental derivation. This identity, however, becomes weakened as the upper harmonic extensions combine and support more positively a select group of tones from the diminished seventh formation. The interchangeability of the diminished seventh tones is interfered with by the added upper tones. In this way, the fundamental root gains more power and its control on the behavior of all chord members is manifested in the progression involved. For example, the interval of the minor ninth, readily accepted above the dominant seventh chord, becomes one of the most harsh dissonances if formed with the lowest tone of a diminished seventh chord. See *example 143a* and *b*. The tone added above the diminished seventh chord, is not a ninth in the dominant hierarchy. It is a natural eleventh, *example 143c*, and conflicts with the major third. (Review natural eleventh chords.) By raising the eleventh, a normal voicing occurs. It is a dominant chord, root omitted, in which all tones function as an augmented dominant eleventh, heard as a chord built on the leading-tone, the first inversion. See *example 143d*.

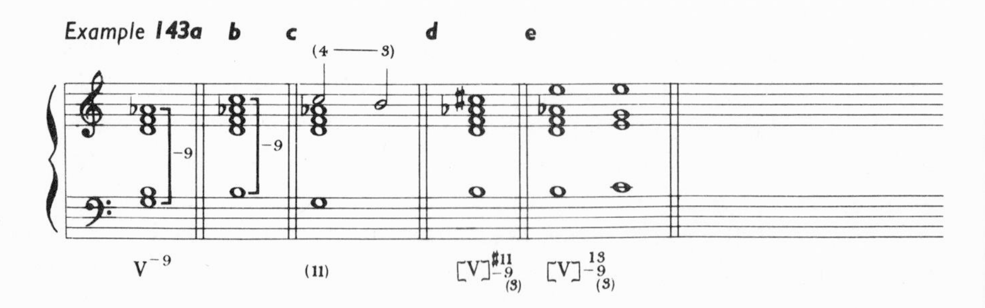

Analogous to this is the tone, one octave and a perfect fourth that may be added above a diminished seventh, as in *example 143e*. Notice its anticipating, or échappée, function. It is not heard as a natural eleventh (whose problems in the dominant hierarchy were noticed) but as a thirteenth, expecting to fulfill the normal cadential progression. In an incomplete thirteenth chord, inversions of the fifth, seventh and minor ninth are equally as possible, as in chords containing the dominant root tone. Nevertheless, any chord in which the root tone is omitted is less securely situated than if the root tone were present and especially if located in the bass. Enharmonic changes may invite surprising resolutions and thereby alter an analysis, as will be seen.

Example 144 illustrates the reenforced dominant sound that occurs when additional chord members are added to diminished or half-diminished quality chords. Each measure includes a dominant quality sound and yet not one dominant root is actually present in the phrase. The diminished seventh chord members in the first measure, are completely devoid of their separate quality as the melody tone of the thirteenth envelops them into the dominant frame. The second measure contains the same chord, with the seventh in the bass. In the third measure, a dominant quality is formed on the root of the submediant but without that tone's presence. The fifth is in the bass, and with a motivic extension moves to the ninth on the next first beat. It resolves by cadential progression. The implied root of B moves to the next implied root of E, the supertonic. The chromatic movement of the tenor part (measure four) contributes largely to this progression. The third of the B chord resolves to the seventh of the E chord in true dominant fashion. Within this measure, the alto takes over the ninth, and lowers it before resolving. The soprano stresses the thirteenth which briefly drops to a neighboring raised fifth. The sound tells the story. The presence of the dominant tone is felt in all of the above mentioned chords. In fact, it can be bewildering to the eye as one hunts for the note that surely must be there!

The symbol for these higher-numbered dominant chords whose root tone is omitted cannot involve the diminished or half-diminished designation because that identity is no longer recognized. The V represents the sound we hear. If the implied root is the true dominant tone of the key, place the dominant symbol V in brackets, *i.e.* [V] as shown in the example, followed by the highest harmonic tone represented in the chord. When the dominant sound is located on a root other than the fifth degree of the scale, use the plan outlined previously for the leading-tone chords. Place the roman numeral designating the parent tone, or implied root in brackets, followed by a semicolon and the dominant symbol. See measures three and four of *example 144*.

The secret behind implied roots is in the behavior of the tritones. The tritone, an interval made up of three major seconds, is either a diminished fifth, or the inversion, an augmented fourth. Its existence in the scale is from the fourth to the seventh tone, and in the dominant seventh chord from the third to the seventh. Its resolution in the dominant seventh chord dictates the implied root. The tritone F and B resolving to C major functions as an implied G dominant. If the B is altered to a C♭, the tone will resolve downward, as a D♭ dominant to G♭ major or minor. To make things a little tougher and more ambiguous, two other tritones may also be found in dominant structures. One tritone may exist from the fifth to a lowered ninth and another from the root to a lowered fifth. This latter one, however, chromatically alters the logical order of intervals of the overtone series. It may be derived from the whole-tone scale and need not function as a dominant chord. As such, it is discussed fully under "whole-tone dominants." In general, all tritones will fall in line and resolve automatically if you discover the main dominant influence, the tritone governing the action of the third and seventh.

One important point to remember is that the leading-tone (the third of the dominant chord) wants to resolve up to the tonic, thereby creating contrary motion with the seventh heading downward. With motion of "dominant to dominant" (cycle of fifths), this leading-tone is frequently thwarted in its upward demand, and falls down by a half step to the seventh of the new root. See *example 145*. This is as true with a seventh chord, or any of its inversions, as it is with a thirteenth chord, and with implied roots suggesting the cycle of dominants. Instead of moving to a root, the leading-tone descends chromatic-

Example 145

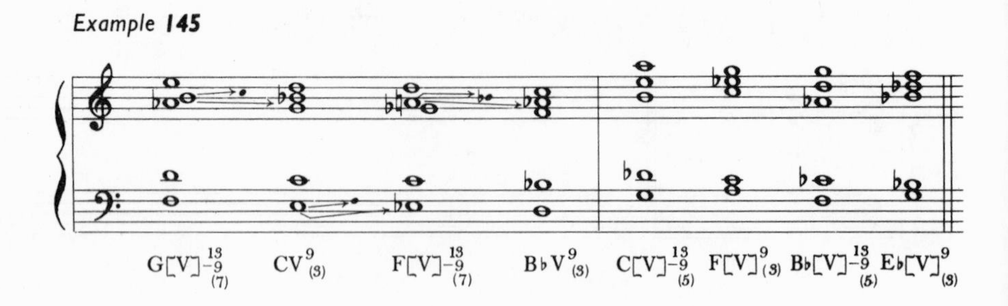

ally, landing alternately on the third and seventh of dominant quality chords. Consequently, there is much parallel downward motion involving tritones. It can't be helped!

Evaded progressions or those involving root movements other than the cadential progression, are feasible but less convincing when using implied roots. You may be planning a certain evaded progression and the resulting sound will be that of another, based upon the dominant to tonic formula. For example, the implied G thirteenth (*example 146a*), intended as an evaded progression to an A dominant ninth, is really an E minor ninth resolving by cadential progression to the A chord. The second example (*146b*), shows an intended G moving down with a mediant relationship to E♭; the result to the ear is B♭ to E♭. The resolution of the tritone which acts as third and seventh of the dominant's structure governs the implied root progression.

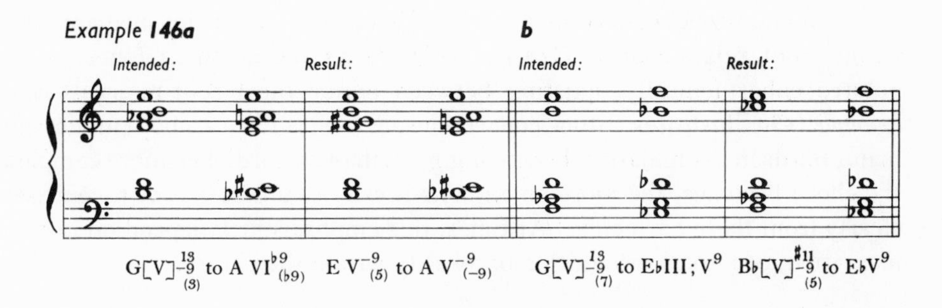

Chromatic movement of roots such as the implied $V^{13}_{\flat 9}$ to a lowered VI is illustrated in *example 147a*. The tritone still resolves as it would in the normal V^7-I progression. The lowered ninth becomes a common tone with the root of the G♭ chord. If the major ninth is used instead of the minor one (*example 147b*), perfect fifths result with the upper thirteenth. This might be objectionable in some situations.

Example **147a** **b** **c**

F[V]$^{13}_{-9}$ (3) VI$_6$ E V^{-9} (3) E♭ D

Parallel chromatic chords may move up or down by half steps (*example 147c*), whether the roots are implied or present. However, it must be recalled that the implied root was recognized because of the resolution tendencies of its chord members. Parallel progressions destroy these tendencies. This generally causes one tone to predominate and declare itself as root, based on an intervallic order of sound. The notation then follows according to tonality and scale organization. See *example 148*.

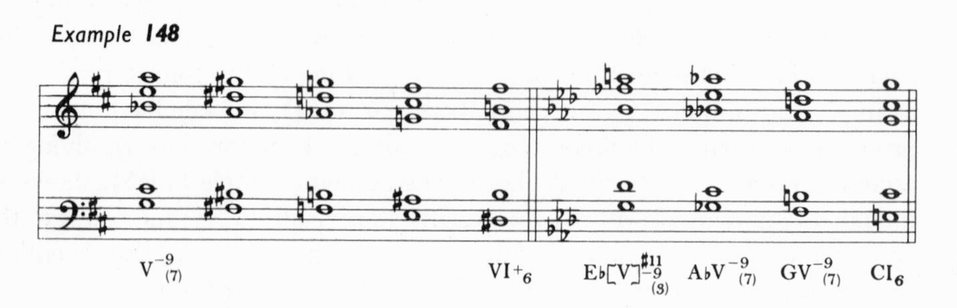

Common-tone connections are particularly evident in mediant and tritone root relationships. *Example 149a* shows the common tones, some notated enharmonically, existing between minor third root intervals, and *example 149b* illustrates tritone connections. *Example 150* uses both minor and major thirds in a cumulative descending growth of a chord. The more complex the chord becomes, the more ambiguous it can be, unless a root tone arises clearly from these harmonies. At times, this emphasis may depend on instrumentation, or a total recognition of tonality within the phrase.

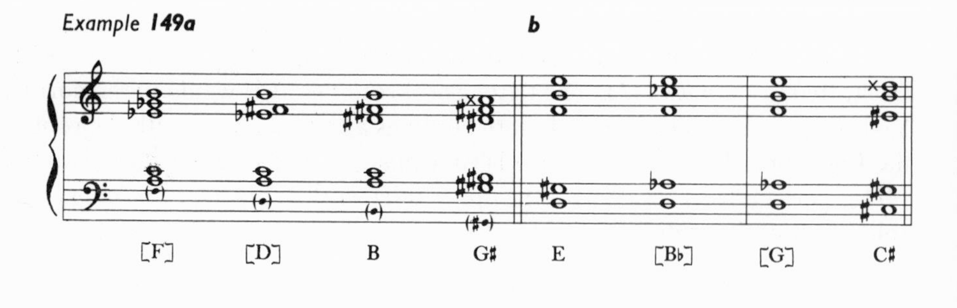

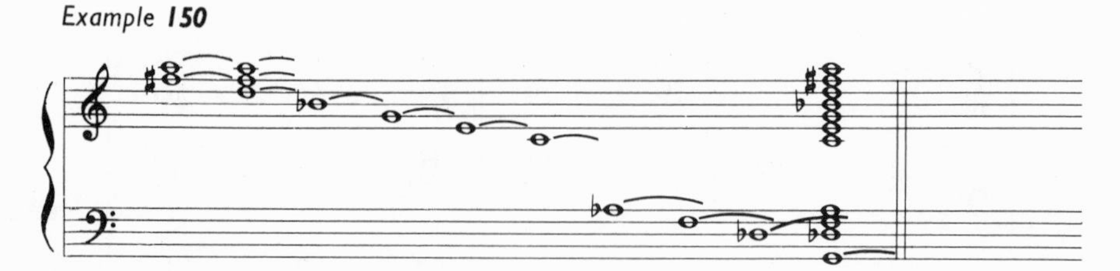

The half-diminished II chord

Up to this point, the qualities of the diminished and half-diminished chords were discussed in terms of a leading-tone function. The $II^{ø7}$ also requires mention both as an independent chord, not associated with the dominant, as well as a chord which so easily fuses itself to the dominant that its independence is in jeopardy. Regarding the latter point, it was noted that when upper chord members are added to a half-diminished seventh, they actually are dominant chord tones which destroy the lower, less secure supertonic root. In the key of A minor, *example 151* builds upon the II ø7 chord. While the tone which forms the ninth, minor or major, does not "prove" a dominant sound, the first indication that the seventh (the alto A) might resolve down would merge even that five note chord into the dominant hierarchy. As the next third is added (supposedly the eleventh), the sound combines that tone with the lower group of tones and definitely links the II into the V organization. Finally the tone that may be computed as a thirteenth adds such a major aura to the lower diminished triad that the bass tone cannot remain independent as a root. The interval association of the bass and soprano tones of this combination form the fifth and third of a major triad. The root is implied, and the dominant quality sound contains a fifth in the bass.

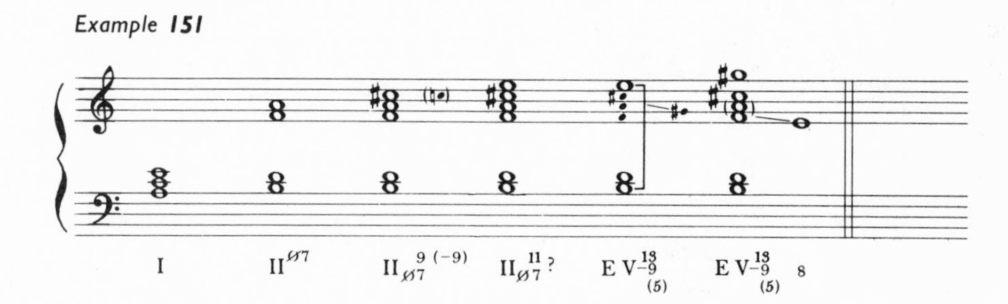

The link between II⁰ and V is close even within the triad and seventh chord harmonization. From Clementi's *Gradus ad Parnassum* comes this simple illustration, *example 152*. Measures seven to ten are of particular interest. The bass motive takes on an arpeggio shape reaching to the minor ninth of measure eight. The harmonic eighth notes of the right hand support the dominant, but begin in measure seven with an appoggiatura eleventh, which does not resolve until two bars later. As the arpeggio rises, this upper incomplete sound forms the half-diminished quality. Whether measure eight is analyzed separately as

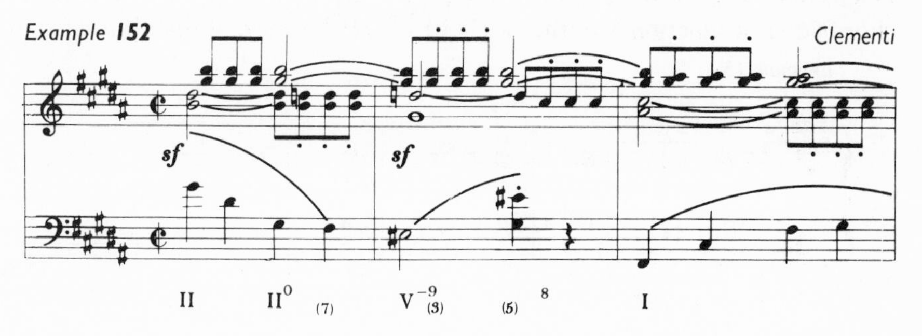

a $\mathrm{II}^{\varnothing 7}$ or retained as part of the dominant minor ninth is not important. What is essential is the understanding that these two chords have a close, almost inseparable, association when used without the strong motion of roots in the bass.

By the same logic, if the bass progression is forthright, it can give the half-diminished chords a degree of independence. A departure from the established progressions may achieve this. *Example 153* illustrates the half-diminished chord as part of an implied plagal and mediant root progression. These chords do not function as either a $\mathrm{II}^{\varnothing}$ or a $\mathrm{VII}^{\varnothing}$ because of the difference in the

Example ***153***

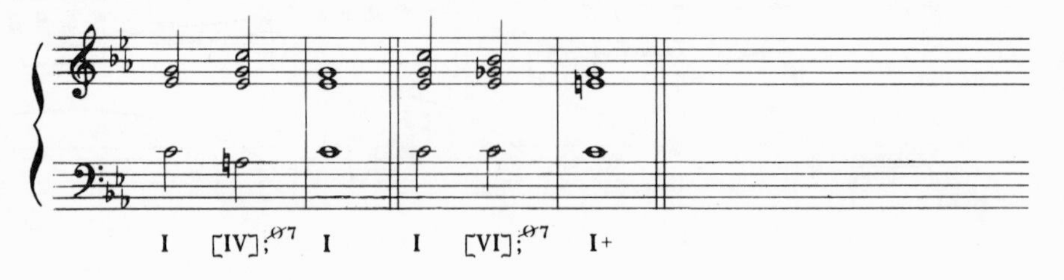

resolution of the respective chord members. Again it must be pointed out that the lowest tone of the half-diminished chords is not a root, but still the third of a dominant heirarchy, regardless of the independent stature the sound may contain. The parent tone is placed in brackets, and the quality symbol ø7 follows.

The quality of a half-diminished seventh is frequently found on the chromatically raised fourth degree of the scale. The implied root is then a supertonic. Generally, this resolves to the dominant, but if it does not, the half-diminished quality has loosened some of its dominant ties. César Franck, in a passage from the second movement of the *Violin Sonata, example 154*, uses such a half-diminished progression. The harmonic plan connects the former key of D minor to its relative major, F. The half-diminished chord serves to remove any one tonal identity. It alternates with an F augmented triad, in which the C♯ functions as a leading-tone, holding on to the lingering D minor tonality. After a forceful repetition, the half-diminished chord resolves chromatically to the minor subdominant, and on to F major. During this phase, there is no indication of an A minor tonality, nor any positive reason to suggest an absent tone of G. Also to be discounted is a B root with a lowered fifth. The F is not a lowered tone; instead, the B is a raised tone in the scale. This leads to the consideration of an implied E dominant eleventh, in which the soprano tone, A, avoids a descending resolution to G♯. The implied E root, as the supertonic of D minor would inherit the B♮ as part of that dominant quality. The eventual movement into F would also be significant, but the immediate progression into the B♭ minor chord is inconclusive. When such an indefinite and uncommon use of the half-diminished chord occurs, the symbol ø7 may be placed next to the roman numeral that denotes the actual bass tone, not an implied root. This analysis is marked in the example.

The augmented sixth chords and added chord members

A different type of leading-tone chord, one built not on the seventh degree of the scale but on the raised fourth degree, is the augmented sixth chord. The three varieties of the augmented sixth chord, known as the Italian, German, and French sixths, each contain the two chromatic tones which neighbor the dominant tone. Their progression, therefore, leads into the dominant (perhaps via the I^6_4) and on to complete the cadence. As the upper chord members are added to the augmented sixth chords, they too lose their special characteristics that distinguish them in diatonic literature.

While augmented sixth chords are frequently referred to as dominant sounds, it is usually for a different reason than the one which will show their merging into the dominant family. This can be best explained by charting the evolution of these chords. *Example 155a–j* starts with the earliest type of progression and expands it by degrees until it assumes the popular cadence in *example 155j*. By following the analysis carefully, you can see the gradual changes that took place so that today the augmented sixths have been swallowed by the expanded dominant foundation.

The roman numeral, ♯IV, represents the chromatically raised subdominant, above which the remaining tones shape into a triad formation, although they are not heard as root, third, or fifth. The augmented symbol is derived from the figured bass, as follows: $\not{6}$ for the Italian sixth which is just a triad; $\begin{smallmatrix}\not{6}\\5\end{smallmatrix}$ for the German sixth, a first inversion of a seventh chord; and $\begin{smallmatrix}\not{6}\\4\\3\end{smallmatrix}$, a second inversion of a seventh chord, known as the French sixth. The Italian and German sixths are built upon the raised subdominant tone, but the French sixth contains the supertonic as root. *Example 155a, b,* and *c* illustrate their Classical function.

Example 155d "inverts" the French sixth, placing the root in the bass. It now behaves as a dominant with the lowered fifth. The augmented sixth interval is contained within the chord rather than appearing against the bass tone.

The German $\begin{smallmatrix}\not{6}\\5\end{smallmatrix}$ is merged with the French sixth in *example 155e* and *f* merely by placing the supertonic root above the German sixth. This forms, in *example 155e*, the D root within which the F♯ retains its leading-tone function and the E♭ is a ninth. The resolution, as a dominant complex, may go to either a major or minor triad, whereas the earlier augmented sixths all lead toward the dominant.

The thirteenth is added in *example 155g*. The illustrations switch to G major, representing V-I, although a progression to a dominant chord is equally possible. Compare *examples 155g* and *h*. They are identical except for one tone and the analytical symbols. The analysis is purposely changed to show the close relationship between the chord built on a lowered II and the V chord. The tritone relationship binds the two possible roots together and if they both lead toward the same resolution, they must have the same function. The F♯ holds the key to the correct solution. One theory respects the F♯ as a leading-tone, while the other requires an enharmonic notation. Priority must be given to the

D root with a preferred analysis of the V-I progression rather than a ♭II-I indication.

Examples 155i and j carry this understanding one step further by omitting the parent tone, the D root. Again, the F♯ functions as a leading-tone within the scale of G, not as a seventh of A♭. The analysis shows the dominant derivation by the implied root abbreviation. No change in the analytical marking need occur if this chord followed the earlier progression and resolved first into a second inversion of the tonic and then to the dominant of the key. The additional tones which may be added to the basic augmented sixth chords minimize the characteristic identity of the latter group and fuse them into the dominant family. See *example* 155k.

Looking backward for a moment, examine *example 155(l)*, the second phrase of Chopin's *Prelude* in G minor. It uses the chord referred to frequently as the "root-position of the German sixth" or the "enharmonic dominant $^{4}_{2}$". By observing the tritone and hearing the resolution of a leading-tone, it becomes apparent that the augmented sixths and all their inversions are outgrowths of a supertonic root. Again, the customary contrapuntal figurations have dimmed the harmonic principles which guide the movement of progressions. It is not necessary to change the figuration for the augmented sixth chords as they occur in Classical literature, but it is important to realize that they are forms of a leading-tone chord. This leading-tone is the chromatic neighbor of the dominant instead of the chromatic neighbor of the tonic. In diatonic passages it employs the implied parent tone of the supertonic chord, and in chromatic passages the same relationship is inferred, but on different degrees of the scale. The Chopin excerpt illustrates this occurrence (*example 155(l)*). (The first phrase of this *Prelude* is analyzed in *example 137*.)

EXERCISES

A *Analysis*

1] In this familiar composition by Grieg, *Example 156*, look for implied roots. Mark the fundamental tone in brackets as was described. Include a complete harmonization.

Example 156 Grieg

2] These three excerpts from the Rachmaninoff *Prelude* provide an opportunity for motivic analysis as well as harmonic. Observe the tonality and use the roman numerals so that they depict the relationship of root tones to the central tonality. Distinguish between chromatic passing chords and those which affect a harmonic scheme.

Find a half-diminished seventh chord which pivots in an interesting way. Also find an unusual thirteenth chord formation.

Example 157a *Rachmaninoff*

Example **157b**

Example **157c**

3] In *Example 158*, mark all harmony noting the flexibility of enharmonic chromatic tones and their grip on a diatonic anchorage. Observe the motivic interest between violin and piano. Mark the particular technique used.

Example **158** Franck

4] One tone in *Example 159* is notated in a manner which may visually confuse its chordal recognition. Find it, change it enharmonically and mark the implied root. Indicate the progression by which the roots move, such as Cad., Ev., Pl., Med. or Tri. (The latter represents a root movement of the tritone interval.) *Example 159b* presents a clue (if one is necessary), toward finding the correct implied root.

5] *Example 160* contains two instances of the merger of a lowered II and a V. Mark the harmonic analysis for both root possibilities, with a specific representation of all chord members.

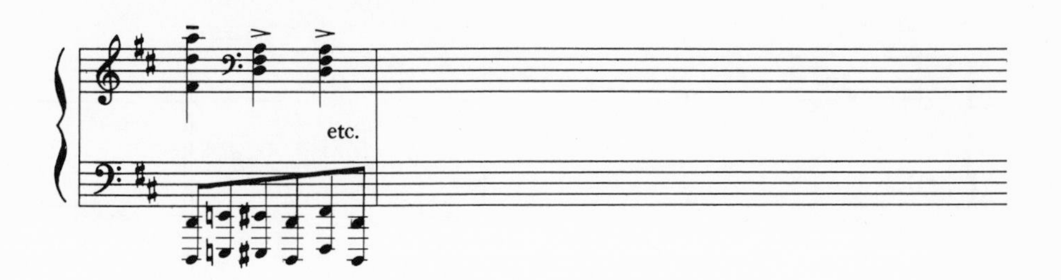

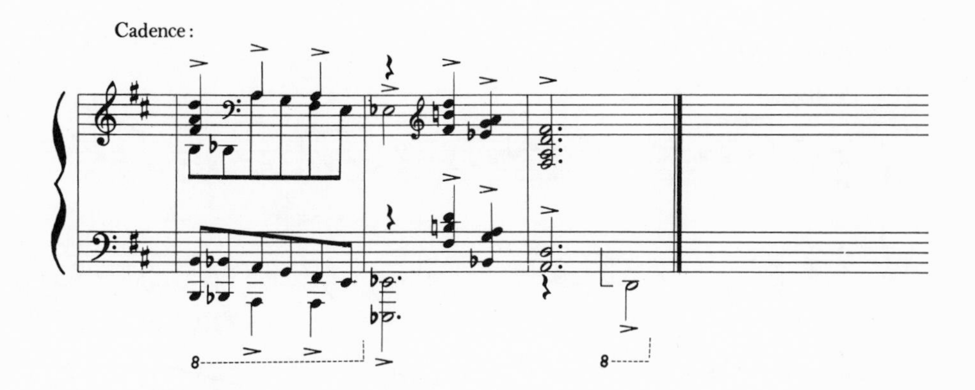

B Fill in the voices of *Example 161* and *162* according to the figuration as described in this chapter. Give the inner voices the same rhythmic freedom that is evident in the given parts. If additional harmonic members are created, add these to the given analysis.

Example 161

C Build the designated chords in *Example 163*. Roman numerals appearing in brackets indicate the implied root. Arabic numbers in parenthesis indicate the chord member denomination of the lowest bass tone, thereby forming inversions based upon the implied root. Compare the enharmonic spelling required within each group. Mark the tritone which controls the notation and resolution of each dominant chord. See model. (Each measure is tonally independent.)

D Write a melody and add the inner voices to the given figured bass of *Examples 164* and *165*. Include additional appoggiatura tones giving prime consideration to a good melody. All voices should include rhythmic divisions.

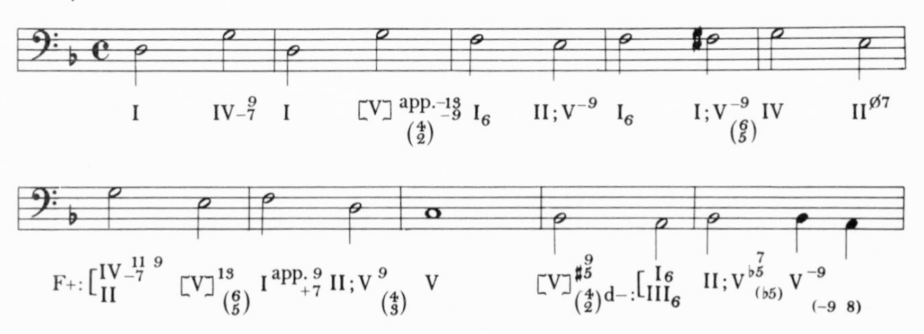

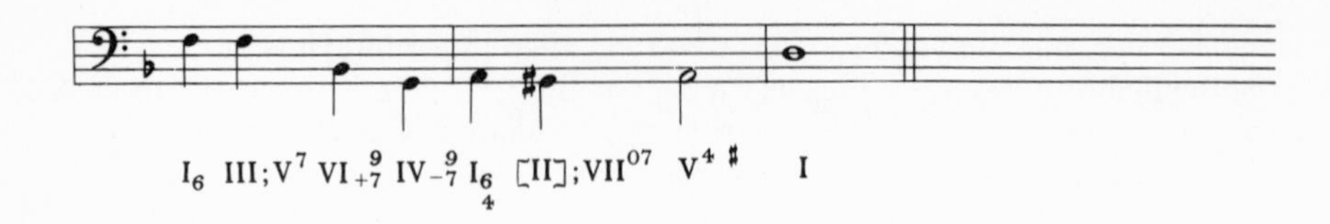

Example ***165***

The following two songs may be of particular interest in the study of implied roots and varied half-diminished seventh chord functions: *Bedeckt mich mit Blumen* by Hugo Wolf; *Far Above the Purple Hills* by Vittorio Giannini.

7 Modern application

Rather than stifle the creative imagination by restricting, at this time, the higher-numbered chords to their conventional usage as has been described in the preceding chapters, the illustrations and exercises which follow are in the Modern idiom and provide an insight into the growth of these chords. It is not the intention here to describe the many aspects of the Modern idiom. The examples are selected to show the utilization of the harmonic materials already described, in a setting that is distinctly forward-looking. The techniques that are listed below are included in the examples which follow. Without detailed explanation, they merely provide a guide for thinking along more modern lines, but within the harmonic controls that have been outlined.

1] Rhythmic and melodic inventiveness. This includes the irregular concepts of motive and phrase construction and the incorporation of changes of meter.

2] Expansion of range and interval within a melody. More leaps, more major sevenths, and more stressed appoggiatura tones are part of a Modern melody.

3] Utilization of all quality seventh chords and their harmonic extensions. The pure dominant qualities stylistically represent an earlier idiom. By chromatic alterations and an application of the more infrequent quality of seventh chord, an austere but not necessarily harsh form of harmony may be experienced.

4] Fewer restrictions on tone resolution. The resolution of upper chord members is frequently delayed and sometimes abandoned in the line itself. The wider leaps of this idiom promote such a non-resolution of these tones. In good musical writing, however, a path can always be traced showing the movement of these unresolved tones.

5] Use of unusual root progression. An overdose of dominant to tonic, or the equivalent root progression involving any tones of the scale, can sound very commonplace. Of course, it is an unbeatable progression and will always produce a smooth continuity of sound. But this same correctness does not produce a tingle of surprise that comes with the many kinds of evaded progressions, and mediant or plagal root movements. As usual, for good results, a varied selection is most desirable.

6] Incomplete chord formations. These frequently support an agile melody. The bass may secure a root tone and then proceed to the ninth or other material without fulfilling the quality of the lower triad or seventh chord. This may produce a feeling of openness in the writing as opposed to the lush sounds of the completely voiced dominant thirteenth, for example.

7] Inversions, instead of continuous root connections, spur on a more contrapuntal style. A bass motive of lyrical importance removes a rigid harmonic concept even though it is within a harmonic frame.

8] Harmonies for dissonant purposes. The selection of chord members which stridently oppose one another may find an advantageous spot in the Modern piece. It was pointed out how the major third clashes with the natural eleventh and is best omitted. But under which conditions must it be omitted? Musical growth of harmonies produced a search for increased dissonance needed for climatic purposes, as a contrast to the new expanded norm of sound. For this reason, purposeful dissonances are employed. Listeners must expect the biting increase of tension, if a span of varying reactions can be accomplished.

ILLUSTRATIONS AND EXERCISES

A 1] The first of the following illustrations, *example 166*, is the beginning of the third movement of Prokofiev's *Piano Sonata No. 4*. It contains a simple diatonic background against which accented melodic tones provide the dissonant vigor. It covers a wide range, and utilizes the principle of motivic contraction combined with an acceleration of harmonic movement, reaching the cadence of C in this case.

Mark the appoggiatura melodic tones by their numerical association with the root, even if they occur only above a triad.

Mark motives and show their contraction.

Example 166 — Prokofiev

2] Incomplete chord formations contribute to the plaintive, lyrical quality of this short choral composition (*example 167*) by Hindemith. Of necessity, only the piano reduction of this excerpt is quoted.

Mark the roots and the upper chord members regardless of the incomplete quality of the total chord. Observe some voice-leading licenses of Modern counterpoint.

Example 167 *Paul Hindemith*

3] The ostinato in *example 168* is of chief interest. Above it, in an improvisatory mood, Prokofiev used many chord tones belonging to a dominant hierarchy, some enharmonically notated. The entire excerpt contains only two chords!

Mark the upper chord members, and observe one particular method of "light-hearted" dissonance.

Example 168 *Sarcasmes, No. 5. Prokofiev*

4] Most dissonant of this group of illustrations is *example 169*, the beginning of the second number from the *Sarcasmes* by Prokofiev. In analyzing, pay heed to the notation as it will reveal, for the most part, the cause of the dissonances. Many roots are implied, producing chords which contain both the natural eleventh and the major third, as well as other harsh combinations.

Mark all chords by letter name and quality, noting the discordant combinations.

B Each of the preceding excerpts may now be considered a model for the exercises which follow. Attempt to carry out the particular characteristic that the analysis of the previous compositions specified. The exercises are arranged in the same order, so that *example 166* is the model for *example 170*. Continue each given phrase either by sequence or by a motive derived from the opening material. The completed exercise may be as long or as short as preferred. Some may happily expand to an ABA form and represent completed miniatures in themselves while other phrases may only be considered as exercises.

The last two, *examples 174* and *175*, suggest a predetermined harmonic plan against which any of the other techniques may be employed. Students may find this method beneficial in seeking out different harmonic combinations. It is doubtful whether composers work this way. A creative impulse is more likely to encompass intuitively all musical aspects that shape a motive or theme; harmony is not the prime consideration. Nevertheless, in studying the growth of chords, priority may be temporarily given to that one detail, until the students' hearing of motives and melodies automatically includes the appropriate harmonization.

1] Continue the given phrase in *example 170* by retaining the bass pattern, and by using sequential melodic material in which accented, higher-numbered chord members are stressed. Follow the model, *example 166*.

Example 170

2] The opening phrases of *example 171* include incomplete chord formations similar to *example 167*. It is not necessary to continue the part writing of a choral setting to achieve this. It may be worked as a piano composition, as given here.

Example 171

3] Treat the bass ostinato in *example 172* as a gay background to a frivolous melody. (See the model, *example 168*.) The bass motive is adaptable to various forms of articulation, that is, combinations of staccato or legato groups. Choose

Example 172

one pattern and hold on to it except for occasional contrasting measures. Transpose the motive whenever desired and feel free to utilize any of the motivic variants (contraction, augmentation, etc.) as outlined in chapter two.

4] Rather than model *example 169* by its own vertical shapes, the phrase given here spreads a chord over the entire measure. The conflicting arrangements of chord members may still be present. Tones expected on top of the tertiary column may be located in lower positions. Notice that the given phrase length is three measures, with the change of harmony suggesting a new phrase as beginning in the fourth measure.

Example 173

As indicated previously, *examples 174* and *175* derive their motives from a harmonic source determined ahead of the melodic inspiration. The advantage may be seen in a more lyrical bass line, and in more coalition of melody and bass. By planning a bass motive first, inversions are simultaneously incorporated into the melodic fragment. Imitation is also more readily available as the harmony remains constant until a decision is made to change it. After this is all accomplished, who can tell which thought came first?

Do not use a key signature until the real tonality is recognized. Even then, it may be best to omit this diatonic element. Select the form of notation that is least complicated and yet accurate. Continue *examples 174* and *175* by planning two or three chord progressions at a time. Expand these into phrases as illustrated.

Example 174

Example 175

REVIEW

A *Analysis*

1] *Example 176* by Brahms contains an unusual treatment of appoggiatura tones. The arpeggio motive starts as part of one harmony, and suspends into a chord formed by the lower triad formation. Analyze this *Intermezzo* in the following manner:

a] Reduce measures one to eight of *Example 176a* and measures one to six of *Example 176b* using block chords as illustrated in the model.

b] Mark the appoggiatura tones by the higher number that they form against the newly created root tone. Include this analysis throughout the excerpt as well as in your reduced portion.

c] With a bracket, as shown, mark the quality of the seventh chord formed by the lower arpeggio members. Indicate this in the reduction and compare the two excerpts.

d] There are three prominent figures utilized in this composition. Mark them in the given material and observe their role in the expansion of a phrase.

e] Apply the analytical method of relating all root tones to the key center of the phrase. The first roman numeral represents the relationship of the root tone to the tonic. It is followed by a semicolon and the quality of that chord (if it is altered from the diatonic formation). Leading-tone chords show their fundamental roots in brackets. Half-diminished sevenths used on the second degree of the scale remain as II⌀7. Modulate, with the composition showing the pivotal or common chord, if there is one. In transitory chromatic passages, decide whether (a) a diatonic progression binds the sequential or chromatic group of chords; or, (b) the chords are connected only by the chromatic scale and are temporarily unattached to any key. In the first instance, mark the inner relationship of the chords, but consider the root of the transitory tonic chord as the over-all binding progression. In the latter instance, mark only the qualities until a key center again becomes established.

Example 176a Brahms

rit.
f
fp
etc.

Example 176b

Example 176c

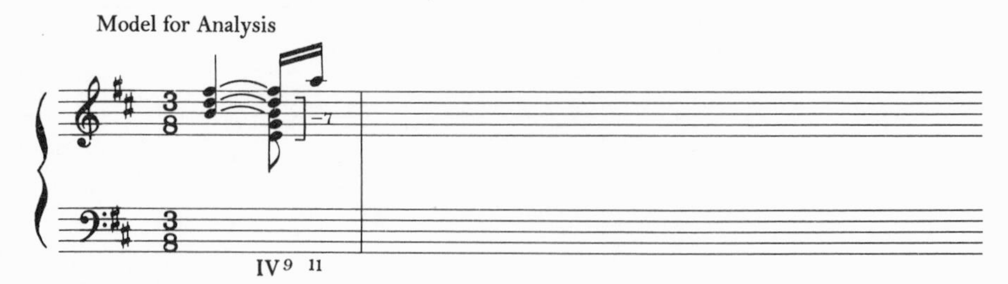

2] The excerpt from *Lohengrin*, *Example* 177, provides a review of intervallic unity.

Mark the motives and the smallest figures within them. Trace their path throughout this excerpt.

Analyze the harmony by the method prescribed for *Example* 176. Be on the lookout for implied roots.

3] Mark a motivic and harmonic analysis for *Example 178*. Observe some instances of the Modern application of the higher-numbered chords.

B Use a chorale setting with the necessary division of parts for the figured bass in *Example 179*. Include an eighth note rhythmic motion wherever desirable. The given higher numbers may occasionally become appoggiatura tones.

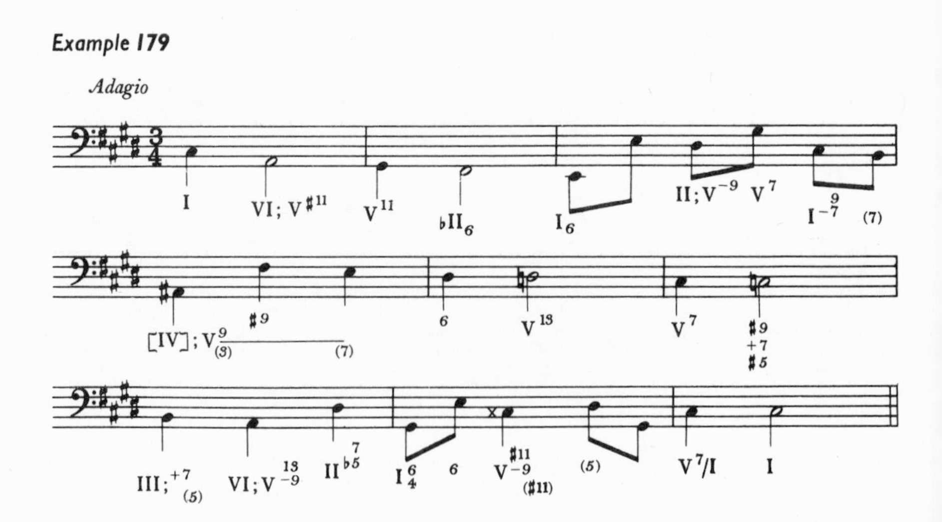

C Harmonize the melodies in *Examples 180* and *181* continuing in the style suggested by the given bass pattern. *Example 181* is notated without a key signature. Add one or two more phrases cadencing in any suitable key. After the piece is written, mark a few of the essential roman numerals which involve a tonal relationship.

Example **180**

Example **181**

D The motives given in *Example 182* may be expanded into short compositions which utilize the harmonic materials of the preceding chapters. Mark your motivic and analytical results.

Example 182a

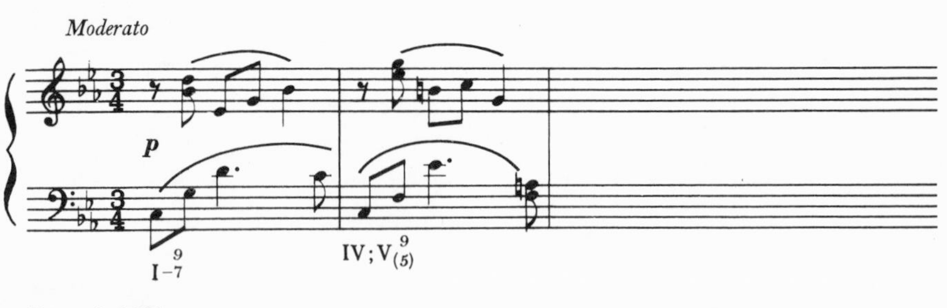

Example 182b

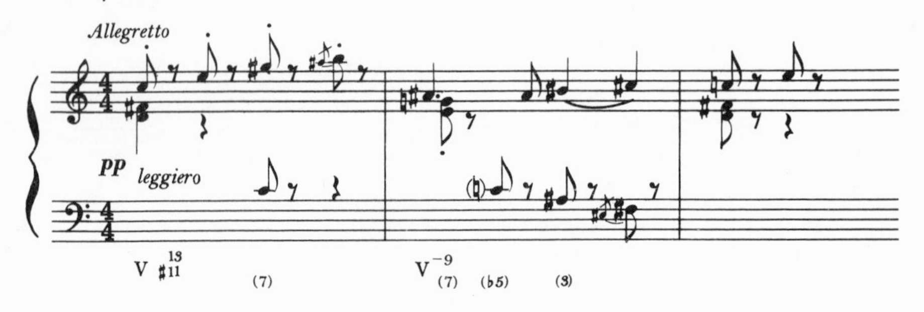

PART II

Impressionism

Many words have been written describing the effect on music of the Impressionistic movement in painting. Color, mood, and shimmering beauty constantly occur in essays attempting to portray this musical setting. No matter how poetic the description may be, words alone cannot suggest the sound.

The music itself is the language, and to understand its beauty one must unfold the musical secrets that lie behind a haunting melody or the undulating waves of *La Mer*. As the painter developed new brush techniques, the composer explored different scales and new harmonies. The painter searched for new subjects in natural settings, and tried to capture a particular expression or momentary image. The composer, using new techniques of orchestration, paralleled this viewpoint by writing more tone poems than symphonies and more songs than sonatas. Debussy's *Preludes* for piano have subtitles, each whetting the imagination as one listens. The beautiful things of life have inspired painters, musicians and poets since man first learned to draw, sing and write. However it is our awareness of a different style and our appreciation of it that gives us a feeling of new beauty in sound. Franz Schubert and Robert

Schumann left to the world their impressions of life in the form of songs, symphonies or even in direct pictoral settings, such as the piano work *Carnival* by Schumann. The many *adagio* movements of Handel or Bach have their own poignant beauty as do the madrigals of Josquin Despres. The meaning of "color", "mood" and "beauty" must be explored through the musical understanding of each style.

8 Modal influence

The musical techniques of Impressionism are so different from the Romantic style that to place any one characteristic above another in importance is difficult. The scale, however, is the structural organization behind both melody and harmony, and when this is substantially changed from former musical practices, herein lies the clue toward the recognition and understanding of this new sound. Although the conventional key signatures were generally retained by Debussy and other composers of this style, modal scales were formed by chromatic alterations of tones of the diatonic scale. Ever since the gradual breakdown of the modes during the seventeenth century, composers of all Western music relied on the major and minor scales for their individual creative expression. Now the Impressionists, as if with a bold stroke of their brush, swept aside centuries of diatonic influence and ushered in a return to the old modal scales. They did not restrict their use to the rigid formulas of the past, but rather added these new patterns to all that chromaticism had already achieved. This blend provided new melodies, enriched harmonies and, when woven with a fresh sparkling orchestration, created a style completely original and intriguing.

To determine the specific mode of a melody, decide upon the rhythmically stressed tone around which the others revolve. Organize the tones in scalewise order around this tonic, called "final" in modal terms. A secondary tone of strength may be the dominant (see chart, *example 183*), capable of receiving melodic stress equal to that of the tonic. The mode need not use all of its scale members to achieve its recognition; nor is it necessary that the starting or ending tone of the phrase be the tonic or dominant. Each mode has a particular characteristic that contrasts it with the major and minor scales. The chart indicates this comparison.—By memorizing these different interval changes, one can quickly learn the new scale formulas and transposition of the modes is facilitated. Not all melodies will fit a specific mode, and many will add chromatic tones, but the modal flavor may still be there. Rarely, will the entire composition fall into a mode. Generally, the theme, or just the main motive, will provide the new color and setting for the piece. The development of the theme continues with full resource of all chromatic elements. Be concerned primarily with the mode in its melodic arrangement. The bass may help to identify the tonic, but the harmonization may be free, just as in a Bach chorale.

Example ***183***

Comparison of Modes to Major or Minor Scales

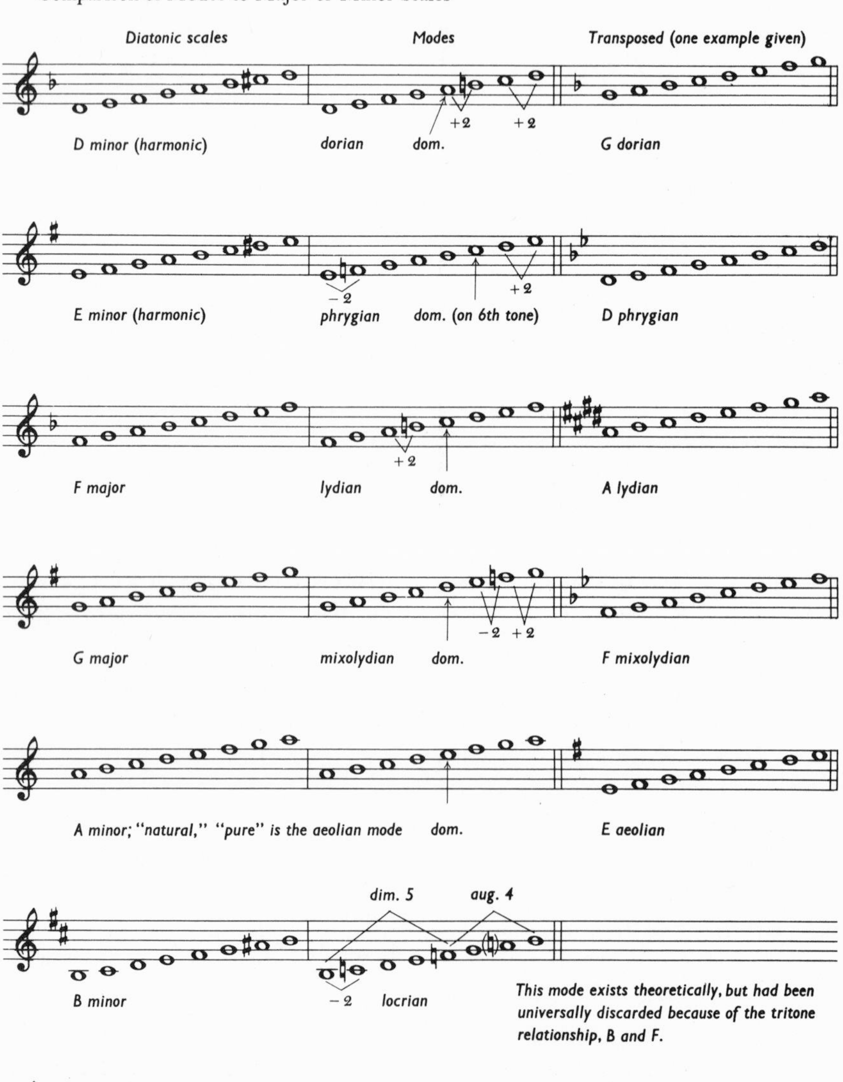

Play the melodies in *examples* **184a**, *b*, *c*, and *d*, and notice how the selection of the proper mode is determined. In *example* **184a**, pitches given the rhythmic stress are B♭ and F. With B♭ as a tonic, the phrygian mode is formed. (In the phrygian mode the dominant is not on the fifth scale tone but on the sixth.)

Both *examples* **184b** and *c* are in the dorian mode transposed from F. Observe that Debussy's key signature in *example* **184c**, confirms it. The range includes the four scale tones below the tonic, F, and this more exactly identifies the mode as hypodorian. Because the instrumental use of all of the modes is less strict today than during the original vocal period, the distinction of range is relatively unimportant.

In the excerpt from "La Cathedral engloutie" (*example 184d*), the theme has been separated from its parallel triad harmonization in order that the mode of the melody be more clearly identified. This section (measure twenty-eight in the prelude) ushers in, for the first time, the chief tonality of C major. Against this firmly established tonic, the mixolydian mode is recognized by the melodic arrangement of tones in which B♭ is present instead of B♮.

Frequently, the melody alone will not give away its modal application. The tonic may be recognized through the total harmonic structure against which the scale tones of the melody may then be properly arranged. The "Musette", *example 185*, from Ravel's *Le Tombeau de Couperin* is indicative of this situation. Without the repeated reference to the tonic and dominant, G and D, in the bass line, the melody might be mistakenly analyzed in B♭. Played alone, this melody would not have a modal conviction.

Example **185** Ravel

It is possible to have a dual reaction to the mode of a certain phrase. The melody may suggest one mode and the harmony another. Generally they merge in favor of the mode that is produced by the harmonic background. Even so, a melody may be so individualistic as to command its own recognition, if only temporarily. In the opening of the song, *La Flûte de Pan* (*example 186*), the ascending sextuplet, suggesting the flute, uses the lydian scale. The starting tone, B, had the strength of a tonic when placed in this scalewise order and also is prominent at the motive's conclusion at the end of the second measure. In the meantime, however, the harmony announces the perfect fifth, D♯ down to G♯ on the very first beat, out of which the chord on beat two is an inversion of this G♯ harmony rather than a switch to a B major large seventh. The return of the chord of G♯ minor in the second measure helps to remind the listener of the opening chord before the motive moves on to B major. The conflict between the melodic reference to the lydian scale from B and the harmonic opening on G♯ as a dorian influence remains unresolved until the voice enters in the third measure. Here, the chant effect stresses the G♯ dorian contour. Nevertheless, the fluctuation between roots of the minor and relative major is a modal characteristic and not uncommon. In this particular song, the final cadence recalls the opening motive and so retains the tonal ambiguity of this modal relationship.

Example 186 *La Flûte de Pan (Chansons de Bilitis). Debussy*

Lent et sans rigueur de rythme

Voice

Piano

pp

Chromatic tones may be added to a modal melody without destroying the original modal feeling. In the following song, *example 187*, the main theme is first presented in the left hand of the piano part. The colorful E♯ dominates the motive and becomes part of the G♯ dorian scale. The descending chromatic passing tones, G and E♮ connect tones of the mode in the same way that they would serve the diatonic scale. The modality is not as obvious, but still is an underlying factor, not to be excluded because of the presence of chromatic elements.

Example 187 *Il pleure dans mon coeur (Ariettes Oubliées). Debussy*

Modérément animé

Piano

pp

p

p

pp

pp

etc.

Motivic construction

Melodies in the Impressionistic style are frequently sporadic in their concept; wishful fleeting images tantalize the listener. This contrasts with the long thematic continuity of the Classical or Romantic conception.

Phrase forms are made up of these motivic units separated by measures of colorful background.

The rhythm sometimes pauses while the harmony provides a restlessness with clusters or whole-tone effects. The phrase may continue by sequential material or move into new melodic thoughts. The total rhythmic effect is one which lessens the rigid movement of pulse, but does not upset its underlying motion.

In songs, this sporadic motivic concept is frequently heard in a recitative style of vocal writing. The text of a poem may be given a setting approximating a prose style. The rhythmic pulsations are not accented, but are delivered in a normal, almost spoken manner, reminiscent of a chant at times. The stress is on the poem and its meaning. This contrasts with the German *lieder*, for example, in that the latter melodies are self-contained. Their flowing lines do not require the text in order to make the musical phrase meaningful. While on the contrary, the Impressionistic song relies heavily on the combination of poem and music.

The preceding techniques are, of course, matters of degree. No song, of any period, regards the text lightly. What is important to understand is the stylistic approach which differs among the vocal art forms of the various musical periods.

Review the vocal writing of *example 186* and look ahead to *example 210*. The text, of necessity, must be omitted in these songs as the fragmentary excerpts would not be sufficient to convey any complete thought.

EXERCISES

The following exercises are designated to produce a familiarity and a recognition of the particular modes. Write the exercises first and then analyze the modes involved in the compositions that follow.

A 1] Change the *minor* scales of D, F♯ and B♭ into the dorian mode.

2] Change the *major* scales of F, E♭ and A into the lydian and mixolydian modes.

3] Write the phrygian scale from C, A and G.

B Organize each melodic phrase in *Example 188* into a scalewise order starting from the tone you select as a "final". Mark the mode, the "final" and the "dominant" tone. Continue each melody by developing some of its motives, as described in chapters one and two. Retain the mode, permitting an occasional chromatic tone.

Example 188a

C *Analysis*

1] Example 189 shows the influence of three modes. Mark
a] the mode in the vocal line alone, basing the judgement upon the opening scale formation and the stressed tones of the first two measures;
b] the mode of the vocal line, apparent at the cadence;
c] the mode which arises from the tonic recognition of the harmony.

Example 189 Sonetto LV. Britten

2] Mark the mode of *Example 190* and observe Bartók's rhythmic interest in the phrase. If possible, listen to the recording of Music for String Instruments, Percussion and Celesta and identify other modal motives in the fourth movement.

3] Example 191 illustrates how the mode of the vocal line is carried through in the harmonization. Observe the Modern touch in the cadence and also note the effect of the meter change upon the phrase length.

For further study of modal applications, listen to:

Symphony of Psalms, "Movement I", by Stravinsky

String Quartet, "Movement II," and the second theme of "Movement I," by Ravel

"Le Vent dans la plaine," "Prelude III", Vol I, by Debussy

9 Influence of modes on harmony

The effect of modes upon a melodic style has been discussed in the preceding paragraphs. Perhaps even more influential to the Impressionistic style as a whole is the profound effect that the modes had on harmonic progressions. The following points help to outline some of the changes that took place between the chromatic concept of harmony and the revolutionary aspects of Impressionistic harmonization:

1] Lack of the leading-tone

2] Triad qualities relating to a mode rather than the diatonic major or minor scale.

3] Root progressions utilizing the full scope of chromaticism.

4] Resolutions of seventh chords in non-traditional ways.

5] Vague sense of "key" due to the non-diatonic effects.

Examining each factor in turn, start by playing *example 192*, the "Sarabande" from *Pour le Piano* by Debussy. It contains many of the new techniques. Notice the cadences, for example. Could you label these with Classical terms, such as "Perfect authentic"?

Lack of the leading-tone

The absence of the leading-tone is one of the most prominent factors that destroys a diatonic relationship. Not only does it remove the sound of our dominant to tonic cadence, but carried further, it lessens the frequency of the dominant to tonic progression within the phrase; the logic being that if the mode does not contain that half-step interval, leading-tone to tonic, then the composition should likewise not stress a formula basically unidentified with the original scale. And of course, Debussy was seeking something new and perhaps deliberately avoided the patterns that could inappropriately mix styles.

In the first eight measure of the "Sarabande" the only significant use of the cadential progression, root movement of a perfect fourth up, occurs

Example 192 *Sarabande from Pour le piano. Debussy*

between measure four and five. But notice, it is G♯ minor to C♯ minor; no B♯ leading-tone!

The next cadential progression occurs in measure fourteen, and this time we hear a hint of diatonic reference. The quality of the A♯ seventh chord, together with its progression to D♯ major, gives us an exact II^7 to V of the key of G♯ minor. Here we do have the raised leading-tone on V, namely F double sharp. However, the diatonic key is not fulfilled; the dominant pivots on its bass tone, changes quality and brings about the return of the theme.

Another example showing the effect of the modal seventh degree is given in *example 193, L'Echelonnement des Haies,* by Debussy. Instead of the usual C♯ minor scale, this song starts immediately in the aeolian mode. The harmonic progression in each of the first three measures is I to V, but because of the mode, both triads are minor. In measure four, the seventh degree becomes a root of the implied B major chord, the VII of the aeolian mode. This closes the first phrase. As the voice enters, the pedal tone B tends to become a dominant of E, but only for two measures. The leading-tone, D♯, in measure six, is immediately lowered by the use of a B minor chord in measure seven. This cancels the brief

Example 193 *L'Echelonnement des Haies. Debussy*

reference to the diatonic key of E. The repeated progression B minor to E major in the eighth measure now facilitates the modal return of the first phrase, being achieved by a drop of a third in the root progression, E to C♯.

Applying roman numerals to a passage in which chromatic alterations take place within a non-diatonic framework can be puzzling. Examining the B minor chord in measure seven of the given example more closely, notice that several logical theories can be applied to its harmonic analysis. The following possibilities are minutely detailed so as to stress the importance of evaluating an accurate tonal setting. Roman numerals represent a tonality and must not be used to satisfy the eye in an apparent visual theory. With reference to measures seven to nine, the harmonic analysis can be applied as follows:

Roman numerals II and V can represent the B minor and E major chords as if in the key of A major. However, the function of the E chord is not that of a dominant, and the progression is too brief to prove any hearing of an A major tonality.

Since no other diatonic key includes both the B minor and E major chords, and since neither chord can be considered merely as an embellishment, a modal analysis may be feasible. Which mode is involved? Again, there are several possibilities: (a) Preserving the E major tonality that was briefly alluded to in measures five and six, the B minor chord of measure seven acting as a minor V to E major as I would be the result of the mixolydian mode from E. (b) On the other hand, the rhythmic duration of the B minor chord and its use on the strong beats in measure eight, may transfer it temporarily to the strength of a tonic. In this case, the IV, E major, would be the product of the dorian mode from B. (c) Another theory can anticipate the return of the C♯ aeolian mode by suggesting that the tone of D♮ (in the B minor chord) be thought of as belonging to a temporary phrygian scale from C♯ and therefore retaining the label of VII!

Which theory do you like the best? Take your pick! Neither the modal alternatives nor the diatonic choice of A major is convincing. The importance in the situation is to recognize that the flexible interpretation is due to the avoidance of diatonic progressions and to the lack of leading-tone resolutions.

Whereas Classical harmony gravitates around the dominant to tonic formula with its leading-tone resolution drawn from both the major and minor scale, only one mode has the half step built in between its seventh and eighth scale tones. This is the lydian mode. (Refer to chart, pp. 162.) It is logical therefore that with the majority of modes not clarifying their tonic by the propelling movement of a raised leading-tone, the sound of modal progressions may become fused, resulting in a loss of specific modal identity. In addition, chromatic alterations erase a particular mode, and no composition adheres strictly to one mode for any length of time.

Use roman numerals to designate areas of tonality and their relationship with one another, but in transitional areas where a key center is elusive, indicate roots by letter name and quality. Recognize this non-diatonic chordal movement as being part of the flavor of Impressionism, a continuation of chromatic flexibility.

Triad qualities relating to modes

The modal scale tones create a unique combination of triad qualities. Already discussed was the modal VII chord, as opposed to its Classic counterpart, the raised leading-tone chord. Other triads also create a refreshing individuality in their movement around a tonic. Listen to the opening of Debussy's *String Quartet, example 194*. In which "key" is the first theme? G minor? Play the first two measures again. Notice the F naturals and the A flats. This is not the scale of the Classical G minor. It is the phrygian mode being used melodically and harmonically. In measure three, the viola brings in chromatics and the mode becomes an influential factor rather than an exact formula. These first two measures, however short, immediately pronounce their individuality and this strength dominates the movement.

Let us compare the triad qualities that the phrygian mode created with those of the usual G minor scale. In the first measure, the root of the second chord is D, the fifth tone of the scale. The "dominant" therefore is now a half-diminished seventh chord! In measure six the A♭ major chord can now be interpreted as the real supertonic of the phrygian mode. Above it, the chromatic B♮ is used as an embellishing leading-tone, part of a G dominant minor ninth chord. In measures nine and ten, the succession of half-diminished qualities can best be interpreted as tonic to dominant root movements. These root tones, G and D, are weakened because of their altered qualities and their location as

Example **194** *Debussy*

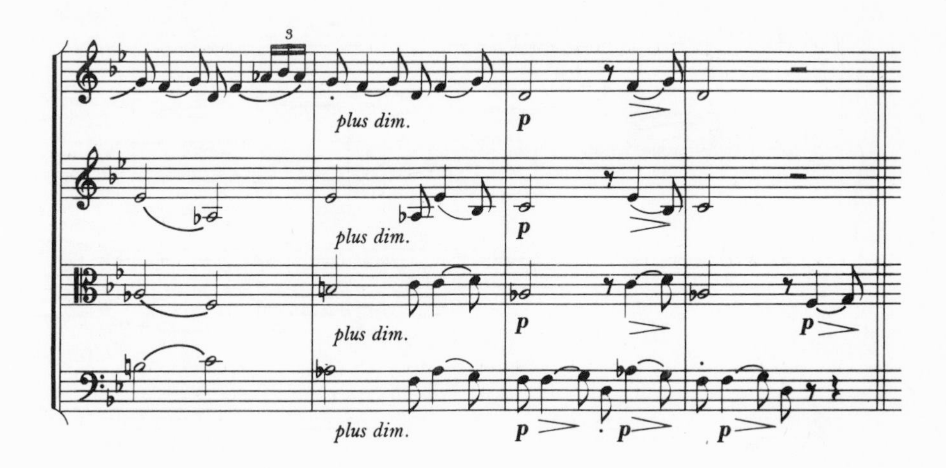

carriers of a melody rather than harmony. However, the melodic emphasis shifts to the cello in measure eleven where the root tone D clarifies the dominant extension. Once again, it is the D half-diminished seventh chord, derived from the phrygian mode.

Structurally, it is interesting that in this first movement, written in sonata form, both the principal theme and the subordinate theme of the exposition use the phrygian mode. Referring back to Example *184a*, notice that the key center for Theme 2 is the traditional B♭, but the scale degrees are modal, thereby forming a structural unity between the two themes.

Another mode which affects the triad qualities in a colorful way is the dorian. Play the opening of the *Violin Sonata, example 195*, also in G minor, and notice the use of the C major chord. It is the subdominant chord made major because of the mode, and is used in measure three to immediately offset a diatonic G minor, and again as a cadential chord to end the first phrase.

All modes produce some subtle changes to the diatonic scales. These engaging alterations are sufficient for recognition of this new style. Refer to the

Example 195 *Sonate. Debussy*

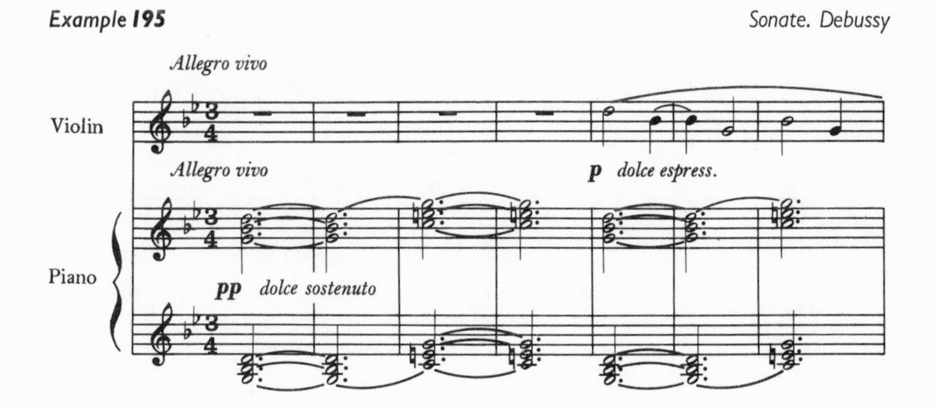

p poco marcoto
Example 196
Bartók
Trpts. (in C)
Strings
I; (V7 in Trpts. only.) V;−7
I
♮VII +6 4
Clts.
Obs.
Bsns.
etc.
(♯5)
V inc.
I; V7

chart again and build triads on the familiar progressions such as I, IV, II, V, I, and see how differently they sound in the various modes.

As a result of these different scales, cadences have lost their labels. They can only be complete or incomplete. The melodic and rhythmic elements in a phrase dictate the cadence with more certainty than does the harmonic progression. The term "semi-cadence" should refer to a pause halfway through a melody or structural theme, not to a chord on the dominant which it has been so frequently associated with in Classical analysis. What will decide if a cadence is complete or incomplete? In contemporary writing, since this trend originated in the Impressionistic period, the completeness of a cadence depends on motivic satisfaction of a certain theme or section of a composition; the vertical component parts of a chord have little to do with it. A series of harmonic structures can prepare the listener for a cadence, which will then be felt by contrast to what has occurred before, but mostly it is the simple fact of rhythmic pause. A complete cadence can be felt on the sound of a dominant seventh, as in the cadence to Alexander Tansman's "Sarabande" from *Suite dans le Style Ancien*, or at the end of the second movement of Bartók's *Concerto for Orchestra*. See *example 196*. The acceptance of such a cadence is contingent upon the structural preparation, motivicly and tonally, that precedes the pause, regardless of its vertical sound at the moment. The Tansman excerpt is described in chapter thirteen, *example 272*.

Illustrating the most convenient method of cadential analysis, examine the familiar prelude, *La fille aux cheveux de lin*, excerpts from which follow.

The function of the chords in measures two to three (*example 197a*), is largely to establish the tonic G♭, and to punctuate the theme. The duration of the G♭ chord nevertheless also gives the effect of our first cadence, the plagal subdominant to tonic. The second phrase cadences on the E♭ major chord in measure six, best described simply as a cadence on a major submediant. The fact that the cadential progression B♭ to E♭ is used, does not make this a complete perfect authentic cadence. The sudden switch of tonality away from G♭, now pausing on a foreign chord, by chance, E♭, gives the impression that the piece must go on. In fact, it connects to a return of the first phrase. The E♭ major chord was used in substitution for the traditional dominant semi-cadence. With the return of the theme, a small ABA form unfolds, concluding with a perfect authentic cadence in measures nine to ten. During the body of the prelude, other cadences rest on the subdominant, major sub-mediant and the dominant. The final complete cadence (see *example 197b*) uses the minor II_4^6 to I. The parallel fourths in the melody carry out a previous parallel design and also suggest the chord tone of the minor seventh as being part of the supertonic chord. Notice also the absence of the leading-tone in this melodic group. Notwithstanding these peculiarities, the cadence is complete, dictated by rhythmic slowing down of the harmonic function, not by a compelling resolution in the melody.

Root progressions

Root progressions are not limited to those arising from the modes. Chromatic additions and mixture of modes must prevail if a composition is not to become boring by its own unique qualities. In the opening of the *Violin Sonata* already referred to in *example 195*, the chromatic addition is the E♭ minor chord in measures eight and nine. This progresses to a D dominant ninth which contains a surprising E♮, as the ninth of a major mode. The phrase cadences on the major subdominant, recalling the dorian opening statement.

Also in the "Sarabande," *example 192*, beginning with the ninth measure, chromatic alterations and free choice of quality are present. The cross relation of the A to the A♯ in the first two chords of measure nine is interesting because this type of movement was not used by a Classicist. The bass A would have moved directly to an A♯ producing an F♯ chord in the first inversion. Try it at the keyboard; make it sound like Bach!

This is the type of control which the chromatic scale enforced upon diatonic writing. By removing such limitations, the chromatic scale in the Impressionistic period as well as now, provides composers with a new uninhibited outlook. Root progressions around a tonic include the possibilities of all the twelve chromatic tones functioning as roots, and this leads to the twelve-tone scale. But for the moment, let's limit this chromaticism to its growth within the Impressionistic period. This treatment includes: (a) Triad alterations to any quality (b) Cross relations of tones involved in chord movement (c) Expanded use of root movement, including, up a third. This was rare in the Classical approach. (Except for I to III, use of II to IV, III to V, IV to VI, is seldom found in triad form. It is possible to see for example, in the key of C major, an F major chord and then an A dominant seventh—altered VI^7, but by hearing it in context, the F chord will be the result of some motive, and the A seventh chord will start the new movement, probably embellishing the II, D minor.)

In the "Sarabande," find the root movement, up a third, in measures one and two. In the *Violin Sonata*, the chromatic chord of E♭ minor is also the result of the same root progression. In *La fille aux cheveux de lin*, the progression IV–VI–I harmonizes the final return to the theme.

Stepwise movement downward is also the result of modal textures. Such progressions as II to I, IV to III, VI to V and others, produce a modal sound, again, simply because they are not prominent in the Classical literature. Notice this treatment in the sixth, seventh and eighth bars of the "Sarabande."

In the preceding illustrations, the emphasis has been to show a modal derivation behind the choice of a particular quality in a chord and its progression to another chord. Chromatic use was included here in order to show more distinctly the opposing features between the strict modal progressions and those which interweave with chromatic additions. In *example 198*, which is the main theme of the Debussy *Quartet* as it appears toward the end of the last movement, most of the original modality is lost. Compare it with *example 194*. The chromatic changes from the tone D to D♯ and back again in the first three chords are part of a forceful declaration of the theme and have no modal intent, in spite of the root progression moving up in thirds. The D♭ chord again removes the D and is a chromatically lowered dominant. It progresses up a third to F minor, which by resolving to G major, restores some of the modal flavor, the use of the lowered VII to I.

Example 198 *Debussy*

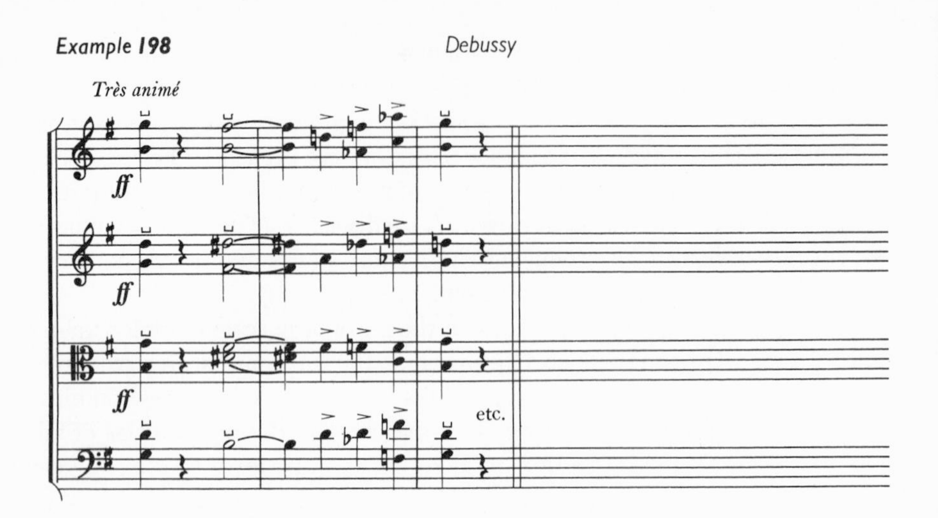

If you have become aware of the unusual resolutions of seventh chords, you have recognized an important step in the harmonic growth taking place in this period. For the moment, this does not directly relate to a modal influence, and so it will be discussed in a following chapter on harmonic expansion.

Tonality

Play the excerpt from the "Sarabande" again (*example 192*). What key is it in? Can you "prove" it? By Classical standards, proof would be in the cadence, if not obviously set up in the first phrase. The Classical cadence would most likely be a dominant to tonic. What do we have in the "Sarabande"?

The two measure motive, and its repetition, emphasizes the E major to G♯ minor progression (measures two and four). This could appear to be in the key of E major, supported by the opening leading-tone seventh chord. But the next phrase makes quite clear that C♯ minor is the focal point of all of the chords and the rhythm of the opening motive. This C♯ minor triad is the tonic, not a submediant to E. Our motive, therefore begins on II^7, leads from III to the minor V; and all of the harmonic progressions, as well as the complete melody for the first eight bars, are in the aeolian mode.

The question might arise as to the cadential function of the B major chord in the eighth bar. Couldn't it be a dominant of E major? Yes, if you look at it—no, if you listen to it. Remember, (a) the focal point was C♯, due to its location, duration, and melodic strength, (b) the harmonic movement, as it leads to the B major chord, is built entirely on the scale of the aeolian mode in both the bass and treble. The ear therefore connects the I of C♯ minor down to the lowered VII of the mode. If anyone needs further proof that the B major chord is not functioning as a V, play the chord adding the seventh. A dominant seventh should not basically alter the function of a dominant triad. It simply increases its tendency to resolve. Does this now sound like the same chord Debussy had in mind? Horrors!

The next section, a small Part 2 of the main theme, develops particularly the figure originating in measure five. Having discussed the interesting use of triads here, now examine the tonality. A diatonic reference to G♯ minor is present at the end of the phrase, II^{ø7} to V (measure fourteen). It is interesting to note the implication of a modulation from tonic to dominant, C♯ to G♯ minor, and also to observe that again the aeolian mode is prominently used, although not exclusively. Notice especially the introduction of the tone of A♯ in measure nine, as part of an F♯ major triad. This same F♯ major chord teeters back and forth with the A♯ seventh chord in measure thirteen, and so provides the modal quality of the implied G♯ aeolian structure. The F double sharp then becomes a raised leading-tone, but not resolved traditionally.

The preceding paragraph suggests the implied tonality of G♯ minor. Is it this time, a foolproof situation? Notice that our conclusion was based on the Classical progression of II to V at the cadence. Disregard this for a moment, and try to find the focal chord of the phrase. Notice the recurrence of the F♯ major, especially when used as the F♯ dominant ninth in measures eleven, twelve, and even in measure thirteen. Here the A♯ seventh chord easily blends as a first inversion of a V^9. What does this suggest then in terms of tonality? B major? If so, how will the D♯ major chord, at the cadence, be analyzed? Altered III?

This is what we have just proven: Tonality for the most part had been based in the past on the major and minor scale, emphasized at cadences by the customary Classical progressions. When enough alterations take place that we do not hear the accustomed progressions, and no single chord takes unquestioned status as a tonic, we lose our foothold on a solid diatonic key center, and must settle for a possible, or perhaps, a probable hypothesis.

The fact that certain passages may not strongly adhere to one tonal center, does not necessarily mean that they have completely lost tonality, or become atonal. Generally this harmonic license will indicate strength of mutual closely related keys such as our deliberation in Part I of the "Sarabande" between C♯ minor and its relative major, E; or Part 2, G♯ minor or B major, or possibly D♯ minor. This reasoning is not due to a lack of tonal recognition, but simply, a lack of diatonic recognition because of the absence of diatonic formulas.

When analyzing doubtful passages, concentrate first on the whole piece, dividing it into large sections, and noticing the cadential areas of these large parts. Once recognizing this overriding tonality, see what relationships occur on the smaller cadences. It is correct to think of them as cadences on the mediant, or dominant, or whichever tonal degree is used. In this way, a unity is woven about the entire tonal focus, and the chromatic passages simply lead toward these more significant structural points.

There are a few compositions arising out of this period in which an unmistakable opening tonality becomes a secondary pivotal sound leading toward a final new tonal center. In the song from *Ariettes Oubliées* (*example 199*) A♭ minor dominates both melody and accompaniment for eight measures. It then moves into a group of changing dominant chords which in themselves have no stability, nor any reference to a single key. In measure sixteen, the last of these dominants resolves and happens to be an E♭ dominant seventh to an A♭ major chord. The V to the major I relationship is most logical. However, two measures later, the A♭ chord resolves to a D♭ dominant ninth which now com-

Example 199 *Green (Ariettes Oubliées). Aquarelle. Debussy*

Joyeusement animé

Voice

Piano

pp *leggierissimo*

pp

pp

p

p

p

dim.

pletely cadences to G♭ major to end the theme. Only at this point can the whole tonal picture be understood with its true significance. The opening A♭ minor area enacts the role of a supertonic. The first of the dominants in measure nine is the real D♭ V^9 and the Classical progression of II to V is present. The following chromatic dominants simply retain a harmonic activity which then resolves to the final key center of G♭ major.

EXERCISES

A 1] Except for an occassional chromatic tone, all of the "Siciliana," by Casella is harmonized by chords derived from modes. The brief quotations in *Example* **200** are sufficient to indicate each mode. In *Example* **200b**, analyze the melody and

Example 200a *Siciliana. A. Casella*

harmony separately. Mark the chromatic alterations that affect the dominant to tonic cadence. In *Example 200c*, find a few interesting higher-numbered relationships that the melody tones form with the accompaniment.

Example 200b

2] All of Debussy's *Preludes* combine chromaticism with the subtleties of modal color.

a] In *Example 201*, mark the modal influence, apparent in the first motive, and observe its growth into a higher-numbered chord in the second measure. This chord may receive three analytical interpretations. Mark all three possible roots and discuss why this sound is so flexible.

Example 201 *Debussy*

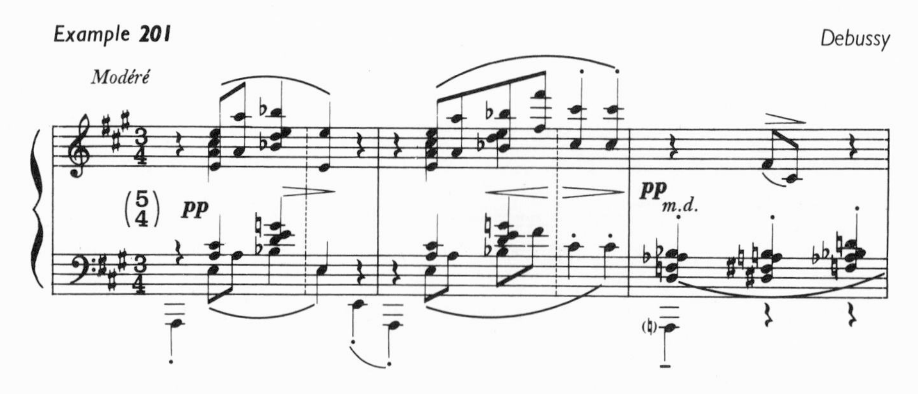

b] In the fifth measure, change the flats to sharps in the chord on the second beat. Name two root tones which may be implied.

c] A development of the motive occurs within this phrase. Which techniques are used?

3] Tonality plays an elusive role in *Example 202*, excerpts from a Debussy song. Play all of the given excerpts before marking the analysis.

a] Which tonality binds the composition?

b] Mark the roman numerals, using raised or lowered designations when necessary.

c] Mark all higher-numbered chords and the bass inversions. Find at least two instances of the ninth in the bass.

Example 202a *Spleen (Ariettes Oubliées). Aquarelle. Debussy*

Example 202b

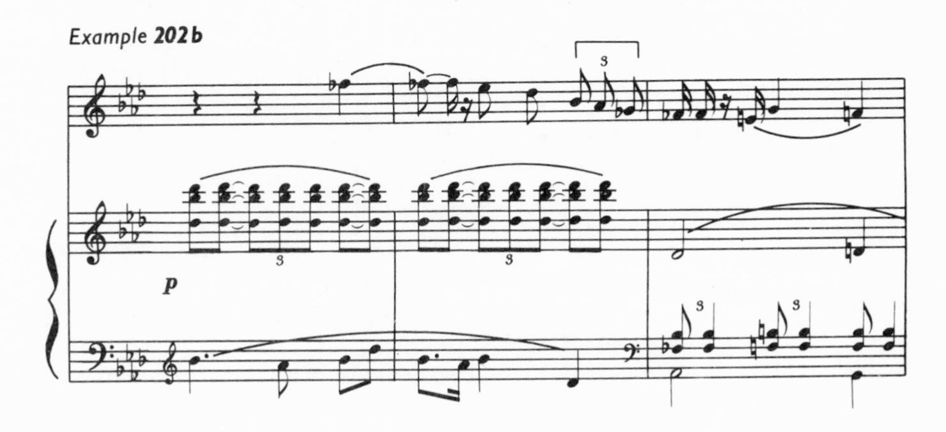

Example 202c — Debussy

B Add the upper voices to the given bass progressions; use a chorale style. Some key signatures reflect the modal qualities involved. The figurations in *Example* **203a** depend upon the key signature. Mark the resulting quality of all chords. The qualities are indicated in *Examples* **203b** and **c**. They require chromatic alterations where necessary.

C Harmonize the following melodies by using harmonies which are derived from the melodic mode. It is not necessary to restrict the harmony to modal derivations, however. An opening bass pattern is suggested. These melodies may be easily adapted for instrumental combinations.

D Continue the motives given in *Example* **205a** and **b**. Add a minimum of three phrases to the *Allegretto, Example* **205a** (forming a "double period") and at least one additional phrase to the slow theme of *Example* **205b**. Retain the modal background in the choice of chords.

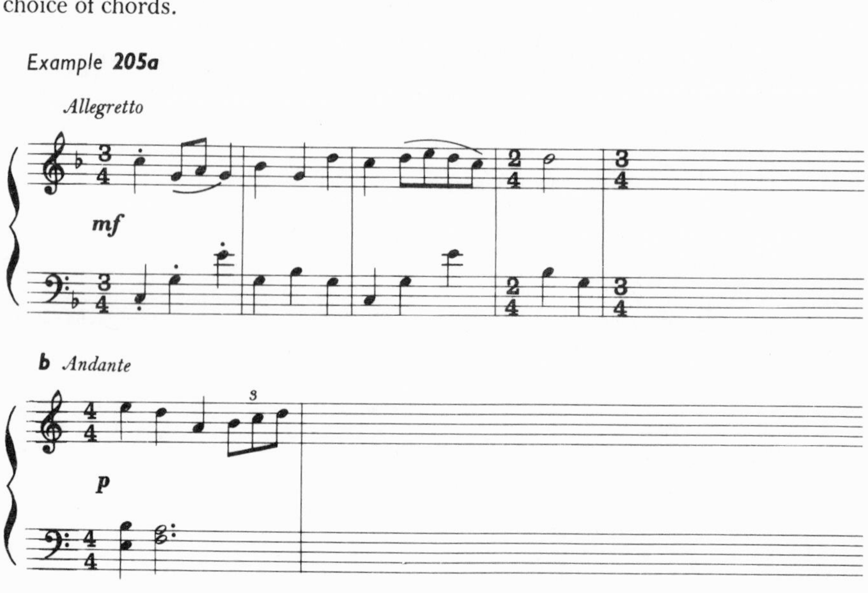

10 Unrestricted melodic movement of all chord members

With the Impressionists, independence came to all seventh, ninth, and higher-numbered chords; they were no longer bound by diatonic resolutions. This was largely due to the fact that diatonic root progressions were not emphasized. New chordal sounds, together with chromatic root movements, created a different atmosphere and this permitted melodies to free themselves from earlier styles.

Every student of diatonic and chromatic harmony will certainly recall one of the foremost "rules"; "the seventh must resolve down", with few exceptions.* Why was this rule practiced with such dogmatic determination? The seventh was first created as a descending passing tone or a suspension, this occurred in the writings of Palestrina and other sixteenth and seventeenth century composers. The Baroque period started using the seventh as an appoggiatura and gradually it gained more and more rhythmic strength, but always retained its downward resolution. The ninth followed the same procedure. The riddle of "when is it a ninth and when is it an appoggiatura", was discussed at length in chapter three. The true ninth chord was resolved by harmonic change to a new chord root, but in so doing, the Classic and Romantic school still preserved its downward tendency for the most part. The Impressionists threw aside these melodic conventions and now the seventh and ninth may resolve up, or move as freely as any other triad member, providing this new treatment is also part of a new harmonic scheme.

Has a "right" been created out of a "wrong"? Positively not! When Debussy wrote a V^7 to I cadence, his seventh resolved down with traditional accuracy. The difference lies in that he chose not to concentrate upon these conventional progressions, but instead, to explore new paths through modal and chromatic means. This new melodic freedom is most frequently associated with harmonic movement of consecutive dominant quality chords, whose roots

* If the bass takes over the tone of resolution, the seventh resolves up. For example, in progressions, V^4_3 to I_6, V^7 to I_6 or IV^7 to II^7.

evade the customary cadential progression, up a perfect fourth. This is illustrated in the three brief excerpts, *examples 206a, b, c.*

In *example 206a*, the dominant root movement is up a major third. The seventh, B♭, moves completely freely while the ninth, D, binds the two chords by the common tone. *Example 206b* has root movement of up a major second and illustrates the melodic stress of the seventh and ninth as they appear on accented beats. The third *example 206c*, has the diminished fifth interval connecting the roots of G and D♭. While the contour of the melody clearly shows the independence of the seventh and ninth, the accompaniment connects the voices as smoothly as possible. Contrary motion is most effective by the uppermost part of the right hand, the ninth, A, resolving up to the thirteenth (B♭) of the D♭ chord. The thirteenth is then retained in the high accompaniment.

The fact that many chords are built with chord tones higher than the seventh in their vertical structure allows for greater freedom of movement for the seventh itself because the listener's attention is focused on the activity of the other chord tones. For example, in this incomplete cadence, quoted from the Ravel *Quartet*, *example* 207, the melodic focus is on the ninth, while the seventh merely bounces into it on the weak fourth beat. In addition, the augmented eleventh is spotlighted in the second violin as a contrapuntal feature. The resolution of this G chord to a C V^{13} uses the melody A as a common tone and shows a momentary descending resolution of both the A and the F. The C♯, also a common tone, sounds a minor ninth enharmonically in the dominant chord, but is notated to show a resolution to D, an added sixth in the F major tonic triad.

In *example* 208, the ascending melody arrives and leans on the D♯, the augmented eleventh, completely overshadowing the seventh, G, of the first measure. The equal major second intervals of the melody, G, A, B, C♯, D♯, suggestive of the whole-tone scale also help to erase the need for the usual downward resolution of the seventh. By contrast, however, the phrase closes on an F♯ V^{-9} which by the progression to B, now uses the Classical resolutions for both the seventh and ninth.

Example ***208*** *Harmonie du Soir. Debussy*

Melodic importance can center on the seventh without the listener being aware of a resolution. If the seventh moves downward to a non-harmonic passing tone, the tension created by the seventh remains, and expects to be resolved at the next chord change. Some motives are so compact and embodied within a single harmonic color that their tones of the seventh tend to disappear rather

Example ***209*** *Nuages. Debussy*

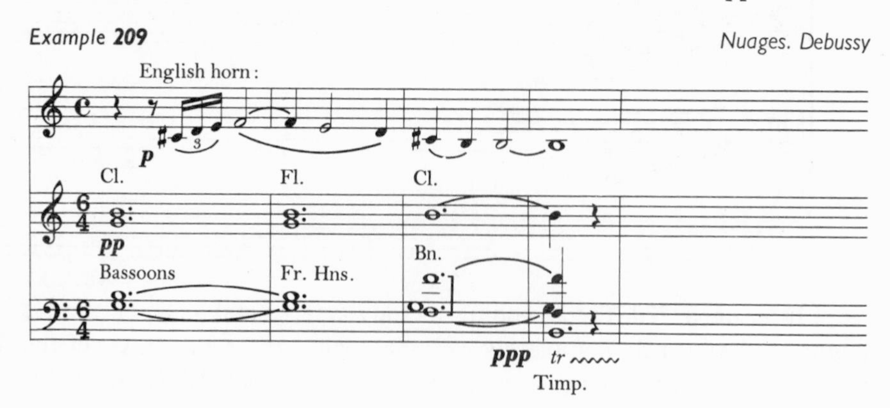

than resolve. For example, the motive given to the English horn in *Nuages*, *example* **209**, is self-contained on the G major chord. The melodic contour rises to the seventh, F, and descends scalewise via passing tones E and C♯. The bassoons restate the seventh in octaves as part of the chord, and before the English horn has ended its motive, the bassoons fade away and rest. No resolution takes place. Listen to this motive throughout all of *Nuages*. The treatment is basically the same, but differing in the surrounding instrumentation.

Frequently, a motive will end as the seventh of a chord. Because of the separation between the end of one thought and the start of another one, the seventh may appear as a stationary chord member, with no resolution demanded. In *example* **210**, the text is included so as to illustrate more clearly the separate figures contained in this short motive. The melody of *Cette nuit* ends on a seventh, as it does at the end of the motive on *j'ai rêvé*. This D♭ in the melody completes a thought, within the limitations of a motive, of course. The accompaniment of the next measure contains the same tone but not as a resolution of the vocal line. This stationary effect, realized by the seventh, is also partly due to the progression of two dominant quality chords moving up and down in intervals of a third. Had the Classical resolution of E♭ to A♭ taken place, the seventh would have insisted on its downward resolution whether it ended the motive or not.

Example 210 *La chevelure. Debussy*

Unrestricted melodic movement for the higher-numbered tones is not limited to dominant quality harmonizations. A minor seventh chord heard in conjunction with a modal melody may use the seventh in any melodic design. The viola theme (*example 211*) from the third movement of the Debussy *Quartet* arises out of the aeolian mode on G♯. The independent treatment of the seventh is heard in measure three against the ostinato accompaniment of the two violins on the I^7 chord. The kinship between the G♯ minor tonality and the relative major, B, is also evident. The absence of the leading-tone, F double sharp, contributes to this modal flexibility.

Example **211** String Quartet. Debussy

Parallelism

Turning back to the "Sarabande," *example 192,* not only does the seventh resolve upward, in the first chord, but all of the chord members move by parallel motion. This was a new approach affecting melody harmonization as well as root progression.

Its effect on melody is to minimize its solo quality. The supporting voices are enjoying the same linear motion and thereby form a unified block of harmonic color out of which the highest voice emerges as the "melody" simply by virtue of being on top. By the same token, the lowest voice, also partaking of this same "melody," loses its role as provider of harmonic root movement. Emphasis is placed on the bass: (1) by rhythmic accent, and (2) by the contrary motion formed as it separates itself from the parallel motive or phrase.

Notice how this applies to the first two bars of the "Sarabande." The opening II^7 chord receives the rhythmic strength of a downbeat. Due to the parallel structure, this chord returns at the end of the measure and resolves by contrary motion to the E major chord, again on an accented pulse. The intervening seventh chords are founded on different roman numerals and so support a tonal setting, but the specific progressions, from one to the other, have no importance. The bass line is part of the melodic contour during this parallel course.

Examples **212**, **213** and **214** are also brief illustrations of a total parallel design. In *example* **212**, the broken form of a triad in the second inversion is used to harmonize the chromatic tones of the uppermost line. Because of the return of the A major chord in measure three, the preceding chromatic $^6_4$ chords all function as part of the melody. Harmonic importance is therefore recognized by the rhythmic stress and duration of chords, since the bass, as a line, is also the melody. In this example, all important chords are chromatic neighbors to the A major chord. In the third measure, a syncopated stress is given to the B♭ dominant $^4_3$, which then descends via the tonic A to the lower neighbor, the A♭ dominant chord. This is held and used as a substitute for a semi-cadence. The A♭ chord is also the first to break the chain of parallels, and by so doing places the harmonic emphasis on the bass, as is normally done.

Example **212** *Fantoches. Debussy*

In *example* **213**, which is taken from the cadence to "Doctor Gradus ad Parnassum" from the *Children's Corner*, the chromatic chords of E♭ and F♯ are merely connecting links between the tonic and the dominant. They do not deserve roman numerals such as a lowered III and a raised IV because it is more coincidence than design that governed this selection. The chords of E♭ and F♯ are there to give a momentary burst of color away from the diatonic setting of C. Other chords could have been used with equal success. To review the issue, parallelism does not give equal values to all the chords which appear to be constructed in the same way. Rhythm and the setting of the entire phrase or composition rule over the harmonic emphasis in situations where the bass is parallel to the melody. The bass, therefore, may shift freely between its normal harmonic role and a new melodic function caused by parallelism.

Example 213 *Dr. Gradus ad Parnassum. Debussy*

Example 214 shows a modulation taking place through the use of parallel dominant ninths. The extensive parallelism negates all association to the former key. The contraction of the sequences and the faster movement of chords build to the goal on the F♯ chord at *Sans retarder*, which gradually provides a return of the main theme in E major. In the first four bars, the parallelism is heard chiefly in the right hand against a repeated cluster effect in the left hand (see chapter eleven). The movement of the treble parts supplies the

Example 214 *Children's Corner, No. II. Debussy*

harmonic background. Measure one is an A♭ dominant ninth, while measure two is a B♭ dominant ninth in the third inversion. The bass cluster remains fixed, but the harmonic emphasis rotates between the two tones. During the final measures of this example, the seconds in the bass are all $\frac{4}{2}$ inversions, making the parallelism totally effective.

One can retain the feeling of parallelism without being entirely chained to an elevator. Look again at the second measure of the "Sarabande" (*example 215*). While the chords are parallel, E to G♯, the bass jumps down to a low G♯ before resuming the upper triad. This subtle treatment creates melodic contrary motion, while retaining harmonic parallel movement.

A similar treatment occurs in the eleventh and twelfth measures of the "Sarabande." The complete parallelism is broken by the sustained melody tone E. The parallel group, composed entirely of dominant quality chords, is contained within one measure and then repeated. Important to this repetition, is the contrary motion formed by the last eighth note of measure eleven and the accented first beat of measure twelve. This emphasizes the F♯ dominant ninth chord which remains prominent during the remainder of the phrase.

Parallel structures may be limited to one setting, such as in a treble group of chords, or in some form of accompaniment, against which a normal contrapuntal line is heard. Such is the case in *example 216*. The melody is harmonized

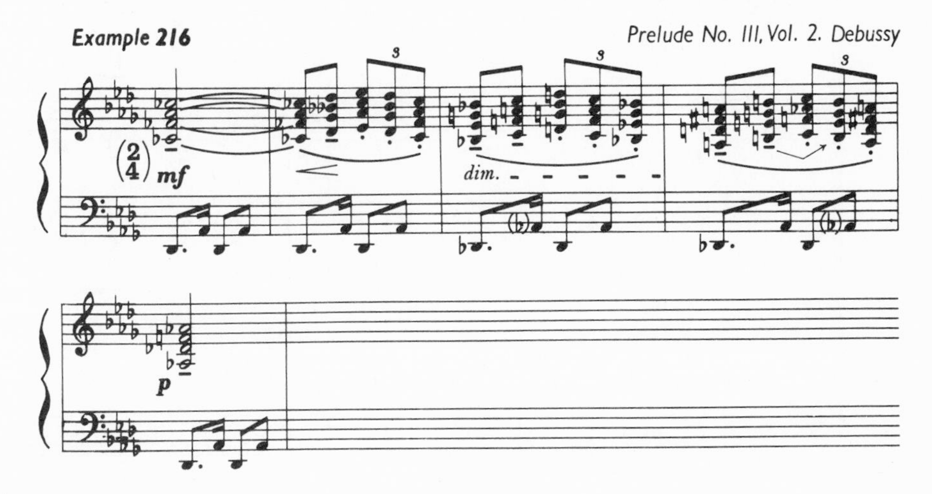

by triads, each spaced in the same manner pianistically convenient for the right hand. Their parallel appearance, however, is only a technicality as the total sound consists of the rise and fall of the melody heard against the repeated ostinato figure in the bass. This counterpoint creates one total result in which the parallel voicing is merely part of a melody harmonization and not part of a complete parallel design.

Example 217

Orchestration can bring out the parallelism of one choir heard against a contrasting line of another section of the orchestra. The excerpt from *Fetes, example 217*, shows parallel triads, appearing first in the woodwinds and then taken over by the strings, against which the main theme in the flutes and oboes rings out in perfect relief.

Parallelism, as already illustrated, can be used with triads as well as with

sevenths, ninths or other combinations. This technique is valuable if it is not overdone; at the same time, it must not appear accidental as if by incorrect voice-leading. The judgement as to how much parallelism is desirable must depend on the composer and the particular idea he is expressing. Generally speaking, one full phrase entirely parallel is too much, and a connection of only two or three chords, especially if not important to the motive, is too little.

Analyzing a complete composition will show a more accurate ratio of the parallel areas to the rest of the music than the limited excerpts here referred to. Above all, however, parallelism must arise as a demand of the motive, as if it couldn't be expressed in any other shape. It is one total thought. Never must a melody be taken for harmonization, and after an hour of desperation, be given a hopeless parallel treatment!

EXERCISES

A 1] Analyze the melody of the excerpt quoted in *Example 218* by observing and marking all chord tones of the seventh and higher. Note their function in the phrase. Mark the root progressions by their intervallic movement.

Example 218 Debussy

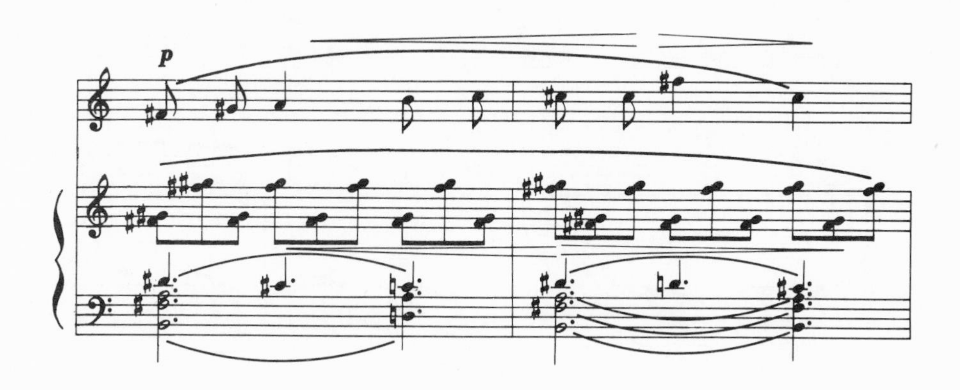

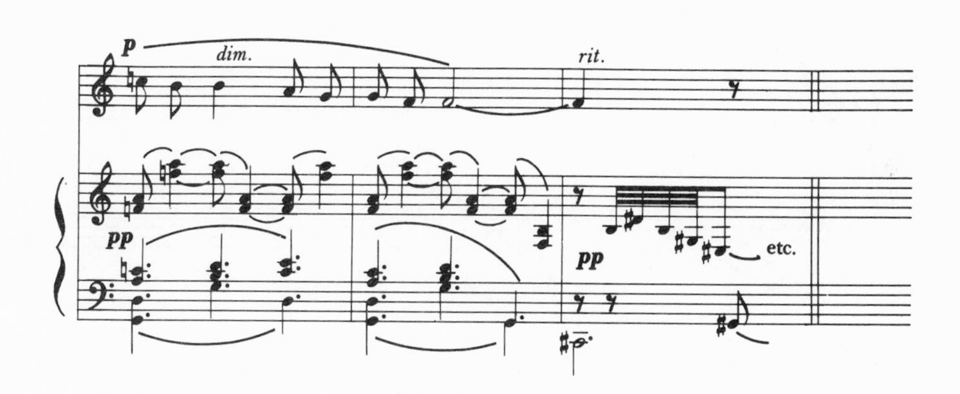

2] In particular, mark the quality of all chords in *Example* **219a** and **b**. Include the same melodic analysis and root progression indications as described before. What mode influences the phrase in *Example* **219a**?

Example 219a *De Reve. Debussy*

pp
Example 219b
p
plus pp
cre - scen - do
p etc.

3] *Example 220* from "Ondine" is a transitional phrase which nevertheless carries a motivic thought and develops it. Trace the motive; mark all chords by letter name, quality and root progression.

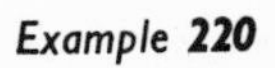

Prelude VIII, Vol. 2. Debussy

(6/8)
pp
pp
etc.

4] Analyze *Example* **221a, b** and **c** in the following way:
a] How does Griffes combine chromaticism with a modal influence?
b] What key is the *Barcarolle* in? Which mode is included?
c] Mark all chords and the melody tones of *Example* **221b**. Look for a few enharmonic notations. Examine the phrases and the motivic contractions.
d] As a review, mark the chords in *Example* **221c**.

Example 221a *Barcarolle, Op. 6, No. 1. Charles T. Griffes*

Example 221b

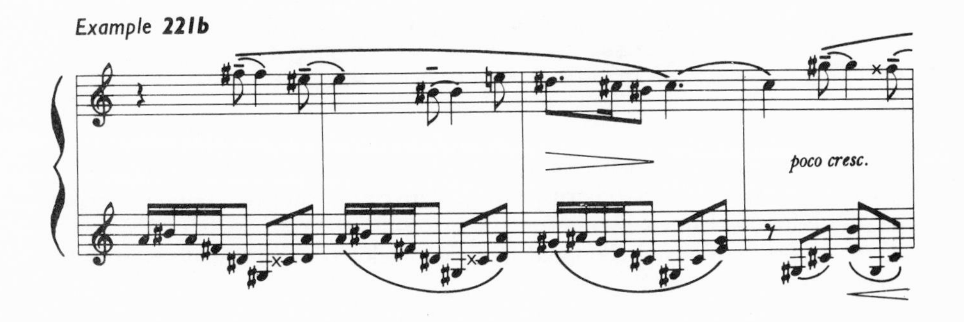

Example 221c

B Harmonize the melodies in *Example 222* by following the designated chord members. Choose your own chord quality and inversion but give preference to dominant chords in this chapter. Do not treat these exercises as chorales but rather as homophonic pieces in which rhythm and motivic development contribute equally to the harmonies involved.

C Work the unfigured basses in *Example 223* in the same manner as the preceding Example, except that you need to think upward instead of down from the melody. Add simple melodic fragments along with the harmonic progressions.

Example 223b

D Develop the given motive by adding one or two phrases. Use a sporadic motivic style.

Example **224**

11 The tritone, the whole-tone scale, and whole-tone dominants

The tritone is an interval which comprises three major seconds, spelled either as an augmented fourth or a diminished fifth. The original definition, however, limited the term to the augmented fourth. In medieval times, this interval was called *diabolus in musica* (the devil in music), and was forbidden at all costs. Gradually, after centuries of careful resolution, it progressed to the point where the Impressionists, delighted with its beauty, gave it a new position of prominence. Rivalling the modes, the tritone influenced melody and harmony in a completely new manner.

The plaintive English horn motive from *Nuages*, previously cited in *example* 209, has the contour of the tritone in the highest and lowest pitches, the F and B.

The *Prelude to the Afternoon of a Faun* opens with a flute solo in which the tritone C♯ and G is outlined amidst connecting chromatic tones. See *example* 225.

Example 225 — *Prelude a L'apres-midi d'un faune. Debussy*

The melodic contour of *The Little Shepherd* revolves around the important pitches of G♯ and D in its opening phrase. See *example* 226.

Example 226 — *The Little Shepherd. Debussy*

In all of these preceding illustrations, notice that the sound of the tritone governs the motive in its shape, but allows any combination of chromatic or diatonic tones to be incorporated into the melody. Such use of a prominent tritone in a motive tends to avoid a key tone or a stable harmonic setting. This is frequently desired by a composer. In *The Little Shepherd*, the eventual key of A is certainly kept a secret by the opening phrase. A more unusual area for the absence of a strong tonality would be a final cadence. But in *Nuages*, this is deliberately sought after. Listen to the entire piece and study the final phrase of *example* 227. Here, the orchestration employs *tremolo* in divided low strings in order to achieve a dark, mysterious color. The bass tones are deliberately diffused, even to the tremolo on two timpani. Against this background, a few of the main motives are hinted at, closing with the tritone leap, sounding B to F, in the muted French horns. Even after the final, soft *pizzicato*, this tritone remains inaudibly present in the mind, to retain a slight feeling of unrest, or a suggestion of infinity.

Example **227** *Nuages. Debussy*

The tritone was not restricted to melodic prominence. Its use in root progressions is very frequent especially as a substitute for the real dominant. Missing, of course, is the traditional leading-tone resolution involved in the dominant to tonic progression, but in its place are two tones which attempt to sound like fair substitutes. An F♯ dominant seventh, or the enharmonic G♭, upon resolving to C major creates the half-step movement from the root, F♯ leading to G, the fifth of C major. (See *example 228.*) Against this, contrary motion is formed by the C♯ (or D♭) leading down to the root, C. In addition, a thirteenth above the dominant chord moves by half step to the third of C major.

Example 228

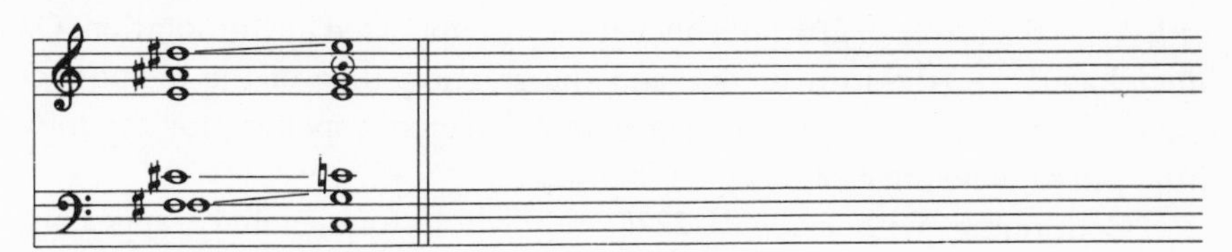

When functioning as the lowered dominant of the key, this chord is called the tritone dominant. This also applies to its use as a dominant embellishment. Otherwise, the interval of the tritone may be used in connecting any chromatic roots with chords of any quality. In the Impressionistic style, however, dominant qualities predominate.

The tritone, if filled in exclusively with the three whole tones that its name implies, becomes part of a whole-tone scale, in fact, exactly half of a whole-tone scale. This is the case in the first four tones of *The Little Shepherd, example 226*. The scale in the next figure is not continued as the half step D to C♯ breaks the whole-step pattern.

The whole-tone scale divides the octave into a series of major second intervals, allowing for at least one enharmonic spelling, chosen at the discretion of the composer. The equidistant intervals actually form only two different-sounding whole-tone scales. Unlike the major or minor scale in which the tonic is recognized by a set ratio or formula of intervals, the whole-tone scale prevents the recognition of one central tone. The repetition of starting on a tone and stopping on its octave might temporarily indicate a resting tone, but this would have to be supported by other musical factors in the composition, not by the scale itself.

Example:

C D E F♯ G♯ A♯ C (A♯ C = dim 3rd) or C D E G♭ A♭ B♭ C (E G♭ = dim 3rd)

C♯ D♯ E♯ G A B C♯ (E♯ G = dim 3rd) or D♭ E♭ F G A B D♭ (B D♭ = dim 3rd)

Examples **229a** and **b** are excerpts from the "Prelude" of *Pour le piano* illustrating first the scale itself and in *example* **229b**, a complete passage, in which the melody and its background figures are entirely derived from the whole-tone scale. In *example* **229a**, the spelling of the scale is in agreement with the A♭ augmented dominant seventh chord. In *example* **229b**, the first four measures show the tritone used as a climax to the preceding phrase and gradually abating in volume in order to introduce the following melody.

What is the harmonic background in this passage? Both the tritone and the whole-tone scale affect the harmony in an interesting way. The tritone cuts the octave in half and leaves the listener wondering which tone is the root and which is the lowered fifth. It works both ways. In this instance, D could be root with A♭ as the lowered fifth; this theory being supported by the notation. On the other hand, A♭, the lowest tone and the starting tone of the melody, could sound like the root with the D being an enharmonic spelling for the lowered fifth. There is no answer to this dilemma.

Continuing with *example* **229b**, the whole-tone melody appearing in measure five, retains this harmonic ambiguity. In measure seven, however, the triplet figure, still derived from the whole-tone scale, creates motion which lands on the major third, B♭ and D. This major third, in spite of its high register, now assumes the role of root and third of the B♭ chord. It remains prominent for the balance of this passage. Listen to this carefully, observing how the lowest tone, A♭, has become a seventh, and its tritone companion, the D, is the third. The whole-tone quality is continued in the "Prelude" for an additional seventeen measures. The tones of B♭ and A♭ eventually resolve, as chromatic neighbors, to A minor, the tonic key. (If possible, listen to the entire "Prelude.")

Factors of rhythm and melodic contour brought forth the hearing of the B♭ major third. These factors must be considered in the determination of roots in any harmonic structure. The tritone and the whole-tone scale add to this complexity. The sound produced by these equidistant intervals is unmistakable, and is valuable because of this distinct recognition. Only the label we attach to this sound may be puzzling and therefore prompts further discussion.

Example **229a**

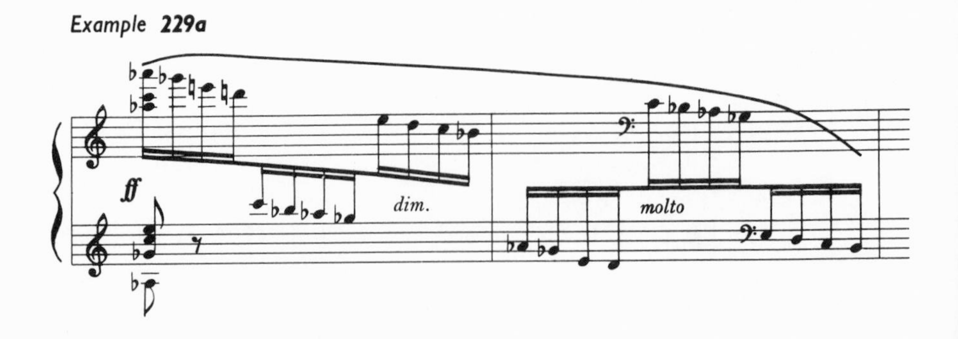

Whole-tone dominants

The whole-tone scale is partly responsible for creating the chord that we shall call a whole-tone dominant. Each tone of this chord, if placed in scalewise order must form all or part of a whole-tone scale, controlled by the interval of the major second. The framework of this sound is the augmented triad or a dominant seventh in which the fifth has been either raised or lowered. The remaining tones that intervene in major second intervals, can then be placed anywhere in this vertical structure. If the root is clear, these added tones will form the major ninth, the raised eleventh or the minor thirteenth (enharmonic to the augmented fifth).

Why does this chord need a special title ? Play *example 230* and notice that the same group of treble sounds blends with a different bass root. The enharmonic notation is adjusted to fit the demands of the overtone series. The low bass tone is the root in each case, simply by priority of range. Now omit the bass tone and play the treble group by itself. This sound is now ambiguous in its root concept and susceptible to any melodic or rhythmic influences for its root determination. Because of the flexibility of such melodic influences, there is a need for a clear name for these sounds.

Example **230**

Use the term, "whole-tone dominant," to represent a chord in which all members are included in a whole-tone scale. The root may or may not be recognized and therefore the naming of the specific chord members is optional. The chord may be complete, using all six tones of the whole-tone frame, or it may be incomplete. The ear does not easily discern the exact number of tones because of the equal ratio of intervals.

Whole-tone dominants with a recognized root tone:

Examples **231*a***, and ***b***, are illustrations of whole-tone dominants whose root is clearly heard in the bass. In the first Example, the chord is an A♭ $V^{9}_{\sharp 5}$, actually lasting through the second measure in spite of the dropping of the A♭ in the left hand. The change of spelling from E♮ to F♭ in the right hand corresponds with the vocal line. This notation preserves the major seconds melodically rather than using the alternating G♭ to E♮, a diminished third. Notice also that the right-hand chord in the first measure has the seventh above the raised fifth. This would not have happened in an earlier period where the raised fifth would have had the greatest tension and would have demanded a resolution up to the third of the chord of D♭. Here, however, the aim is one whole-tone sound, in which the individuality of the chord members is not present.

Example **231*a*** *Le son du Cor s'afflige. Debussy*

In *example* **231*b***, the accompaniment suggests a chord change on each quarter beat, regardless of the fact that all tones occur within the same whole-tone scale. This is due to an orderly use of the overtone series in which the major third is heard as root and third of each dominant chord. The passage starts with a B♭ chord in the third inversion, and with a hint of parallelism, moves to a C root sustaining the lower notes as pedal tones.

Example **231b** *L'Echelonnement des Haies. Debussy*

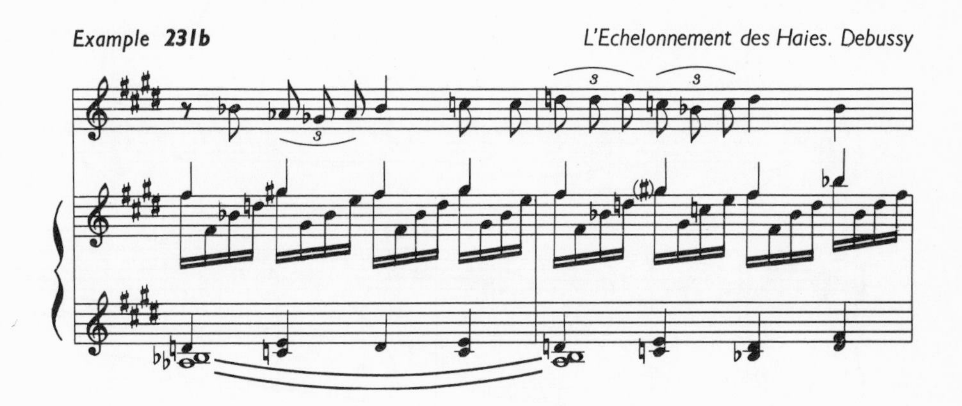

In selecting the proper notation for whole-tone dominants, choose the spelling that is most appropriate to the general tonal area. Do not be misled by the thought that all sharps go up and flats come down. Chromatic tones connect known chord members or diatonic scale tones and are spelled within that reference. Melodic direction is a contributing factor but not to the exclusion of the tonal setting.

The root of a whole-tone dominant is frequently recognized only after a resolution of the chord is heard. If the familiar cadential progression (root movement of up a perfect fourth or down a perfect fifth) is present, the ear will follow the resolving tones and will pick out the root as a result of that movement. This method of analysis becomes necessary in whole-tone dominants if the lower tones of the chord are clustered together, or if the order of intervals prevent the hearing of a root in the chord. Unfortunately, this root recognition works only with dominant to tonic progressions or with the similar use of dominant embellishments. Any other progression is not expected and would not employ the necessary tonal tendencies that uncover the hidden root. One way to facilitate this root detection is to focus on the tritones of the chord and see which one functions as the third and seventh of a dominant chord. While the full use of the whole-tone scale includes three tritones, the resolving tendencies of the third (heard as a leading-tone) and the seventh can be easily singled out in the normal cadential progression. (Remember also that the third, instead of heading upward to the root of the next dominant, can resolve down to the seventh of the new chord. Refer to chapter six, which discusses implied roots.)

The passage from Debussy's *Violin Sonata, example* **232**, has whole-tone dominants whose roots are easily recognized in the first five bars, largely because the first low B♭ leaves no doubt as to its harmonic priority. Parallel techniques move the root to C in the third measure, back to B♭ and again to C in the fifth measure. In spite of the chord's clustered appearance, the first bass B♭ still acts as an anchor to these upper structures. The sixth measure, how-

Example 232 *Sonata for Violin. Debussy*

ever, illustrates the point of the preceding paragraph. Played as an isolated measure, the chord has no outstanding tone that can claim itself as a root. It could be a D chord based on the preceding parallel technique, although this melody differs from the prior motive. It looks like a B♭ chord by its notation. Even a C chord is not totally improbable. Only upon resolution to the B minor chord in measure seven is the true root revealed to the listener. The tone of B♭, strongest in the violin, functions as the leading-tone, A♯. The F♯ becomes the dominant of B minor and therefore functions as the root of the whole-tone dominant. The chosen notation retains the key signature instead of giving away its eventual dominant function. Notice the correct spelling of the F♯ whole-tone dominant in the piano part in measure eight. More important, however, is the point that Debussy chose this ambiguous sound deliberately. Measure six acts as a pivot between the old B♭ dominant harmony and the forthcoming dominant on D, beginning in measure twelve. The intervening B minor chords allow a more refreshing return of this whole-tone harmony which in the final four measures of this climactic passage is combined with the real D dominant ninth. It prepares the return of the main theme, in G minor.

Whole-tone dominants without an audible root tone:

Examples 233a, b, and c show the use of the whole-tone dominant sound in which not one tone can be singled out as the unquestioned root of the chord. Reasons for this ambiguity can generally be found in one or more of the following situations: (1) the lack of a prominent bass tone, (2) a melodic movement in the bass register, (3) the abnormal order of intervals in the vertical structure which negate the strength of the overtone series, (4) a conspicuous use of the tritone, melodic or harmonic, in which either tone may claim its right as a root and (5) an absence of the cadential root progression by which an association of tonal movement could either anticipate a root or recognize it following the chord's resolution.

Example 223a is the midway point of a phrase in which descending chromatic tones predominate, without a strong root conviction. The whole-tone dominant, reached in this manner has no prior tonal commitments or relationships. It is notated as a C dominant seventh with a lowered fifth, but this does

Example **233a** *La Chevelure. Debussy*

not mean that the tone, C, is heard as a root. The quality of the whole-tone sound is all that is essential within these restless measures. The counterpoint formed by the differing directions of the whole-tone scale adds a motivic interest, while harmonically, all of the major seconds become fused together. The resolution of this whole-tone dominant (in the $\frac{9}{4}$ measure) is to a D V^9 whose clarity is so welcome in contrast to the preceding harmony.

The whole-tone writing in *example 233b* starts in the second measure of this excerpt from "The Snow is Dancing." As with the preceding illustration, it is necessary to evaluate the content in which the whole-tone dominant is found. The understanding of the proper melodic emphasis, or the reasoning behind a particular notation may be revealed in prior measures. In this example, the selection of the notation of G♭ in the second measure, arises from the preceding material, as is evident. The tone of G♭ may begin the whole-tone passage with a moderate degree of root strength, but the moment the melodic contour emphasizes the sound of the major third (G♭ and D) as prominent melodic tones, G♭ can no longer be thought of as a root tone. The major third produces an emphasis on the lower of the two notes which form the interval. While the tone D may temporarily lay a claim as a root, it would be short-lived. The melodic movement in the bass demands an analysis based upon melody, and so hampers a harmonic result. The subtleties in the reasoning between possible root tones in this quality of sound are so refined, that a decision made simply in favor of a whole-tone dominant, root unclear, is best.

The excerpt from the third movement of Debussy's *String Quartet, example* 233c, starts with a whole-tone dominant whose root is G. The melody line, doubled in the second violin and cello, stresses the tones of the augmented triad in such a way that the correct order of intervals results in a G chord. The resolution is made in the fifth measure to an F^6_4 triad, heard perhaps as a substitute for the C chord suggested by the bass skip of a fourth. The whole-tone sound returns in measure nine. Listen carefully from here through the G♯ minor resolution and test the feasibility of several possible roots. Measure nine starts out as an F augmented triad. Measure ten throws the accent on the A. Measure eleven cancels the previous F possibility because of the melodic major third occurring between the tenth and eleventh measures and therefore places a stress on C♯. Measures thirteen and fourteen are a contraction of the motive. A faster harmonic rhythm is heard due to the accompaniment figure rising on each third beat. But upon which root is this momentum created? Upon the resolution to G♯ minor in measure fifteen, the viola clearly uses the G♮ as an F double sharp. This might suggest a D♯ dominant motion, effective at the last moment. To conclude, the whole-tone scale appearing melodically in the bass, prevents the listener from grasping with certainty a single tone upon which to establish a harmonic structure.

Example **233c** *String Quartet. Debussy*

In deciding upon a root for a whole-tone dominant, arguments can be given in favor of a solid vertical structure, or if that is not possible, upon the strength of intervals in a horizontal, linear line. When these two factors do not agree in their suggested roots, an indeterminable result occurs. A final short example showing the conflict between a melodic design and its harmonization is illustrated in the beginning of the second movement of the *Sonata for Violin, example 233d*. The first chord of the accompaniment is clearly a G♯ V^9, omitting the fifth, which progresses via parallelism to a G and an F♯ ninth. However, the violin, by leaping from F♯ to D, which resolves by sequence to G, is stressing a melodic use of the cadential progression D to G. Which is the stronger root, the melodic D or harmonic G♯? Notice that once again, the tritone causes this dilemma. If at first glance this chord may seem too easy, namely, that the D fits into the G♯ chord by being a lowered fifth, place more attention on the function of the first tone, the F♯. It doesn't behave like a seventh, but does resolve to G as a leading-tone. To summarize, both tones of the tritone are equally important. This results in a whole-tone dominant chord whose root may be heard in a melodic design, or recognized by an expected harmonic resolution, or left unclear due to the conflicting stresses of melody versus harmony.

Example **233d** *Sonata for Violin. Debussy*

Clusters

Several adjacent tones, mainly major or minor seconds, sounding simultaneously comprise a cluster. Its purpose is not to establish harmonic movement for a melody, but to give a colorful block effect that in itself is noncommittal as to a specific harmony. A cluster drawn from the whole-tone scale is therefore similar to a whole-tone dominant in which the spacing of the intervals is tight. See *example* 234.

Example **234**

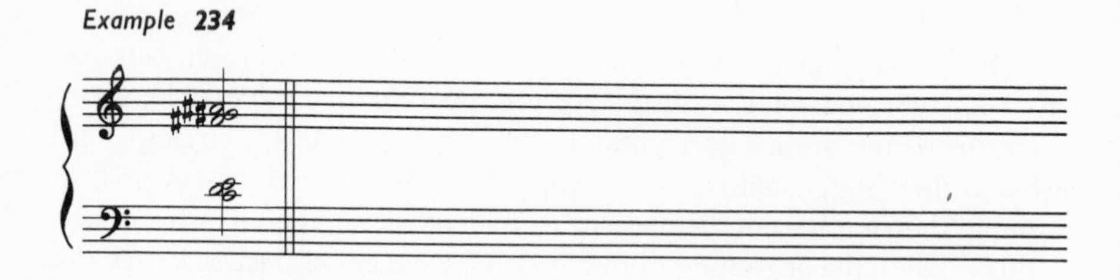

The range that a cluster may cover depends upon the instrumentation. In a symphonic composition, the range could span several octaves, especially if the composer uses divided strings. Obvious limitations are placed upon other ensembles, as well as on piano compositions. Perhaps with the orchestra in mind, some composers have directed the pianist to use the entire forearm upon both black and white keys for a somewhat uncontrolled cluster. In greater use, however, is a padded stick of specific length that can depress either the white or black keys. This is called for in Charles Ives's *Piano Sonata No. 2*, "Concord."

The cluster which includes just a few adjacent tones is in more common use than the extreme type mentioned. Even two tones can be called a cluster under certain conditions. *Examples* **235a, b** illustrate clusters formed by striking all tones simultaneously while *examples* **236a, b** show clusters being formed by arpeggiated movement and then held. Trills are an excellent means of producing the sound of a cluster. In the excerpt from the "Third Movement" of *Music for String Instruments, Percussion and Celesta* by Bartók, *example* **237**, all half steps are sounding within the range of a perfect fifth. The cluster is formed gradually by the entrances of the divided strings. In the third measure, the *glissando* intensifies this shimmering color while the piano has the only harmonic role, that of parallel major sevenths.

Example **237** Bartók

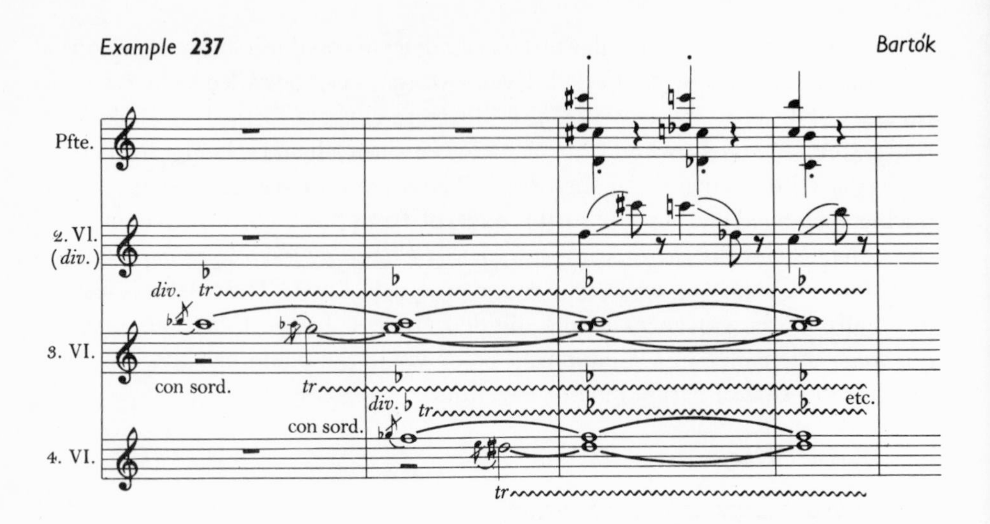

Clusters of two or three tones used as a harmonic interval rather than as a chord may be part of a melodic design in which one tone is part of the harmony while the other adjacent tone merely adds color. It may be added for reasons of desired dissonance or even humor, as in the accompaniment figure for *Minstrels.* (See *example* 238a.) This type of cluster becomes a pattern in the musical idea and in order to be effective, must last for at least a motive or phrase length. The harmonic intentions of the composer become clear as the design of the cluster

Example **238a** Minstrels. Debussy

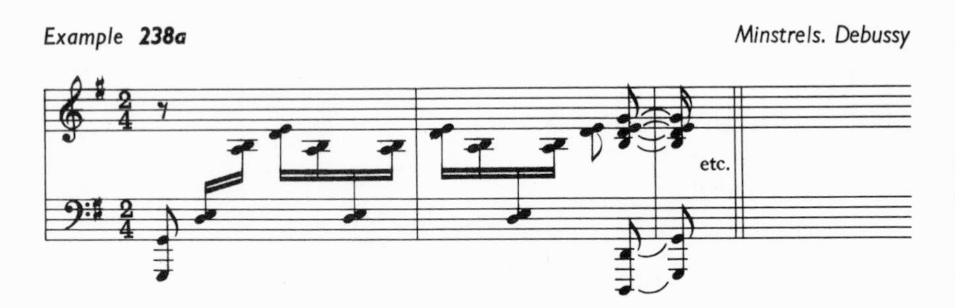

continues. For example, in the first measure of the excerpt from the "Gavotte" of Alexandre Tansman's *Suite dans le style Ancien*, *example* 238b, the first chord may be labeled as an A♭ major seventh. As such, both members of the cluster are labeled as chord members. Continuing with this plan, the second measure would start as an A♭ augmented eleventh. However, an eleventh chord is built upon the framework of a seventh chord, not just a triad. The reasoning follows therefore, that the D is present as an added tone forming an intervallic cluster with the chord tone E♭. This recognition of the use of clusters in the melody reduces the harmonic plan to a very simple rotation of diatonic harmonies around the tonic triad of A♭. The adjacent dissonant tones are not indicated as higher numbered chord members.

Another way of using a two tone cluster can be seen in the left-hand pattern of "Golliwogg's Cakewalk," *example 238c*. Instead of striking the plain triad of E♭, the thumb deliberately hits the white keys F and G together, producing the intervallic cluster. The F does not function as a ninth. Its location is in the bass, below the third, in the setting of a triad rather than that of a seventh or ninth chord.

Sometimes a chord may appear to be a cluster, but when fully analyzed, is actually a higher-numbered chord in close position. For instance, in this cadence to *Prelude No. 6* by Kabalevsky, *example 238d*, the C♯ and D on the fourth beat are clustered together and create a dissonant sound. Nevertheless, they are both chord tones belonging to the F♯ V^{13} whose octave root precedes it. The organization of the chord tones above the minor ninth, G, are not in the overtone order, nor is the seventh present. But in spite of this abnormal position, all of the chord tones are recognized because the root is so clear in its advance announcement.

Example **238d** *Prelude No. 6. Kabalevsky*

A composer may want the sound of a cluster but may still use chord tones to achieve it. *Examples* **239a, b** illustrate such "middle of the road" instances. Always analyze these by identifying the root and all chord tones. If you wish, you may add "in close position" or "in the position of a cluster" which would represent the knowledge that the order of intervals is deliberately squeezed into a tight range.

Describing these examples briefly, "Prelude VIII," *example* **239a**, opens with the sound of a three note cluster in the right hand. As the music unfolds, however, the harmonic setting of the A V^{13} becomes clear. Therefore measure one would be analyzed as containing a minor ninth and a minor thirteenth, while in measure two, these chord tones are major. They prepare the key of D major. The cluster effect is created by the seventh, root, and ninth in close position.

Example **239a** *Ondine, Prelude VIII. Debussy*

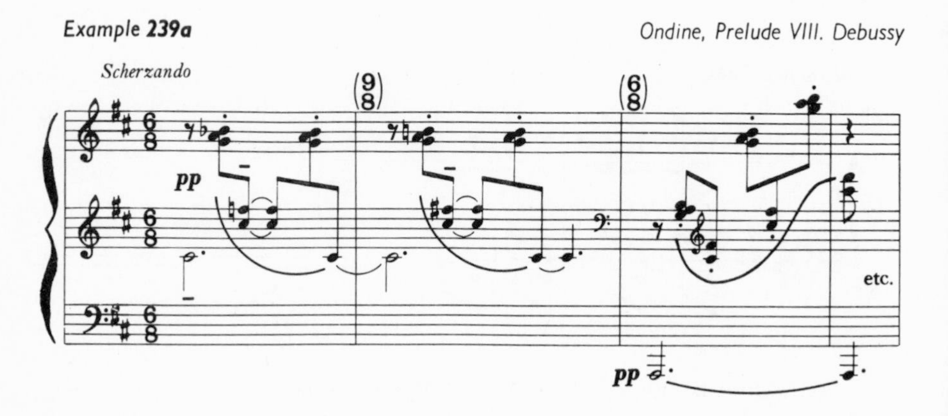

Prokofiev, near the beginning of his *Sonata No. 2, example* **239b**, wanted this dissonant, rhythmic effect. He used a BV^9 and clustered the ninth and third together. The melodic movement in the left hand then attacks the adjacent minor ninth to form this powerful dissonance, especially striking in the context of the whole movement.

Example **239b** *Sonata No 2. Prokofiev*

Added tones of the sixth and ninth

Harmonic expansion, during the Impressionistic period, included the use of the popular added sixth. This tone is actually a thirteenth, but called the added sixth because it is most frequently used directly adjacent to the fifth of a triad, generally a tonic triad. As a chord member of a thirteenth, this tone would be heard above a seventh chord, thereby building up on the overtone series. Nevertheless, the terminology is a matter of preference. With today's complicated harmonic sounds, the thirteenth is not likely to appear solely with a triad. This tends to make the term, added sixth, a cliché, already dated, belonging to a style of harmonization made popular in the twenties. There is nothing commonplace, however, in its cadential use in the following songs by Debussy. See *example* **240a** and **240b**. In both instances, the added sixth, present in the final chord, has been prompted by an earlier motivic suggestion. In the first illustration *example* **240a**, the piano accompaniment in measures four and five states for the last time the simple three-note motive that was the chief melodic binder for the entire song. The chord of the added sixth supports this motive, not only in the desired duplication of the tone, A, but also in its own vertical make-up, a third adjacent to a second, in the right hand.

Also interesting in this excerpt is the vocal line and the chord of the first measure. The vocal line alters the motive by first using the third and then the second. These tones, C, A and G become the crucial members of the final C major chord with the added sixth as if predestined for this cadence. Accompanying this motive in measure one, is a chord with a dual purpose. Primarily, it establishes the true dominant. The added emphasis gained by the repetition then allows for the entrance of the foreign chords, in measure three, which directly enhance the tonic. Secondly, the vertical structure of the chord is such that the C which supports the vocal line is placed directly above the bass tone G. Ordinarily this placement calls for a C^6_4 chord but Debussy topped it with D minor. The tone C, in a sense, joins together the upper D minor as a supertonic with the dominant G. This chord can be added up as a V^{11} but a doubtful glance at the location of the so-called eleventh is worth a more painstaking analysis. The selection of this particular harmonic sound was based upon the smooth support it gives to the vocal line and upon its similar texture to the final chord of the added sixth. This connection between the first two measures and the resolution in measure four is even noticeable in the highest voice of the accompaniment. The uppermost D of the first measure becomes the first motivic note in the fourth measure. This understanding behind the selection of chords is much more valuable than a quick decision upon a label for them. Call the first chord either a 11^7 over a dominant or a dominant eleventh, and the cadence chord either a tonic with an added sixth or a tonic thirteenth. In all analysis, describe the sound as thoroughly as possible, using the labels as an aid, not as a means.

Example **240a** *Debussy*

In *example* **240b,** the motivic reason behind the selection of a final tonic chord with the added sixth is apparent in several ways. The figure of four sixteenth notes, used in a scalewise manner, is carried through into the cadential measure, providing an interesting rhythmic displacement as it then appears on the first beat. The tone of D♯ is not recognized as a chord member until the second beat of this final bar. Slowly, the realization is made that this tone will not resolve down, and so is heard as an added sixth.

The reinforcement of this tone in the left hand is motivicly allied to the grace-note pattern three measures earlier, as well as to the two-note group of a sixteenth to a dotted eighth occuring at the beginning of this phrase. Still another reason behind the selection of D♯ as a final tone, lies in the connection between the first use of the dominant chord (measure three), and its complete resolution in the last measure. The vocal line ends on a D♯, the ninth of the C♯

dominant. The piano accompaniment retains this dominant sound as a suspended chord, but lowers the ninth to a minor ninth, D♮, for two bars. The tension so created by this D♮ is then resolved by the half step rise which restores the original D♯ that was left stranded in the vocal part. The result is a delayed resolution of the vocal dominant ninth to the added sixth of the tonic chord in the piano part.

In the foregoing illustrations, the added sixth was seen as a member of the cadential tonic triad. As such, it could never be misconstrued as a first inversion of a seventh chord. However, if one attempts to add the sixth to other roman numerals, the active propulsion already inherent in these triads would not permit the ear to separate an added tone from the normal activity of a seventh chord. For example, if a chord made up of C, E, G and A is present in the key of G major, it will lead toward the dominant and tonic of G major. The decision as to whether this chord is a IV with an added sixth or a II^6_5 would be negligible in terms of the function of the sound. It would be improper, however, to attach a modern label to an old diatonic principle that was originally conceived through contrapuntal techniques in the sixteenth century. The new term became necessary when the function of this chord changed from its active role to the new stationary result on a tonic triad. In this usage, history shows no precedent.

Exceptions to the use of the added sixth solely on the tonic can be found, and the excerpt from Debussy's *Prelude*, subtitled "Bruyères," *example 241a*, is worth debating. The manner by which the parallel fifths are placed in the lowest part (measure one), suggests the root movement of A♭, D♭ and A♭. The vertical formation also runs up a complete D♭ major chord before the B♭ as a possible added sixth is heard. This vertical support for D♭ as a root plus the parallelism is convincing enough that Debussy heard a basic subdominant harmony to which the B♭ is added in a melodic role rather than planned as a harmonic root. Joining the B♭ melodically is the ninth, the E♭ in the sixteenth group, forming a subdominant thirteenth chord which omits the seventh.

Compare this first measure with a similar bass movement heard in *example 241b*. The parallelism is present, but gone is the depth and the duplication of D♭. Furthermore, the B♭ is now the starting tone of this fanciful

Example 241a — Debussy

Example 241b — Debussy

melodic figure. The melodic function of the tone of B♭ is that of a passing appoggiatura (6 to 5). The chord starts as a II^6_5 and becomes a IV^9 just prior to resolving to the tonic chord. What is important in the comparison of these two instances is that in both cases a general plagal motion from D♭ to A♭ is recognized. The specific location of tones, and the melodic emphasis, however, can cast a different light on chords which appear to be the same.

The added sixth, when adjacent to the fifth of the triad, may be heard as a cluster. In this excerpt from the second movement of Debussy's *Violin Sonata* (*example 242a*), the accompaniment uses the position of the cluster in the C major chord. The violin, by separating the A from the G by the interval of a ninth, designates the A as a chord member. It also becomes a common tone with the following A dominant seventh chord. The preferred analysis would therefore include the A as an added sixth, rather than the simple label of a cluster which would imply a non significant harmonic activity, and could only apply to the piano part in this case.

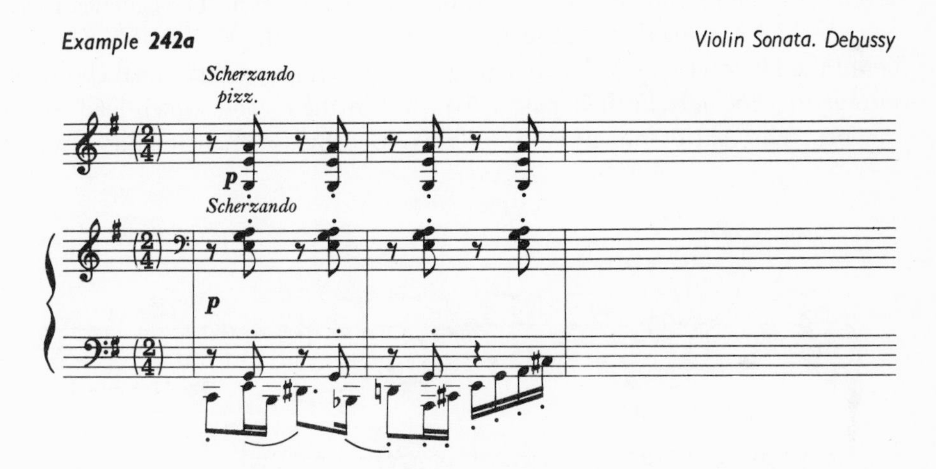

A perfect merger of the cluster and the added sixth is heard at the cadence of *Prelude VII* of the first volume, *example 242b*. A turbulent crescendo on a

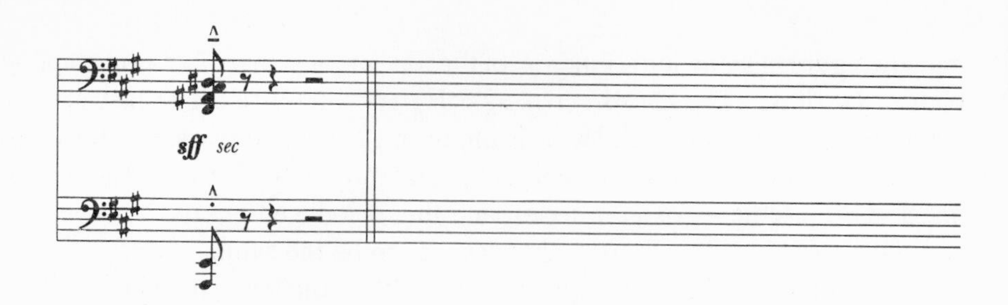

D^6_5 chord resolves to an intervallic cluster of C♯ and D♯ spread over three octaves. Within this measure, the cluster becomes part of a C♯ whole-tone dominant and resolves to the tonic F♯. The motive, having been presented throughout the *Prelude* in this clustered form retains the cluster upon this F♯ resolution, thereby also forming the added sixth.

The ninth may be heard as an added tone, especially when combined as a cluster. Again, it would appear with tonic triad or its stationary equivalent; no seventh can be present if it is to be called an added ninth. The cadence to *La puerta del Vino, example* **242c**, illustrates the added ninth (E♭) as a chord member of the D♭ tonic chord. The two measures which prepare the final chord are interesting not only in their parallelism but in their roots which lead to the cadence. The real dominant is cleverly avoided by dominant quality seventh

Example **242c** *Prelude III, Vol. II. Debussy*

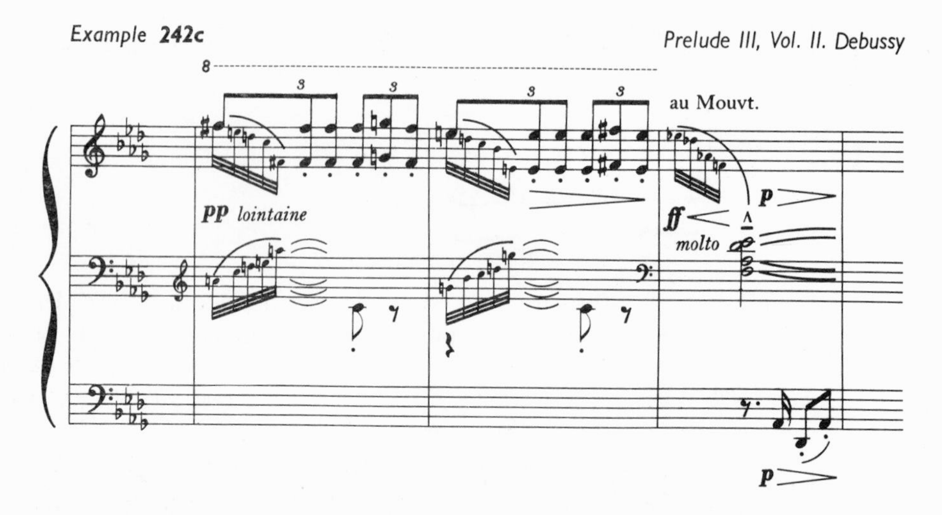

chords whose roots are the two half-step neighbors to D♭. All of the tones in both of these measures move to the chord tones of D♭ with not a single anticipation, or common tone amongst them. This activity is a necessary factor for all dominant substitutes. In the second measure, the melodic movement of the high E leads to the E♭ as the added ninth, and thus helps distinguish it as an important chord member.

Adding a minor sixth or a minor ninth to a major triad is more apt to result in a cluster sound rather than a recognition of an added tone.

Added tones to the minor triad are possible but not heard very frequently in serious writing. The minor triad, by being an alteration of the fundamental overtone series, does not have the same solidity as the major triad. An added tone might switch its position from an inactive triad to one which might need some further resolution. For example, play the triad of C minor and then add the A as an added major sixth. The existing tritone between the third, E♭, and the added A suggests motion. The degree of activity heard would depend upon the context in which the chord is found. Located at the final cadence, its stature would remain unchallenged because undoubtedly the preparation for the cadence would be thorough. However, within a composition, this chord becomes a half-diminished seventh chord in the first inversion. This problem restricts the use of this chord to areas where the root of the minor triad is inflexible.

To show the questionable analysis of this chord when used within a phrase, play *example 243a*, an excerpt from "Canope" (Prelude X). The root movement of the D dominant seventh chord toward G minor in the third measure gives strength to G as the root. The vertical construction supports G minor thoroughly, saving the E for the highest position. Coming from the preceding octaves, it is as if the melody was accidentally stretched by one degree. This high register in which the E is placed, also helps to dissuade it from sounding as a root. The chord is heard as G minor with the added sixth. It moves into a G major chord with the added sixth still present, and here, the comparison between the sound of the two chords is most distinct. The activity engendered by the minor chord in the third measure is entirely satisfied by the repose of the major chord.

This tension, felt in the third measure, may promote the opinion that after all, the chord should be labeled as having a half-diminished quality. In fact,

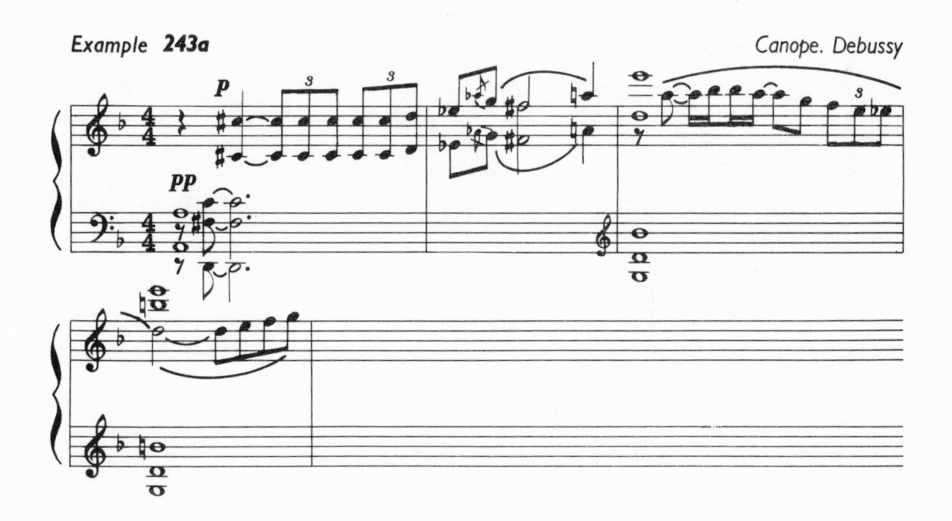

if you play the third and fourth measures alone, omitting the dominant preparation, the E may well sound as the root. This unconvincing attitude that the chord has, accounts for its rare appearance as a minor triad with an added sixth, while its form as a half-diminished $^{6}_{5}$ is most prevalent.

The loss of a solid root footing also applies to inversions of chords and is the reason why added tones would not be heard as such. In a more complex harmonic situation, there may be many added tones but each tone would not be singled out for separate comment.

The pentatonic scale can be the influencing factor behind the added sixth when used in a melody. In this excerpt from the sixth prelude, "General Lavine," *example* **243b**, the key center is F major, against which the bass pentatonic melody bounces around; the D as an added sixth is used freely in the melody and is also supported by the harmonic accompaniment. The pentatonic scale may also stress an added ninth. In this case, the G is not used harmonically, but is given clever melodic stress in measures five and six. Actually heard as a non-harmonic tone, it nevertheless creates accented parallel ninths with the "oom-pah" bass! The six measures march along on the F chord until the dissonant clash of the cluster brings the motion to a halt. A resolution of supertonic to dominant, and the melody starts once again, adding a further development.

Observe that the last measure of *example* **243b** may appear to contain an added fourth. The chord, nevertheless, is a C dominant with an adjacent ninth placed next to the root. While added fourths do occur in the Impressionistic writing, their usage and evaluation is best discussed in a later chapter. See chapter seventeen.

Example 243b *"General Lavine"—eccentric. Debussy*

EXERCISES

A *Analysis*

1] Analyze harmonically the excerpt from Griffes, *Example* **244**. What quality predominates within this theme? Which mode influences the opening arpeggios?

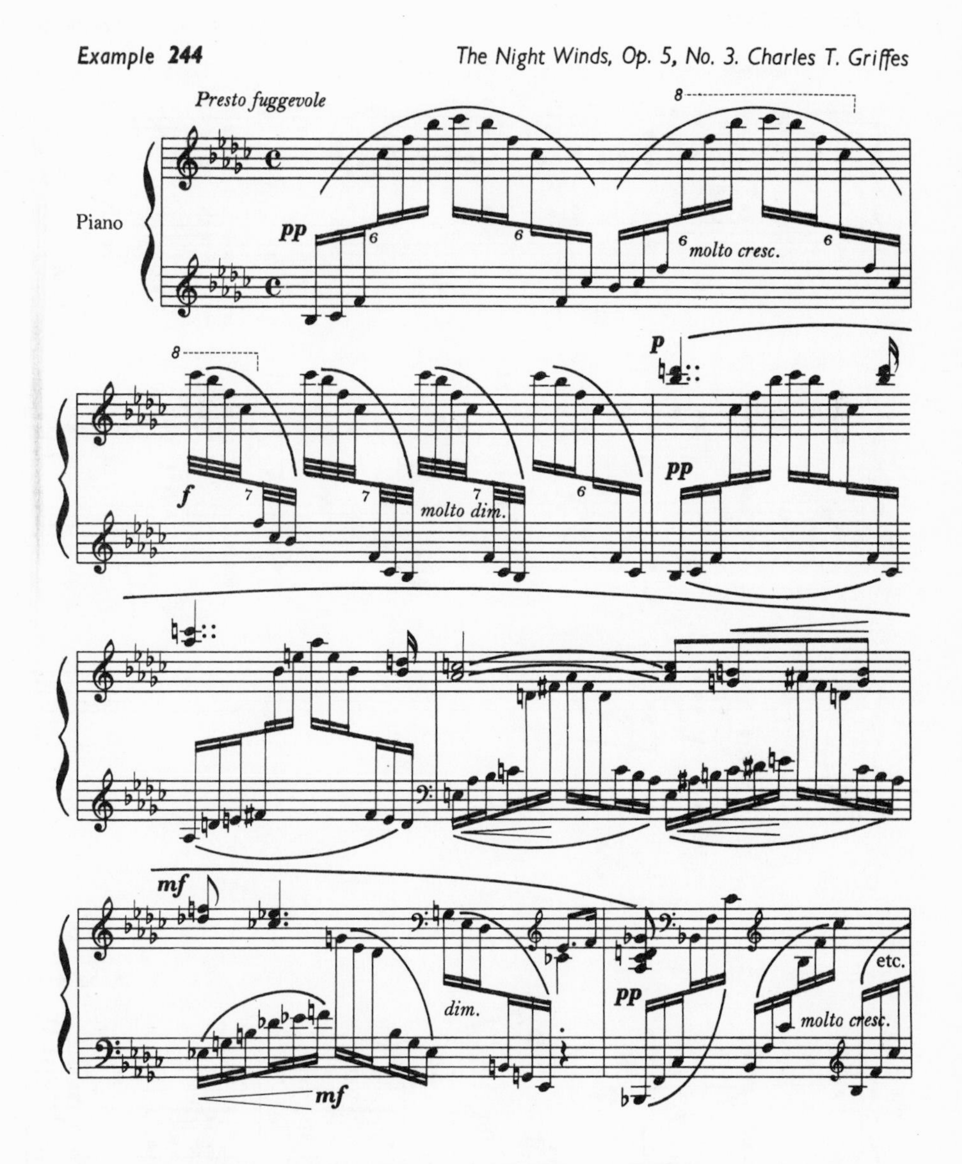

Example 244 The Night Winds, Op. 5, No. 3. Charles T. Griffes

2a] Tones of the added sixth and added ninth are given a vigorous appoggiatura type treatment in this *Prelude* by Kabalevsky, *Example* **245**. Circle each such tone and mark its numerical relationship with the root. You may also find an added fourth. Some chords on the weaker beats may be interpreted two ways. They are incomplete, and the tempo moves quickly.

b] Mark the motivic construction in the melody. Observe the meter changes in *Example 245a*.

c] Compare *Example 245b* with the first excerpt with respect to contrasting idea, key, melody.

Example 245a *Prelude No. 21. Kabalevsky*

Example 245b *Kabalevsky*

3a] In *Example* 246, *En Sourdine*, differentiate between added sixths, chords of the thirteenth, clusters and appoggiaturas.

b] Which mode is present in the vocal line itself? Which is heard within the harmonic reference of the tonic tonality? Which scale influences the motive of the accompaniment?

c] Use the roman numeral analysis as described in the preceding chapters for a tonal evaluation.

Example 246b

Example 247a

L'Ombre des Arbres. Debussy

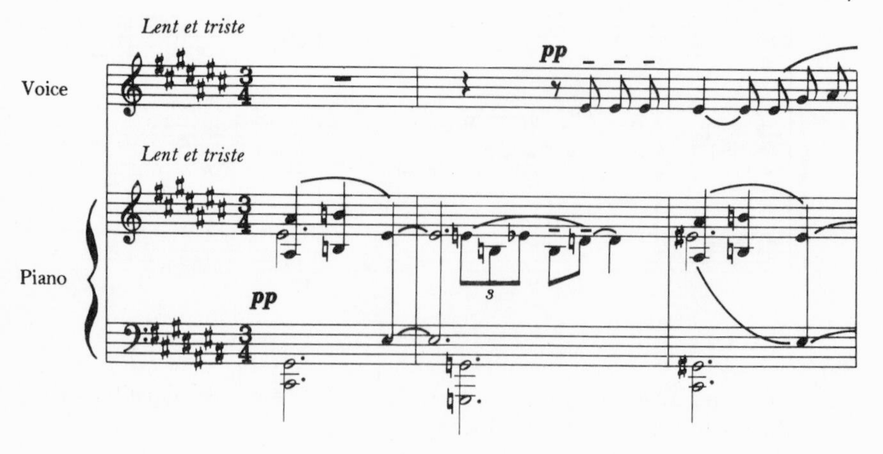

4a] In the first excerpt of *Example* **247**, analyze the melody tones and their harmonic relationship. Which root progression is utilized? What key is this first phrase in?

b] Treat the second excerpt, *Example* **247b** as a review of implied roots, one substantial and interesting progression may be found. Mark all chords and indicate the root progressions that arise from them.

(*Continued on p.* 242)

c] The final cadence reveals the tonality. Mark the roman numeral relationships.
d] Mark the motivic material throughout.

B Build a complete whole-tone dominant from the tone of E♭. Starting from this chord in each of the following groups of *Example 248*, progress to a chord of your own choice, moving the voices accordingly. Use enharmonic spelling where necessary. Mark chords.

Example 248

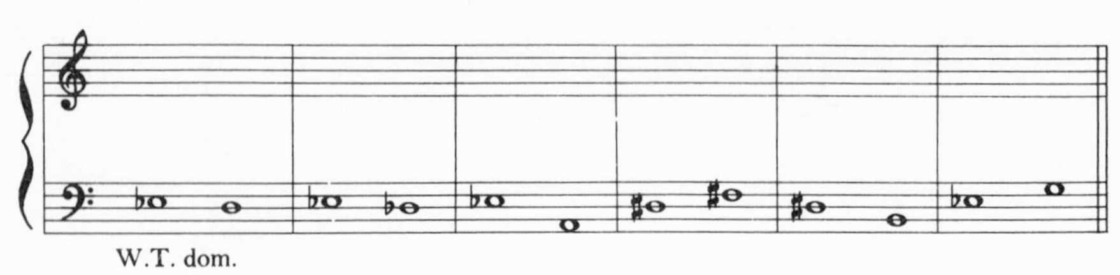

C Write a vocal line above the harmonies given in *Example 249*. Tones may duplicate those of the given harmonies, but concentrate on adding the higher harmonic extensions. Use a sporadic motivic treatment, selecting your own rhythm for the harmonic movement as well as for the melody. If desired, repetitions of some progressions may be used for rhythmic balance, and additional passing harmonies may be included. Add your own cadence.

Example 249

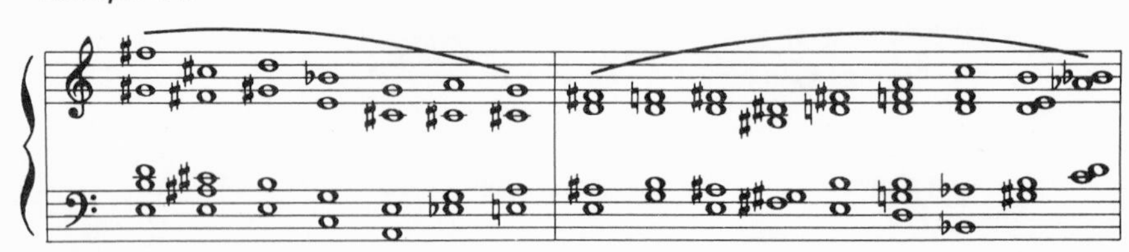

Example 250a

D Harmonize the melodies of *Example 250* by including whole-tone harmonies, clusters and chords with added tones. Remember to consider the melody tones as higher-numbered relationships and those of the tritone. Do not change chords too frequently. Use clusters and whole-tone effects in a free, rhythmical piano style. These melodies will adapt to many good solutions. There is no single tonality that is "right" or "wrong"!

REVIEW

A Write a melody in the phrygian mode from F♯. Harmonize it chiefly by chords derived from the mode.

Other modal suggestions are as follows:

dorian from C
lydian from D
mixolydian from B♭
aeolian from G♯
locrian from B

B Write a chord progression starting in the key of D which includes:

a] Mediant progressions of up and down a third
b] Tritone progressions
c] Whole-tone dominants
d] Clusters of two tones, and of six tones
e] Added tones of the sixth and ninth

Mark all chords and progressions. If desired, add a vocal melody line above.

C Select one or more of the following motives and expand into an Impressionistic "Prelude."

Example 251a

Example 251b

Example 251c

D Choose a poem, and write an original song in the Impressionistic style. Select a poem which inspires imagery or mood rather than a philosophical thought. Use the text in a free rhythmical manner but with an accurate scansion of the words involved.

E The excerpts from the following songs are substantial so as to give some degree of motivic material. Mark a complete analysis, noting as many of the Impressionistic techniques as possible.

Example 252c
mf
pp
ppp
ppp

Example 253a *Dans le Jardin. Debussy*

Example 253b

Example 253c

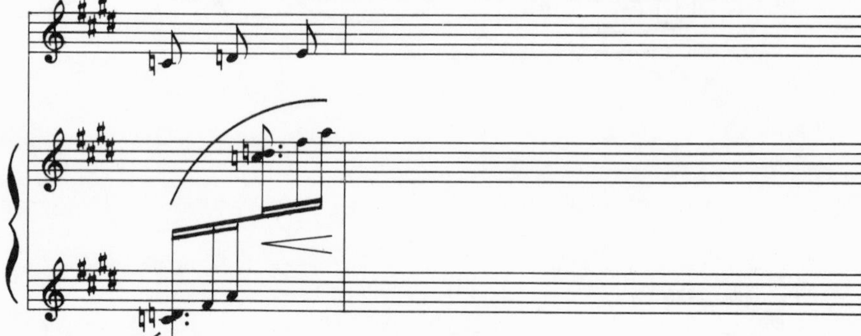

Example 253d

PART III

The rise of modern dissonance

12 Free counterpoint and the twelve-tone scale

Rhythmic vigor and contrapuntal independence

As the Impressionistic style waned in the latter twenties, a trend toward greater dissonance was started throughout Europe and America. The early writings of Stravinsky, Prokofiev, Berg, and Copland show each composer's unique individuality, but the one ingredient that is present in all, is added dissonance. The smoothness of modal textures and dominant qualities gave way to vertical structures whose added tones deliberately clash with other chord tones. Experiments in polytonality aided this harmonic massing of dissonance. In addition, a new excitement in rhythm was achieved by the increased use of changing metric designs and complex rhythmic divisions.

Together with this harmonic and rhythmic growth, a contrapuntal style evolved which stresses complete independence of melodic lines. Melodies move against one another without regard to former harmonic dictates. The intervals formed by the union of these melodies are not diatonically controlled. They have complete chromatic freedom, and as a result of this independent function, the concepts of the twelve-tone scale are recognized.

The preponderance of seconds, sevenths and tritones also contributed to a changing pattern of harmonic sound. Instead of hearing harmonic movement by clear vertical progressions, the listener's attention is drawn toward one central tonality within which the contrapuntal lines create the fluctuations of dissonance that become the basis for the new harmonic sound. From a conservative beginning within clear concepts of tonality to today's serial compositions, the contrapuntal impetus influenced all composers alike. A passage from a Bartók string quartet may require the same contrapuntal listening as a Schoenberg quartet, or one by Roger Sessions. The concentration on melodic structure and contour becomes the guide for hearing movement of pitch rather than movement of complete harmonies. This trend toward the complex contrapuntal texture was gradual and in order to understand it today, it is necessary to trace the rise of the modern dissonance in all of its aspects: the melodic advance through the use of the twelve-tone scale; the harmonic growth resulting from the freedom of the scale, and from experiments in polytonality as well as in chords containing conflicting chord members; also, an essential, new rhythmic strength reflecting a changing attitude and temperament within the creative impulse. It is this vigorous style that overpowered and snuffed out Impressionism.

No composition could better illustrate the new rhythmic strength than *Le Sacre du Printemps* of Igor Stravinsky. First performed in 1913, it literally shocked the musical world; it also made music history. It ushered in a harsh harmonic idiom which composers of the following decades, as well as Stravinsky himself, continued to exploit. Not all is violent, however. The opening passage, *example* **254a**, has a lyrical softness not entirely devoid of an Impressionistic sentiment. The bassoon, in a very high register, announces a plaintive motive, modal in tonality. Joined by the French horn in the second measure, the modal melody receives a simple background made up of only two tones. But within this outward simplicity lies the nucleus of non-harmonic linear counterpoint. The opening tone of the horn, C♯, directly conflicts with the A minor setting of the bassoon motive. The two lines function independently, but not opposingly. The vertical intervals do not conform diatonically, nor are they without tonality. The motive and its repeated emphasis on A establishes this first tonal area as being A, heard horizontally rather than by vertical recognition. Details regarding this linear analysis are fully explained in the chapter, "Linear Roots."

Example 254a *Stravinsky*

Aside from the hints of Impressionistic influence and Russian folklore, the dynamic strength in the composition is rhythm. To quote just one passage is to select a diamond amongst many. Nevertheless, the following excerpt from "Danses des Adolescentes," *example* **254b**, is appropriate. Within the steady pulsation of a $\frac{2}{4}$ meter, violent accents on a constantly changing irregular design remove any association to the basic $\frac{2}{4}$ pulse. Strength on the downbeat, as part of normal notation must be avoided here in order to emphasize the indicated accents. The rough harmonic structure is built with two roots, but the passage is not polytonal. (See chapter thirteen.) The root of an E♭ dominant seventh is placed above an F♭ major triad and for a few measures the dual conflict between

E♭ as the highest tone and F♭, the lowest, might be heard. As soon as the melody enters, however, the tonality of E♭ is assured and the association of the bass tone to the chord becomes that of a minor ninth.

Example 254b

Throughout *Le Sacre dù Printemps*, the difficult rhythms and metric changes challenge the abilities of conductors and orchestras alike. Virtuoso playing is demanded. To fully appreciate the complexities of the score, examine it from a melodic and rhythmic point of view. The complete harmonic scope of the score need not be worked over at this time. Most of the melodies are easily recognized amidst the full orchestral score and can be sung readily, being in a simple diatonic or modal context. They are generally embodied within one motive which is expanded by shifted rhythmic accents and metric changes. After this study, try to follow the score while listening to the music, even if only for a few pages. The full meaning of the flexible bar line and its resulting intricacies can then be realized, and a brilliant performance marveled upon.

This new vigorous style took root amongst young composers in the thirties, having been spearheaded by Prokofiev and Bartók, as well as Stravinsky. Before analyzing the many melodic and harmonic aspects of this style, as detailed in the following chapters, play the beginning of Anis Fuleihan's *Sonata No. I, example* **255**; written in 1939, it is representative of what can now be called, a conservative Modern idiom. It starts with an energetic three-note figure which expands to a normal four-bar phrase. The tonality of F♯ minor is suggested at the outset, but devoid of any raised leading-tone (E♯), the tonal feeling of a lydian D major becomes more convincing. Not to be discounted is the A major grouping of melody tones, especially at the first two cadences in the fourth and eighth measures. This type of tonality, fused between modal and diatonic influences, is the result of a flexible counterpoint out of which mildly dissonant intervals contradict a single strong diatonic tonality, but do not deter a more general tonal setting. Such ambiguity is usually temporary, as in this movement, which gradually settles on D major. However, there is never an obviousness of diatonic progression.

Another trait of this style is the adherence to specific intervals during the course of a motive's development. Brahms had explored this way of thinking in many of his compositions, and undoubtedly influenced this generation of composers. In some compositions of this period, however, the intervallic preoccupation superseded the more important musical demands of a phrase, such as harmonic movement and structure; and the notion arose, especially amongst students, that a development had to retain the original motivic intervals. Such a self-imposed limitation can stifle melodic exploration as it did in many compositions which have not survived the test of time. Schoenberg's development of the twelve-tone row, which completely retains an intervallic formula, also contributed to this type of developmental process, even amongst composers who did not use the tone-row itself.

In this piano sonata by Fuleihan, interval retention is evident, mainly by repetition or transposition of the first phrase. Although the opening interval of a third changes to that of a major second occasionally, the intervals of measures three and four remain intact. Notice in measure seven, the bass inversion of the motive in the third bar. Also indicative of this intervallic preoccupation is the balance created between the lowest bass tones of the first two measures, E to D, and their parallel use in the fifth and sixth measures, D to E, as the highest tones used in retrograde.

In the seventh measure, harmonization by perfect fourth intervals, and by arpeggio use of fourths as in the ninth bar, is idiomatic to this period. Perfect fourths are a substitute for the parallel thirds or sixths of the diatonic age. They adhere to a horizontal sense of tonality without declaring a particular root tone in their harmonic organization. This tends to create a smooth continuity between chord roots, or a desirable ambiguity, thereby permitting the strong harmonic areas to stand out. The left hand arpeggio group in the ninth measure has such a purpose. Following the bitonal suggestion in measure eight (A major in the right hand versus a progression of D^6_4 to E in the left hand), the first three arpeggio fourths are neatly noncommittal. The main motive, returning in the treble, supports the B, as II of A major. At the same time, the arpeggio arises from the previous E chord of the bass, and is heard as its inversion. At the end of the ninth measure all tones merge into a G dominant of the next strong C root.

A similar instance of a vague arpeggio becoming strong in its root recognition occurs in measure twelve. Although G major, as a subdominant, is

Example 255 *Sonata No. 1. Anis Fuleihan*

present on the first two half beats, the fusion of non-harmonic tones within the descending arpeggio removes its certainty. The second beat, with its accent on A, anticipates the forthcoming resolution to A major, while retaining a few supporting intervals for the half note B. This "free counterpoint" adds to the harmonic motion and strengthens the consonant intervals reserved for the goal of the phrase.

Free counterpoint, a practice often abused by students unaware of stylistic consistency, permits the use of dissonant intervals, no longer bound by Classical conventions. In this example, the parallel triads in measures fifteen and sixteen are especially indicative of this dissonant style of counterpoint. The dissonances involved are deliberately chosen and placed carefully amongst the less harsh intervals so as to achieve more contrast in sound and tension. Examine, for example, the effect of the dissonant interval of the minor ninth on the third quarter beat of measure fifteen. The clash of the E major triad against the melody tone A, comes at a moment when such an increase in dissonance is desirable. Following the pure consonances of the B minor triad (with its parallel fifths), the increase of dissonance against the E chord adds to the tension which is then partially relaxed on the F♯ minor triad and reactivated by the last triad of the group, B major. A cursory analysis of this measure might reveal only the presence of four ascending triads used to harmonize the original motive of measure three. An analysis which shows the effect of these triads on the motion within the phrase and helps to discern the structural arrival points within phrases, can then aid the understanding of the total composition. Everyone responds to the large crescendo and climactic arrival within a composition, but equally important, is the response to the less obvious areas of tension that exist in all phrases. Only then can a harmonic and melodic analysis be really worth while, and an interpretation satisfying. Free counterpoint, therefore, is controlled by the demands of each particular phrase. Further examination of dissonant intervals and their role in harmonic fluctuation is discussed in chapter nineteen, "The Control of Dissonance."

One more development in Modern writing needs to be pointed out. This is simply the free choice of any of the twelve chromatic tones for either melodic or harmonic purposes, regardless of the initial tonality. This function of the twelve-tone scale is described in the chapter immediately following. In *example 255*, the first evidence of such freedom created the partly modal, partly diatonic tonality. More radical use occurs in measure twenty when the independent tones create a bichordal passage, A major over C major. In measure twenty-two, a climatic A major over the bass chord of D, starts a descending passage in which non-diatonic triads function equally in importance to those belonging to D major. To summarize, many characteristics of Modern writing are heard in the Fuleihan *Sonata No. 1*, which by being uncomplicated and straightforward in its approach, is beneficial as a first acquaintance in this style. The many facets that have been touched on will now be explored thoroughly.

The twelve-tone scale

The twelve-tone scale has the unfortunate distinction of being surrounded by terms such as atonality, tone-row, twelve-tone system and, of course, Schoenberg. During any evolution of art, it is natural that the meanings of words become confused in the attempt to define changing techniques. A new trend is usually molded by more than one person and a little time must elapse before the specialized terms can be universally accepted in their specific meanings. Today, too many people think that if one is using the twelve-tone scale, one is using the tone-row. Actually, these terms, the tone-row, twelve-tone system, atonality, are by-products of the scale, which unnamed, has its roots inherent in literature as far back as Wagner. The twelve-tone scale itself is nothing more than the chromatic scale, but in application, it differs so noticeably that it easily separates Modern music from all of its predecessors.

To explore the function of the twelve-tone scale, it must be placed historically in line with the other scales. Out of the modes arose the diatonic major and minor scales. The chromatic scale added the half steps as embellishments to the diatonic scale. For example, if we add the chromatic tones to the E Major scale, we preserve its diatonic key signature and raise or lower the tones so as to form correct embellishments to the diatonic scale. See *examples 256a* and *b*. Usage demanded these resolutions, hence, the chromatic scale indicates the correct use of all embellishing tones.

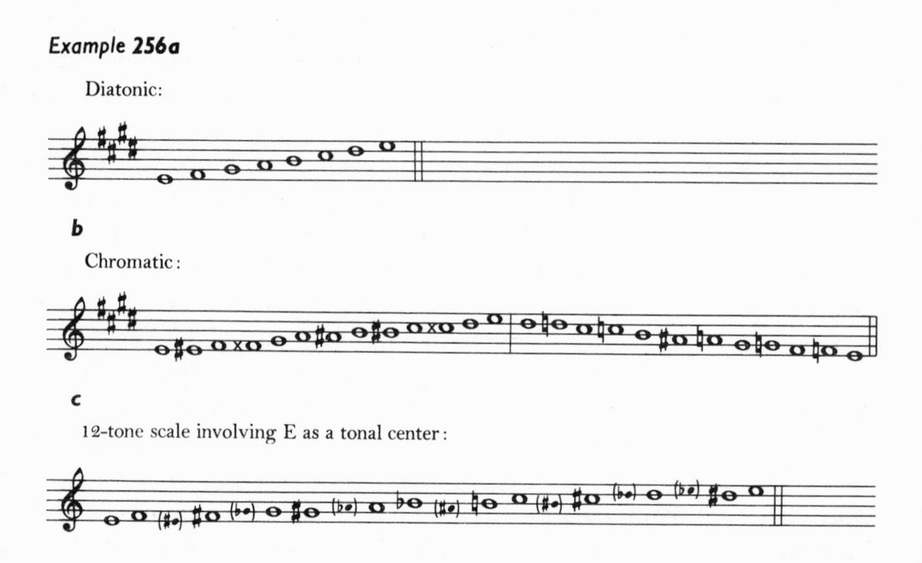

The twelve-tone scale indicates the independent use of all of the chromatic tones, with no demand for specific resolutions. The tones are not subordinate to a diatonic scale and therefore may be spelled in any way logical to the particular instance involved. See *example 256c*. With this equality for all twelve tones, there may still be a tonal center, or a tonic. The roman numerals surrounding this tonic would theoretically be twelve, but to devise such a new order would be too impractical. Consequently, the more conservative compositions in this Modern style can still retain some diatonic principles, and be analyzed accordingly. The compositions which veer sharply away from establishing any tonal center are generally organized by a twelve-tone row, which is a particular method of using this scale. Arnold Schoenberg laid the foundations for this type of composition and called this procedure, "Method of Composing with Twelve Tones which are Related only with One Another." From his book *Style and Idea*, we quote: "Curiously and wrongly, most people speak of the 'system' of the chromatic scale. Mine is no system but only a method, which means 'modus' of applying regularly a preconceived formula." The details of writing with a tone-row are discussed in a later chapter.

Example 257a illustrates a melody written with the free choice of tones as indicative of the twelve-tone scale. All twelve tones are used within the first three measures, but they are not organized into a fixed pattern as would be necessary in a tone-row series. The starting and ending tone of E produces a general tonality of E, not restricted, however, to the diatonic concept. For this reason, a key signature is avoided, and the melody tones are not committed to the former dictates of chromatic harmonization. Play the melody and consider the following questions:

(1) How can you decide if a tonal center is present?

(2) Does this melody completely abandon former scale patterns?

Break it down into its smallest figures and find a few places where conventional chromatic embellishment and resolution patterns might be used. By contrast, find the places which will not fit these earlier harmonizations and discuss why not.

(1) The melody has a tonal center of E, known not just by the first and last tones, but by the rhythmic pause on the third and fifth tones of the E minor triad in the first motive. Any tone which is given more stress either by rhythmic strength, repetition, or by diatonic association with another important tone, may result in being heard as a tonic.

Play the melody again and decide which tone is given strength during the body of the phrase (measures three and four).

Due to the repetition, the sound of E♭ lingers in one's ear, and as the melody cadences, the realization comes that the E♭ acted as an accented

Example **257a**

leading-tone. It was also strengthened by the following B♭, just before the cadence. Notice therefore, that the next to the last note, D, has very little importance.

Why not use a key signature of E minor? Yes, it could be used, but it is usually more convenient to add the accidentals as needed. The ear does not retain the diatonic background when the modern skips are present. Each melody, however, must be judged individually, and the decision made in favor of the more readable version.

Still, with regard to spelling of tones, the question might arise as to the possible use of G♭ to F in the first measure. It would not be preferred because (1) The interval of a diminished third from the first beat, E, is awkward. (2) The F♯ does aid our understanding of E as a tonic. (3) The G on the third beat would then require a natural sign anyway.

(2) As to chromatic treatment, one can force the second measure into the following embellishments: (*example* **257b**).

Example **257b**

Example **257c**

If the melody used the half step resolution, A♯ to B, then many more opportunities would be present. The same is true of the cadence. Notice that in *example* **257c** the spelling conforms to the harmonic background. A chromatic realization, complete with a V^9—I cadence (the leading-tone is raised for this illustration), removes all of the intended independence of the original melody. These altered examples perhaps illustrate better than words can describe the difference between the chromatic scale and the application of the twelve-tone scale. To use the preceding harmonizations in the setting as a whole, would be inappropriate in its mixture of styles, and would cancel the inference of the twelve-tone scale.

Play the contemporary setting in *example* 257*d*. The analytical techniques which apply to this type of contrapuntal writing are discussed thoroughly in chapter fourteen. At this moment, observe the general use of the twelve-tone scale and some of its idiomatic expressions as used in both the treble and bass of this example. In addition to the rhythmic asymmetry examined earlier, modern melodies take advantage of, (1) all of the twelve tones, (2) leaps of sevenths and ninths, (3) the outlining of such intervals in the melodic contour by several skips in the same direction, and (4) increased vertical dissonance. This does not mean, however, that every measure must include these new radical procedures. If it did, the melody might resemble a game of leapfrog in which not one stepwise motion would be tolerated.

Example 257d

Apply these same principles to the opening of *Symphony No. 5* by Dimitri Shostakovich, *example* 258. We know from listening to the entire symphony that this tonality is D minor, in spite of the lack of key signature. In the following reduced excerpt, compare the measures which create a diatonic association of sound with those which belong in the twelve-tone scale concept. Notice how easy it is to apply diatonic roman numerals where they fit. But what about the second measure, or later, the movement toward E♭ minor? These tones have equal strength in their organization around D minor, but our diatonic chart cannot show it.

More specifically, the opening figure of a minor sixth may be considered as the VI of D minor moving to V. It is answered rhythmically by tones which depart from the diatonic scale. The "foreign" tones, C♮, F♯ and D♯ are not embellishments but motivic responses. From the wider interval of the sixth, the motive becomes smaller in size, the tones being chosen on a melodic, not harmonic basis.

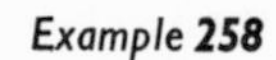

A second instance of the twelve-tone scale at work is heard in the modulation to E♭ minor occurring in measure eight. The approach to the temporary setting of E♭ minor is done without a chromatic series of embellishments but with a simple transference of the A minor triad into an A diminished triad. Moving out of E♭ minor is just as simple. Measure ten illustrates the use of the tritone progression, a direct move from E♭ minor to the A minor chord which acts as a semi-cadence to the theme.

Within two measures, a singular ascending melodic line leads the tonality into C minor (measure thirteen). A sequential use of the introductory motives follows. The counterpoint forms a subtle movement of pitch, utilizing any tones of the twelve-tone scale which are motivicly suitable. Whatever harmony there is, arises out of the union of contrapuntal parts. Sometimes a diatonic grouping of tones is retained, while in other instances the parts move independently, as inherent to the twelve-tone scale.

Independent triad technique

The freedom that the twelve-tone scale extended to melodies, that is the ability to use any tone at any time, can be applied to harmony by the same logic. Any triad of any quality can progress from one to the other. The chord need not be limited to a triad, of course, but a restriction to triads at this time is beneficial to the understanding of the early Modern school. Dissonance is not necessary. The simplest connection of non-diatonic triads will produce a modern flavor. Prokofiev used this technique in the *Classical Symphony*. The opening chords of the "Gavotta," *example 259a*, are D major, C major in the first inversion, and B major in the second inversion. There is no diatonic association between these three chords. As the theme continues, D major becomes the tonal center, not for the limited D major scale, but the tonic for all of the surrounding triads of any quality as understood by the principles of the twelve-tone scale.

Example 259a *Classical Symphony. Prokofiev*

The "Gavotte" Op. 32, No. 3, also by Prokofiev, *example 259b*, illustrates the free choice of triads circling the tonic of F♯ minor. The first motive, true to the rhythmic characteristics of a gavotte, starts in the middle of a bar, and ends a measure and a half later. The pedal tones, root and fifth of F♯ minor, last the full length of this motive and establish the key center very clearly. In the melody, the two tones which add a touch of modern dissonance are the G♮ and C♮. Actually they are the fifth and root of an incomplete C major triad, the tritone dominant, chosen deliberately for this dissonant effect of the clashing half steps. The second motive, after modifying the F♯ minor arpeggiated figure, moves to a B♭ major chord in the second inversion, and cadences on B♭

Example 259b *Op. 32. No. 3. Prokofiev*

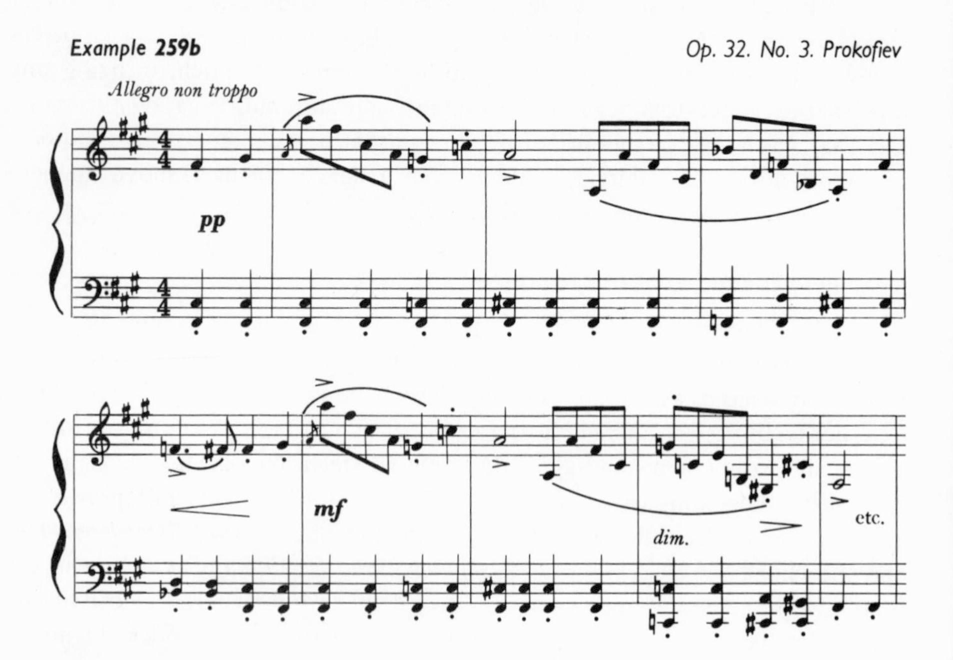

in the fourth measure. Here, the independent connection of triads is most pronounced; F♯ minor to B♭ major followed by an abrupt return to F♯ minor for the second phrase. Which roman numeral, or what association should be attached to the B♭ major chords in this setting? To force this chord into a diatonic terminology, a result of either an enharmonic major III or a lowered major IV would have to be chosen. Neither wording describes the triad for what it is; namely, an independent triad functioning within the twelve-tone scale, which cannot be forced into a diatonic framework. Seven roman numerals are now insufficient. Their value in recognizing diatonic areas, however, will never diminish. But there is no need to chain modern sounds into a system for which it was never intended. In the F♯ minor *Gavotte,* the roman numerals will indicate the tonic, and the perfect authentic cadence, dominant to tonic at the end. The remaining triads are simply referred to by letter name and quality, thereby acknowledging their independent status. Another look at the C major chord and its two different resolutions in the first and seventh measures deserves comment. In the first case, the C major chord clearly substitutes for the real dominant, and the term "tritone dominant" is applicable in showing its function and in distinguishing it from its diatonic counterpart. However, in the approach to the cadence which is accomplished by the real dominant and tonic, the C major chord is used as an independent triad. Its resolution to C♯ is unexpected and consequently cannot be said to function as a dominant. To label it, therefore, as a lowered dominant would be more satisfactory to the eye than to the ear.

This harmonic freedom is a logical outgrowth of the expanded root movement used by the late Romantic and Impressionistic composers. The Romanticist wove together distant tonal regions but with diatonic controls binding each area. Debussy's expansion occurred largely as the result of his free connection of dominant quality higher-numbered chords. Being active chords, they tend to sound like a series of non-related embellishments, settling on an occasional triad or modal region. Triads, on the other hand, do not have the motion that would shift them about as embellishments. They have their own secure footing and may progress anywhere. With this lack of compulsory chromatic direction, these triads become representatives of the twelve-tone scale. Sometimes they are referred to as "foreign chords." Foreign to what? The answer is easy. They are foreign to the diatonic scale and do not function within the laws of the chromatic scale. To acknowledge their role more positively, therefore, these independent chords are actually members of the twelve-tone scale.

Since musical growth represents a continuous evolvement of material, it is fitting that an illustration by Debussy is included in the discussion of independent triads. The opening of "General Lavine" (Prelude VI of Vol II) combines the parallel technique with a free choice of triads. See *example 259c*. Anchored to C major, these triads do not function harmonically, as they do in the Prokofiev *Gavotte*, but they open the gate for further exploration. They are not chosen with the thought of altered diatonic triads; they are not embellishments. They progress melodically by a mediant interval relationship and within the tones which make up the triads, almost all of the twelve tones are included. Their modernism is not in a dissonant vertical idiom, but in the connection of these unrelated triads.

Example 259c *Prelude VI. Debussy*

EXERCISES

A *Analysis*

1] Analyze the themes of *Example 260* by contrasting the diatonic areas with the independent treatment of the twelve-tone scale. Mark the letter names of all tonal regions. Add roman numerals only where they show a significant diatonic relationship.

Example 260a *String Quartet No. 4. Hindemith*

Example 260b *Capricorn Concerto for Flute, Oboe, Trumpet and Strings. Samuel Barber*

2] Analyze the arpeggiated triads of *Example 261a* by marking letter names and diatonic relationships as described. In *Example 261b*, the closing passage of this Prelude, mark all chords and observe some contrapuntal modern dissonance.

Example 261a *Prelude No. 10. Kabalevsky*

Example 261b

3] Apply the harmonic analysis as outlined in chapter six for the Hindemith theme quoted in *Example 262*. In this example, roots for all twelve tones may be indicated by the raising or lowering of the seven diatonic roman numerals. Mark all qualities and inversions as previously described.

4] The opening phrase of *Example 263*, an excerpt from the second movement of R. Vaughan Williams' *Symphony in E minor*, is played by a brass choir and supported by the timpani on the bass part. It connects to the second phrase in measure four which is a complete contrast in sound, and is played softly by unison strings. Analyze the independent triads of the first phrase and the application of the twelve-tone scale in the second phrase.

Example 263 *Symphony No. 6. R. Vaughan Williams*

B The melodies which are incomplete in *Example 264* use the principles of the twelve-tone scale. Play them and mark a few tonal areas that you hear by circling the tones which combine to indicate a tonal area. Look for rhythmic strength of certain tones, repetition of tones, and a diatonic interval association. Complete the melodies, choosing an appropriate ending tone. Use motives derived from the given material.

Example 264a

C The technique of independent triads can produce beautiful results in choral writing. Analyze the given model, *Example 265*, and continue by adding two or more phrases.

Example 265

D Harmonize and complete the melodies of *Example 266* with independent triads (and inversions) in a freely chosen piano style. It is not necessary to restrict the harmony to triads, but give them priority in this chapter.

Example 266a

Example 266b

Example 266c

The following compositions are recommended for further study of independent triads:

Hymn to St. Cecilia for chorus; S.S.A.T.B., by Britten
Sonata No. 3 for piano, by Prokofiev
Symphony No. 3, "Andante," by Haieff
I Hear an Army for voice and piano, by Barber

13 Bichordal writing and polytonality

Polychords

A harmonic vertical structure that simultaneously sounds the roots of two chords is called bichordal or polychordal. It is an extension of the Classical pedal tone which represents a strong bass root above which other chords move. A bichordal structure may have the complete bass chord against which a treble chord of a different root clashes. No preparation of pitch is necessary for either chord. By definition, a polychord may have two or more roots, while the term, bichordal, would pertain to a harmonic structure of two roots. Only in rare instances would a chord of three roots seem possible (see *example* **271**, described later), but bichordal passages, although infrequent, are feasible and effective under the right conditions.

Relationship of roots in polychords: Charles Ives experimented with polychords in the given passage from "Thoreau," *example* **267**, the last movement of the *Piano Sonata No. 2*, entitled "Concord, Mass. 1840–1860." The treble chords oppose the bass triads as they gradually meet in the middle register. The plan is clearly visible but as you listen to each chord, the resulting sound differs in the degree of its bichordal effect. The treble triad of F major in the first chord joins the bass and is heard as a D minor seventh, not a polychord. The second chord is perhaps a trifle more successful in separating the roots, but the opening grace note, E, being doubled, takes away the root strength of the C in the upper triad. Even the clash of the G♮ against the lower G♯ is not severe, and in fact is one of the frequently used double inflections (discussed in the next chapter). The third chord is similar to the second one in that the treble root is again a minor sixth above the bass root. This time, the root D, appears first as a grace note of the upper triad, and its distinction as a root is greater. While listening to the following chord (number four), mentally transform the sharps in the bass to the enharmonic triad of A♭ major. Now the treble fits quite smoothly into the bass triad, permitting just a slight conflict between the E as an augmented fifth in the treble, and the perfect fifth E♭ in the bass.

The bichordal status of the next harmonic structure (number five) is indisputable. The respective roots are a minor second apart and consequently each of the three chord members of one triad opposes its counterpart in the other. The resulting dissonance is greater than any preceding intervallic clash. In the next chord (number six), the pattern of triads in the treble is dropped, and an A dominant seventh is pinned above C major. However, the G of the right hand belongs to the lower C major, negating any sound of a seventh chord. The closer range of the entire structure also minimizes the strength of the upper A major, and actually sounds like a single chord, C major with the added sixth, plus an out of tune C♯! The merger into a single root chord is completely realized in the following D dominant eleventh (number seven). The deliberate use of the natural eleventh, in the presence of the major third, is recognized. This is followed by the E major chord (number eight), in which the melody tone F is the minor ninth, heard against suspended tones of the thirteenth and major ninth. The *diminuendo* has been accomplished by the lessening of tensions within the last three chords.

This bichordal passage, when played fluently, is convincing in its deliberate plan of clashing triads. The wide separation of range and the continuing pattern help to isolate each root. Removing the factor of range, and adding

sevenths in both the bass and treble, play *example 268* and try to hear a separation of root. You can't! The treble tones completely unite with the bass root and form a single higher-numbered chord.

Polychords, and the dominant seventh: Example 269 illustrates the single chord which results from an attempted major treble chord placed over a lower dominant seventh chord. All twelve chromatic roots have been placed over an E dominant seventh. In the first group of four chords (*example 269a*), the relationship between upper and lower root is mediant, that is, the minor and major third above, and minor and major third below the bass root of E. The conflicting upper G against the lower G♯ is not harsh. The lower major third dominates the quality because of its proper placement in the overtone series while the minor third above fits in as an augmented ninth. The minor third may also be analyzed as a minor tenth above the dominant quality, and is discussed later in this chapter. Except for the two different sevenths in the second chord, all chord tones above, fit the lower root, as illustrated.

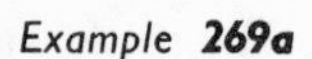
Example 269a

The upper root which is a second above the bass root, becomes a ninth as seen in the next group (*example 269b*). The dissonant conflict occurs between the G♯, as third, and the upper natural eleventh, A. If this dissonance is undesirable, either tone may be omitted but the result will not be a polychord. The seventh binds the upper tones to the lower root.

Example 269b

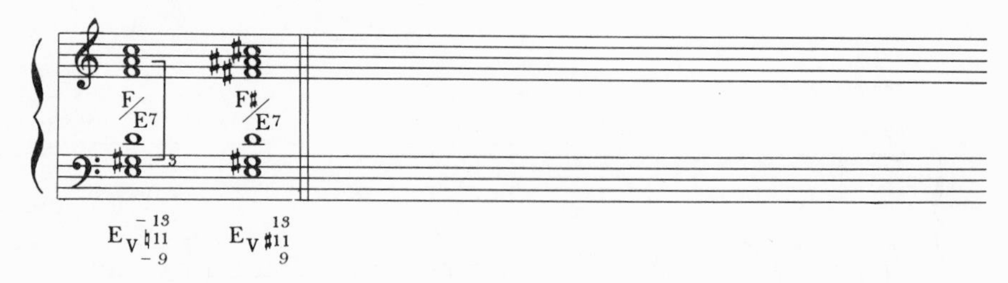

The upper chord whose root is a minor second below the bass root, *example 269c*, forms a major seventh, augmented ninth and augmented eleventh respectively. Although the major seventh is discordant, the dominant quality is not harmed by the two sevenths whether they are clustered together or separated, as long as the minor seventh is the lower one. The following D chord over the E seventh again has the conflict of the third and natural eleventh. As already noted, either tone may be omitted or forcefully maintained. This also applies to *example 269d* in which the A, now as root, is placed above the E seventh. This combination may be heard and used as a polychord, a tonic over its dominant seventh.

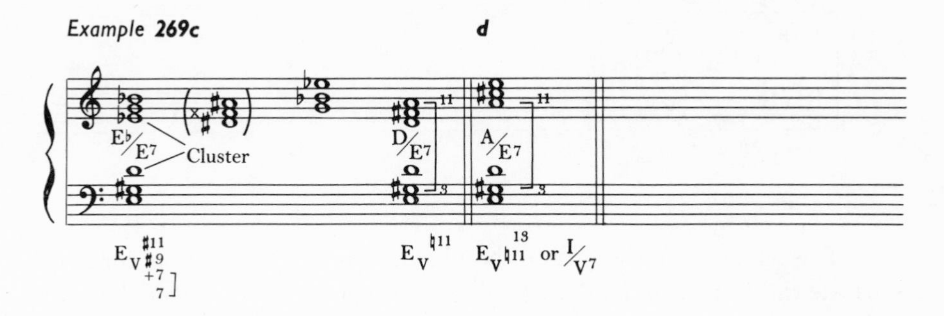

The tritone relationship between upper and lower roots creates a very smooth blend of chord tones. See *example 269e*. Even if both fifths are present, there is no conflict as long as the perfect fifth is the lower. The diminished fifth is enharmonically the augmented eleventh. The seventh of the lower chord is automatically the third of the upper triad and vice versa. As a vertical structure, it is not very apt to be heard as a polychord. And yet, paradoxically, this combination can make a very successful polytonal passage, for the very reason that all chord members combine together so willingly, but are notated so oppositely.

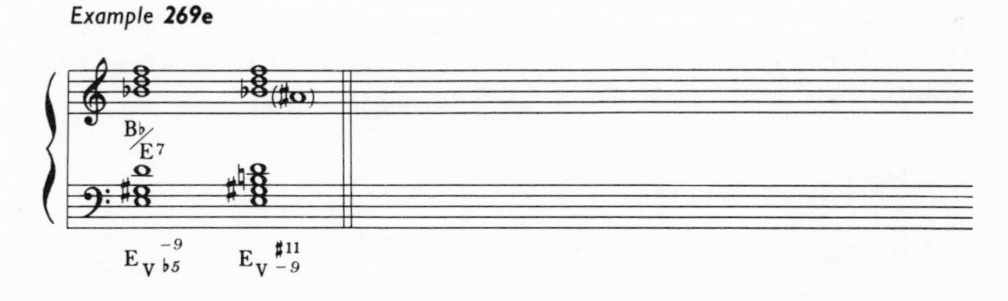

The last group of chords (*example 269f*), have a more familiar relationship, known as the "dominant over tonic" or "dominant over dominant." Earlier usage would have represented the lower chord only by its root, or root and fifth. Notice that in the last chord, when the triad, B major, is placed above the E seventh, the two sevenths are more harsh than in the previous instances. This is due to the lack of other higher-numbered dissonances, which increase the tension in a graduated manner. Here, the sevenths are directly exposed.

The B of the upper triad is merely a fifth of the lower E seventh and the F♯ as ninth is still closely related. This leaves the two sevenths, an augmented octave apart, in direct conflict. Note that by comparison, the second chord in the third group (*example 269c*), has the augmented ninth and augmented eleventh intervening between the sevenths.

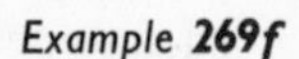

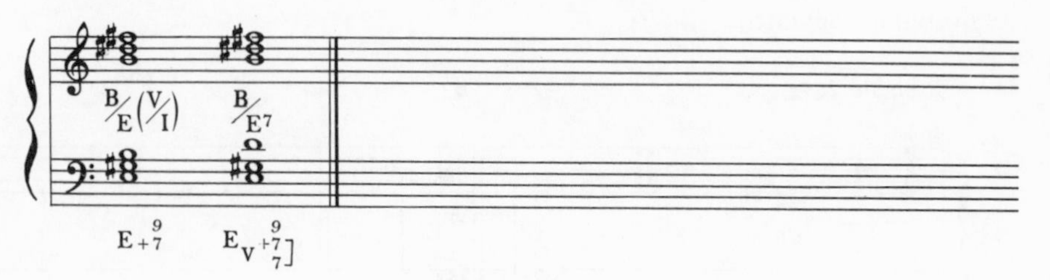

The omission of the fifth in the illustrations within *example 269* helps to separate rather than cloud the attempted roots of upper and lower chords. The fifth is inherent in the lower chord. If it is included, it thickens but does not alter the complete chord.

If the lower chord is minor, it automatically loses the strength of the overtone series and generally results in a support of the higher root. Both *example 268* and *269* can be tried by substituting the minor third for the given major third. For the most part, the chord will be an inversion, the upper root (a major triad), dominating. The chords of *example 268* are changed and illustrated in *example 270,* and become dominant ninths in the first inversion. Where dissonant clashes occur, the judgement as to the degree of desirable dissonance must be made in the same manner as with major triads. Remember that these sounds have been presented devoid of an established tonality. Melodic writing can give strength to minor chords as well as imply other chord tones. This is discussed in the following paragraphs.

Example 270

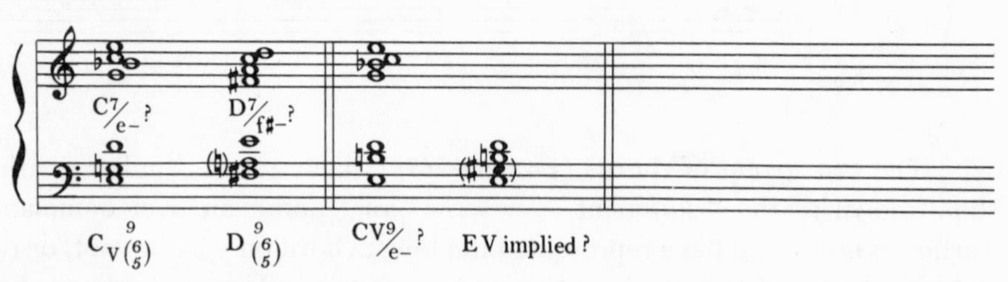

To summarize, a polychord is most readily heard when two triads oppose one other, intent on a separation of melodic ideas and range. If a seventh links the potential polychord, a separate identity for each root is unlikely.

A polychord of more than two roots is extremely rare. Also from "Thoreau," *example 271* comes close to having three opposing roots. Analyzing the preparation for the forte chord, the three registers are already distinct. The bass F is a pedal tone above which a C dominant ninth is heard in the parallel thirds of the middle register, and two octaves above, in the melody. The resolution of this chord, which already implies two roots, is threefold. The bass tone F moves by deceptive resolution to F♯, announcing it heavily by an arpeggio technique. The middle register chord ordinarily would conform to this bass anticipation, but here, a second deceptive resolution takes place, by a B major chord substituting for the expected continuation of F♯. High above in the melody, as if unmindful of this bass conflict, a diatonic progression of C to F is forcefully struck. As a result of the three-way resolution, the momentary impact of F♯ versus B versus F suggests three roots. It is the result of motion, however; a static playing of only the forte chord would not reveal the independence of the high F at all.

Example **271** Ives

Polychords in melodic writing: To gain a bichordal feeling, there is more reliance upon the movement of sound than upon the use of isolated polychords. This is the same principle that prompted the Classical pedal tone. Once established as a chord member, the pedal tone could then be held while other chords moved above it. If the pedal tone is not first recognized within one chord, or tonality, a simultaneous striking of this bass note and an upper chord might not result in the same double root connotation. Numerous bichordal passages exist as the result of melodic motion in one part heard against a contrary harmonic background. A simple, short example is present in the cadence to the "Sarabande" from Alexander Tansman's *Suite dans le style Ancien, example 272.* The first beat of the next to the last measure uses the E♭ minor triad as an embellishment into the B diminished sixth. The second beat, however, shows the independent declaration of E minor in the right hand, accompanied by two opposing triads, the G♭ and F in their first inversions. This bichordal instance is the result of the motion of the E minor triad heard against a differing harmonic background. By suspension techniques, both parts resolve into the dominant seventh on the third beat. The last measure is interesting in that its tonic chord of E minor colorfully changes into the quality of a dominant seventh and rests upon that sound. Throughout the composition, the E was maintained as a tonic so that its status at the ending is unquestioned. The switch from the minor to the raised G♯ is symbolic of the *Tierce de Picardie* and although the seventh is present, a curious mixture of the retained tonic of E and its new dominant quality leaves the listener somewhat puzzled. A resolution is not demanded, nor is the tonic motionless.

The following bichordal passage (*example* 273) is from the third movement of Prokofiev's *Sonata No. 7*. The tempo is very rapid, marked *precipitato*, which accounts for the three measure introductory setting on the single chord of E♭ V ♭9 $\binom{4}{3}$. Against this, the left hand enters forcefully with the theme of this middle section. It outlines the triad of C major heard with complete opposition to the continuing E♭ ostinato. The phrase starts with the *marcato* motive which is immediately repeated, then developed, and cadences in the eighth measure of this excerpt. During its development on the irregularly repeated tones of A♭, the tonal reference is still associated with the preceding triad of C major. The A♭ is non-harmonic, both to C and to the upper E♭ ninth. It resolves at the end of the figure in measure eight to G, now part of the E♭ chord. The role of the pitch of A♭ can be summarized as starting as an upper neighbor to C major and resolving as a 4–3 suspension on E♭.

Chromatic tones, still retaining the E♭ root, link and prepare the second phrase which starts as a modified sequential phrase in the eleventh measure. The marcato motive is now spread over a wider range, but more important, it does not have its own independent tonal grouping as in the first phrase. The upper ostinato, now on a G V♭9, incorporates into itself the tones of the left hand motive. Observe that if played alone, the lower motive might appear as a B seventh, which does not conform to the triad principle as did the C major in the first phrase. Two ninths are present in this harmonic structure. The ostinato retains the A♭ as a minor ninth, and it becomes a melodic neighboring tone of G. The left hand motive contains the other major ninth clustered in the bass. The only harmonic movement within the two phrases is the opening bichordal sound, E♭ over C (resolving into E♭), and the G ninth for the entire sequential second phrase.

Where polychords are effective: Polychords thrive on dissonant, clashing chord members. Their successful use depends on their location, not only within the phrase, but within the context of the entire composition. The listener must be ready to respond to this war of chord roots. The tension created by polychords may be prepared by a gradual motivic agitation and abated by the return to non-conflicting harmonies. This type of musical phrase is so related to the structure of a composition that it cannot be used indiscriminately.

Samuel Barber in the second movement of his *Sonata for Piano*, Op. 26, *example* 274, has such a perfectly controlled passage. The motivic material is appropriate for bichordal writing; the tension is increased gradually toward the clash of the two roots; and the location of this section within the movement lies approximately midway, allowing the bichordal area to be felt as a structural point of emphasis. Before analyzing this example in detail, it is important to represent this second movement in its proper relationship to the first. It is a study in contrast. While the first movement is extremely dramatic and turbulent, marked *allegro energico*, the second movement opens with a very soft, and very rapid theme, high in the treble clef. Its lightly articulated motive retains a constant fluent rhythm, similar to a *moto perpetuo*. After an expansion of this first theme, the middle section (*example* 274) follows as an outgrowth of one of the motives. It is an outgrowth, not only from the technical motivic point of view, but also in its jovial spirit. The motive is given a comical accompaniment, perhaps as a satirical reference to the traditional waltz. If possible, listen to a recording of the entire sonata, so as to fully appreciate the humor in this excerpt, especially as a contrast to the profound and serious disposition of the other movements.

The harmonic analysis of this excerpt (*example* 274), starts with the tonic triad of C major, followed by the subdominant F, altered to dominant seventh quality. The first bichordal implication, in measure five, presents the motive as if it were in E major, against a conflicting bass. The C on the first beat of the left hand suggests a momentary C augmented triad, but this is unfulfilled by the following minor sixth, whose root is D♭. Adding it all up, the conflict occurs between D♭ and C, both bass tones. The E of the melodic motive cannot stand out strongly as an upper root as it forms the major third to the lower C root. The tones of G♯ fit two ways, as the augmented fifths to C and as the enharmonic perfect fifths to D♭. Although the bass tone C can be analyzed as a pedal tone, each time the melody strikes the pitch of E, the tonic C root is revitalized. On the other hand, the same E is actually heard simultaneously with the D♭ chord, in which it fits as an augmented ninth. The bichordal impression results in a teetering harmonic frame of C augmented versus D♭ major, against a melodic suggestion of E.

The motive in this third sequence has been stretched to a three-bar length in which the melody, repeating the last figure (measures seven, eight and nine), is heard above a D chord, D♭, and again a D dominant chord respectively. The F♮ above the D major is the normal use of the minor third heard above the dominant setting. This opening phrase of the theme accomplishes an increased drive toward the fifth measure, retains this mild dissonance and softly echoes it in measure nine. The second phrase starts in the tenth measure with the same original treble motive, this time harmonized by F major. The union of both parts forms an F major large seventh, thereby increasing the level of dissonance in comparison to the previous phrase. A change to the F minor seventh balances

the former sequence and pushes toward the dissonant culmination in the fourteenth measure. The bichordal technique here is at its best. It is in keeping with the former motivic content and yet supplies the added punch for this satirical instance. G major above is pinned against the B♭ major below. Both are triads. The opening dissonance, B♮ against the bass B♭, refuses to blend with the lower chord. The two roots remain incompatible, increasing their drive toward measure sixteen where they merge into a single harmonic sound. Even at this point, a dual reaction is likely because of the tritone, D♭ and G. The melody tone of A♭ blends as the fifth of D♭ and as the minor ninth, correctly resolves to the root of a G $\mathrm{V}\begin{smallmatrix}\flat 9\\6\\5\end{smallmatrix}$ with a lowered fifth. Measure seventeen carries this dual impression also, but because of the clear tertiary organization the chord is a B♭ $\mathrm{V}\begin{smallmatrix}\flat 9\\7\end{smallmatrix}$ with an enharmonic appearance of the minor ninth. This may have been intended to simulate an extension of G major above B♭. After another repetition of the last figure, as in measure seventeen, a resolution to C ushers in a melodic return to the first motive of this section. The "oom-pah-pah" is omitted so as to prepare for the opening theme. The impetus generated by the secondary theme had intensified and been fulfilled. The bichordal passage of B♭ over G is the dissonant and structural point of emphasis in the middle section. With the imminent return of the first theme, this bichordal passage becomes the focal point, at the center of the structural arc of the entire movement. No tremendous double forte has taken place, just a normal acceleration of intensity toward a goal, followed by a decline of tension toward the modified reprise.

Polytonality

Just as polychords demand the simultaneous hearing of two roots in a vertical structure, polytonality is the simultaneous use of two or more keys or tonalities. It can be deduced that in a polytonal passage, polychords will, of necessity, be present. The reverse is not true. As already seen in the former examples, an occasional instance of a polychord or a short bichordal passage need not affect the single tonality in which they are present.

Prokofiev, in *Sarcasmes*, Op. 17, No. III (see *example 275a*), used polytonality for his opening theme. By marking a different key signature for each hand, his intent on the separation of the two keys is clear. Polytonality (or bitonality), at its best, is heard intermittently. The control of dissonance, its increase and decrease, must be present in all phrases, regardless of tonality. If a polytonal effect is to be constantly maintained, the dual harmonies would have to prohibit any merger of polychords into a single-root chord. Having already seen how easily certain well-meaning polychords lose their double identity, a polytonal composition generally includes both the single-root chords as well as the polychords.

Play, or listen to *example 275a* and distinguish the areas of greater and lesser dissonance. (It can be played one octave higher for a clearer discernment of pitch.) Starting in F♯ minor, the two bar introduction establishes a priority for that key. The melody's entrance in the left hand does not announce a new tonality immediately. The earliest hint is in the fifth measure where the melodic triad of B♭ minor has been completed. The full recognition of the polytonal writing comes with the dynamic cadence, dominant to tonic, heard simultaneously in two keys (measures six and seven). It is interesting to note that although the lower key is B♭ minor, the cadential skip of C to F would appear as either a modulation or a forceful preparation of a dominant. However, the upper movement of C♯ to F♯ is supported by chord members, resulting in a definitive dominant to tonic cadence. As polychords, note that the roots directly oppose one another, that is, C against C♯ and F against F♯.

Example 275a *Sarcasmes, Op. 17, No. III. Prokofiev*

Allegro precipitato

Piano

pp

ff pp

ff pp

ff pp

f etc.

Example 275b shows the harmonic results of measures three and four, by the simpler enharmonic notation that temporarily supports the upper key. Notice the emphasis upon the F♯ minor $^{6}_{4}$. The binding tone between the two keys is C♯ (or D♭). The ascending scale tones in measure five begin the polytonal effect by persuasively reiterating the would-be leading-tone, E♯ (F♮), and by not permitting its fulfillment as a leading-tone. Instead, its melodic association is formed with the tone a perfect fifth below (B♭), thereby placing in opposition two minor triads. Notice that the ear does not link the upper A as a major seventh to the lower B♭ minor key. Its own relationship to F♯ minor does not waver.

In the phrase starting in measure eleven, the melodic emphasis in the bass revolves around its relative major, D♭, or enharmonically, C♯. The polytonal effect results in the right hand repeated thirds being still heard as tonic now placed over a dominant harmony in the left hand. Observe the merger into a diminished seventh on the first beat of measure thirteen. It resolves as a leading-tone chord to the tonality of the lower part. (See the analysis illustrated.)

Example **275b**

Polytonality need not be expressed by a different key signature. *Example 276* is a passage from the second movement, "Vivace," of Aaron Copland's *Piano Sonata* (1939–41). At first glance, there is no appearance of a polytonal design. Clusters are evident and the highest melodic tones support the key signature of B major. It is not until the entire passage is heard that the polytonal writing is recognized. The insistent repetitions of the first motive grow in intensity and strengthen the polytonal convictions of the listener.

Tonality is created by the movement of sound. By playing the right hand alone, B major will be easily recognized. Perhaps a modal inference can also be drawn by the use of A♮ throughout this excerpt. The polytonal hearing is also the result of movement of tones. In order to understand the analytic details as discussed in the next paragraph, play this excerpt several times so that the continuity of the melodic groups will be recognized within each tonality.

Example 276 *Piano Sonata. Aaron Copland*

The first three measures are not necessarily heard in a polytonal setting. B major is outlined in the melody and the third left hand cluster merges as an $F\sharp\ V^{13}_{\left(\substack{4\\2}\right)}$. After the five eighth-note motive (the main motive of this movement), the polychord of B major over D is forcefully pronounced. Observe that the B is actually omitted in this upper root. Its implication is assured, however, as a result of the strong opening B major tonality and its retention through the preceding eighth-note motive. Measures eight and nine repeat the first motive, but devoid of the cluster, the left hand defies the upper B tonality by itself declaring the motive to be on C major. The ensuing repetitions keep hammering away at this tonal conflict. The upper B major gains in strength while the lower voice moves melodically in C with the occasional harmonic punctuations on D. By means of hindsight, the first three measures can be re-examined to note that the clusters actually combine the two tonal areas of the left hand, C and D, each rising on their own first three scale tones.

The repetitions within this excerpt have been retained in this reprinting, not only for reasons of tonality as already discussed, but also to preserve Copland's style. The metric and rhythmic asymmetry of the motives, their concise length, the preoccupation with intervallic concepts and controlled dissonance are all part of Copland's writing within this period.

Double inflections

The trend toward greater harmonic dissonance gave rise to chords which include two intervals of the same numerical distance from the root but of differing qualities. For example, a chord may have two thirds, one major and the other minor; or two fifths, a perfect fifth as well as a diminished or augmented one. Heretofore, a selection of chord members would have made up one total structure emanating from the triad, permitting no conflicting chord members.

It is easy to recognize chords which contain double inflections because the notation generally includes both accidentals, the natural sign and the sharp or flat, so as to positively identify the two conflicting notes. It is not as easy to hear the differing chord members because they may not sound in the same opposing manner as would be expected from their appearance. For example, the chord built in *example* **277a** includes two thirds, the B and B♭. It is then rewritten with the enharmonic notation of A♯, and as an augmented ninth, replaces the minor third. *Example* **277b** illustrates first a chord with the double inflection of the fifth and then altered to a G $V^{\sharp 11}_{\substack{\flat 9\\7}}$. Both forms of the chord are correct. The decision must be made upon the melodic context and the resolution of the notes in question. *Examples* **277c** and **d** show possible resolutions for each instance. In the first group, the tonality of C minor creates the double inflection as the minor melodic scale is used against the V to IV_6 and V to VI^7 progressions. By contrast, the next setting in C major shows an ascending resolution of the augmented ninth to the major seventh of the C chord. In both cases, the minor third or augmented ninth serve a melodic function. This does not, however, lessen their harmonic involvement.To show the distinction between the tone that functions as a minor third and the one that is an augmented ninth, the marking – 10 may be used. The dominant symbol includes the major third, and consequently, the upper minor third is located in a higher octave, at least a tenth above the root. These symbols are illustrated in *example* 277c.

Bichordal passages frequently result in the notation of double inflections. In *example* 277d, a cadence is approached by a telescoped Neapolitan sixth over a dominant. Although it is doubtful that the ear would separate the two roots as a polychord (see preceding chapter), the notation requires the double inflection of D♮, in support of the G root, and the D♭ in its melodic role leading toward C. By contrast, the same sound spelled with C♯ in place of D♭ would require an upward resolution as is illustrated.

Double inflections of the third and fifth are more commonly found in this idiom than altered sevenths or roots. When placed above a dominant seventh foundation, they retain a structural force which cannot be destroyed by added qualities. This means that the major third must be the lower one, allowing the minor third the equivalent placement of an augmented ninth. By the same reasoning, the perfect fifth is generally the lower one. Since the perfect fifth is more of an unconscious supporter of the root of a dominant quality chord, it is frequently omitted, thereby avoiding a double inflection without basically changing the harmonic intent. Play *examples* 277b and d again, omitting the lower perfect fifth. The result is simpler in sound and improves the voice-leading if a purity of line is desired. The inclusion of the perfect fifth, by contrast, thickens the sound and suggests a harmonic massing of tones rather than a smoothness of part writing.

Conceivably, any double inflection will sound well if placed in a suitable melodic context. *Examples* 278a, b and c illustrate a double inflection of the root, seventh and ninth respectively. In *example* 278a, the altered root in the second measure is the result of a polychord by appearance, correctly showing the upper F♯, as a member of the B major triad, resolving to the third of E, against the lower F♮ (as the lowered II), also leading toward E. Rewritten enharmonically, the chord fits into an F V$^{\sharp 11}_{\flat 9}$.

The Prokofiev excerpt, *example 278b*, avoids the notation of a double inflection by enharmonically spelling the sound of the lower seventh as a D♯. Nevertheless, it fits into the lower F dominant $^{6}_{5}$ and sounds like an E♭, sharply opposed by the insistent major seventh E, in the treble. The resolution of D♯ down to D♮ (measure four) also helps to indicate that the notation was chosen merely to prevent the appearance of the double inflection, which would look especially awkward in this right hand part. The resulting dissonance is deliberate. Even if the double inflection is discounted in favor of a B over F analysis, the clash of E against the D♯ is still present, and does not enhance a B root.

Example 278c shows the conflict of two ninths, one harmonic and the other serving a melodic function in the bass. The mellow quality of the upper dominant ninth is disturbed, as if punctured by a pin, when the D♭ is interjected into the chord. The dissonance attained adds an opposing strident motion into the bass part, giving the effect of a complete separation of ideas, the harmonic treble versus the motivic bass.

The clamor for added dissonance and tension as part of the musical creativity can be felt in the opening to Prokofiev's *Sonata No. 6, example 279.* The persistent rotation of the minor and major thirds tends to leave the listener bewildered upon hearing these unsettled tonal qualities. The tritone leap in the bass from A to D♯ adds to the unrest. The double inflection is seen between the bass D♯ and the melodic passing tone D, but is heard also as an opposing fifth,

Example 279 *Op. 82. Prokofiev*

an enharmonic E♭ clashing against the accented E of the melody. After three measures of this forceful repetition, the fourth measure cadences temporarily on F♯ minor, each hand approaching it independently. The right hand retains the pitch of E, and by choosing the lower octave, melodically cadences E to A. The bass turns the D♯ pitches into an E♭ $^6_4$ and resolves to F♯ minor, an evasion of A. The double inflection pertains to the roots of the polychord, the upper E over the lower E♭.

The fifth measure, which extends the phrase and connects to a repetition of the previous cadence, also includes an interesting double inflection. Parallel techniques produce a motive of four eighth notes harmonically moving from C♯

to G♯. An altered repetition of this motive shows the C♯ major changed to C♯ minor, followed by the lowering of the parallel tenths in the bass by a half step. The double inflection is seen as the bass voice drops to the root G, while the soprano voice repeats the original perfect fourth motive, thereby landing on G♯. The sound of this G♯ is clearly that of a minor ninth. Ordinarily, the notation would reflect this progression of G dominant minor ninth to C minor, by the use of the A♭ as the minor ninth. However, the usage here is one of chromatic extension to the tonality of A rather than of a fundamental harmonic progression in C minor. To preserve the original key center, the upper melodic line was left in sharps. The G♯ also maintains its role as a leading-tone, heading toward the resolution to A in the sixth measure.

The arpeggio which follows in the seventh measure restores a rhythmic propulsion by including four chord changes within the one ascending drive. While the chords are related to F♯ minor (which is VI of A), they give the effect of moving independently toward the real goal of the returning tonic, and repetition of the first phrase. It may be noted that this type of linking measure, in the Classical period would be built on the dominant seventh chord, thereby resolving the inherent tritone, D and G♯. By contrast, this arpeggio gains excitement through the changing chords which deliberately avoid the dominant tone E. However, tritones are included on the third and fourth beats. A linear D to G♯ in the lower voice moves to a G^{4}_{2} just prior to the resolution on A. No leading-tone moves directly to A, and yet the secure sense of arrival has not been thwarted. The substitute tritones supply the necessary harmonic activity. The melodic movement of pitch may be more directed toward the returning pitches of E on the second beat, rather than the first climactic A. Within the arpeggio, the pitch of F♯ leads to the last F♮, which in turn is resolved by the original motive. In the bass, the pitches of D on the second and third beats directly prepare the pounding tritone, A and D♯.

So far, we have discussed double inflections in chords as being the result of (a) bichordal passages, (b) melodic movement that conflicts with the normal resolutions of higher-numbered chords and (c) the desire to preserve an overriding tonality. The notation is a matter of judgement. In the following short excerpt from the second movement of Paul Hindemith's *Second Sonata, example* ***280a***, the forces of melodic versus harmonic reasoning for the selection of proper spelling are easily noted. In measures one through three, the canonic imitation is the chief musical factor and in order to see, as well as to hear it, the double inflection of G against G♭ was selected. The F♯ spelling, as the leading-tone to G would have been suitable harmonically but would have created an awkward augmented second melodically. By contrast, the sixth measure correctly avoids a double inflection by building the sounds above a G♯ root. Rather than choosing a plain C for the alto and G♮ for the soprano, which would have been easy but harmonically distorted, the alto and bass sound the root and third of G♯, above which the F double sharp is the major seventh, actively leading toward its upper resolution on G♯ in the next measure. A compromise in favor of simple notation is evident in the tenor part. Acting as an augmented fifth, it nevertheless is spelled as E instead of a D double sharp. The spelling of E also supports the brief suggestion of a melodic diminished seventh at the end of the measure.

Do you hear any parallel fifths in this sixth measure? If spelled with the double inflection, C and G natural, you certainly would see them, and probably mistakenly hear them also, as the parallels would suggest C and G as root and

fifth, moving directly to C♯ and G♯ in the next measure. The fifth caused by the third and the major seventh, actually functioning as a raised tone to the dominant quality, is not heard with the same "perfect" tuning as is a root and its second overtone partial. Many parallel fifths of this sort occur when dealing with the more complex harmonic structures. If the voice-leading of the lower part of the chord is smooth, the fifths caused by the added upper tones will probably not be too noticeable and, therefore, not harmful.

The last two measures of this excerpt show the minor and major third within a melodic pattern. Notice that the major third is the lower one and the upper minor third could function as an augmented ninth. From a notation standpoint, either spelling for the minor third is suitable, that is, C♭ or B♮ in measure ten and D♭ or C♯ in measure eleven. Hindemith's preference is based on the motivic design of the major-minor contrast evident throughout this movement. The notation therefore helps the performer to identify this pattern. While the performance may not show a discernible difference between the choice of a C♭ or B♮, there is a differing attitude that each spelling suggests. The confrontation of the minor third, altered to a major third, poses the two thirds as if in a conflict for tonal power. This suggestion would be impossible with an augmented ninth, heard as a non-harmonic tone resolving to the major triad. The minor–major conflict would not be seen, and the tone in question would be played as an embellishment, probably with less power than when recognized as an equally important minor third placed next to its opposing major third.

The conflict of the two thirds is extraordinarily harsh if the overtone series is destroyed by the placement of the minor third below the major third. Nevertheless, such an ugly sound may be wanted for an occasional area. This must not be confused with the constant demand for fluctuation of harmonic tension, which is heard without a destruction of harmonic principles. This double inflection with the reversed thirds occurs in the development section of the first movement of Prokofiev's *Sonata No. 7*. *Example* **280b** includes just the first usage of this sound, which is then maintained within the following phrases, each powerfully stressing this dissonant mixture of thirds. In the first measure, the roots of C and F♯ are mingled. The chord is F♯ minor with the major third, enharmonically spelled as B♭ on top. In the third measure, the design is even more distinct. A C minor-ninth chord includes the major third E♮ as an accented harmonic tone, intent on shocking the listener. Observe the convenient +10 analytical notation that clearly designates the higher third as being major, above the minor third that forms the basic triad. Listen to the entire first movement of *Sonata No. 7* so as to fully appreciate the significance of this harmonic usage within the development section. The contrast later achieved with the lyrical second theme is especially rewarding.

Example ***280b*** *Prokofiev*

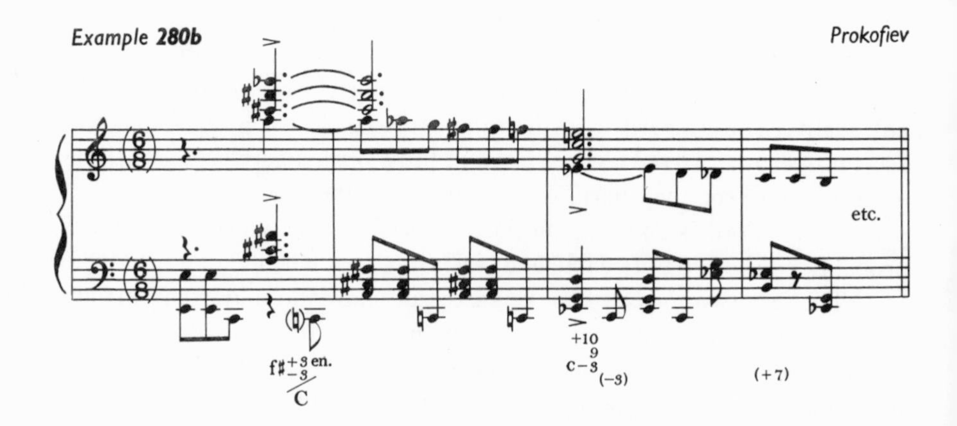

EXERCISES

A *Analysis*

1] Find the double inflection in *Example 281*, an excerpt from the Mozart *Requiem.* What causes this notation? Mark all chords.

Example 281 *Requiem. Mozart*

2] Circle all tones involved in a double inflection. Simultaneous sounding of double inflections is not necessary when arpeggio divisions are used. Complete the harmonic analysis of *Example 282* by marking the roman numerals which have a diatonic relationship.

Example 282 *Hindemith*

3] Analyze *Example 283*. Is there any merger of tonalities? Examine the rhythmic pulse.

Example **283** Ives

4] Are any polychords present in *Example 284*? Mark the complete harmonic analysis. Listen especially for a melodic reference to tonality.

Example **284** Prelude No. 18. Kabalevsky

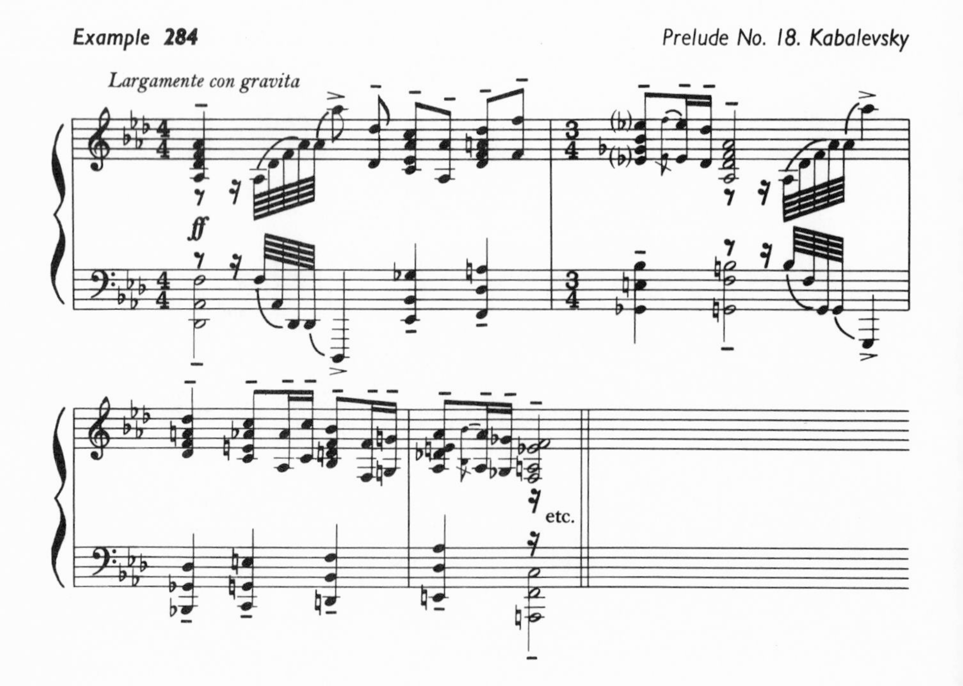

5] The Copland excerpt, *Example* 285, is another fragment from the same illustration quoted in *Example* 276. Review the previous explanation and analyze the polytonal suggestions given in the motives of *Example* 285.

Example **285** Copland

B Build the indicated polychords of *Example* 286 and mark their common tones as illustrated. Are all true polychords? Indicate an alternate analysis.

Example **286**

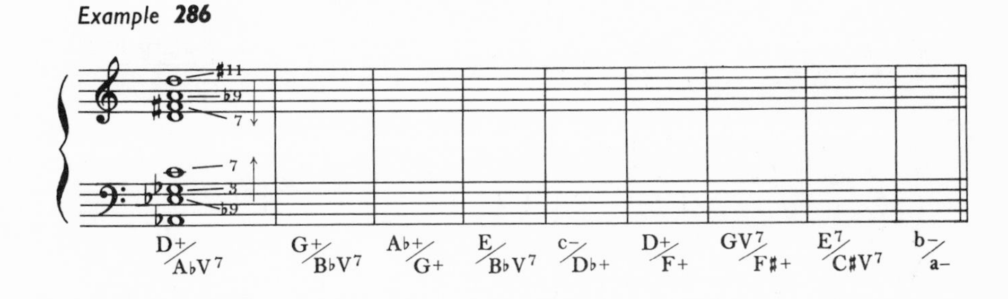

C 1] Fill in the inner voices of *Example* 287. Follow the given designations in *Example* 287*a* and try to hear similar polychords and single rooted chords with double inflections in *Example* 287*b*. While many double inflections are given, inner voices may also supply some. Mark your harmonic result.

2] The following melody is suitable for a polytonal setting. Use the given rhythmic pattern, but choose any triad, or tonal background that you wish for the lower part. Do not restrict your thinking to diatonic triads.

D 1] Use the excerpts from the *Sonetto XXX* by Benjamin Britten as a model for a polychordal composition. Analyze the root relationship between the opposing triads. Observe the motivic contraction and the selection of triads for increased tension as the goal is approached. Score your composition for a solo instrument or voice and use the polychords in a similarly simple setting.

Example **288b**

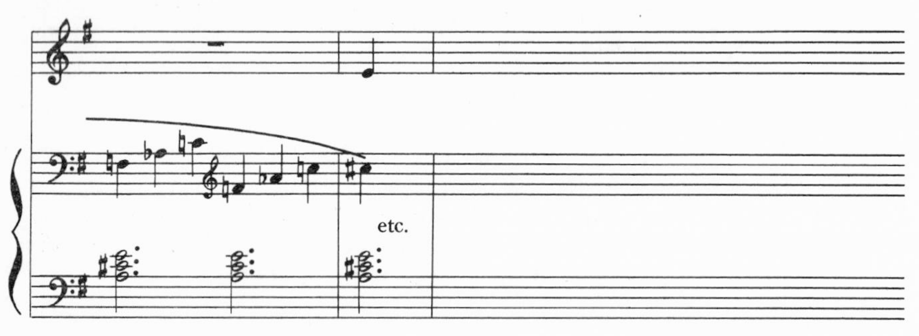

Example **288c** Sonetto XXX Britten

2] Complete the following polytonal motive. Its visual appearance is startling, but the sound is comfortable. Why?

Example 288d

For further polytonal study, see:

Eleven Pieces for Children: "Preludio," "Carillon," "Giga," by A. Casella

Symphony in Three Movements, by Stravinsky

For study of double inflections, see:

Sonata No. 3, Variation II of "Movement I," by N. Dello Joio

PART IV

Contrapuntal writing

Together with the growth of vertical harmonic dissonance, a contrapuntal style evolved in which the movement of tones, not necessarily conforming to a chordal association, guides the tonal setting. Instead of hearing the melodic lines merge into a recognizable harmonic movement, the listener tends to feel a greater independence amongst the contrapuntal melodies. The tonality may seem vague, especially if the twelve-tone scale is fully realized in all of the participating voices. Nevertheless, whenever tones of several melodies coincide, harmony is automatically formed, and it moves together with the movement of the melodies. The analytical problem lies in the fact that the familiar, traditional harmonic groupings of tones are not present. Newer combinations have replaced them. Sounds merge which are "incomplete" to the diatonic ear. The strength of a solid major or minor tonic triad, used in the past to establish tonality, is absent. Taking the place of triads and seventh chords, are intervallic combinations which create varying degrees of consonance or dissonance. Tonality is heard when intervals of strength predominate either in a vertical formation or during the course of a melodic line.

14 Linear roots

Diatonic melodies rely upon a scale formation from which a central tone arises as the keytone of a major or minor scale. In compositions where all twelve tones have equal status in a scale formation, the key tone, or predominating tone, must be identified by some other means. Such a tone may gain stature rhythmically, either by receiving metric stresses or merely by being held longer than the surrounding tones. Or, a tone may be part of a melodic interval from which a harmonic association may be derived.

Intervals which form an important harmonic nucleus are, the perfect fifth, perfect fourth and major third. The overtone series support their standing. These intervals, if given prominence within a melodic line, suggest a harmony built upon the parent chord (in which the intervals exist as chord members). The perfect fifth is recognized as representing the lower tone as a root and the upper as a fifth of a chord, unknown in specific quality, however. The perfect fourth, as the inversion of the fifth, refers to the upper tone as root, and the lower as the fifth of a chord. The interval of a major third gives strength to a major or dominant quality chord. Its inversion, the minor sixth, may represent the third and root. Beyond this point, the intervals decrease in their value of harmonic suggestion. For example, the minor third could represent the third and fifth members of a major triad, or be heard as part of a diminished fifth context. The function of this interval as root and third of a minor triad, is not automatic when the fifth is omitted, whereas the harmonic function of the major third does not require the supporting fifth in order to be heard as root and third of a major triad, or higher-numbered chord.

The interval of a major sixth may represent a fifth and third of a major triad; but with the implied root missing, there is less certainty in this evaluation. The minor sixth, on the other hand, generally includes the root as the upper tone of a suggested major triad. The opening of the Shostakovich *Fifth Symphony* (please turn back to *example* 256), starts with the melodic minor sixth, D to B♭, and is immediately balanced by another minor sixth, A to C♯ below. These melodic minor sixths unquestionably create the roots of B♭, followed by A, which in turn establish the tonal setting of D minor. The next interval, a perfect fifth, C to G, contains C as the root, and tonally moves away from D minor. The following minor third, F♯ to D♯, which ends the two-bar motive, is completely removed from the diatonic scale of D minor, and being a minor third, has no positive harmonic association. Do not be tempted to call this minor third an embellishment of the following supertonic seventh chord. Although the pitch movement of D♯ to the bass tone of E is recognized, there is no rhythmic propulsion toward the forthcoming new motive. Rather, it ends the first motive, fulfilling a contrapuntal balance. The selection of F♯ and D♯ is inherent in the freedom afforded by the twelve-tone scale and should not be forced into an unfitting diatonic analysis.

It cannot be said that all perfect fifths or fourths found in a melodic line automatically include a known root. Factors involving rhythm and the placement of the intervals within the melodic contour have a bearing on the amount of emphasis the intervals receive. Before examining such melodies, complete with rhythmic detail, study the given illustrations (*examples 289a* to *d*), which show very simply, the linear roots obtained from the perfect fifth, perfect fourth, major third and minor sixth. Seconds function as passing tones and when inverted to form sevenths, they either remain as non-harmonic tones functioning in different registers, or may suggest a seventh chord. This is especially true if a dominant quality is outlined within a melodic contour that involves the seventh.

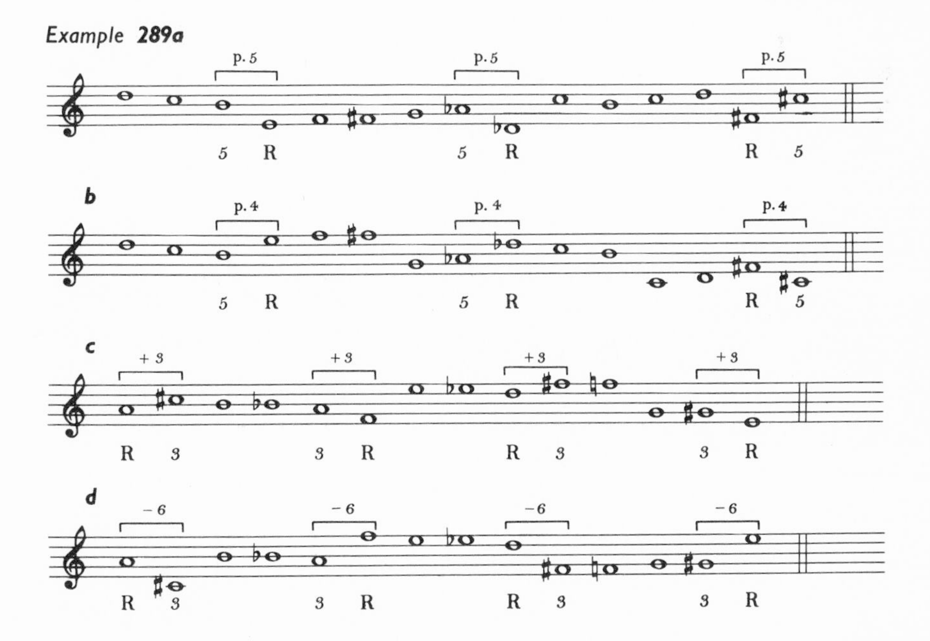

The contour of a melody is made up of many groups of ascending or descending tones. The tones which occupy the highest or lowest position of each small "peak" are more prominent than the connecting tones between them. The change of direction that necessarily follows a higher or lower tone of a melodic group tends to stress such outer tones and permits their pitches to linger in one's mind. These outer tones shape the entire contour of the melody. The intervals thus formed by the highest and lowest tones of each melodic curve, have a greater harmonic association than the intervals formed within a succession of tones in the same direction. *Example 290a* shows how the major thirds C♯ to A and later E to C become part of the total descending group and do not retain their identity as third and root. Instead, the continuing descending line forms first the contour of a perfect fifth, C♯ to F♯, followed by a descending major seventh, E down to F, in which the perfect fifth also supports the lower root F. Compare this with *example 290b*, in which the same notes are used, but are placed in different registers, thereby altering the outer tones of the melodic contour. Here, the A is the lowest tone, and becomes the linear root outlining a dominant seventh quality until the perfect fourth C to F cancels it.

A second factor governing the hearing of linear roots is present amongst these opening tones of *example 290*. When a tone is established as a linear root, it will remain prominent as long as the companion tones can be embodied into its chordal reign. To illustrate, the root A in *example 290b* (the fourth tone) retains its root significance, incorporating the high G as a seventh and the E as a fifth, until the C♮ removes the dominant quality that had been set up. Viewing this only on the basis of melodic direction, it will be seen that the high G forms a perfect fifth contour with the lowest tone of the group, C. By itself, this group would suggest a C root immediately resolving to F. But when heard in context, following the major third C♯ to A, the tones fulfill the harmonic association started from the tone A and cannot gain a new identity until all traces of the former harmonic grouping are removed. In this case, the C♮ is the first tone to cancel the A dominant setup, and the following F becomes the next linear root.

The last seven notes of both *examples 290a* and *b* also sum up the two principles which control the hearing of linear roots, namely, the prominence of the outer tones of a melodic curve and the lasting quality of a root, once established. By changing the tone D (seventh tone from the end) to its octave placement in *example 290b*, a different melodic contour results in each example. In the first instance (*example 290a*), the D, by being the lowest tone of the group, commands the role of root for all of the remaining ascending tones. By contrast, in *example 290b*, the G is the lowest, and is the linear root, resulting from the perfect fifth approach, D to G below. The two endings therefore differ in that the first stresses a lengthy dominant resolving to the tonic only on the last one, G, while the second version lands on the tonic G and retains it as a codetta for the remaining five tones. In both cases, once the tone received its stress as a root, the remaining tones heard in ascending succession succumb to the former root regardless of their own interval make-up. The fifth, A to E, is incorporated into the D dominant association easily (*example 290a*), and in a melodic fashion, supports the tonality of G, in *example 290b*.

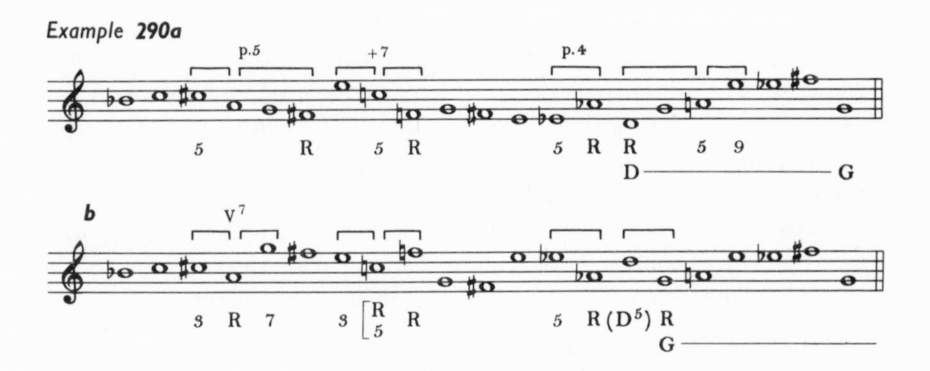

How do tritones affect the hearing of linear roots? Derived from the leading-tone and its companion the diminished fifth, or augmented fourth, the tritone retains its active tendency within a linear treatment. As an embellishing interval, it seeks a resolution, generally accomplished by one of the harmonically associated intervals such as the major third. If not immediately resolved, the search for a stronger stable interval continues, hopefully formed somewhere within the melodic contour. *Example 291* contains many tritones, none satisfactorily resolved. By itself, the tritone has no root, each tone equally cutting the octave in half. A harmonic association can be heard only by the assimilation of other tones into the melodic contour, and then the quality, including the tritone, can only be an active dominant one. A persistent succession of tritones, therefore, creates unrest and motivates all phrase members to push forward toward a decisive goal. Experiment with *example 291* by adding a cadential

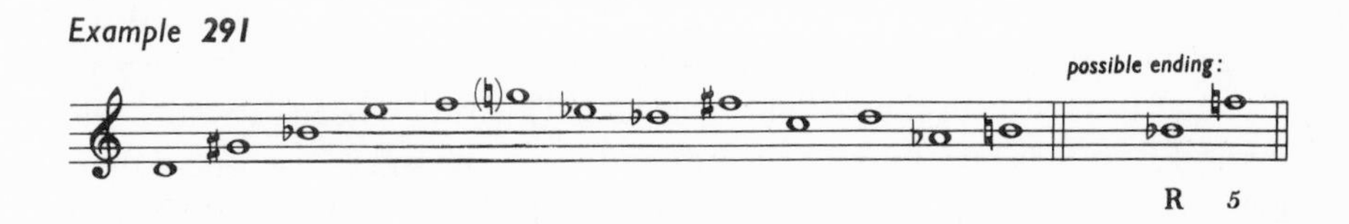

interval such as a perfect fifth or a perfect fourth, using any tones other than the last three of the given exercise. For example, the fifth, B♭ up to F, would be one possibility. Play this exercise first without and then with the added ending. Notice how all of the tritones become meaningful when given the opportunity to fulfill an inherent demand for resolution.

Directional tones

In addition to the careful selection of intervals needed for good melodic writing, the complete tonal contour of the phrase or theme must be considered. This is as true of Modern melodies as it is of Classical melodies. The many melodic curves that make up the total span of the theme have a directional control. They lead toward a focal point, forming an overriding melodic arc or a comparable pitch design. The subject from Bach's B minor fugue (No. 24, Vol. I of *The Well Tempered Clavichord*), *example 292,* illustrates this so well. Its extraordinarily chromatic texture can be likened to the pitch contour of a Modern fugue. The two tones which make up the half-step figure (Figure b), start in the center of the melodic range. From this central location, two lines emerge, one ascends toward the highest group D to C♯, while the lower line moves contrarily to E and D♯ and then also ascends toward the new tonic of F♯. The focal point of both lines is the transposed return of the opening motive, Figure a. A melody from which one can extract two or more distinct lines (as if denoting a soprano and alto part, as in the Bach subject) is called a compound melody. Within such a compound melody, certain tones lead the way and form a melodic span in both the upper and lower registers of the melody. These tones may be called "directional tones." They guide the over-all pitch movement of the melody. In the Bach, the two tones making up the half-step figure are really inseparable, and both act as directional tones serving an upper and lower pitch contour.

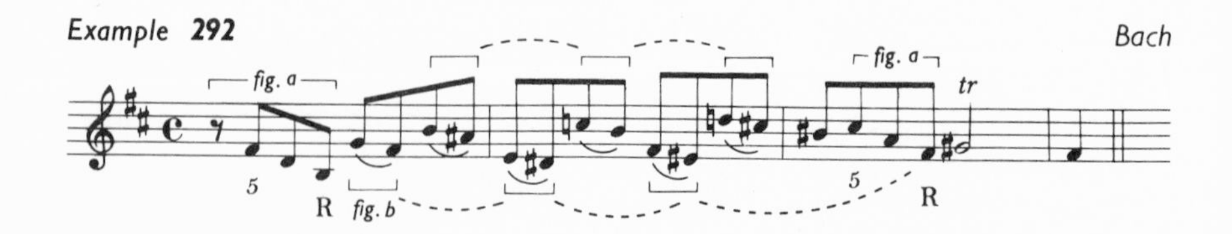

The theme from the "Andante" of Beethoven's *Fifth Symphony, example 293,* illustrates a compound melody in which the directional tones cover a larger distance in terms of time. In the upper line, the tone C on the downbeat, progresses toward D♭ two bars later. Meanwhile, the opening E♭ pitch is directed toward F in the second measure, which then heads toward the chromatic E♮ in measure four. The fifth and sixth measures use one-bar motivic groupings and accordingly, the directional pitches tighten their rhythmic movement. The most essential tone within this melodic contour is the E♭ in the next to the last measure of the theme. The opening directional tones of C and D♭ guide the entire melodic movement toward its culmination on E♭. The design created by this melodic contour is not the rounded arc, centering the highest and lowest tones near the center of the melody, but rather, approximating an elliptical shape in which an elastic band stretches the upper curve toward its peak at the conclusion of the phrase. Perhaps from feeling this stretched shape, Beethoven added a cadential extension in which the climactic E♭ is reiterated twice in expanding ranges before starting a descending melodic contour.

Example **293** *Beethoven*

Directional tones may move by "resolution" in other registers. (The word "resolution" frequently suggests a necessary act of pitch movement. Directional tones do not require any resolution; they guide the melodic contour which is frequently stepwise.) Everyone is familiar with the melodic cadence occasionally used in Baroque literature (see *example 294*), where the leading-tone resolves to the tonic by the downward leap of a major seventh, instead of the usual ascending half-step resolution. The directional tone on the second degree of the scale prepares for the tonic a whole step lower, while the upper leading-tone completes a higher pitch contour. Both resolve to the single lower tonic note. In *example 294*, a sonata for violin, Bach uses a two octave span in the downward leap.

Example **294** *Bach*

Directional tones which change register expand a melody's range and in so doing may shape the phrase differently in terms of the over-all contour. This is illustrated in *example 295a*, a plaintive melody by Charles Ives from his *Piano Sonata No. 2* in the movement entitled "Emerson." The melody of five bars contains one basic motive followed by several variations of it, one per bar, each ending on the tonic tone of C. The repetition of this melody, illustrated in *example 295b* without the arpeggiated background, shows the wide leaps resulting from the change of register.

The tune is quite different as the directional tones change the melodic emphasis. For example, in the first setting, the melodic strength falls on the

Example 295a Ives

first tone, A, which descends to C. The stress on C is retained in the second measure. Upon the repetition, in the varied *example 295b,* a new peak is created. The uppermost directional pitch movement involves F (the third tone), which leads toward G, a step above, located in the second measure. This switch of register widens the scope of the melody and is partially responsible for the continued upward expansion culminating in the highest C in the fourth measure.

In the third motivic group, the descending and ascending intervals are reversed, but the same tones control the contour of the group. In the fourth "variation," the separation of range is most noticeable. The tone which gains attention upon the repetition is the sixth note, D. (The preceding D♭ does not apply in this notation.) In the original fourth bar (*example 295a*), the high D is an upper neighbor, surrounded by the essential tones of C. Upon the repetition, the D below the staff is now associated with the former D♭ and links that tone with the bass C. The final group is differentiated by the predominant stepwise approach of the original idea, as opposed to the leaps in the variation. The latter treatment emphasizes the tones which result from the skips involved, while the stepwise use incorporates them as less noticeable passing tones.

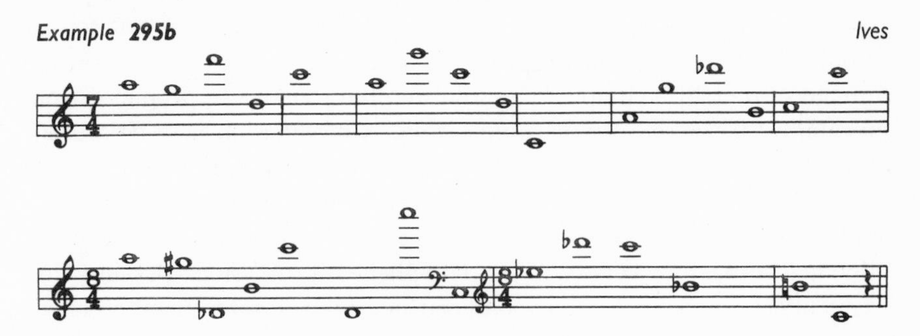

The understanding of how directional tones may operate in many registers, or octaves, is helpful toward the appreciation of many contemporary melodies. A chief complaint of Modern writing is that it is "not melodic." It is true that melodies cannot be sung readily if they skip about in range, but the wide leaps scored instrumentally should not evoke a totally unmelodic response.

Schoenberg was an exponent of writing for maximum instrumental ranges within brief motives. A quote from the third movement of the *Fourth String Quartet* is typical. See *example 296*. The first measure of the excerpt is one which introduces the melody in the "Poco Adagio" section. The most essential pitches that lead toward the new theme are noticeably located in the lowest and highest registers of this measure. The first two tones, F♯ and G combine with the high half notes, A and G♯, and together prepare the starting tones of E♯ and F♯ in the forthcoming melody. Within the group, the C above the staff, drops to D♭, a major seventh below and then leaps up to high A. If all of the intervals of the seventh and sixth were inverted to seconds and thirds, this group of tones would take on a singable shape, but as they exist, they still connect pitches, providing the ear is flexible enough to permit the range differential.

Example 296 Schoenberg

The melody (quoted here without the accompanying instruments) is typical of Modern writing in its use of seventh and minor ninth intervals. Dotted lines show the movement of the more important directional pitches.

One particular type of directional tone can be singled out for special comment, namely, the leading-tone. It would be recognized if upon the fulfillment of its half-step upward resolution, the tonality so produced would be meaningful to the phrase or composition. A modulation may be caused by a tone which, through melodic or rhythmic prominence, is then heard to resolve as a leading-tone regardless of register, establishing a new key center. Dominant harmonies may be absent in this preparation. All that is necessary is a prominent leading-tone, one which accomplishes its mission. Because this is a frequent occurrence in Modern composition, it can be appropriately called "the leading-tone technique."

To illustrate, *example 297a* contains a hypothetical introductory measure to the Ives melody quoted in *example 295*. The directional tone in the first measure is B, and as a result of the forthcoming tonality of C major, it would be recognized as the leading-tone. It differs from a dominant setting, in that it functions either as a single leading-tone not associated with the dominant

Example 297a

chord; or it may be present within other harmonic structures and detected only by the significance of the leading-tone resolution. *Example* 297b places the leading-tone in a harmonic setting whose root recognition is secondary to the leading-tone function. Other directional tones are marked by dotted lines.

In combining the analysis of linear roots and directional tones, the introductory theme to the *Sixth String Quartet* by Bela Bartók, *example* 298a, is particularly suitable. Written as a viola solo, the theme can be discussed, not only in the selection of pitch from bar to bar as the melody unfolds, but from a large structural standpoint, as it leads toward the principle theme of the movement. Two reductions illustrate; first, the most significant directional tones *example* 298b, and second, *example* 298c shows the linear roots. They are explained in that order.

The opening three-bar motive divides into two segments, the first being the more significant of the two. Containing only stepwise motion, the directional tones merely follow the rise and fall of the melody. In the fourth measure, C♯ begins the lower line of a compound melody, rising to its sequential tone D♯, in the fifth measure. The higher contour moves from the F♯ in measure four to the following G♯. In this case, the F♯ is a starting tone of the four-note figure (derived from the opening motive) and although the highest note of this group (F double sharp) rises one half-step above the F♯, the motivic emphasis given to the F♯ takes precedence over its rhythmically weaker neighbor. The compound melodic treatment merges into a single expanding line, reaching its peak in measures seven and eight. The tone, C double sharp, is a rhythmic augmentation of the opening pitch, and with the accompanying crescendo leads forcefully into D♯. Descending sequences, still outgrowths of the first motive, follow (measure eight), in which the directional tones drop a distance of a seventh. The ninth measure starts the sequence on E, a tone motivicly equivalent to the previous C double sharp. This motive, in turn, is followed by another partial sequence, beginning on G♭ in the tenth bar. Within these rhythmically stressed tones, other directional tones link them chromatically, but by a lowering of the range. For example, the highest tone of the climax, D♯, is a directional tone to E, a seventh below. From E, the motive rises to F which prepares the following sequence starting on G♭. It is true that the eighth notes are rhythmically short and are followed by other tones not directly involved with the contour. Nevertheless, the selection of pitch for these sequences is influenced by their presence, as they form the small peaks within the motive. The melody returns to a compound treatment as the final expansion of the motive brings out two significant pitches, in measures twelve and thirteen. The pitch of A♭ is important as a leading-tone, preparing the dominant tone A of the forthcoming tonal center of D. In turn, E♭ leads downward to the tonic D of the principal theme.

Next, study this theme from the standpoint of linear roots. Which directional tones combine with strong intervals that may suggest passing harmonic movement? *Example 298c* illustrates a maximum number of linear roots, together with the more prominent intervals that make up the melody. The roots marked in parenthesis are less distinct than the others, and may be omitted. Such roots, for the most part, do not have a rhythmic emphasis and are the results of stepwise movement.

The opening G♯ gains its significance upon the completion of the entire theme, rather than as a result of the minor third contour. The pitch of G♯ returns at the end of the phrase (measure twelve), as the enharmonic linear root of A♭, thus uniting the pitch span. In the second measure, the stepwise scale association of B major blends with the former G♯, but rhythmically, the major third within the eighth notes places F♯ as the linear root. Cancelled to F♮ in the third measure, the descending scale continues and concludes the motive on D. At this point, it suggests D minor, but this quality is not carried forth in any meaningful way, although D is later recognized as the tonic (within the twelve-tone scale concept) for the first movement.

In measures four and five, the perfect fourth interval creates the linear roots of F♯, followed sequentially by G♯. The intervening tone between D♯ and G♯ in the fifth measure in no way disturbs the outer contour of the perfect fourth. The tritone, stressed in the sixth measure, activates the rising line, climaxing in the eighth measure on the tone of D♯. Combined with the immediate major third, B becomes the linear root, but within the tonal reign of G♯ minor.

Good notation aids the understanding of passages like this one. Bartók's choice of sharps and double sharps conveys the tonal association he heard with the starting suggestions of G♯ minor. Had the C double sharp been notated as a D, and in the preceding measure, the F double sharp chosen as a G, it is possible that a fake image of G, root to fifth, could arise, removing much of the excitement and activity inherent in the C double sharp, as representing the raised fourth degree of G♯ minor.

Bartók's theme illustrates the value of directional tones, not only in the smaller motivic pitch connections (as in the sequences of measures four and five), but more importantly, in the connection between the stress on G♯ (later enharmonically A♭) and its motion into the first tones of the principal theme, A and D. The leading-tone technique applies to the A♭ as it chromatically prepares the dominant of D. This structural planning of pitch is necessary in order to create modulation, the large movement of tonal areas. The contemporary contrapuntal setting requires that more attention be placed on the tones themselves which control this motion, rather than on a harmonic combination. A single tone may have the strength of a tonic, but this tone may not be anchored to its triad chord members. In the "Vivace" theme of this same example, Bartók includes both the minor and major thirds in the main motive (*example 298d*). Should it be labeled D minor or D major? Although the major third is the latter one, it did not arise from a diatonic association with D. The inherent

Example 298d

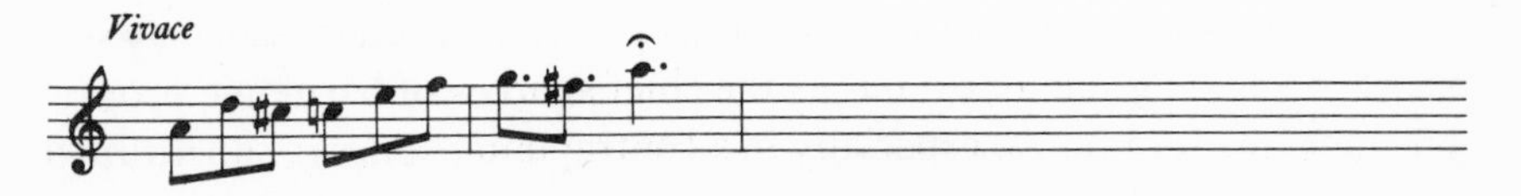

privileges of the twelve-tone scale give D, the tone itself, stature as a tonic, with all eleven surrounding tones equal participation in their melodic, supporting functions.

The subordinate theme of this *Quartet* is prepared by careful long-range planning of the directional pitches. See *example 299.* A motive consisting of an augmentation of the first three tones of the principal theme, A, D, and C♯, is used as an ostinato in the first violin and repeated six times. This emphasis prolongs the harmonic sound of a select group of tones as the other instruments also reiterate a few pitches. When the connection to the second theme is made by a stepwise lowering of D♭ (C♯) to C♮, the impact of the modulation is most rewarding. An entirely new set of important pitches is now present with the new theme.

Descending from C for the distance of a perfect fifth, the second theme forms a linear root of F. This alignment of the tones C and F produces the tonality of F (indeterminate as to major or minor) in which the starting tone of C acts as a dominant tone. The modulation from the tonality of D of the first theme to F for the second theme fits the Classical pattern of key relationships. Instead of focusing on a harmonic progression for a binding analysis, however, the connection in Bartók's usage can only be explained by the stress given to certain tones of one area and their departure and movement into other tones signifying the next tonal area. Bartók planned his second theme to be in F, and therefore carefully avoided any accented or noticeable use of the tone of F, and in this case C, prior to the theme's exact beginning. (Unimportant occurrences of passing tones, and others, would not have any adverse effect on a modulation as the ear would not single out such tones.) A traditional "rule" of modulation: "do not arrive prematurely on the root position tonic chord" can be applied to a Modern usage in this way: "do not include the directional tones of a new section in the material intended to prepare it." In other words, don't show your aces until the bidding is over!

Example 299

Applying this analysis to melodies of the contemporary idiom: the controls that a composer places upon the melodic contour of a theme, may serve not only as melodic guide lines, but as the chief sources of harmonic progression. The movement of tones, especially in a contrapuntal setting, substitute for the movement of chords. The fleeting vertical combinations may involve many different tones which together do not organize themselves into traditional harmonic structures. The listener therefore responds to the most outstanding pitches which may be either based on the melodic contour, or derived from an intervallic strength, heard melodically or vertically.

EXERCISES

A *Analysis*

1] Analyze the compound melody, *Example 300a*, which is the theme of an early piano sonata by Stravinsky. Observe a Baroque quality and note the leading-tone resolution.

Example **300a** Stravinsky

2] Study and mark the directional tones of *Examples* 300b and c. They control the pitch movement of this brief composition. Observe the linear roots only in the bass part, where, in this excerpt, the writing is no longer unison.

In excerpts that follow, connect the directional pitches by dotted lines and mark the linear roots by brackets to indicate the interval that contains a harmonic association.

In addition, mark the bichordal harmony of *Example 301*.

Example **300b** Wm. Schuman

Example **300c** Wm. Schuman

Example **301** Prokofiev

3] In *Example* 302, reduce the measures which contain the pizzicato into a melody line devoid of the large skips and register changes.
b] Mark the intervals that denote motion in contrast to those that establish tonal roots.
c] Mark long-range directional tones as well as those described previously.

4] Separate the theme of *Example 303* into small figures and trace them throughout the given excerpts. Observe the intervallic unity. Analyze as before.

Example 303a *Riegger*

Example 303b

B 1] Mark the linear roots occurring within the melodic lines of *Examples* **304a**, **b**, and **c**.

2] Rewrite *Examples* **304a**, **b**, and **c**, changing the register of several tones of your own choice. Observe the new directional tone pattern, and mark the resulting linear roots.

3] Add rhythm to the tones of *Example* **304**, filling in with extra melody tones where desired. Within your "theme" mark the motives and long-range tonal movement.

Example **304a**

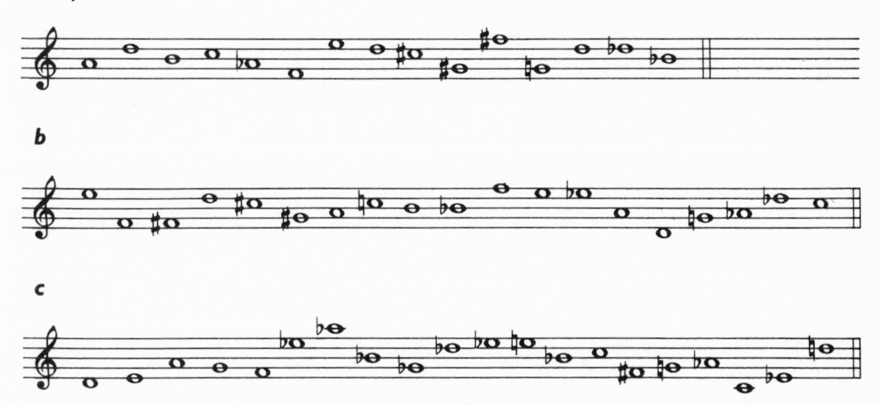

C Write three original melodies by following these suggestions:
a] write the tones (in the twelve-tone scale concept) without rhythm, observing the directional tones, and
b] add the rhythm and mark a few linear roots

D Continue the motives given in *Example* **305**. Choose your own tempo.

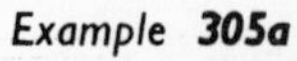

For further study of directional tones see:

"Temptation of Saint Anthony" from *Mathis der Maler*, by Hindemith
Symphony for Strings, by William Schuman
Ludus Tonalis, "Interludium" after "Fuga Seconda," by Hindemith

For hearing the tritone influence, listen to:

Symphony No. 6, "Scherzo," III movement, by R. Vaughan Williams

15 Two-part writing

The analysis of linear roots and directional tones in a single line is carried forth into two-part writing in the same manner, except that an additional factor must be considered, namely, the harmonic union of intervals. Fortunately, all intervals retain their basic characteristics, in terms of their consonant or dissonant attitudes, whether applied in a melody or heard in a chord. The intervals which are derived from a triad, especially the major triad because it is contained in the natural overtone series, are the strongest intervals that evoke a harmonic association. The perfect fifth, as a harmonic interval, establishes the lower tone as a root so strongly, that it will retain its tonal stature through much contrapuntal activity until another combination of strong intervals takes over. *Example* **306a** starts with the perfect fifth, after which the melody's meandering includes all of the twelve chromatic tones, but through it all, C remains the root. Melodic designs like this can be realized as long as the upper tones do not form their own triad combinations. *Example* **306b** illustrates the arrival of a linear root, D♭, occurring above the pedal tone, C. It moves to an implied dominant because of the leading-tone resolution. Directional tones influence the movement of these upper triads. The starting tone G helps to put the spotlight on the high A♭ because of its leading-tone characteristic. In turn, an implied resolution to G is felt, due to the dominant to tonic cadence and the

Example 306a

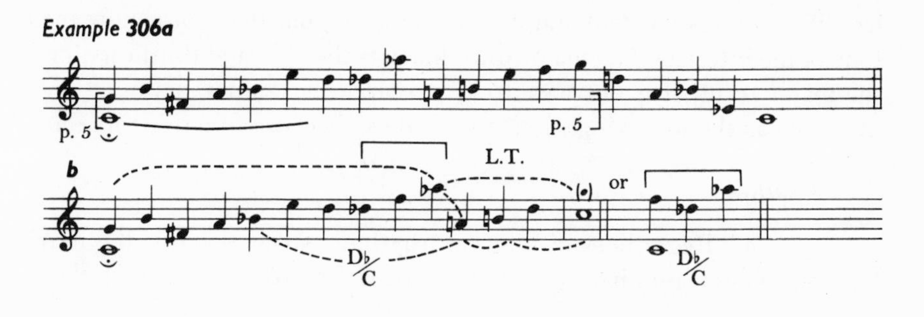

octave C, in which the presence of the fifth is understood. Dotted lines illustrate other directional motion.

The perfect fifth need not be the starting harmonic interval, in order to "rule the roost." In *example* **306c**, it occurs after three other tones begin the melody. It must be noted that these first three vertical intervals, the major seventh, sixth, and ninth, do not within themselves form any harmonic coalition, but sound like they are searching for a root. The arrival of a perfect fifth supplies the need and C remains the root for the entire melodic span. It is reaffirmed by the top G and by the brief diatonic scale influence of E, F, G in the center of the line. Suppose the first G of this same example was not there. Omitting it, *example* **306d** shows the resulting D major triad forming a D^4_2 combination with the lowest tone C. The chromatic tone of F♯ is so active, that in spite of its cancellation to F♮, it becomes a directional tone strengthening the top G. At this point, the perfect fifth again commands the root of C. It would be easy to permit the top G to become a root of a dominant chord, as the D^4_2 would prefer a G over C pedal combination, rather than the cadence of *example* **306d**. Illustrated in *example* **306e**, the tones of the original cadential group are merely given the crucial leading-tone at the last moment. This ties in with the high G and unifies the six tones preceding the cadential C as dominant members.

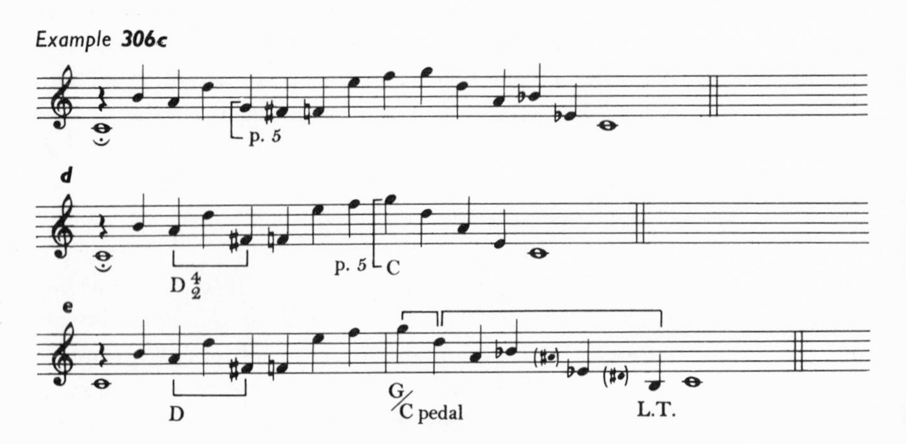

As harmonic intervals, the perfect fourth and major third follow the fifth in the strength of a root association. The fourth, being an inversion of the perfect fifth, retains the root and fifth connotation, but the root is now the upper tone of the interval. The major third inherits the root and third relationship of the major triad. It is not wise to try to place these intervals in any order of priority (as the following discussion shows) because other factors intervene.

Rhythm

a] Regardless of interval, rhythmic stress dictates the hearing of harmonic versus non-harmonic tones. *Examples* **307a** to **307e** show the perfect fifth, fourth, and major third in non-harmonic situations. In all cases, the established root at the start of the example retains its tonal strength, negating both the linear and harmonic influences of the weaker beats. In *example* **307e**, the brief tenth, supporting C, is sufficient to delay the linear perfect fourth D to A in establishing a D chord until the stress is given to a supporting tone, F♯. By contrast, all notes in *example* **308a** to **e** have been rhythmically shifted to produce the opposite root from their previous setting. Tonal strength is therefore subjugated to rhythmic influences.

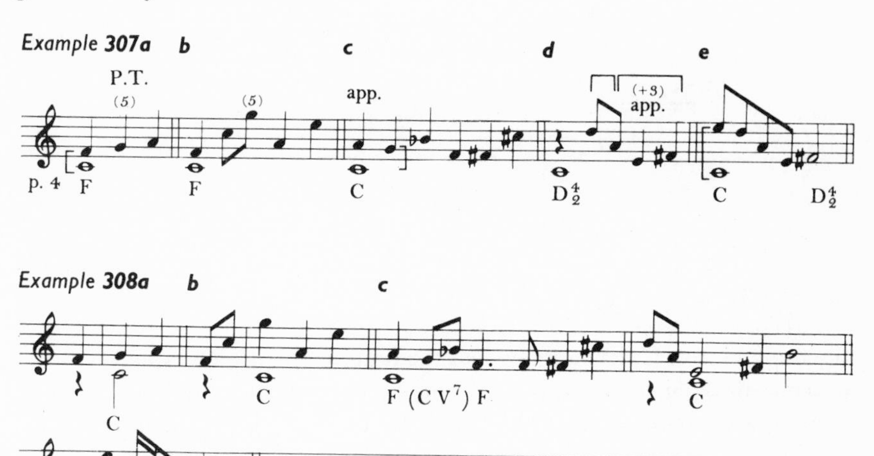

b] Harmonic rhythm, that is, the movement of chords, affects root determination in the same manner as above. The appearance of complete chords on an unessential rhythmic occurrence may conjure a non-harmonic response, because rhythmically, the ear is not ready to receive harmonic associations. *Example* **309a** sets up an energetic duple beat which contains a harmonic stability of C throughout. Due to the melodic formation of a B^7 chord, harmonic pulse of two chords per bar is recognized. Directional tones influence this also, as the bass C responds to the melody contour of the tone B, and vice versa. At the end of the measure, an enharmonic A♭ minor chord is seen, but not heard. The tones are placed rhythmically so as to connect to the tonic members of C on the strong beat.

c] Similar to the rhythmic demands of movement of harmony, the duration of a root is equally affected by rhythm. Once a pitch is established as a root, the ear connects as many companion tones to this central root as is possible. A new root may take over only when the rhythmic pulsations suggest a change, and the new association of chord tones overrules the former root. The chromatic scale, by its nature, a scale which connects diatonic tones, is used in *example* **309b** to illustrate its non-harmonic activity, and to show its constant support of

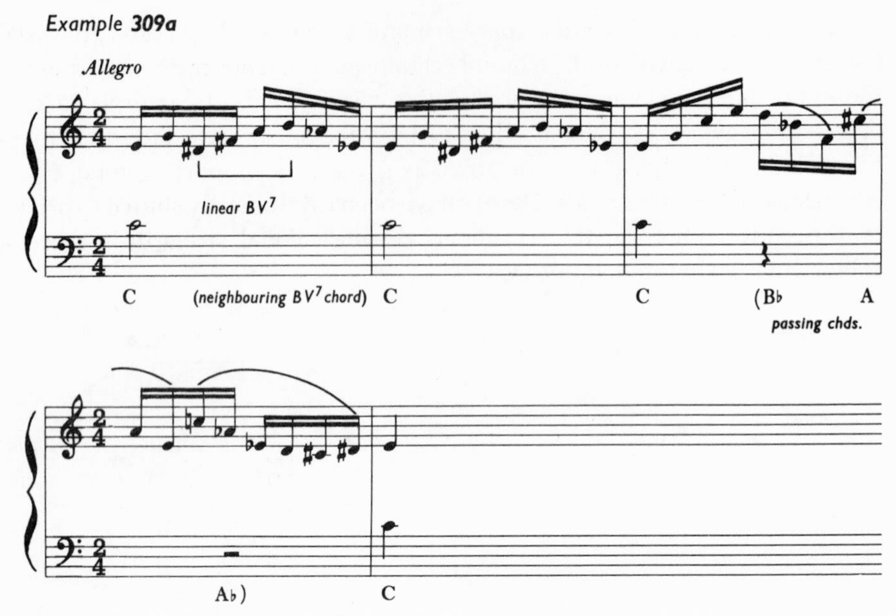

the tonic tone of C. Remember that the tempo moves along quickly, so that the passing dissonances do not have a chance to associate with other chord implications. This is even true of the linear B^7 outline; it does not get a chance in *example* **309b** to be recognized (except by an analysis of the melody alone), because the chromatic scale keeps reaffirming the C root. For example, the second eighth beat of the first measure surely looks like a B major triad (and, if played at a snail's pace, it must be heard as B major also). In tempo, the ear has just recognized C and is unwilling to abandon it so immediately. Therefore, when the chromatic B♭ is heard on the next eighth beat, a C^4_2 connotation is felt, regardless of the vertical dissonances formed by the contrary melody. The repetition of the motive in the second measure affirms the C root by containing the third and fifth, while the chromatic bass, A♭, is non-harmonic and moves directly to the powerful fifth, G, of the C tonality. Notice how this strength is entirely linear and unless you play or hear the phrase continuously, these harmonic relationships cannot be comprehended. In the third measure, C major is recognized in the treble, and therefore, the bass contains the third and the major seventh (B) of the C major chord, notwithstanding the linear fifth. The first harmonic change occurs emphatically with a new convergence of chord tones both in the melody and in the bass, as B♭ clears the air of chromatics. From this point until the return of C, the movement of melodic pitches takes over, rather than the movement of chords. The B♭ lasts as long as it can, but the influencing tone that brings about the return of C major is B♮, the leading-tone, in the fourth measure. It is interesting to realize that if the music stopped prior to the fourth eighth beat of this cadential measure, all of the tones would find their associations with B♭. It is the movement of the leading-tone to C that finally removes the strength of B♭. To illustrate this retention of sound, *example 309c* repeats this identical B♭ structure, and leads the chord to E♭. The sound of B♮ now functions as a minor ninth throughout the passage. *Examples 309b* and *c* can be combined into a parallel period form by repeating the first two bars of *example 309b* and then considering *example 309c* as a second ending. This fluent playing will clearly permit the hearing of only the two chords per phrase, and will enable the melodic trimming to be recognized as directional influences.

Example **309b**

Range

a] All intervals which have a closer placement to the bass or lowest tone, have a greater harmonic contribution than do intervals rising above them. Even the perfect fifth, if spread by octave expansion, may relinquish its strength to the perfect fourth or major third, whose lower location would enforce a different root. *Example 310a* illustrates the vertical perfect fourth, and a linear major third, both shaping the F chord, above which the high G adds the ninth. It does not sound like a resolution because the lower tones command the tonal setting. Compared with *example 310b*, the G, now in the same register as the tones forming the F chord, is the tone of resolution and creates a C root.

Example 311a illustrates linear fifths and one vertical fifth. The moment the vertical fifth is struck, the clarity of the C root is certified. By contrast, if the G is located in the higher octave, the linear influence of the perfect fourth, D to G, would suggest a G over C pedal connotation. See *example 311b*.

Range also affects the general statement that the vertical interval which contains a harmonic association will contribute to the tonal hearing more so than linear intervals. The linear writing generally will be in a higher register than that which denotes harmony. *Example 311c* shows the strength of the B♭, which is the chief tone that establishes the dominant harmony. The linear perfect fifth, and the linear major thirds are swallowed into the C V^{13} the moment it is heard via the B♭.

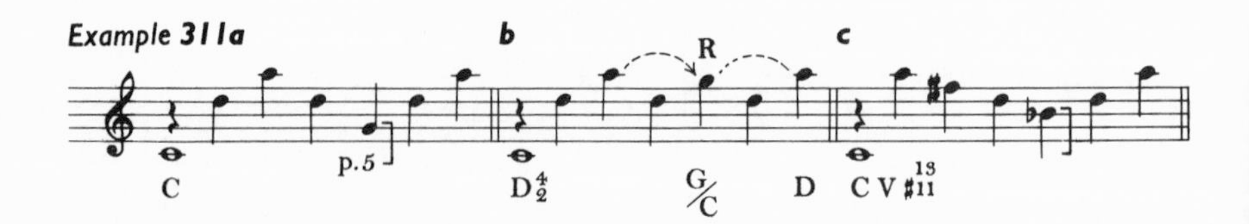

b] Amongst linear intervals, those occurring in the bass line (which produce a tonal association), have greater root strength than the linear intervals of the upper parts. This is illustrated in *example 312a*, in which the bass intervals, fifths and fourths produce the root tones, while the fifths and fourths of the melody line contribute additional chord tones and non-harmonic tones. The first measure root is F, not D minor. The bass linear perfect fifth, even when starting on the chord tone of the fifth instead of the root, establishes the tonal association because it is the lower of the two possible roots. The third measure uses the roots in reverse; D minor is the root, again resulting from a fifth to root chord member motion, while the linear outline of F only adds to the D minor seventh quality. The second measure contains the perfect fourth interval in the bass part, of which the root is the higher tone, B♭. The quality is a major seventh sound. Both the melody E of this measure, and the D within the first measure are freely chosen melodic tones, having more significance as melodic directional tones, than as contributing chord members. (This is explained more fully in the paragraph immediately following.) In the fourth measure, the root this time is derived from the minor sixth interval, in which the root is the upper tone, G. A more elaborate variation on this phrase is illustrated in *example 312b*. The upper line contains fewer supporting chord members, but with all of this free chromatic writing, the bass movement holds to the same roots as in the previous setting.

Melodic associations

Since the melody does not affect the root recognition as much as does the bass line, it logically follows that the melody tones may be largely non-harmonic. This freedom of melodic choice extends to all of the chromatic tones, and with such an unlimited scope, the relationship of all of the melody tones to the root become less significant. If the root is recognized, it matters little whether the melody, in a complex motive, includes the augmented eleventh or the augmented ninth. Chances are that the sound of the tones would be gone before the ear had a chance to clearly evaluate such upper chromatic extensions, and secondly, their normal resolutions which would help identify them, might not be forthcoming. Modern contrapuntal writing permits all intervallic leaps and requires no resolutions for any tones other than those which the composer hears and selects. Consequently, the decision as to which melody tone is harmonic and which is not, rests largely on the recognition of the tones which strengthen the root. The identification of a root, third, fifth, and the dominant seventh quality can be detected because they support the single root. The remaining tones are too far removed from the root to sound convincing as upper partials in a contrapuntal setting. Remember that a two-part invention is not apt to produce a clear dominant thirteenth, with all of the chord tones neatly organized!

a] Melodic motives may suggest scale associations. The D♭ major scale in *example 313* discloses the presence of the D♭ root, while the bass conforms to a diatonic practice of leaving the non-harmonic tones by step and thus identifying the chord tones, as they are left by skip. On the last quarter beat, the vertical perfect fifth may suggest a brief A♭ root, which is, of course, the dominant relationship to D♭. Whether it is recognized or not would depend on tempo and resolution of the last eighth note F. If F is left by skip, a D♭ chord will prevail; if left stepwise, both root recognitions are possible.

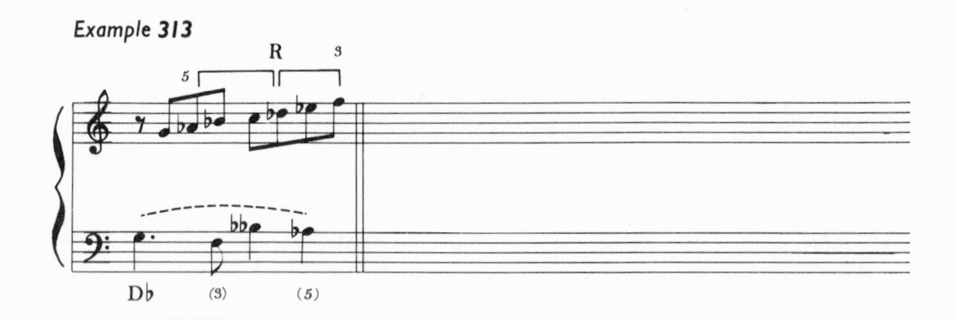

b] Tones preceded by directional leading-tones gain more melodic emphasis than others and may contribute toward a root recognition. In *example 314a*, the vertical intervals are ambiguous and could fit an A minor or C major root. By adding an appropriate directional leading-tone, the melodic association is clarified and the root is strengthened. The leading-tone, G♯, of *example 314b* pinpoints the passage into an A minor scale association while in

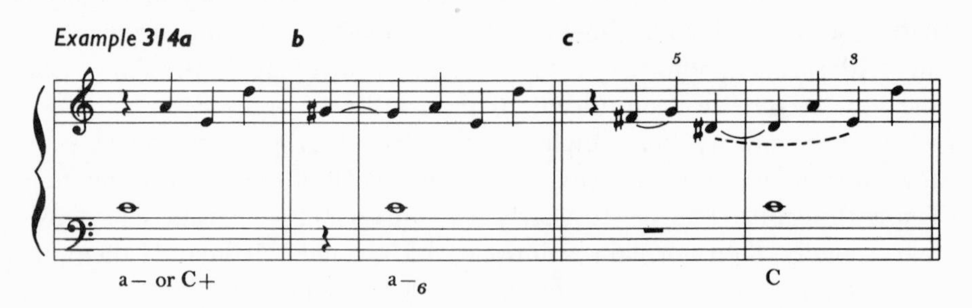

example 314c, the directional tone, F♯ emphasizes G, and D♯ leads to E, strengthening the vertical C major third.

c] The root of a major triad or a dominant quality grouping of tones will sound more clearly than the root of a minor triad which may appear to be present in the same passage. This is based on the overtone principle in which the lower partials produce the major triad. To mention just one easy experiment that helps to prove the predominance of a major sound, play a minor third interval and without thinking of any scale association, or any chord, sing immediately a tone that would fit as another chord member. If done spontaneously, that is, without any preconceived pitch association, invariably the third sound produced will be the root of a major triad, not the perfect fifth which would place the given minor third into a minor triad frame. (This basic audibility of a major triad also explains to a large degree why some students in the early stages of ear training have a difficult time distinguishing between minor and major sixths. They may both be heard within a major triad setting, so that only precise interval distinction will separate them.)

Illustrated in *example* 315a, the A minor triad is completely outlined, but the moment the G enters, the support for the root C is immediate. Looking at this group of tones, the G appears as a neighboring tone, but due to the lower perfect fifth placement, and to the major sound winning over the minor, the group emerges in a C major setting. *Example* 315b starts with a C chord. Notice that the fifth of C is not present, but inherent within the major third or tenth. The second beat is clearly F because of the vertical major third. The third beat strikes the minor third interval and in spite of the complete E minor triad occurring within the arpeggio, the major quality is heard. It is also recognized right on the third beat and merely confirmed by the last sixteenth note. This is due to the start of the C major setting and the basic feeling that there is no need to change to the mediant unless more melodic influences for the minor triad would be evident. *Example* 315c removes the last sixteenth and does not alter the chord progression. The strength of the C in the preceding patterns carries through the third beat.

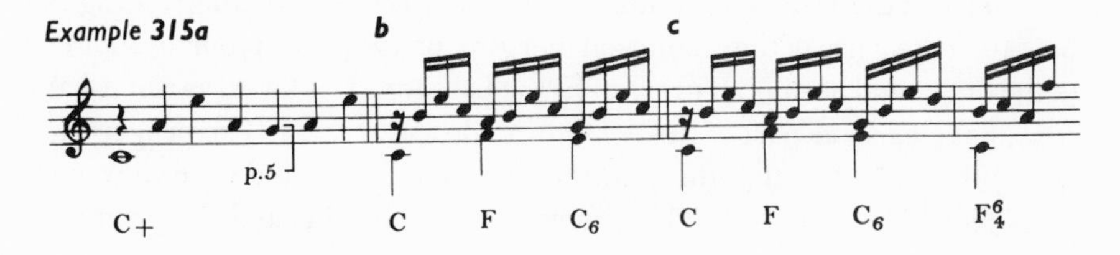

The sounds which merge into dominant qualities will be more outstanding than other root suggestions. Frequently, these sounds become clear at the end of a motive group and then bind the other pitches within the dominant cloak. The opening tones of *example* 316a may suggest B minor over C, but with the sound of the last B♭, all tones suddenly become unified into the C dominant augmented eleventh chord. The bass tone is always a factor, and the first opportunity it has to become a root or another important chord tone, it will assume that position. This is also illustrated in *example 316b*, as the C dominant chord is clarified at the end of the descending arpeggio, while in the second bar, an uncertain diminished triad finally receives a strong companion tone at the end of the ascending arpeggio, in the high A. Suppose the top A is omitted. The tones will still group together, centering on those which occupy the lower position in the arpeggio. The chord members are marked in *example 316c* indicating a root possibility of either the C chord, with the held tone being an enharmonic minor ninth, or an implied A dominant as the arpeggio still rises in this tertiary expansion. A clearer picture would be revealed upon the resolution or progression of the tones involved, especially in the movement of the starting tritone.

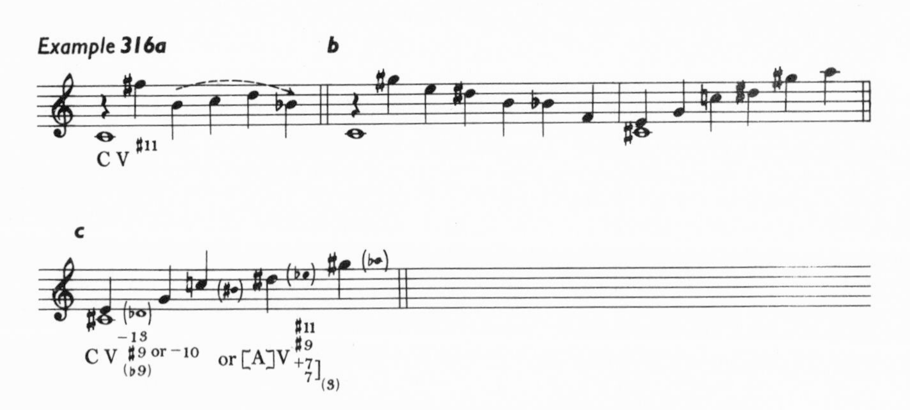

d] Root progressions which suggest movement of the cycle of fifths, regardless of the quality of the chords involved, will stress the tones which form the essential intervals of that progression. *Example 317a* includes incomplete outlines of the chords E and A minor. The melodic group of tones is entirely in the scale of A minor, starting just as a discordant group against the bass tone. Because of the resolution merging on the perfect fourth, and resulting in the linear and harmonic stress of E, the bass tone C is heard as a non-harmonic tone, but clearly as part of the A minor scale association. The progression of E to A follows. Notice that this minor third (A and C) could never be considered an F chord if F is absent. The difference between this and the prominence of major over minor lies in the dominant preparation and in the tonal association of the minor key which began the motive. Compare this with *example 317b*. The selection of a B♭ passing half note alters the scale association from A minor to F major. The vertical tritone now forms a C dominant chord which does not resolve to a complete F chord, but neither is it thwarted in any way from implying the intended movement of the dominant tones. As in *example* 317a, the progression of roots in the normal, up a perfect fourth cycle (or down a perfect fifth) is expected, and given a partial indication of such a resolution, the ear can easily imagine the missing chord members.

e] Intervals which may hamper a root association are a series of perfect fourths or a series of unresolved tritones. In a former example (*examples* 316b and c), the tritone was depicted as having the capability of participating in either of two roots. Actually, the tritone by itself cannot anticipate any tonality. The tones around it will aid in the tritone's eventual progression and its actual role. This is equally true in a harmonic structure or in a melodic passage. However, if the tritones are not given further melodic expansion, they will sound simply as a group of active intervals, without a root association. Such is the case in *example* 318a which contains three parallel tritones in the first two measures, a linear tritone in the third measure and another vertical one in the fourth measure. No root can be assumed in this exercise until the last perfect fourth is heard creating the root A. Once the direction has been recognized, the passage can be repeated, and certain directional tones will take on more meaning. In this case, the second measure contains the D and G♯ which lead toward the eventual A. Nevertheless, the impact within the phrase is chaotic because of the excess of tritones.

Unlike tritones, which demand a resolution, a series of linear perfect fourths do not contain much agitation, but neither do they contain a strong central root. As inversions of the perfect fifth, their stronger tone is the upper one. In a series, this feeling of shooting upward for the root is present with each forthcoming fourth interval. If at the peak of the fourth, the root is the highest tone, the confusion created is only temporary; but this is rarely the case because the lower tones still maintain their priority and they form some melodic association in which they contribute to a root manifestation. The fourths in *example* 318b become part of a general B♭ major setting. Because of this melodic direction, the first and third measures contain tones derived from the dominant suggestion while the second and fourth measures imply tonic formation. (Also see "Perfect Fourth Chords.")

Example 318b

The preceding factors regarding the influence of rhythm, range and melodic association or root recognition can be summarized with one basic analytical concept. Don't juggle the notes! Consider the value of the tones exactly as they progress. Which tones receive rhythmic stress? Which tones shape the contour of the melody and perhaps contain linear tonal associations? Allow the music to furnish these answers. Do not look for a root in every measure. Connect the roots that you hear and recognize that areas of transition are areas of tonal movement which are not intended to evoke root stability.

Putting this into practice, *example 319*, an excerpt from a two-voiced invention by Lukas Foss, illustrates this contrapuntal analysis. Brackets are drawn between the strongest linear intervals and between the tones forming the vertical tonal associations. Dotted lines connect directional pitches. (Only a minimum number are marked.) The letter of the root is indicated below the chord change even if the actual root tone does not appear until later in the measure. This letter name represents a single tone as a root whether the chord quality is known or unknown as in the case of incomplete combinations. A chord quality may frequently be presumed from scale associations which precede it. In such probable instances, as well as in the known chords, a capital letter denotes a major quality and the small letter, a minor quality. Dominants are marked with the symbol V, representing a quality and not necessarily the dominant scale association. Inversions in this example are not indicated. Roots marked in parenthesis indicate passing harmonies, generally occurring on rhythmically weaker pulses and resulting from passing melodic movement.

Focusing on a few measures which may require further clarification, notice that the tone which concludes the sequential development of the first motive, is the D in the third measure. This cadential D has been rhythmically emphasized by the ascending sequential group which in each case starts with a pair of sixteenths. The directional tones accompany this rise of pitch, shaping the D major tonality as the high F♯ drops a major third to the D. At this point, a new bridging motive starts, and forms a linear E♭ root. The perfect fifth that you see between the D and the following sixteenth G cannot be given any root significance because both tones have separate motivic functions. The D ends a thought and the G begins a new one.

The increased chromatic material in the third measure later corresponds with the sixth measure. In both cases, the added harmonic movement is bringing the invention subject to a close. In measure four, an elision is created as the bass voice enters simultaneously with the upper part's cadence. Its imitation is exact only for part of the first motive. Reaching the sixth measure, the bass line adheres only to the increased harmonic activity, which then slackens in the seventh measure and comes to a complete cadence on D. The sixth measure also supplies directional tones for the cadence as well as a more dissonant combination of pitches. For example, the whole-tone scale which starts in the lower voice from C♯, moves through a G♮ to an A, causing tonal conflicts with both the melody's G♯ and the dotted eighth B♭. Because of this cancellation of C♯ sound, the passing roots of B♭ and A are worth noting. Of the two, B♭ is least essential, functioning only as an appoggiatura to A. Both are very brief but they do provide the connection between C♯ and the G dominant thirteenth which starts on the second pulse of the sixth bar.

In recognizing this G dominant chord, it is important to note the linear tritone of the lower line and its resolution. Upon hearing C minor, one recognizes that the tones of the dominant have moved to it without any abnormal pitch treatment. The conflict between the upper B♭ and the lower B♮ is first recognized in melodic terms as a reiteration of the previous appoggiatura B♭ leading toward the final sixteenth, the tone of the ninth, A. Neither is the B♭ improper harmonically, as it refers to the usage of the minor third placed above the major third or dominant seventh chord. (This may be marked as a minor tenth, – 10.) The realization that all tones have merged together in the support of one root, eliminates any further guesswork involving the vertical perfect fourth, present within the counterpoint.

The dominant cycle, starting in measure nine, illustrates the ease of hearing this progression. After the complete B dominant seventh is heard, all that is necessary to fulfill the expected resolution is the root. In this case, the seventh appears below it. Notwithstanding the conflicting non-harmonic E♭, all tones resolve and continue the dominant movement sequentially.

The *Fughetta, example 320,* by Vittorio Giannini provides opportunity to study linear movement of perfect fourths. Starting without any preconceived tonality, the ascending fourths in the first measure could become part of several different tonal or root associations. Each rising fourth gives a temporary tonal stress to its upper tone so that in rapid succession, the roots of F, B♭ and E♭ are suggested. In addition, the sound of the first tone, C, doesn't vanish, but links itself particularly to the highest and most prominent tone of the series, the E♭, producing a possible C minor harmonic outline. Without looking ahead to see the future direction of these tones, there is no positive root that the series of perfect fourths conjures. In this *Fughetta,* the tonality of F minor becomes apparent during the first and future phrases, permitting the understanding of a dominant minor outline of pitches for this opening motive. Nevertheless, the analysis of fourth chords, either harmonic, or as contained within a linear design, may be simply marked "p 4" denoting their ambiguous root quality.

The second measure contains both linear perfect fifths and perfect fourths. The rhythmic stress and the lower location of the tones involving the perfect fourth produce the roots of A♭ followed by B♭ minor, diatonically, mediant to subdominant of the F minor tonality. The subject's answer on the perfect fifth imitation enters in the third measure against a held dominant tone of C. Starting with the vertical perfect fifth, there is no question of the dominant root of C in this case. The sound of F within the series of fourths can be thought of as the eleventh substituting for the third. Notice that as a directional tone it leads to the E♭ in the next measure.

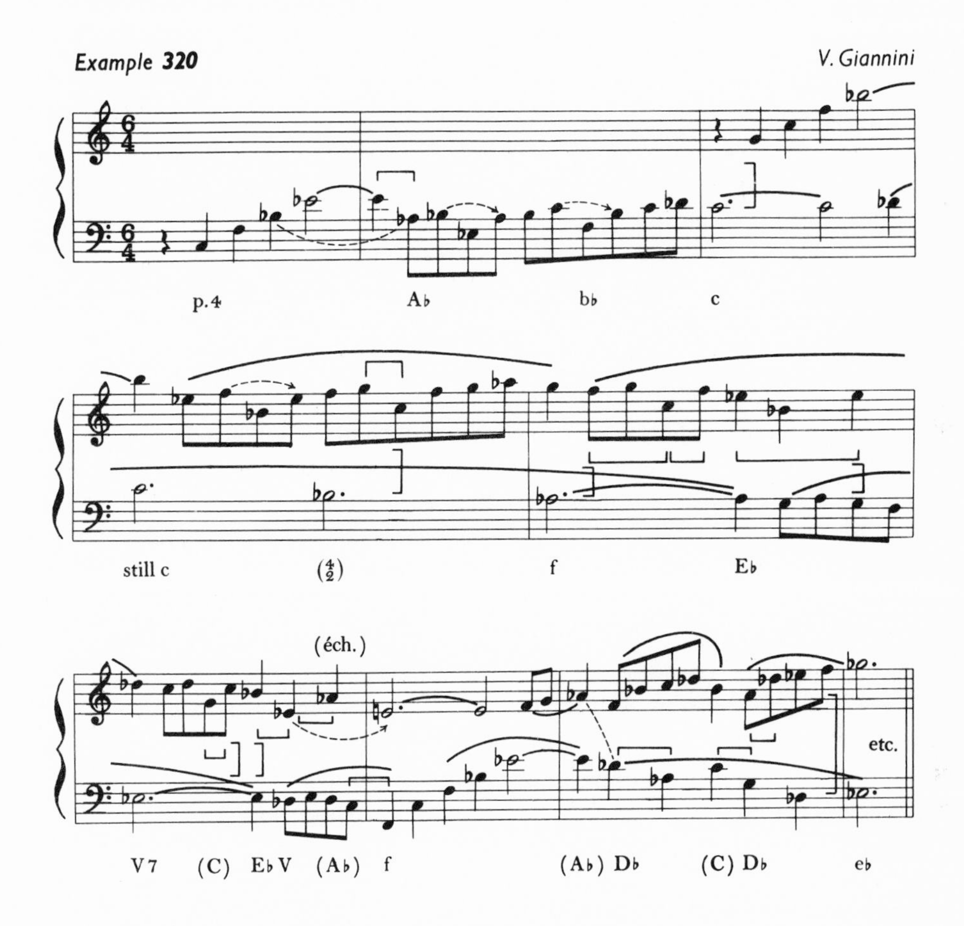

The fourth measure illustrates the ear's retention of a root sound. The bass movement from C to B♭ is the movement of a root to its seventh, and needs only the slightest melodic support to verify it. Compare the upper line in measure four to its original in the second measure. The intervals are identical but the analysis must stem from the influence of the lower part. The first eighth-note group emerges as a C minor seventh chord and the second group is still C minor against the seventh of the chord in the bass; this, in spite of the vertical perfect fifth announced strongly on the beat, and in spite of the same pattern of eighth notes which now group themselves in support of the C root. The linear perfect fifth helps the established root; the root C is the lowest tone of the upper group; but most important, the dominant to tonic resolution is present as the bass seventh resolves to the F minor chord, I_6, in the fifth measure.

The approach to the cadence of this phrase is especially interesting. The sixth measure contains an E♭ dominant seventh, which at the very end of the measure resolves briefly to A♭. However, the function of this A♭ is to prepare the cadence. More important than an A♭ harmony, is the movement of pitch, both in the upper as well as the lower part. The linear fifth, C down to F functions as a dominant to tonic tonal suggestion. The melody A♭ anticipates the F minor cadence in the manner of an échapée. A very engaging chromatic move now takes place as the major seventh is struck against the tonic root of F. This causes a discordant quality, together with the feeling of resolution that accompanies the cadence. It is especially meaningful because of the fresh sound that the E♮ brings. As a tone, it did not appear at all up to this point—all the dominants were either incomplete or minor—so that its timing is well chosen, and well prepared by the directional tone of E♭. Retained against the reappearance of the first motive, the leading-tone E then slides up to F itself, to combine with an episodic phrase.

In measure eight the fourths are developed in the lower voice, including a tritone fourth at the end of the measure. There are passing contrapuntal suggestions marked in parenthesis, but D♭ major is the over-all root. It is possible to hear a B♭ minor seventh chord on the second and third quarter beats, but the major quality predominates through the bass motion and the bass A♭ does not sound active enough to represent a seventh. The tritone motion from G to D♭ on the fifth and sixth quarter beats provides the intervallic motion which progresses to the next measure. The overlapping of root ideas is a normal contrapuntal function. While the bass line suggests the C root in the movements from C to G, the melody at this point skips the perfect fourth A♭ to D♭, returning to the prior D♭ harmony. Both parts form the vertical major third, which then summarizes the D♭ root for that measure.

Enharmonic notation may at times be misleading as the eye does not immediately focus on the interval that is sounding. This is true in *example 321a* starting from the fourth measure, which has also been quoted with reference to the double inflections. Hindemith chose to prompt the visual response of the canonic imitation, rather than the direct recognition of the harmonic roots. If the lower voice changed its first tone of the imitative pattern from the G♭ to an F♯ in measure four, and substituted G♯ in place of A♭ in the sixth measure, the roots of D moving to E would be clear. *Example 321b* illustrates these enharmonic changes. The crisscrossing of directional tones is also involved in this illustration. From the highest melody tone, G (measure four), the imitation takes over a minor ninth below, first through a clashing vertical dissonance, then settling on a harmonic minor sixth which promotes the D root. The lower motive concludes on D itself, forming a vertical octave which, through the retention of sound (even through the following quarter beat rests), combines with the melody A in continuing the root of D. By sequence, the soprano A again changes register in its directional move, as the lower voice starts on the enharmonic G♯, the third of E.

The singular melody line with which this excerpt begins, is included here chiefly as a further illustration of root retention and the selection of directional

pitches. It happens to be the main theme of this second movement of Hindemith's *Second Piano Sonata,* and in this excerpt, it returns as part of the ABA form. (A comparison with the opening material would be of interest, as it contains subtle differences in pitch selection.) The theme starts with a strong tonality of E. This solidarity withstands all of the chromatic ascending material and connects to the new sound of G♮ at the peak of the line. The ear does not actually hold the sound of E as a sustaining pedal note, because the ensuing chromatics prevent such a complete suspension, but neither is it dislodged or cancelled by another root during the melodic movement. Areas which contain unstable harmonic motion are frequent in Modern writing just as areas of embellishing diminished and dominant sevenths are frequent in the Classical period. Due to the added chromatic mixture of tones, the Modern sound may not emerge with root identifications, unlike the Classical period's harmonic blending of chord members. Where there is no clear replacement of a former root, the last tonal stronghold acts as an anchor until lifted. In this example, the progression from E major to the pitch of G♮ corresponds to a harmonic movement of the tonic to its mediant. Notice that G arrives as a fresh tone, not anticipated within the preceding run. This is part of the well-designed selection of pitches. The directional pitches which descend from the melody's peak are equally well chosen. The highest tones form a perfect fourth directional outline, in which the tones D and A, in measures five and six, in addition to the high G, do not occur at all in the preceding material. This results in harmonic motion, which in the most reduced form, is illustrated in *example* **321b**.

Tritones help to create unstable harmonic areas. Sometimes they merge with root tones adding their restless quality, but frequently they agitate a melodic line whose harmony is formed by the tritone itself. This is illustrated in *example* **322**, an excerpt from Stravinsky's *Sonate pour Piano* written in 1924. (Review *example* **300a** from the chapter on directional tones, as this excerpt is the development of the theme quoted in the former chapter.) Almost every measure contains a tritone, either in a linear usage or as a vertical result of the counterpoint. Being imitative, the motives overlap, resulting in a greater linear influence on harmony than in clearly defined vertical associations. The tritone contained in the opening motive sets forth an active pace and permits the starting root of A minor only a brief moment with which to begin the phrase. Do not anticipate the harmony of the diminished triad, especially since the phrase has just begun, and follows a previous A minor cadence. The tone of E♭ enters on the second pulse and at that moment fulfills the diminished quality. The bass imitation continues the tritone motion from the root, B. Notice how the melody tone of E♭ doubles as a D♯ in further establishing the B root even when it continues as a diminished triad. The precise moment when B blends into D minor is not easy to determine because of the rhythmic overlapping of motives. The first beat of the second measure concludes the bass motive and continues the treble response which also started from B. Therefore, the vertical D minor cannot, at that moment, be separated from the preceding root, especially when the sounds of D minor can be incorporated into the B chord very easily. The imitation suggests that the third eighth note, D (of the upper part), starts D minor, and is answered two octaves below by a strong announcement of the D root, this time in the major quality. Again, motivicly moving into the first beat, the figure represents C as the seventh, fixing a dominant quality for the first half of this third measure. The tritone motion is twofold, D♯ to A in the melody (the D♯ is an enharmonic minor ninth) and vertically, F♯ against C.

The quality of D minor returns on the second half of this measure. The ear retains the root D and does not change to an F chord as might seem possible when scanning the bass part.

The fourth measure illustrates tonal movement which is not intended to fit a triadic vertical organization. Directional tones take over and provide the melodic understanding of this passage. The bass C♯ is heard as a leading-tone, arising from the D root. At the same moment, the E♭ is a directional tone connecting the previous F of the right hand's compound melody to the mutually stressed tone of D. Further dissonance is added as the uppermost tones of C conflict with the leading-tone C♯. The selection of the upper C♮ serves to continue the sequential pattern from the preceeding D minor arpeggio and finally, to anticipate the forthcoming root of C. Looking at the fourth measure, an analysis of a bitonal nature is possible, namely C minor over the leading-tone of

D minor. However, the ear does not separate the bass C♯ from the first two tones of the arpeggio. The tritone (C♯ and the middle tone, G), connects the active members of both the upper and lower parts. Together, the tones converge on D and their analysis need show only this directional movement. Do not force the tones to form chords where the vertical stability of a central root is not intended. The measure in question could be construed as an enharmonic E♭$^{4}_{2}$ with a non-harmonic upper C♮—surely not a thirteenth! But this harmonic conclusion has no meaning whatsoever in terms of tonal movement that here exists in D minor, and is progressing to the next root of C. A more accurate harmonic conclusion recognizes the implied A dominant root from which the tritone is derived. The E♭ may be considered a lowered fifth. There is no question that this derivation supports the tonal movement as it is used. But there is no need to make a chord out of the fragmentary pieces of an implied dominant, when the contrapuntal motion does not demand a definitive chordal acknowledgement.

The fifth measure is approached by the motivic group in the bass, which contains the tritone, and leading-tone to C. The upper line, having already suggested the C tonality, descends chromatically, supporting the C by scale association rather than by vertical means. The lowering of B to B♭ suggests a dominant quality which, however, is not planned to progress in a dominant role. The brief D major chord in the latter half of the sixth measure is important in that its motion strengthens the arrival of G in bar seven, which begins the cadential drive.

Harmonically, the seventh measure can be likened to the first measure, in that the letter name root arrives first and is then followed by a diminished quality. The motive this time starts on the beat, causing the tritone to appear rapidly on the second eighth note. Nevertheless, the dominant to tonic motion provided by D to G minor secures the root G. Functioning as a pedal tone, the compound melody above retains the motivic diminished triad and descends sequentially with a shifting rhythmic stress. Once again, the chords formed by the diminished triad are not intended to be analyzed vertically. They are there to activate the pitch, and direct the tones to their culmination in the ninth measure. The root movement involves only the bass tone G, which can be thought of as a subdominant pedal, moving through a leading-tone, G♯ (implied E) to the A V^9, the expanded focal point of the entire phrase. Notice the anticipation of the pitch of A in the compound melody in measures seven and eight. They provide an excellent increase of tension especially when used against the G♯ leading-tone. It will be recalled that this dissonant structure contains the A as a natural eleventh heard conflicting against, not one, but two major thirds as part of the implied E dominant chord. The dissonance abates in the fruition of the passage. At last, the counterpoint is completely enveloped by the harmonic structure, and in this way, provides the contrasting satisfaction that is achieved on the A dominant minor ninth chord.

No rules

In Modern contrapuntal writing, all twelve tones are at the composer's disposal and able to be arranged in any manner he wishes. Since rules come about after the fact, and are only manifestations of what has been done, the writing today has not yet been scrutinized with a predetermination for discovering the "dos" and "don'ts" of Modern counterpoint. It might be possible to detect certain practices within a particular composer's style, but in an age in which creativity is being expressed in so many individual ways, any specific presentation of musical doctrines would be challenged.

The writing of Modern counterpoint is best approached by a comparison with former practices. The basic principles of good writing have not changed. Each part requires an undulating melodic contour; a rhythmic diversity between the voices aids in their distinction; a harmonic selection of interval should be varied, changing between consonance and dissonance. The difference in the contrapuntal rules is only applicable to the intervals themselves. Today, all intervals may be used, on any beat, and approached or left in any manner the composer selects. Some sounds are more harsh than others, and the well written phrase contains a proper degree of dissonance and consonance proportioned to the demands of the specific areas of the phrase and of the composition. An understanding of which contrapuntal techniques are more jarring than others, can be helpful in the handling of the new set of available intervals. The explanation and illustrations which follow will show these Modern privileges, separating the most common practices from those occurring less frequently.

1] Dissonant intervals, formerly limited to certain melodic uses, may now be used without any rhythmic, melodic, or harmonic restrictions. These include all seconds, sevenths, ninths, the tritone, and chromatically augmented or diminished intervals. For practical reasons, these will be termed "dissonant," as opposed to the "consonant" intervals of the perfect fifth, fourth and octave, and the major and minor thirds and sixths. (For a further reference to dissonance and consonance, read the chapter on the control of dissonance.)

2] All dissonant intervals are most frequently approached by opposite or oblique motion. See *example 323* and *example 324*.

Example 323

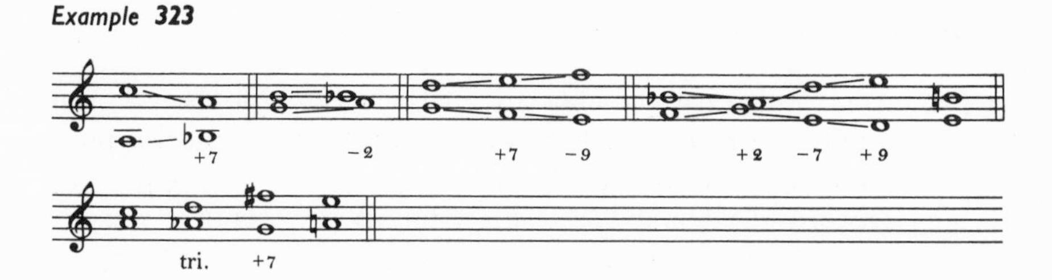

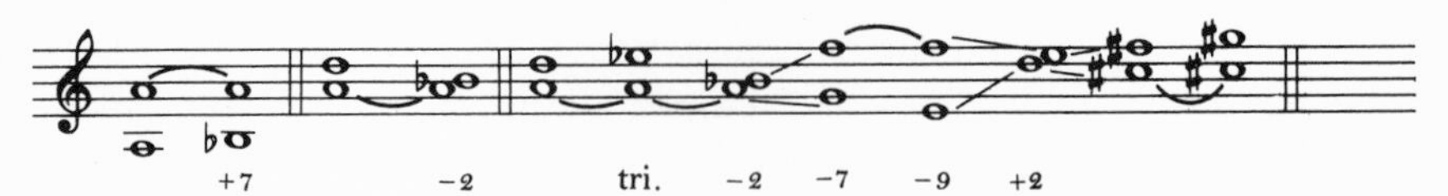

3] Many dissonant intervals are also left by opposite or oblique motion (*examples 325a, b*), but may move in the same direction especially if a] they are harmonically allied to each other (*example 325c*); b] one voice moves by step (*example 325d*); c] the voices move as direct parallels. See *examples 325a* through e.

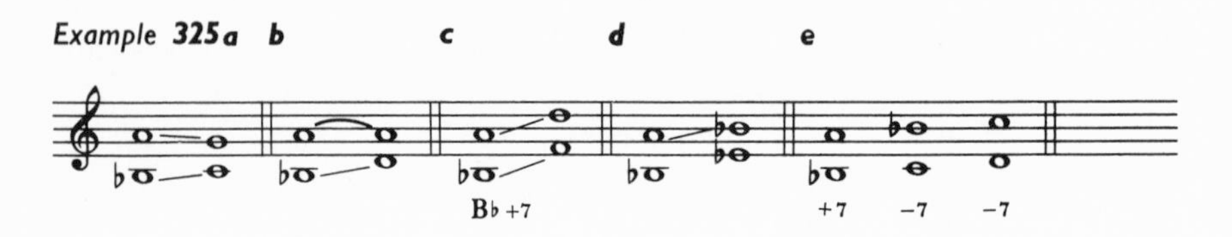

4] Either the approach or the movement away from a dissonant interval contains a stepwise progression or a common tone, generally. Compare this usage within *example 326*.

Example 326

5] Parallel motion into a discordant interval may or may not be desirable, depending on specific intervals and usage in the phrase.

a] One voice may move stepwise, if a tonal combination unites the interval. See *examples 327a* and *b*.

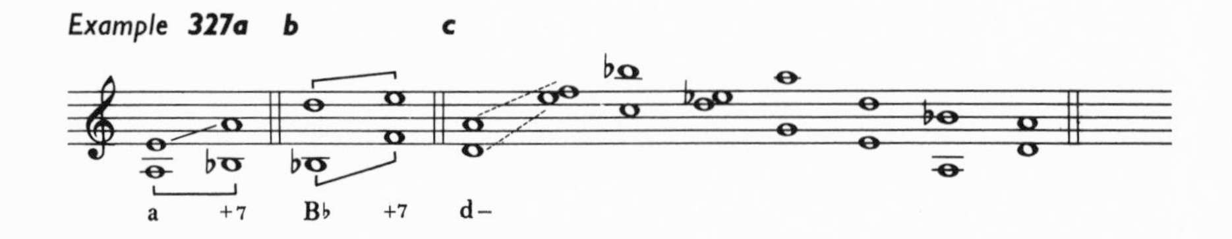

b] Wide range may be idiomatic, particularly with the use of instruments, permitting greater tonal associations within the parallel approach to dissonant intervals. See *example 327c*.

c] Discordant intervals, particularly the major seventh or minor ninth may be extremely harsh if preceded by an octave, or perfect fifth and approached by parallel motion. The change from the pure consonances to the radical dissonances may sound too abrupt. The tension is generally gradated with mildly dissonant intervals. Compare *examples* **328a** and **b** with *examples* **328c**, **d**, and **e**.

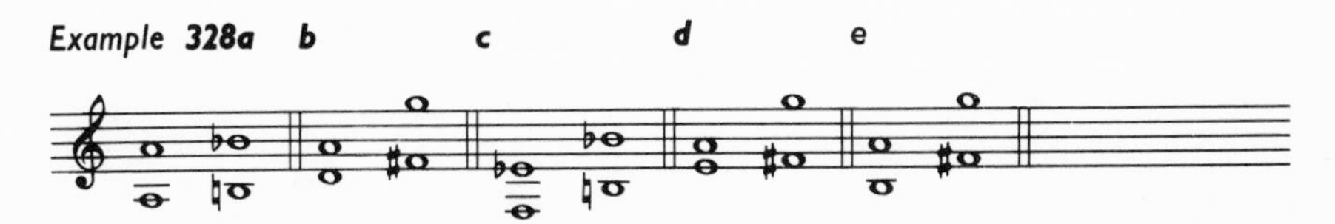

d] Where the phrase demands an intense dissonance, these practices may be used. *Example* **329a** places the intervals depicted in *example* **328a** at the end of an insistent crescendo, thereby utilizing the harsh effect deliberately, for emphasis. *Example* **329b** adds a rhythmical figure to the perfect fifth of *example* **328b** which lessens its purity as a consonance. Both examples contain an increased level of dissonance which could not be presumed when the intervals are stripped of the musical thought.

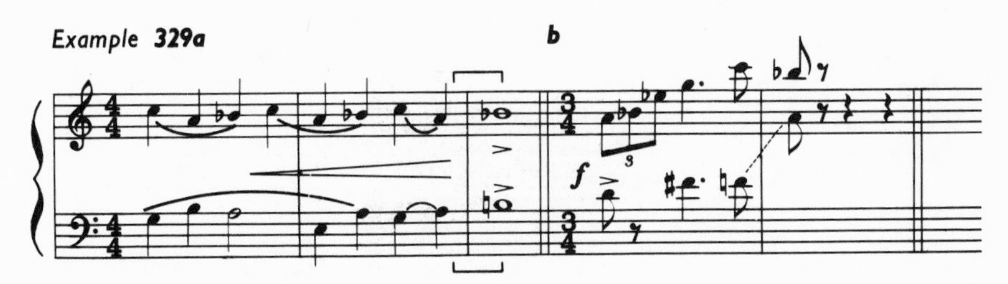

6] Double inflections, approached by too consonant a selection of intervals are also generally ineffectual. *Example* **330a** would not start a phrase, but *example* **330b** places it appropriately at the end of a phrase, where its discordant quality is beneficial.

7] Awkward switching between a recognized major tonality and its parallel minor, or vice versa, within a phrase, does not contribute to a smooth blending of parts. *Example 331a* starts with an obvious G major tonality. Before the measure is over, the quality shifts three times. *Example 331b* coordinates the major and minor shifting into a rhythmic pattern, designed for a lighthearted piece in a more homophonic character.

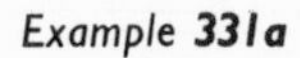
Example 331a

Example 331b

8] Parallel motion may be applied to all intervals, and is particularly effective if used for emphasis and contrast in a composition.

a] *Example 332* is imitative via contrary motion, but not identical in interval distance. The mixture of parallel major and minor thirds in the sixth measure provides both a rhythmic and melodic contrast for the phrase.

Example 332

b] Parallel fifths, fourths and sevenths, particularly if used on weak beats, may be thought of as substitutes for the Classical use of parallel thirds and sixths. Compare *examples 333a* and *b*.

c] Due to the privilege of leaping with wider intervals, a compound melody may appear to involve the voices entirely in the same direction, when actually it is unfolding a larger contour of contrary motion. See *example 334*.

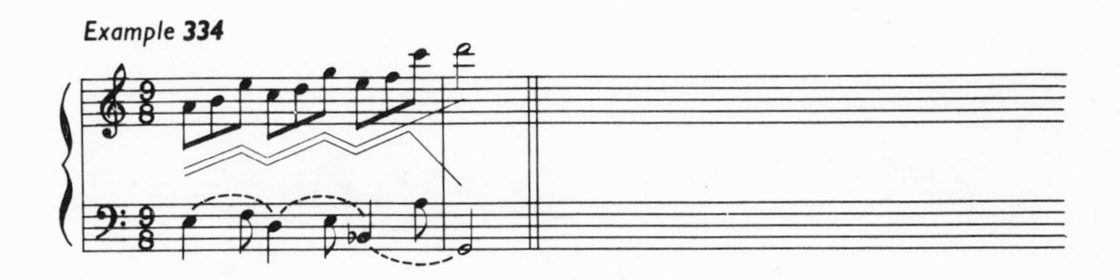

In brief, the success of good contrapuntal writing is contained in the adherence to the stylistic demands set up by the initial ideas of the composition. To begin with a traditional flavor and burst into contemporary uses is inconsistent and illogical. By the same reasoning, a composition beginning with disjunct major sevenths, would sound uncomfortable if its middle episode was handled traditionally with thirds and sixths. An excess of any one contrapuntal mannerism is apt to erase other musical qualities. A happy balance is achieved when all of the rhythmic, melodic and harmonic forces combine for a continuous blend of diversified techniques.

EXERCISES

A *Analysis*

1] Mark all of the discordant intervals (seconds, sevenths and tritones) and observe the opposite, oblique or parallel motion that precedes and follows the dissonant interval. Where is a dissonant interval used to the greatest advantage?

Example 335 *Prelude No. 4, Op. 34. Shostakovich*

Moderato

2a] Mark the root tones of *Example* **336** by hearing the strongest interval, whether present horizontally as a linear root or vertically in a harmonic interval association. Bracket the intervals involved. Use letter name root indications. (If desired, as a second step, mark the chords more fully taking into account all chord members and root relationships.)
b] Mark the important directional tones either with dotted lines or by copying separately only the tones that directly influence the pitch movement.
c] Observe the contrapuntal techniques that affect the principal motive.

Example 336 *Lukas Foss*

Andante

3a] *Example 337* illustrates the mellow blend that can be achieved by a fluctuation of harmonic and melodic influences. Compare the arpeggio root suggestions with the upper linear intervals. Mark both and listen to their changing associations.
b] In the second, cadential excerpt, observe the selection of bass tones and their directional progression to the final chord.
c] Compare the consonant and dissonant qualities, produced by the inner motive. Analyze all harmonies.

Example 337a *Sonata for Harp. Nicolas Flagello*

Example **337b**

4] Review the melody, *Example* **225**, harmonized in the twelve-tone scale chapter. Mark directional tones, and linear and harmonic roots.

B Following the rhythmic models of strict counterpoint, use the free intervals of dissonant counterpoint to complete the exercises of *Example* **338**. Some given interval indications are provided so that by practice, moving in and out of dissonant intervals can be easily accomplished.

a] The groups in *Example* **338a** are to be given a note against note rhythmic motion.

b] Use two notes of your melody to one of the given line in *Example* **338b**.

c] In *Example* **338c**, use three notes or four notes against one, selecting the dissonances at will.

d] Analogous to the older "florid species," *Example* **338d** may use a free division of rhythm including suspensions and eighth note groups. Unlike the older style, the Modern counterpoint does not preserve the intervallic restrictions. Continue each example marking all intervals, seeking a variety of consonant and dissonant sounds together with a good directional pitch contour.

Example **338a**

Note against note:

1.

2.

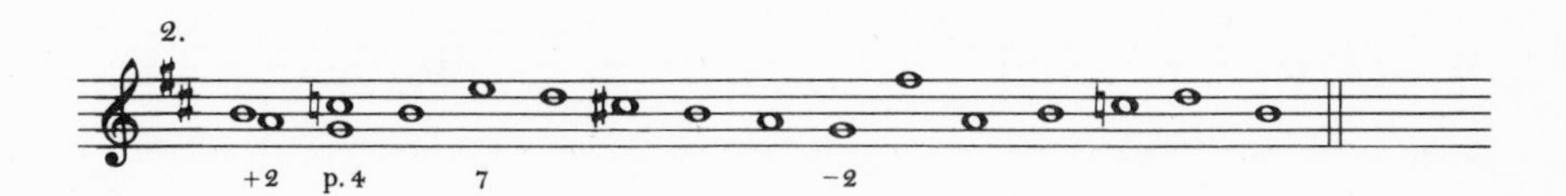

3.

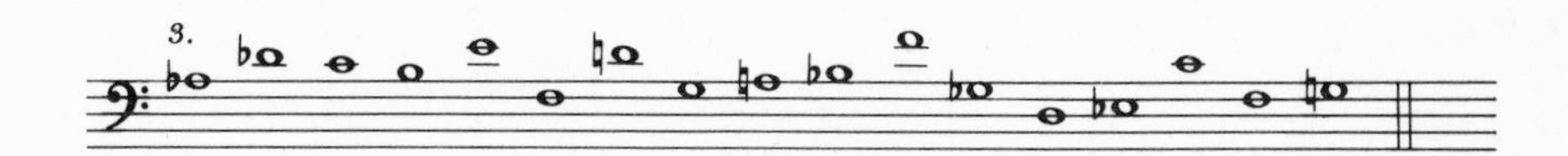

Example **338b**

Two notes against one:

1.

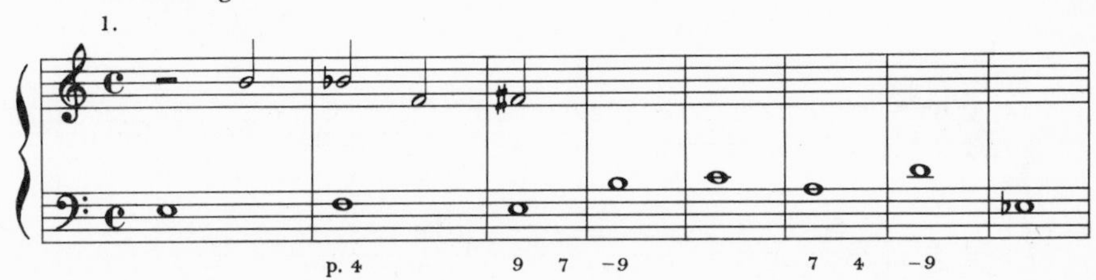

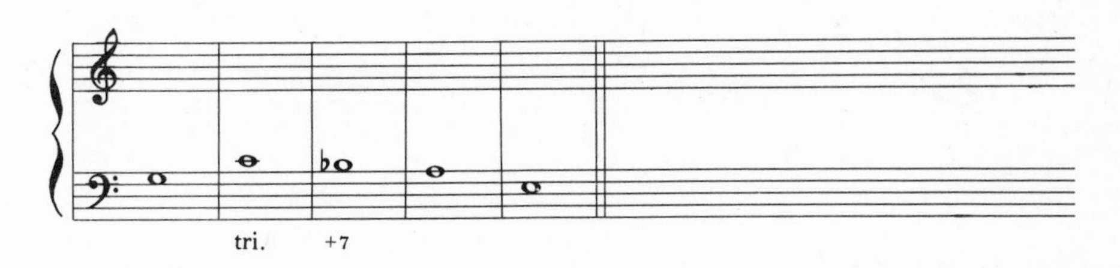

2.

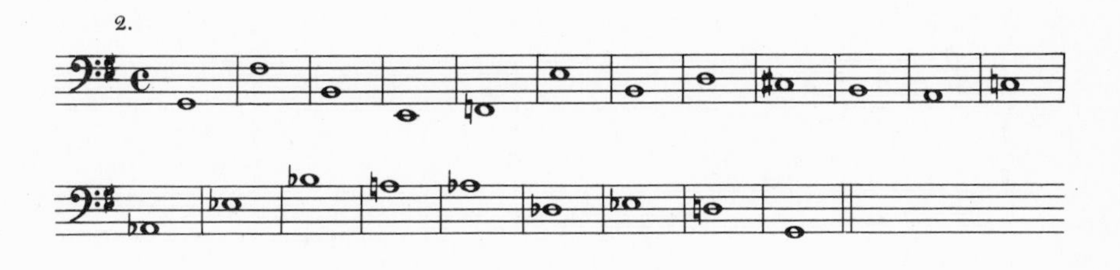

3.

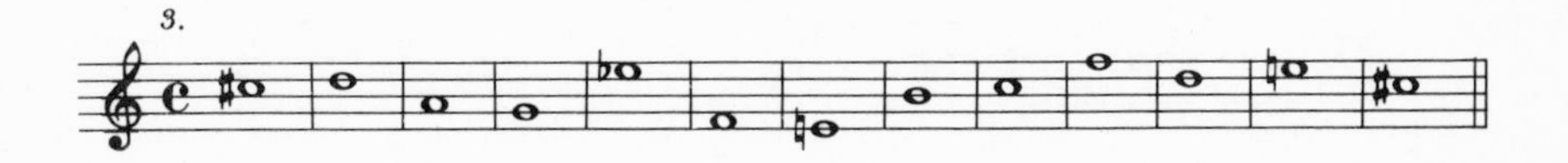

Example ***338c***

Four notes (or three in $\frac{3}{2}$) against one:

1.

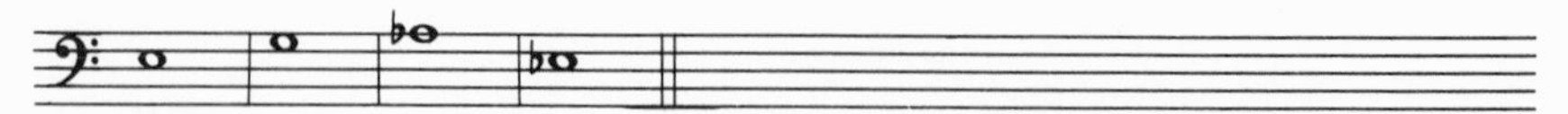

2.

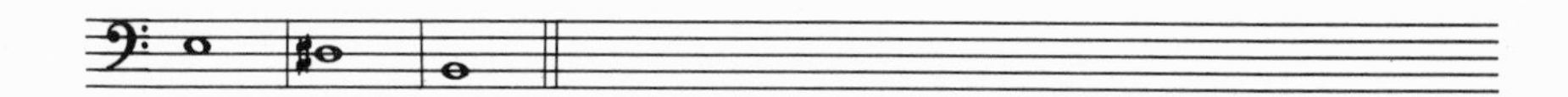

3.

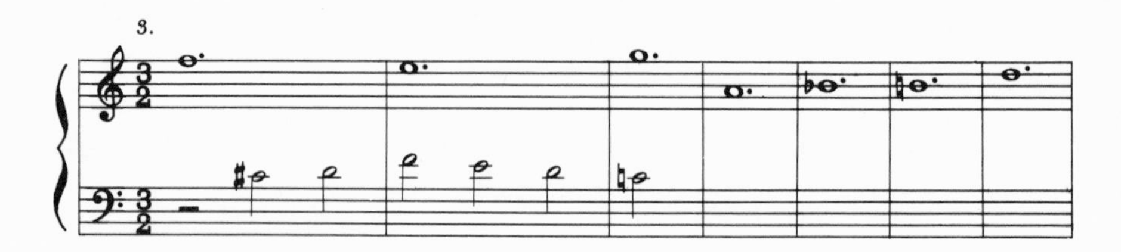

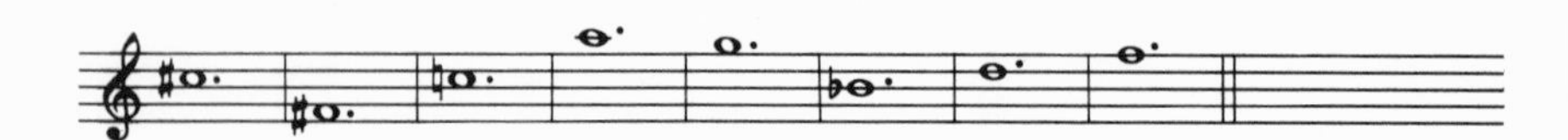

Example ***338d***

Florid

1.

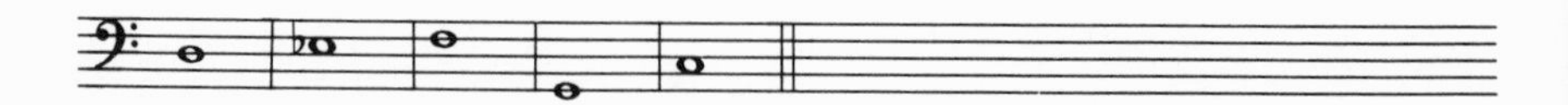

C Add an upper voice to the given bass lines of *Example 339*. Use brackets to denote the strongest harmonic intervals, whether linear or vertical.

Example **339a**

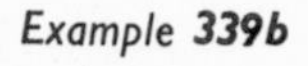
Example 339b

D Add a lower voice in canonic imitation to the given melody lines of *Examples* ***340a, b***. Try the imitations in different rhythmic locations and with different interval relationships. Do not adhere rigidly to the form of the canon. Try to achieve rhythmic fluency between the two voices.

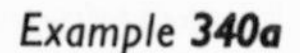
Example 340a

Example 340b

For further study of two-part Modern writing, see:

Four two-voiced Inventions by Lukas Foss
Preludes, Nos. 9 and 22 of Op. 34, by Shostakovich
Tanz und Spielstücke, Nos. 4, 6, 8, 9, Op. 40, by Ernst Toch
Visions Fugitives Op. 22, No. VI, by Prokofiev
"Chromatic Invention," *Mikrokosmos*, No. 145a, b, by Bartók

16 Intervallic structures in the writing of three or more parts

Incomplete chords

The principles which guide the understanding of two-part writing apply to all other forms of composition whether completely polyphonic or partly so. Compositions which by definition are considered homophonic nevertheless contain a contrapuntal movement between the outer parts at least. This shapes a basic two-part contour in which inner voices may contribute to a more defined harmonic concept. In the pure two-part composition, intervals, rather than complete chord formations, create the tonal movement. When three or more voices unite, the vertical intervallic combinations that may be formed are endless. Some, through a positive placement of the perfect fifth, perfect fourth or major third will produce a root tone, while others may not be definitive and will function as passing harmonies. With an unlimited interval selection, it is possible to recognize a root tone, but it may be contained among other vertical tones whose relationship to the root may be distant. The term "chord" implies a diatonic merging of harmonious chord members. In contemporary usage, as in *example* **341**, the term "G chord" is incorrectly applied when the highest melody tones radically depart from the lower tertiary organization of chord members; nevertheless, the "root tone of G" dominates the passage. A "chord" permits identification of all chord members based upon the tertiary concept of harmonic organization. An appropriate term for all vertical formations based upon any arrangement of intervals, is "intervallic structures." This includes harmonies which may or may not be centered around a root tone, and may contain as few as three tones or the maximum, twelve. Intervallic structures containing only three tones may sound like incomplete chords, particularly when the root tone is heard. Complete sounding chords may also bring forth only a root tone around which other harmonic members are massed without regard to the traditional spacing of chord members. Both types are formed by the sound of vertically spaced intervals, selected with or without a predetermined root.

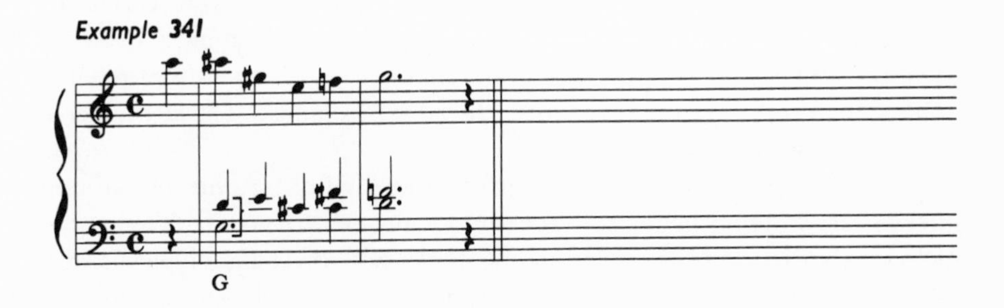

Root tones

As in two-part writing, root tones are identified by the harmonic association produced by a "strong" interval and by the concurrent melodic association. A third voice expands this procedure simply by involving more tones. This may result in a greater complexity or on the other hand, may clarify some two-part writing. The root producing intervals, located in the lower range, preferably including the bass or lowest tone, are still likely to contain the audible root movement. If the perfect fifth, fourth, or major third is higher in the vertical structure, more thought must be focused on melodic associations than on the vertical formation alone. *Example 342a* illustrates an intervallic structure consisting of a bass tone G, above which at the distance of a major ninth, is a perfect fifth A and E. As an incomplete chord, it may represent a G thirteenth (minus the very parts needed for a higher-numbered chord), or an incomplete A chord with the seventh in the bass. *Examples 342b, c,* and *d* contain this vertical formation in a three-part setting; each through a different melodic

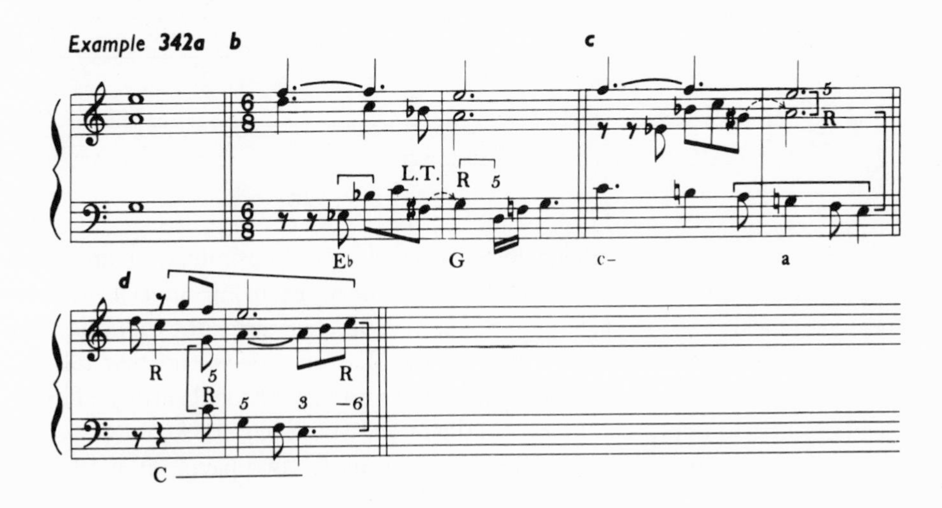

association, emphasizes a different root tone. *Example 342b* shows the influence of the leading-tone F♯, also associated with the preceding leap of a tritone producing the root G. *Example 342c* contains the rhythmical motive in the alto voice in which the leading-tone, G♯, places the tonal stress on A. The bass approaches the seventh, G, via the descending scale of A minor. In *example 342d*, the first established root is C and with the two outer voices of the intervallic structure fitting the C tonality, the root is retained. The alto tone A is recognized as a passing tone.

The perfect fourth is subject to the same kind of scrutiny. As an upper interval, separated from the bass tone by a wide, non-harmonic placement, the melodic association of the surrounding tones will affect the emphasis of the particular root tone. To illustrate, *example 343a*, by itself, appears as an incomplete E minor seventh chord. In context, *examples 343b, c,* and *d* respectively, show the tonal association creating the root tones of C, E, and G. In the first instance, the preparatory F in the bass, and the leading-tone, B, in the alto motive, suggest the resolution to C, which occurs amidst some rhythmic shifting. The ear supplies the expected sound rather than surmising an evaded chord that is incomplete also. *Example 343c* clarifies the E minor seventh chord while *example 343d* starts with G major and retains it through the passing bass tones.

Examples 344a to *d* illustrate the variable root possibilities of an intervallic structure in which the major third is the most harmonic interval. Again, located in the upper portion of the I.S. (intervallic structure), the root relationship sways with the contrapuntal thoughts that precede it and that follow, adding further intervals which may support a particular tonal setting. The G dominant ninth chord, resulting from the melody in *example 344b*, is "proven" by the last vertical perfect fifth between the upper two parts, D and G. In

example 344c, the first two beats suggest a tonality in which the E "silently" supports the following harmony by filling in the presumed perfect fifth. The root tone is the bass A. *Example* 344d focuses attention on the root of B, proven only by the melodic scale of the alto part. Notice how the highest part outlines a G triad, which nevertheless is dependent on the movement of the lower parts. As the alto reaches D♯, the total harmonic group reflects B as a root. It is possible to employ a G augmented analysis, but in hearing the resolution of the tone of G, the recognition of the F double sharp function is more appropriate. On the other hand, *example* 344e shows how strongly a change to a supporting interval affects the whole group. The last alto eighth note is altered to D♮, forming a perfect fourth which supports G. Regardless of resolution, the G has been reinforced and controls the sound of the entire measure.

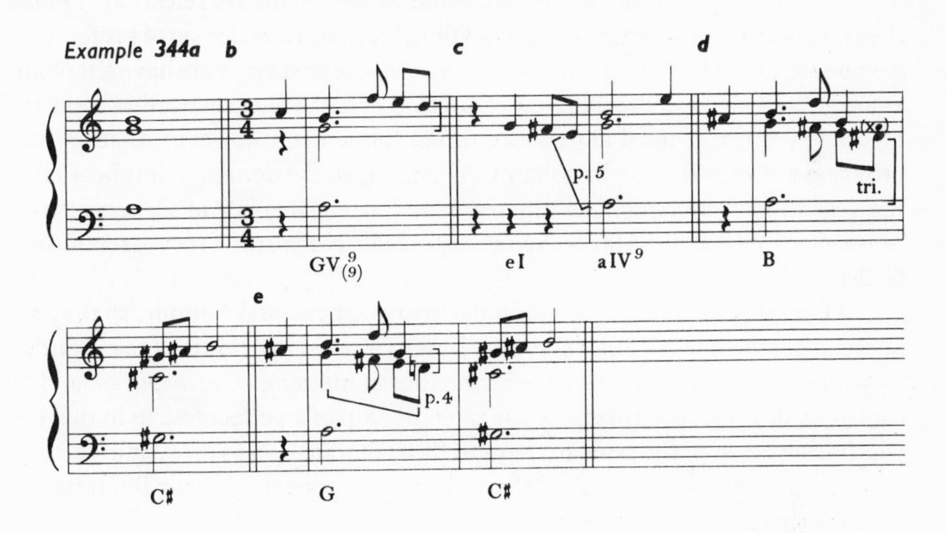

In examining the preceding examples, it is apparent that a correct analysis of root tones must depend upon an evaluation of the entire tonal scheme. In many instances, a positive conclusion is not possible. Contradictory melodic forces may negate a strong vertical interval, creating two or more analytical theories. In such dubious cases, the sound is as unsettled as is the theorist's pen. Don't insist on finding one solution. Instead, play the entire phrase, or theme, and consider the phrase cadences which are the final receivers of the pitch motion. By understanding the goal, certain prior elements may take on an added significance. But even so, all measures will not conveniently form positive root tones.

Intervallic structures of fewer tones are frequently more ambiguous than those which contain a greater number of tones. For example, the sound of a lower perfect fourth heard together with the outer voices forming a widespread perfect fifth (see *example* 345), creates a root conflict. Each possible root, G or

C, has a supporting fifth. The tonality involving this chord may or may not be solved by the course of the melodic associations, or by cadences. The short composition in *example* **345a** starts with this I.S. and progresses to a semi-cadence on the root tone of E♭. Such a harmonic pause is inconclusive because it is intended as a tonal departure from the starting sound, which can be either C or G. The second or a later cadence is more apt to furnish a clue as to the composer's hearing of this type of opening passage. Play this example, noting that the repetition of this first phrase is harmonized three different ways; whichever is selected will promote a tonal reference and an assumption of the root in the opening bar. If the root of C gains stature during the composition, then one gains the confidence in the premise that C may be the underlying tonality. If the root G becomes apparent, as in the second alternative, then it will be the central tone. But if neither gains a foothold as seen in the B♭ selection of pitch, then the opening measure remains questionable, and a smaller set of preferences may be suggested. Namely, the outer voices in the first two bars have a melodic association which is more akin to G than to C. This is then vertically supported by the lower major third in measure three. Remember, however, that one can progress to G via the subdominant C, changing to the dominant implication in the second bar. Secondly, any instrumental strengthening of C, can also be persuasive in the latter's favor. See *example* **345b**. No positive root assertion can be declared.

Outer voices generally contain the main contrapuntal contour, so they are likely to convey the root associations. Inner voices support rather than conflict with these lines. This is the case in the fourth measure of *example* **345a**. The root tone of E♭ is recognized by the melodic skip of a perfect fourth in this I.S. which is made up of the same fourth and fifth combination as present in the first measure. Rewritten in *example* **345c** without the supporting tenor B♭, it nevertheless remains as an E♭ measure.

The second phrase of *example* **345a** (measure five) starts with an I.S. in which the perfect fourth is the lower interval and a widespread major third, or tenth, forms the outer distance. The vertical perfect fourth declares the root, G♭, and the melody "fits" as a major seventh. No conflict exists because only one root and its supporting fifth are present, as opposed to the perfect fourth and fifth combination in which both possible roots are supported. The melody with its own linear perfect fourth is subservient to the stronger harmonic impact, which is also lower in range.

Examine the second beat of this same measure (bar five of *example* **345a**). Does it deserve a root representation? In a quick tempo, no, because the tones are connecting, as passing chords, returning to the solid G♭ in the following measure. In a slow tempo which permits the hearing of these secondary intervallic structures, a root tone may be discerned by the same logic as would be applied to the strong beat. *Example* **345d** illustrates this by suggesting the slower movement of sound in this manner of notation. The melody tone of F in the first measure, combines vertically with the bass tone A, forming a minor sixth; the root is F. In the second measure, the second beat on D combines with the bass tone A, this time forming a perfect fourth; the root is D. Following another return to G♭, the second beat of the third measure starts with the most discordant grouping of this passage. The make-up of this I.S. consists of a major second, and an outer enharmonic major seventh. No root combination can be derived from these three tones alone. As they resolve, the bass tone A is supported by the minor third in the tenor but a perfect fifth forms between alto and soprano. Where do both quarter notes lead? The cadence contains the root tone of F because of the preceding perfect fourth leap. Therefore, measure three contributes passing tones preparing the next root of F, and does not, by itself, contain a root other than the starting G♭, and a passing suggestion of C on the fourth beat.

Example 345b

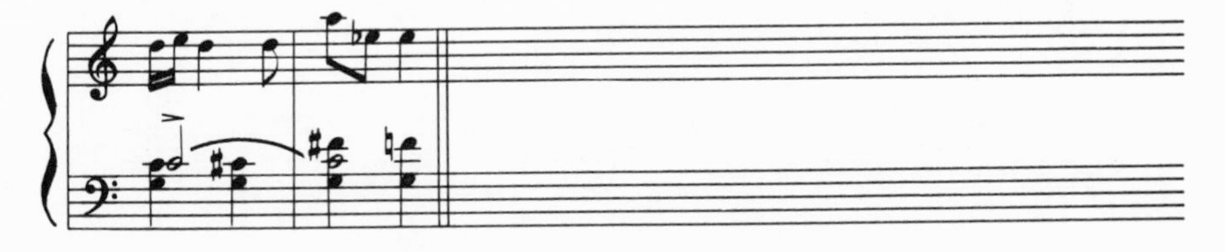

Example 345c

Example 345d

Tonal ambiguity

Don't look for root tones in passages where tritones predominate, whether vertically situated or as part of the linear writing. Such measures are transient and must lead somewhere. The value of root recognition is in the comprehension of the tones which stabilize certain areas. These are the sounds which mold the entire composition and permit the hearing of modulation within highly complex compositions. One can think of these transient elusive sounds as a series of passing tones involving not just one or two notes, but several measures of connecting material. Such passages must have melodic strength, and the analysis involved should depict the directional tones as they lead toward the stronger harmonic areas. *Example 346* contains several tritones in each of the first three measures. At the outset, the tritone, C and F♯ prevents any tonal foothold. Nor is there any conventional resolution that would suggest the dominant function. Consequently, no tonal area can be heard until this active harmony settles in the fourth measure on the root tone of F♯. If desired, the analytical marking for measures that are under the influence of tritones, may be simply abbreviated as "tri."

Example 346

In contrast to tritones, many three-part compositions contain a vague tonal feeling due to a preponderance of consonant intervals, especially perfect fourths. The tonal movement is generally not highly chromatic and the lack of a strong central tone comes about through a mixture of modal references. This is illustrated in *example 347* which begins with the linear motion of two successive perfect fourths in the bass. As has already been described, each perfect fourth suggests the upper tone as a root. In a series, none portray a clear root. Combined with vertical intervals of the major ninth, and melodic associations which also prevent one root from being recognized, the first measure cannot be given a positive root tone. The sounds generally suggest either a modal reference of D, giving preference to the first, and lowest bass tone, or C major resulting from the highest perfect fourth and a crisscross reference to the starting melody tone of E. Do not attempt to identify each beat as a changing root. Most of these sounds are incomplete. They blend together as a kaleidoscope of pastel colors. Harmonically, this measure forms an intervallic structure based on the perfect fourth. Label it I.S.p4. (Details follow in chapter seventeen.)

Example 347

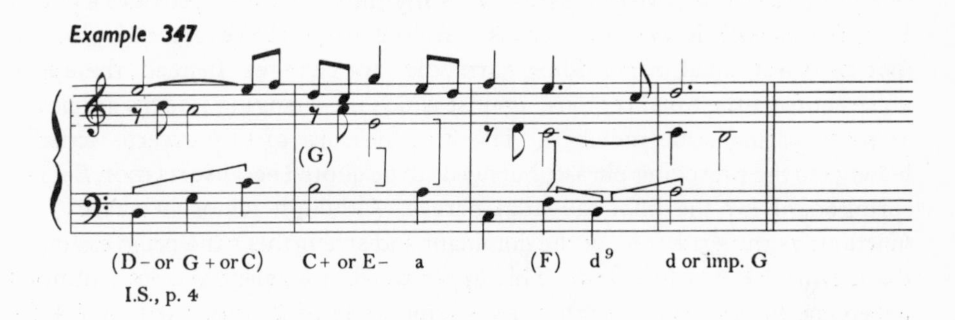

The second measure contains a linear influence of C against a vertical strengthening of E minor. These sounds do resolve on the third beat to an A root. Notice the positive root feeling when the two lowest tones form the perfect fifth. The rhythmic and melodic stress in the third measure falls on the second beat, and once again, the perfect fifth is heard. The bass tone descends, however, and the third beat supplies a lower tone which accomodates all of the preceding tones into a tertiary D minor ninth chord.

The fourth measure is one of the most interesting, analytically, because it puts into play the elements of melodic suggestion against harmonic overtones. Melodic motion in both the outer voices leads to a cadence on D with the fifth in the bass. As the alto resolves the seventh, C, downward to B, a different set of harmonic colors are brought forth. The progression from C to B unsettles the D root by forming a minor third, which is felt as a resolution, and as such, suggests an implied G root. Which root wins? Neither! The cadence relaxes by a melodic motion toward D supported by the bass, while an active inner voice keeps the wheel in motion, gradually subduing the former root influence. These incomplete harmonic sounds are typical of three-part writing. The changing interval patterns do not solidify a tonal center except where such cadential emphasis is purposely created. Every interval contributes toward the subtle increase and decrease of harmonic tensions without a down-to-earth rooted sense of progression. The melodic writing in the three parts is the more controlling and more significant aspect in this style of composition. This phrase is sufficiently analyzed, in harmonic terms, as being in the general region of a modal D. Preference for uniting the cadence with the starting bass tone accounts largely for this summary. The future role of this phrase may then be discerned by the long-range directional motion of D. It may have a close diatonic relationship, perhaps as a supertonic to C, or a distant chromatic relationship that holds no restrictions.

Two cadential excerpts from Hindemith's three voice fugues contained in *Ludus Tonalis* are quoted in *examples 348* and *349*. They illustrate the hearing of tonal regions, caused by melodic associations, periodically strengthened by vertical intervallic structures. *Example 348* is almost totally devoted to a descending pattern of perfect fourths. This rhythmical pattern provides a pulsation, felt as each lowest tone drops a scale degree. However, each unit of fourths is not equal in providing harmonic root changes. Instead, the upper voice controls the tonal regions, against which the changing fourths are heard as participating scale members. The first measure of this excerpt actually belongs to the preceding phrase, but needs to be quoted because its root, B♭, is a springboard for the final cadential phrase. Although minor in quality, B♭ functions as the scale tone of the dominant and strengthens the progression to the melody E♭ which follows. This upper tonal movement and its continued adherence to E♭ minor negates any strong sense of C minor that is briefly suggested on the first beat. The role of the bass, C, is that of the sixth degree of an E♭ scale, heading downward, and contributing to the tonal region of the melody. On the second beat, the first perfect fourth, B♭ to E♭, supports the tonic similarly to a I^{6}_{4}. In the third measure, the triad formation of A♭, followed by the I.S. which supports G♭, may be thought of as a progression of subdominant to mediant, continuing on to a modified supertonic. However, these are passing references, disrupted by the added fourths, resulting only in the recognized scale motion. Analyze the two and one-half measure group simply as being in E♭ minor and containing intervallic structures based on the perfect fourth.

A harmonic change occurs as the bass descends to E♮ in measure four. This combines with the sequential use of the motive. Notice the deliberate dissonance caused by the upper melody E♮, heard conflicting with the bass perfect fourth, E♭. This is a desirable effect because its pungency then sweetens the forthcoming resolution. It alerts one to the harmonic change that accompanies the sequence. The scale is now E minor, the preceding E♭ having functioned as a directional leading-tone. Vertical support is also given to E. As the motive leaps a fifth, the outer voices also strike the perfect fifth. The inner voice, adding a perfect fourth, does not cause any deterrent to E minor, in view of the strong melodic approach by the outer voices. The activating dissonance within this sequence occurs in a different location. On the second beat of measure five, the alto and bass form a tritone which also clashes on the next eighth note, F♯ against the bass F♮. This active choice of interval promotes a resolution on the

first beat of measure six into the tonal region of B♭ minor. Although the alto holds over an F♯, its pitch at this point is not protruding, and does not interfere with the more noticeable root preparation of B♭ in the bass. It can be considered a suspension on the sixth degree of the B♭ minor scale.

The third sequential group, contracted this time, starts with the leap of the perfect fifth, C to G. The intervallic structure now contains the greater consonant interval between alto and bass, forming a root tone of F, and heard as a brief dominant to the preceding B♭ root. Passing through C minor, tritones reappear on the second beat of measure seven, in the outer voices. This last perfect fourth bass group begins as a D root but immediately provides dissonance through the B♮. Not only does it conflict with the quarter beat C, but also causes a cross relation with the B♭ on the last beat. This activity pauses on D minor, and is followed by a concluding motive, actually an augmentation of the starting motive of the fugue's subject. The intervallic structures which form the cadence have a simple melodic association producing a tonic to dominant to tonic progression. The first three dotted quarter notes group together and with a combination of linear roots and vertical support, result in a root tone of E. As the other voices change direction, a harmonic change to the dominant, B, engulfs the next two measures. Utilizing the tierce de Picardie, the E major triad represents the goal, not only of the printed excerpt, but of the entire fugue. The reserve in using the complete triad only at structural points in a composition, increases the sense of finality. With styles that predominate in incomplete harmonies, this forthrightness at the cadence is frequently felt to be necessary. The summary of the tonal movement in this excerpt, starting from the phrase beginning in the second measure is: E♭, E, B♭, D, E, B, E.

The tonality of *example* **349**, the cadence to the "Fuga Secunda" from the *Ludus Tonalis*, is unmistakably G. Yet the intervallic structures form a network of passing roots above the pedal, ostinato motive. The subject of the fugue is illustrated in *example* **349b** so that the rhythmic shifting which occurs at the cadence may be more meaningful. In contrast to the preceding fugal example, the intervallic structures in this cadence contain very few ambiguous perfect fourths. Starting motivically on the last eighth beat, the bass G commands more root strength than the higher perfect fifth. The reason for this is the relationship of the alto F, as a seventh to the bass G. Spreading by contrary motion, the upper voices move into an E♭ root followed by D♭ in the form of a perfect fifth. The lack of a close association with G (a tritone), now separates this fifth from the bass, and permits its own root to be recognized. The root tone of C follows, returning to G together with the bass on the second eighth note of measure two. The minor third in the lower two voices then forms an F root, sustained through the dominant quality at the end of the bar. The A♮, as a leading-tone, emphasizes B♭ as the root of the perfect fourth I.S. in the third measure. The motive brings back G, followed by the root tones of E♭, F, D♭, and a phrygian cadential effect of F minor to G major.

The last two measure particularly show care in the selection of vertical intervals as the increase and decrease of tension is felt within these structures. Starting with a consonant fifth and fourth combination in measure three, the level of dissonance increases to the E♭, a minor ninth with the bass. This is followed by the major seventh, in which the E♮ also has the urgency of a leading-tone to F. As this is resolved, all intervals become consonant in the approach to G major. Tonal movement, root recognition and vertical awareness of intervallic dissonance all play an equal part in good contrapuntal writing.

EXERCISES

A *Analysis*

1] The melodic movement provides one root tone for *Example 350*, an excerpt from one of the *Mikrokosmos*. Observe the one tonality holding forth in spite of the vertical dissonances. Mark intervals, motivic treatment, and a few directional tones. (Indicate only those intervals which significantly support the tonality, linear or vertical, and those which contribute to dissonant activity).

Example 350b

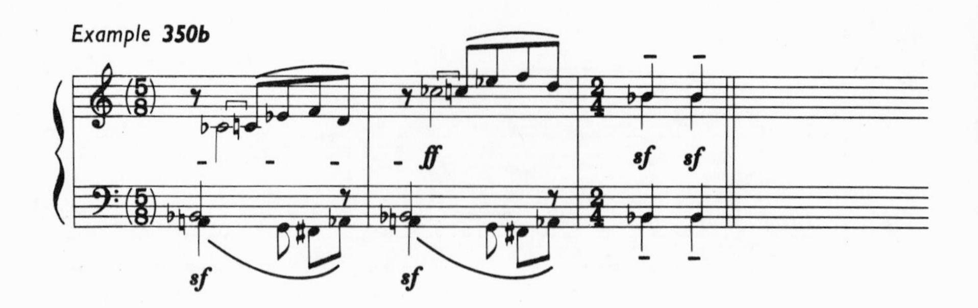

2] *Fugue No. 2* by Shostakovich has a Classically orientated subject but is used with free choice of intervals.

a] Mark the dissonant intervals and observe how they spruce up the phrase.
b] Mark the independent triads.
c] Find several important directional pitches.
d] Show the development of the subject matter by designating motives and figures.

Example 351a Shostakovich

Example 351b

Example 351c

3] The second theme from Prokofiev's *Sonata No. 7* is written in a linear style but without the strict adherence to three voices as occurs in the above examples.
a] Mark the strongest intervals (those producing a harmonic association) whether harmonic or linear.
b] Indicate the letter name root.
c] There are two tonal centers in this excerpt. Each has one or two supporting diatonic chords. Use roman numerals to show this relationship.
d] Find some double inflections and an interesting suggestion of a polychord, which briefly gives the melody its own linear tonality, as a polytonal phrase.

Example 352 Prokofiev

B In the contrapuntal exercises, *Examples* **353a** to **d**, complete the two unfinished voices. Mark the root tones by letter name. Use a bracket to indicate the effective interval.

Example 353a

1. Note against note:

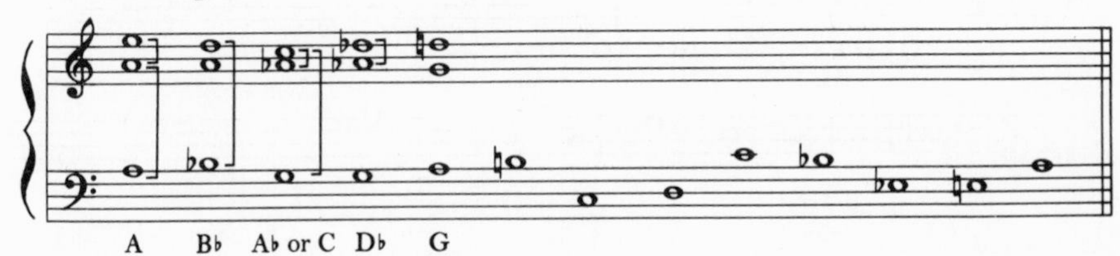

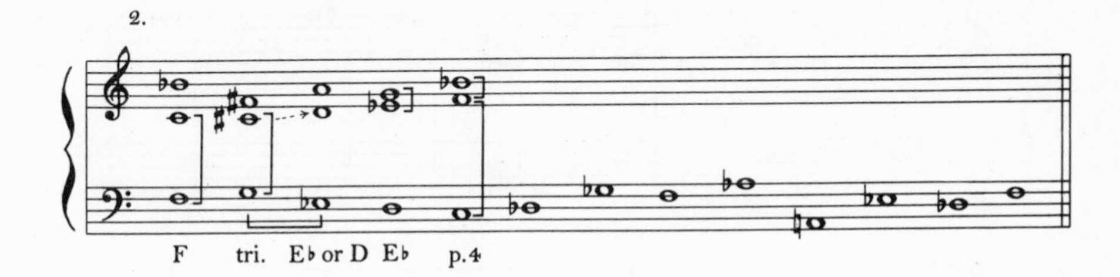

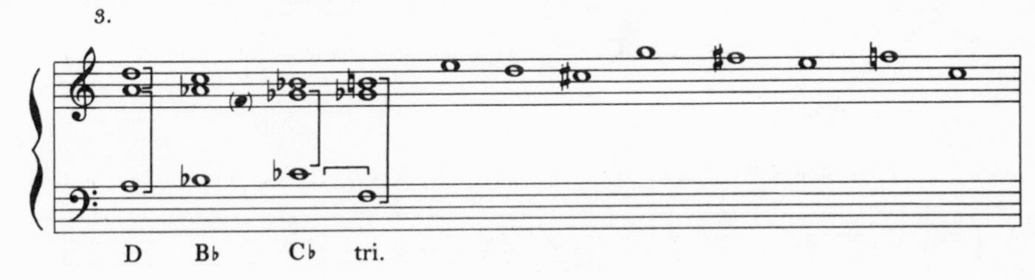

Example 353b

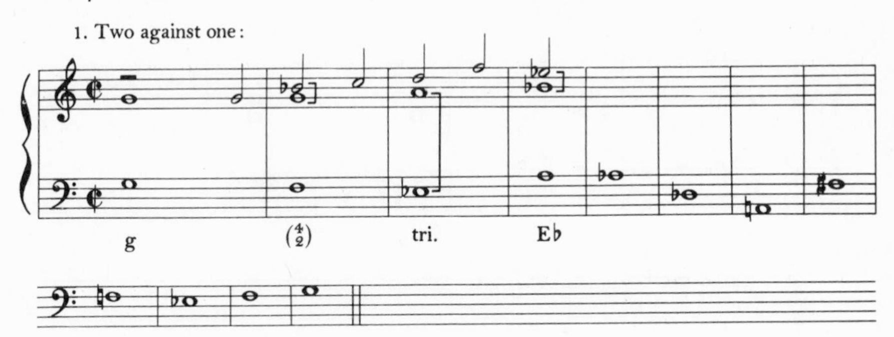

2.

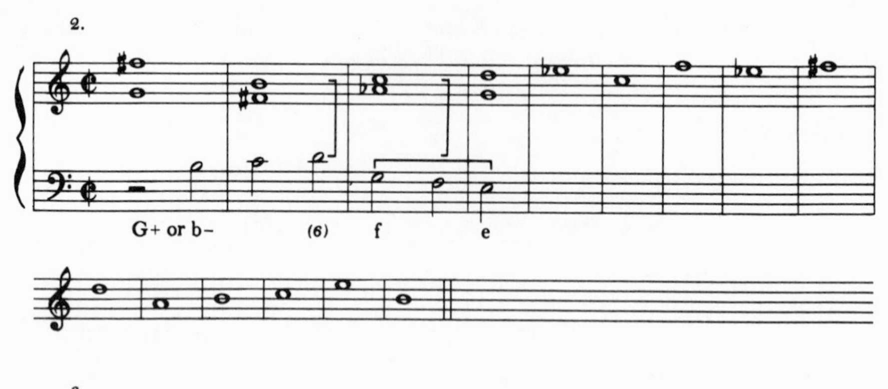

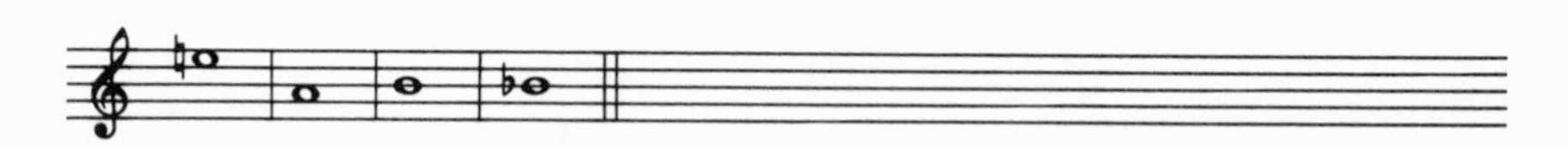

3.

Example 353c

1. Four against one:

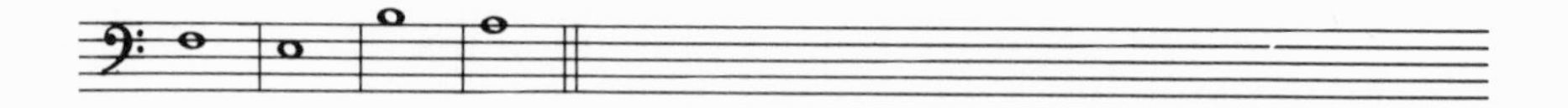

2.

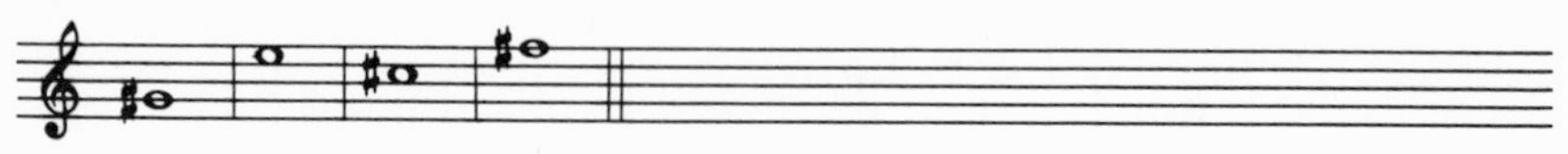

3.
Example 353d
Florid 1.
2.
3.

C 1] Harmonize *Example 354a* by continuing the intervallic structures used for the accompaniment to the melody. Use the more dissonant intervals to highlight a particular part of the phrase. Mark letter name roots.
2] *Example 354b* has the reverse situation. The intervallic background is given in the upper voices. Supply a melodic bass and mark resulting root tones.

D Try a short three-voiced invention on one or more of the following subjects. Develop the figures contained in the subject. Choose three instruments for an individual, creative result.

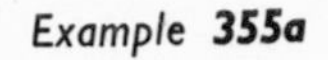

For further study of three-part writing, see:

Ludus Tonalis, by Hindemith

Fugues, Op. 40, by Shostakovich

PART V

Intervallic structures in homophonic textures

17 Fourth chords and perfect fifths

Perfect fourth chords

While the tertiary organization of tones stems from the triad, the quartan organization, that of superimposed fourths, has no particular diatonic origin. The closest reference to the triad is in the obvious recognition that the perfect fourth is the inversion of the perfect fifth. This would seem that the lowest tone is a fifth, the middle tone, the root and on up. It doesn't work that way. In a simultaneous chord formation of perfect fourths an equality of intervals is formed, avoiding any particular root stress.

Fourth chords may be used on any degree of the scale, diatonic or chromatic. They are frequently given two connotations: (1) The fourth is used as a substitute for the third, see *example 356a*; and (2) The chord of fourths derives from the natural eleventh chord, see *example 356b*. If the tone of the

Example 356

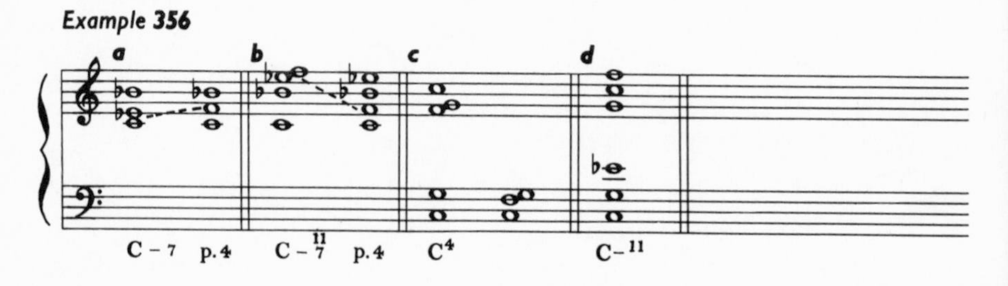

eleventh is lowered from its tertiary placement, it no longer carries with it the harmonic extension of sound. Instead, it takes over part of the chordal foundation, hence the need for the new category of fourth chords.

Do not confuse a chord which contains an added tone of the fourth, as in *example 356c*, with that of a fourth chord. *Example 356d* also illustrates a tertiary

C minor chord with an added eleventh. The difference between the term, added fourth, and added eleventh, is insignificant. The eleventh is favored if the tone has an upper location in the chord.

All twelve chromatic tones may be placed in a quartan organization. See *example 357a*. This forms a massive harmonic structure that cannot be broken down into particular chord members and their associations to a single root tone. While the first six tones of a perfect fourth chord unite in forming consonant intervallic relationships among themselves, the seventh tone of the column provides a tritone relationship with the bass tone. Each succeeding tone continues the tritone conflict in the vertical structure, as illustrated in *example 357b*. Mounting tension accompanies this harmonic growth. The perfect fourth ascendancy is nevertheless maintained, giving the chord of any number of successive fourths its name, "fourth chord."

Example 357

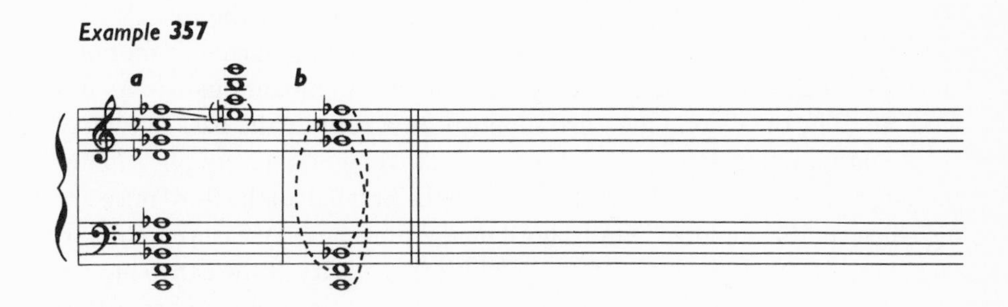

Function: The superimposed perfect fourths by their opposition to the overtone series create a vertical, tonal equality in each tone of the formation. While the outer voices may assume a more binding relationship, only the inclusion of melodic associations may sometimes suggest a root of a fourth chord, and even then, a tonal uncertainty must naturally prevail. *Examples 358a, b* and *c* place a fourth chord into three different tonal associations. Because the tonal reference is unquestionably established at the start of each motive, the fourth chord continues the melodic tendencies that a simpler two or three part plan would entail. In *example 358a*, the quarter-note melody tones of C and D progress to E♭ within the fourth chord. Against the contrary motion in the bass, and an alto B leading-tone, the lowest tone, C, of the perfect fourth chord gains priority as a root.

Example 358b places this same perfect fourth chord into an F minor setting. Preceded by its dominant, the F of the fourth chord gains melodic emphasis and may be considered the root in this situation.

The motion of the outer voices in *example 358c* places the melodic emphasis on the highest tone, A♭. By continuing in a parallel design, but not with true perfect fourth chords, the root remains in the top voice for the succeeding harmonies.

Example 358

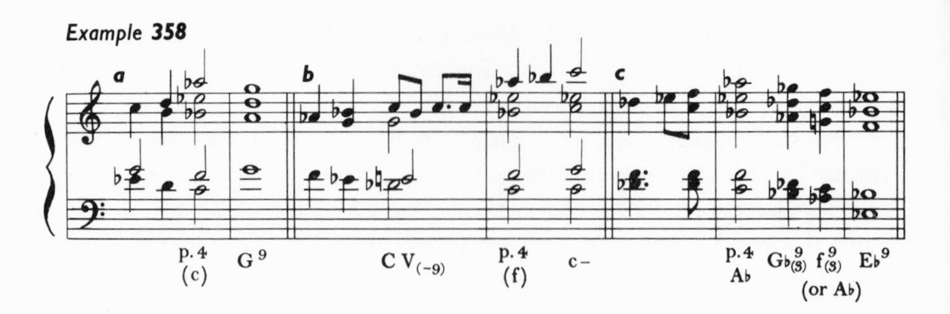

Because of the tonal ambiguity that fourth chords contain, they are frequently used to gain a Modern effect that poses few harmonic problems. They fit so easily into many different areas. With the changing melodic attitudes, a subtle harmonic change also occurs, as the tones of the fourth chord alternate their stress in combining with the melody. Illustrated in *example 359* is a bass ostinato made up of perfect fourths. Notice how the tones which are re-enforced by melodic duplication supply an undulating harmonic motion. The re-enforced C, in the first measure gives rise to a dominant quality. As it leaps a fourth to F, the second measure supports an F root by the bass motion of the third and fourth quarter beats. Harmonic movement and a duplication of the melody tone G, change the tonal context in the first half of the third measure and also form an incomplete C ninth chord on the third beat. Measure four emphasizes B♭ by its melodic duplication, and by a receptivity of the ear to hear whatever motion can be implied within the static repetitions of the bass pattern.

As the complete change of harmony occurs in the fifth measure, all directional tones move into new tonal areas. This forthright motion is a welcome change from the intricate root references of the former passage. It again

Example 359

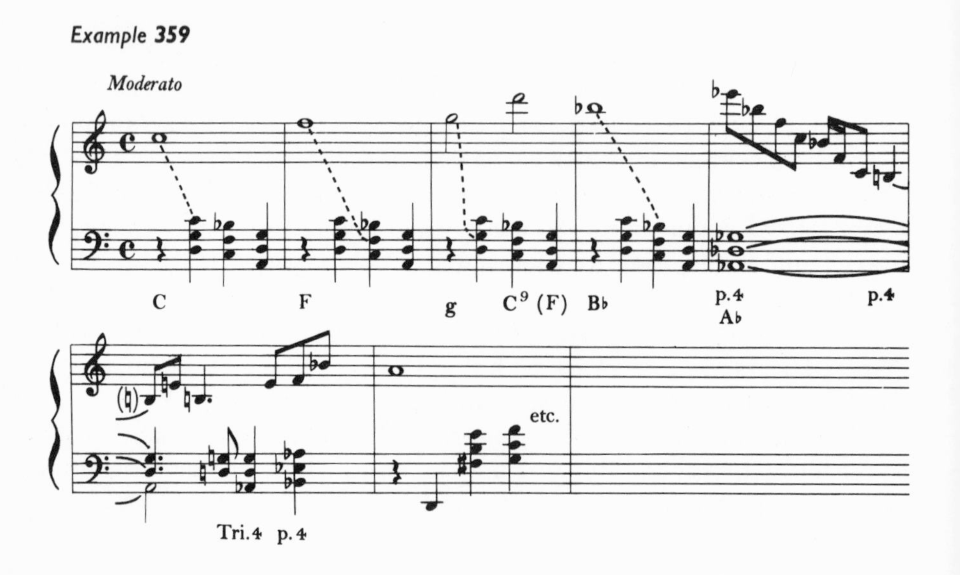

illustrates the linear force that ultimately controls musical progression. Also built upon perfect fourths, this pitch motion from one set of sounds to another propels the progression while rhythmic motion aids the goal. Not only is it expressed in the melodic divisions in measure five, but in the directional movement taking place from B♭ to B♮ in a syncopated effect, and from the high E♭ to the lower E♮ in the sixth measure. Harmonically, the ascending fourth chords on the third and fourth beats provide tonal motion that becomes stabilized on the forthcoming D root. These are typical fourth chords with indecisive roots. Their strength lies in their melodic preparation of D. All tones resolve by half-step, and thereby provide an excellent approach for either a cadence or the start of another phrase.

Tritone fourths

Intervallic structures which are made up of a mixture of perfect fourth intervals and augmented fourths, or their enharmonic diminished fifths may be called "tritone fourths." The location of the tritone may occur between the lowest two tones of the I.S. or between any of the upper successive fourth intervals. See *example 360a*.

Any number of tritones may be included, but they must alternate between the perfect fourths if a duplication of pitch is to be prevented. The additional tritones increase the harmonic tension. See *example 360b*.

Example 360

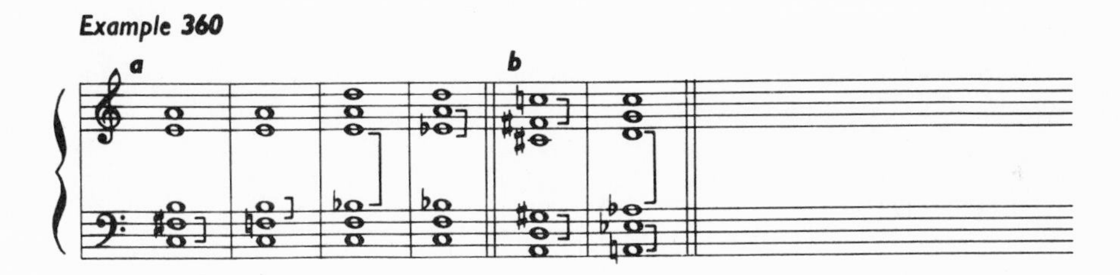

A phrase consisting entirely of fourth chords is illustrated in *example 361*. In spite of the same harmonic textures, it has enough variety of tension, heard through the melodic contour and the contrast between the two types of fourth chords. The perfect fourths start and end the phrase, while the tritone fourths widen the range and activate the development within the phrase. Notice that the first chord of measure three contains seven tones, producing a tritone interval between melody and bass. Its ascendancy is nevertheless a perfect fourth structure.

Tonal ambiguity is as prevalent among tritone fourths as with perfect fourths. In this same example, each intervallic structure is accepted on its own terms. There is no single compelling tone that insists on a specific resolution of pitch, tritone notwithstanding. This "isolated" quality is the result of intervallic structures which defy any significant root tone. It leaves the entire effect of movement to the melodic contour and the slight deviations in the vertical quality.

Example 361

Omission and Juxtaposition of Chord Members

The quality of fourth chords may be retained in intervallic structures which do not adhere rigidly to the exact quartan organization. Omissions of some "middle" members do not affect the basic chord quality.

a] In *example 362a*, tones which would rank fourth and fifth in the column of perfect fourths are omitted. No change occurs in the fourth chord quality. The missing chord members, however, are not implied or suggested in the sound of the I.S.

b] Above the initial three tones which make up the fourth chord, a gap in the spacing may occur between any of the upper fourths. See *example 362b*.

Example 362

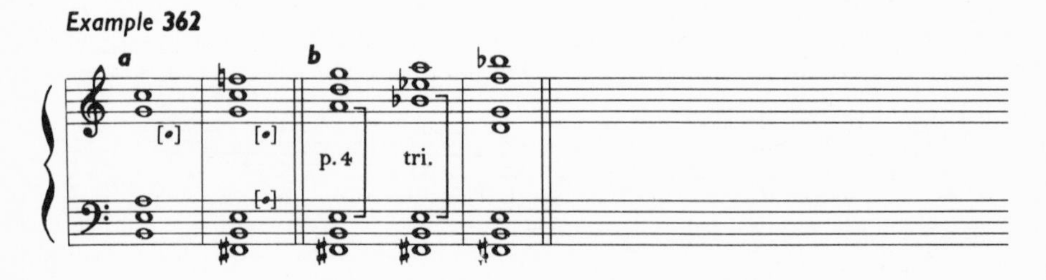

c] A centrally located interval may deviate from the fourth ascendancy without causing a noticeable change in the fourth chord quality. This can be thought of as an extraction of upper fourth formations from the complete column of twelve notes. *Example 363a* shows how the highest three tones are brought down by an octave forming an intervallic gap of a major seventh in the center of the I.S. In *example 363b*, the seventh, eighth and ninth tones of the column form a gap of a minor sixth, which can be either widely or closely spaced. A closer placement may sound more dissonant as the conflicting tones are nearer each other. The formation in this example is particularly strident as each upper tone stresses the tritone and minor ninth intervals in its relationship with the lower group. In these discordant combinations, the eye comprehends the predominating quartan organization, but the ear responds mostly to the tritones and almost erases the perfect fourth ascendancy. In analyzing these intervallic structures which are mutations from the pure fourth column, judge them by their total intervallic effect. Generally, concordant fourth structures do not contain any tritone relationship, while those labeled as discordant do. *Example 363c* gives a convenient analysis.

Example 363

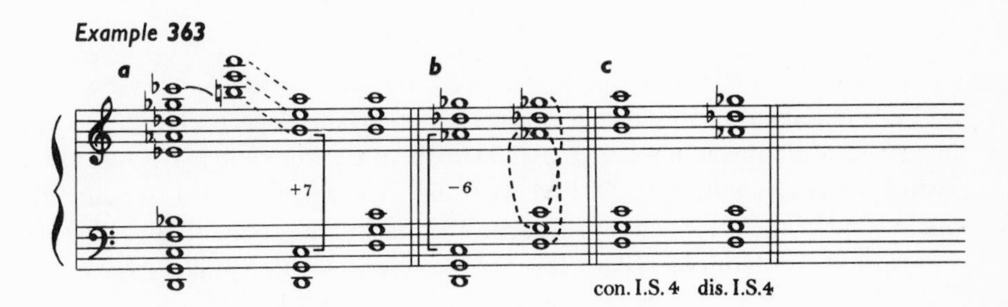

d] Fourth formations appearing above a single bass tone, or above one perfect fourth interval, may or may not qualify as fourth chords.

A perfect fourth structure may remain intact if an octave or more separates a single bass tone from the rest of the fourths, as in *example 364a*.

A tritone fourth may reflect a dominant quality, as the gap between the single tone and the upper arrangement may provide its own overtones which, if supported in the above group, will disclaim a fourth hierarchy. See *examples 364b* and *c*.

Example 364

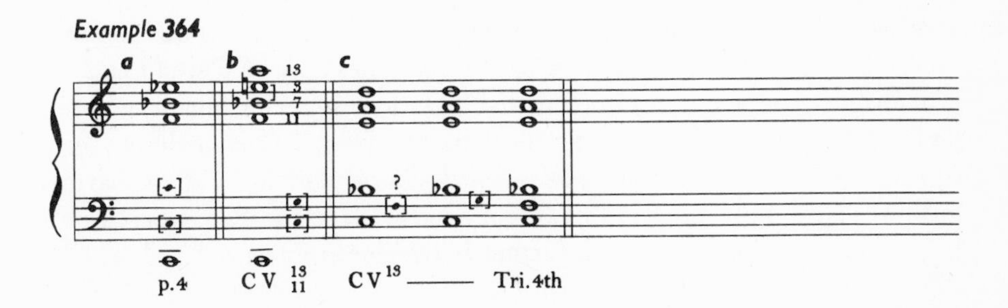

Above two tones which form a perfect fourth interval, the analysis must reflect the presence or absence of tertiary organized tones. This is necessary particularly in the first tone of the upper group which breaks away from the fourth formation and from the lower pair of tones. Compare the different qualities given in *example 365*. The root tone of G is either emphasized or not by the upper formation. Notice that the low bass placement of the G aids in its harmonic association.

Example 365

e] Juxtaposition of chord members may also take place, preferably among the perfect fourth structures. *Example 366a* illustrates the switch in range as the second perfect fourth, A to D, inverts to become a perfect fifth, sending the fourth tone of the series up one octave. This reshuffling may involve the first six tones of a column of perfect fourths. See *examples 366b* and *c*. Above that, tritones may set up conflicting harmonies, removing the bland, tonal ambiguity that is characteristic of fourth chords.

Example 366

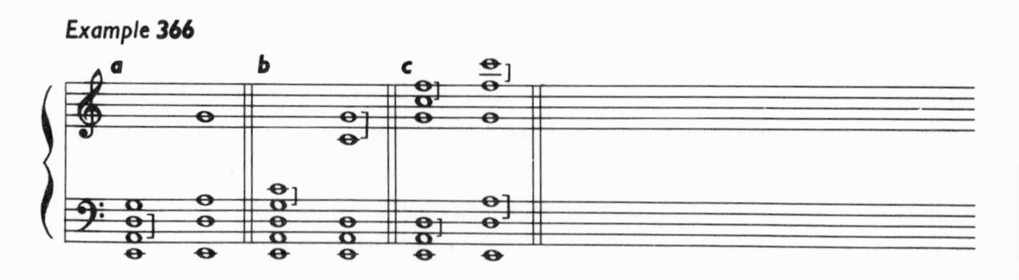

Other forms of reshuffling of the first six tones are illustrated in *example 367*. Similar to an inversion, the lowest three tones may be placed in a perfect fifth formation above a series of fourths. In a wide range, the fourths will retain their individuality, but the greater the departure from the basic column, the less significance can be attributed to a fourth-chord planning. These harmonic mixtures fall simply into an I. S. category and are labeled I.S. p. 4 based on the lowest fourth. This is discussed further in chapter eighteen.

Example 367

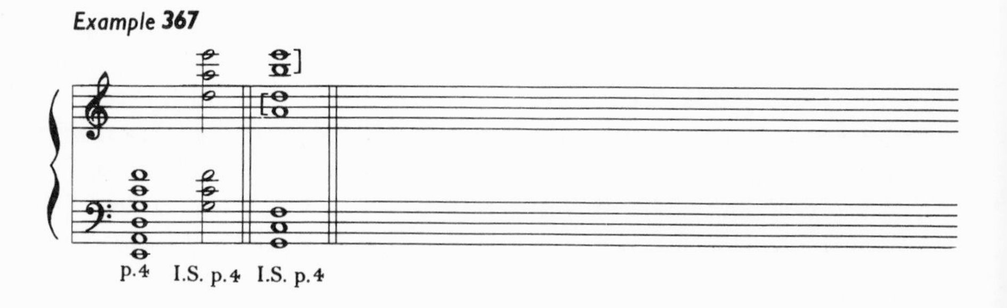

The perfect fifth "anchor"

Any combination of intervals can be mounted upon a low perfect fifth. It can be likened to an anchor gripping the sands of tonality. The lowest tone, by having the support of the immediate perfect fifth receives a root strength that cannot be shaken by any amount of upper dissonance. Higher tones may conflict and tug at this anchorage, but at best, they may emerge as polychords, or move independently above the rooted bass pedal. Orchestrally, the lowest tone (and sometimes the fifth) is frequently doubled in the next octave, thereby producing additional root strength. The intervals illustrating this in *example 368* are chosen at random, each providing a variance of tension, but none disturbs the root tone of E.

Example 368

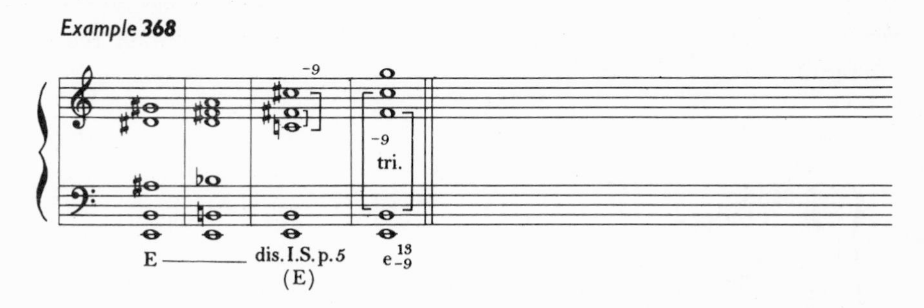

In a series of perfect fifths (*example 369*), the lowest fifth retains its root stature. In this way it differs from a perfect fourth chord which does not give root emphasis to any particular tone. The wider interval spread that is contained in the perfect fifth chord usually limits the number of tones used in such a structure. From a pianist's point of view, it is more clumsy than the fourth chord; and orchestrally, the fifths are apt to cause more intonation problems. Nevertheless, when used in a vertical column, the texture is similar to that of the column of fourths, especially perfect fourths.

Example 369

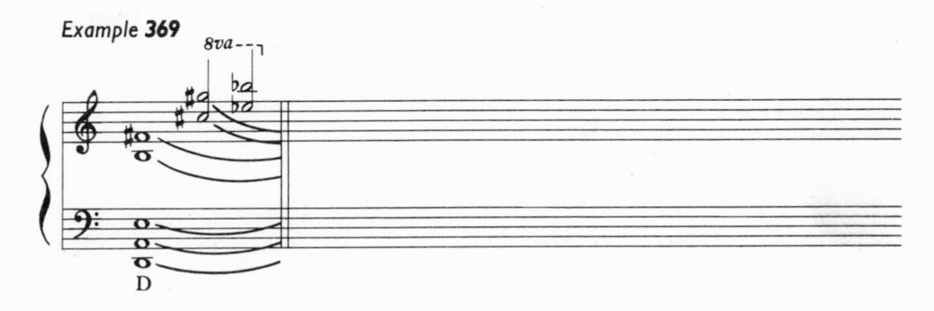

Pianists particularly, become adept at "right hand fourths." These are not fourth chords as they are built above the perfect fifth root, but they can be heard as fourth combinations. These "right hand fourths" replace the triad. *Example*

370 shows how the root is replaced by the ninth, and the fifth is taken over by the major or minor added sixth. These are familiar cadence varieties.

Example 370

Fourths built below the tones of a scale, as in *example 371*, provide a soft blend of sound over a positive tonality. They are diatonically conceived and are readily available for any root progression. They do not contain the tonal ambiguity of the fourth chord.

Example 371

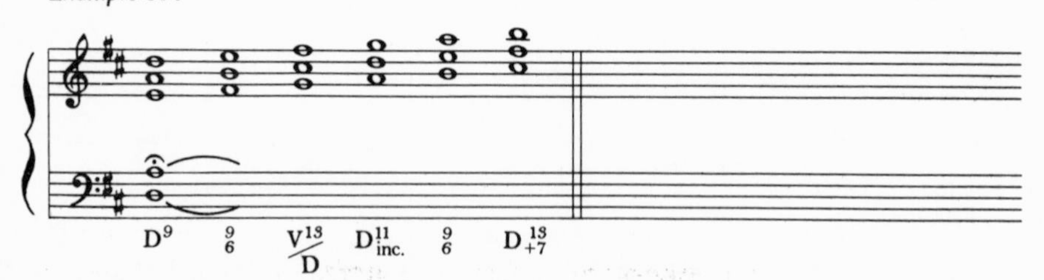

The power of the bass fifth is perhaps more evident in *example 372*. The root tone of D remains unshaken by the arpeggio which contains all discordant tones. Label it "I.S. p. 5" because the tones are chosen for their intervallic tension rather than conceived in an orderly tertiary harmonic plan. The rush of tones progresses to a C root which includes a major seventh and a raised eleventh. Approaching the cadence via the tritone progression is a "right hand fourth" group containing the tones of the major seventh and thirteenth. The cadence rests on a perfect fifth chord, on the root of E.

Example 372

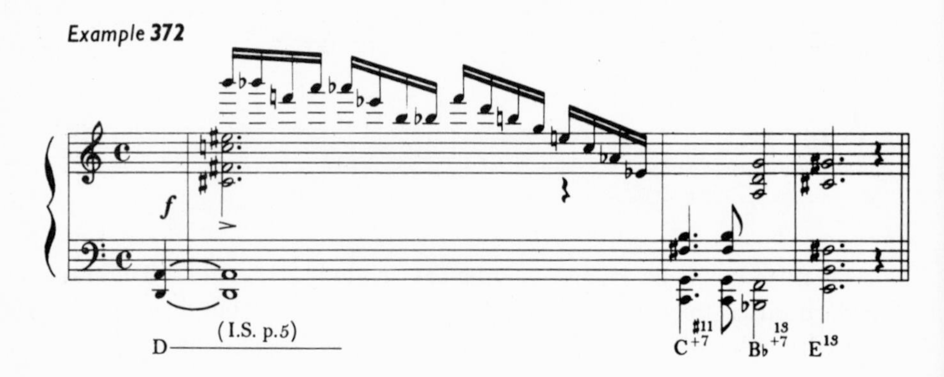

In a short composition, *Prelude and Fughetta* (an excerpt from the "Prelude" is quoted), Vittorio Giannini combines perfect fourths and perfect fifths into an interesting motivic blend, *example 373a*. A lively motive settles on F as the tonal center. The scale, however, is largely modal as it incorporates the tones of the phrygian mode, both in its harmony and in the motivic development. Observe the slight differences in the quality of the chords which do contain the tritone amidst the fourth formations, and those which because of the scale, do not. *Example 373b* is drawn from the second phrase. It illustrates the possessiveness of all root tones when part of the perfect fifth bass interval. Derived from the first motive, this middle section contracts its material, quickens the harmonic pace, and arrives climactically at the return of Motive 1 in the dominant tonality. In the $\frac{3}{4}$ measure, notice how the tritone on the third beat of the bass part adds an extra ingredient of motion; it literally pushes into the measure's repetition, as it does to the following G♭ major seventh chord. Here, the tritone is used as a lowered dominant root leading to C.

In quite a different idiom is *example 374*, an excerpt from the last movement of Paul Hindemith's *String Quartet IV.* It illustrates the secure foundation that perfect fifths establish against considerable dissonant counterpoint occurring above. The contrast between these solid roots and the inversions of chords is very noticeable. For example, compare the first and third measures with the second, fourth and fifth. The alternate exchange of qualities is deliberate. Notice how the harmonic movement is focused on the solidly rooted chords of G in measure one, moving to A♭ in the third measure. In between, the second measure, containing more contrapuntal material, moves from an implied C root through G and connects to A♭ in a melodic style. Measures four and five are very active, designed to return to C in the sixth measure. The general tonal suggestion of A♭ is continued in the fourth bar while the fifth contains three passing harmonies controlled by the chromatic bass. Observe also the contrary motion of the outer voices, almost forming a "mirror" design in the beginning of the phrase.

Example **374** *String Quartet IV. Hindemith*

This excerpt represents a harmonic climactic goal within a very contrapuntal movement, a "Passacaglia." If possible, listen to the entire movement, tracing the "Passacaglia" theme within the masterful string writing.

EXERCISE

A *Analysis*

1] Analyze all of the fourth chords in *Example* **375** in the following manner:
a] Distinguish between the pure perfect fourth chord (labeled p. 4) and those containing tone omissions or juxtapositions. Mark the latter with a bracket showing the interval that replaces the fourth, as illustrated in the second measure.
b] Where fourth chords are not present, separate the melodic part from the harmony and observe a bichordal quality.
c] Note the contrapuntal and linear usage of the fourth interval.
d] Mark the essential directional tones.
e] Is this excerpt in a "key"?

Example **375** *Bartók*

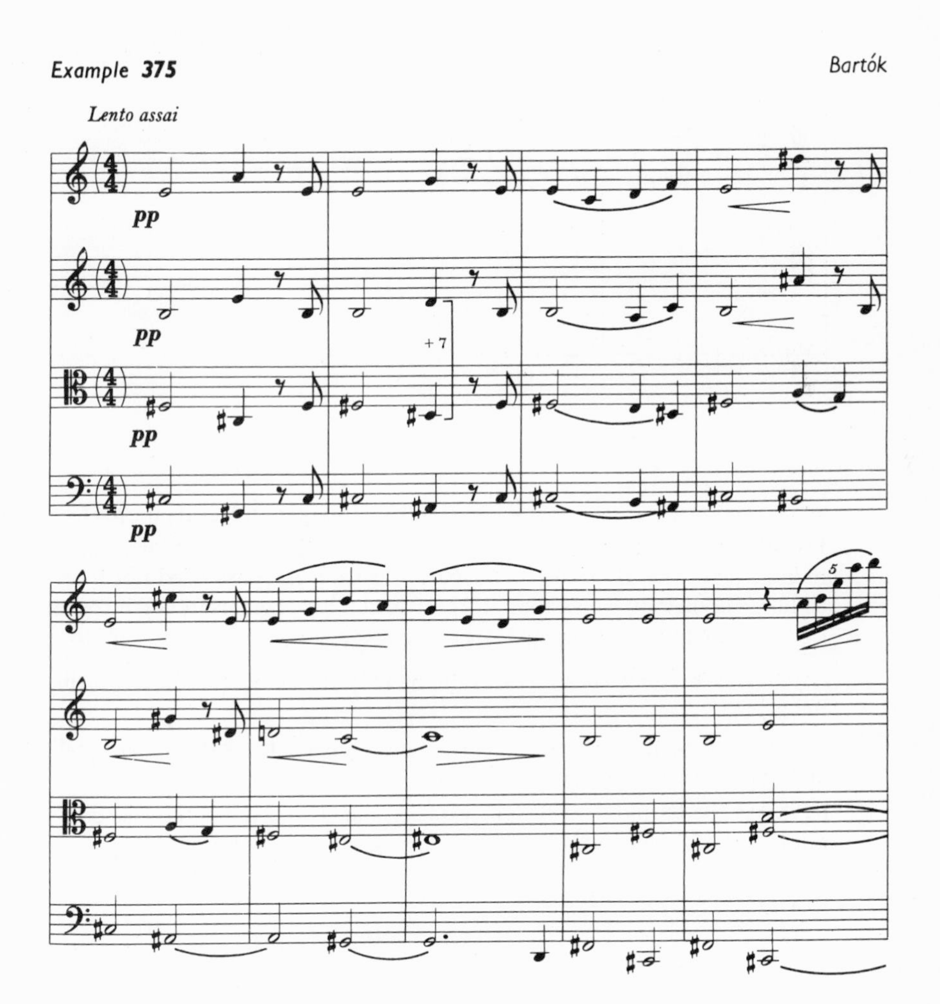

2a] Differentiate between perfect and tritone fourth chords in *Example 376.* For the most part, the melody moves separately from its fourth chord harmonization. The intervals that separate it from the bass need not be marked. Find some melody tones that are part of the lower quartan organization.

b] Do the tritone fourths suggest a dominant control?

c] Mark the directional tones in the melody. Is there any linear tonality suggested?

d] In the two-part writing, measures nine to eleven, mark the linear tonality and an important leading-tone.

e] Mark the harmony of the last cadence and compare its influence on the first phrase. Where does a fourth substitute for the third of a chord?

3] Which melodic associations suggest a tonal center in *Example* 377? Find a dominant to tonic progression and relate the other tonal influences to that tonality. Analyze as above.

Example 377 Toch

4] *Example* 378 illustrates a brief approach to a semi-cadence. Analyze the tone formations of the third measure. Where is the dominant tone located? How does this chord relate to a fourth chord? (The beginning of this quartet is quoted in *Example* 298.)

Example 378 Bartók

B Fill in the inner voices (using divisi where desired) of *Examples* 379a, b, c. Tritone fourths may contain the tritone between any of the voices. (Other chords are indicated by the analysis procedure as described in chapter seven.)

Example 379a

Lento
e–: p.4 Tri.4 p.4 IV–7 9 V;–7 IV;V 9 C+: III +7 V; (4 2) –7 I +7 9 p.4
Tri.4 II–7 F/G♭ Tri.4 I

b
Scherzando
f♯–: p.4 p.4 p.4 p.4 p.4 p.4 p.4 p.4 p.4 Tri.4 –7 Tri.4 –7
D+: III V
IV; ♯11 +7 (4 3) V 6 4 IV; ♯11 +7 (4 3) p.4 II; –11 7 III 9 II –11 7 b: VI 9 I
Tri.4 –7 IV–9 7 V I+

C Harmonize the given melodies of *Example 380* by fourth chords predominantly. Use *Example 376* as a model. Score for instruments if desired.

D Bartók wrote a six-voiced canon on this theme (*Example 381*) in the first movement (measure 363) of the *Concerto for Orchestra.* Reproduce the canon starting with three trumpets on unison imitation and followed by three trombones entering one octave lower. Entrances are spaced one measure apart. After scoring, compare and listen to the original.

Example 381 Bartók

For further study of fourths in their linear motion, listen to:

Concerto for Orchestra, the "Introduction," by Bartók

Sixth String Quartet, the lyrical theme present in the movement, "Marcia," by Bartók

Sonata for Piano, Op. 26, movements I and IV, by Samuel Barber

18 Intervallic structures emanating from bass intervals of sixths, thirds, sevenths, and seconds

Intervallic structures built upon a bass interval of a sixth have less diatonic footing than either the perfect fifth, fourth (except in the exact quartan organization), or the seventh. This is, of course, presuming that the upper tones do not complete an inversion of a diatonic chord. A review of the overtone series indicates the proximity of the tones forming the sixth to the fundamental root. The major sixth is contained between the third and fifth partials (by-passing the root on the fourth partial), while the minor sixth is not formed until outlined by the fifth and eighth partials. Both sixths may be the foundation for very diffuse and discordant intervallic structures.

a] I.S. above a minor sixth: The potential root implication within a minor sixth interval is in the upper tone, the lower note representing the third. If a discordant, non-diatonic harmony is desired, tones may be built above the minor sixth which do not belong to the potential root tone of the minor sixth interval. Particularly, the first tone of this upper discordant group should not be a conforming one. *Example 382* illustrates the contrast between dissonances added above a tertiary foundation of three notes, versus the group as described above which is chosen to defy the potential root tone. In *example 382a*, the tertiary order is maintained, as the tone of the fifth in the first chord, and the tone of the seventh in the second chord supply sufficient tonal anchorage above which the dissonances relate to the root tone of A. *Example 382b* starts the upper discordant group by the tone of D which immediately conflicts with the minor sixth bass interval. It upsets the A root by also suggesting its own root capabilities. The remaining upper tones support neither D nor A and form a sound which, out of context, can be described only as a discordant intervallic structure.

The chord is identified by the abbreviation, I.S., followed by the designated bass interval, in this case the minor sixth, -6. By marking the interval, an awareness of the potential root tone is always present. Some melodic support or a larger harmonic significance may be observed, which initially could go unnoticed in the confined study of analytical detail.

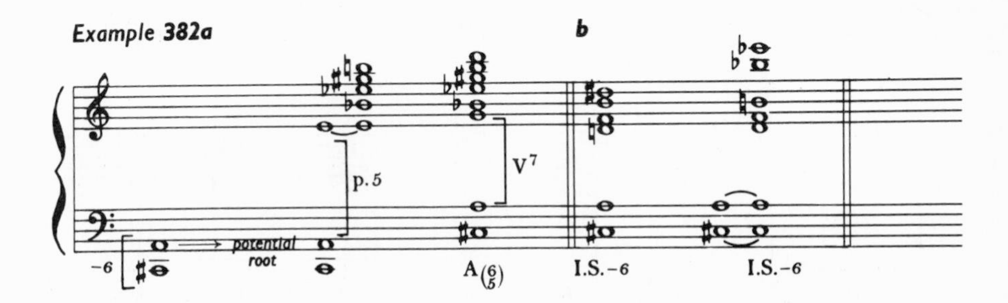

Fourth formations, placed above the sixth interval, continue their tonal ambiguity above the insecure sixth below. They may form discordant or concordant results as illustrated in *examples* 383a and *b*. The judgement is made largely upon the interval relationships contained within the chord. A concordant I.S. generally does not contain a tritone or an excess of major sevenths or minor ninths within its complement of tones. (Exceptions to these intervals may always be noted in recognition of the chord's function in the phrase.)

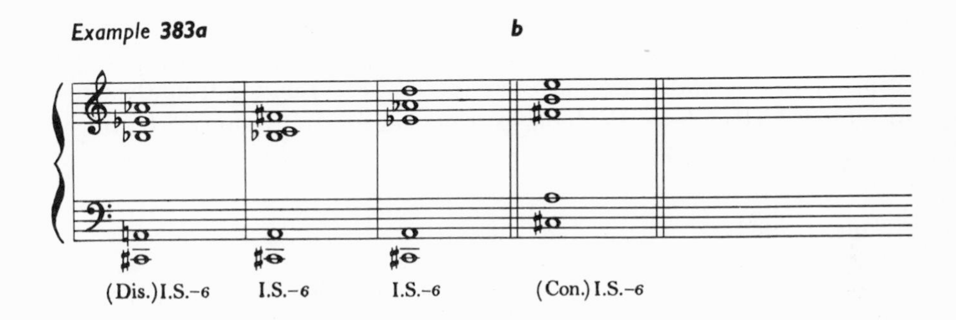

A comparison between a non-diatonic I.S. built above a minor sixth and the identical group of tones placed above a perfect fifth may be made by playing the illustrations in *example* 384. In each instance, the root security of the chord founded upon the perfect fifth is felt. Such a chord acts as a receiver of the motion supplied by the preceding intervallic structure. It does not pertain to the concordant or discordant quality of the I.S., but relates to the firmness that a root position chord emits. The first chord of *example* 384a progresses clearly to the tonic D♭ major thirteenth, and yet it will be noted that there is no tritone present in the I.S., and only one minor ninth is resolved. It illustrates, convincingly, that if dissonant intervals are organized into a tertiary ascendancy, they combine into a mutual coordinated sound. The one differing tone of the I.S., the A, placed directly above the bass tone, is sufficient in dislodging the other tonal relationships.

Examples 384b and *c* retain a discordant quality in both the I.S. and the rooted chord. One still feels the contrast between the conflicting tonal associations of the former and the solid dissonance of the latter. The rooted chord achieves dissonance through double inflections and tritone relationships.

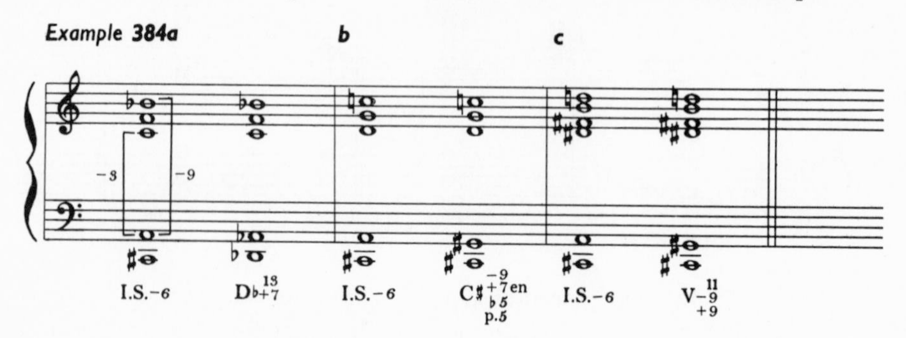

b] I.S. above a major sixth: The major sixth has as its potential root tone, the implied but not real presence of the fourth partial in the overtone series, or the tone that lies a perfect fourth above the bass tone. See *example 385*. It is amazing how effective this implied root can be in interjecting its quality into the vertical chord formation. *Example 385a* illustrates an upper placement of a perfect fourth formation in which the more positive lower major sixth suggests the G root. The same exists in *example 385b* where the possible B minor root may also be interpreted as G, barring a definite B minor tonality. The dominant qualities are shown in *example 385c*, ranging from the smooth, unaltered thirteenth to the discordant perfect fourth group which still has a strong inference of G.

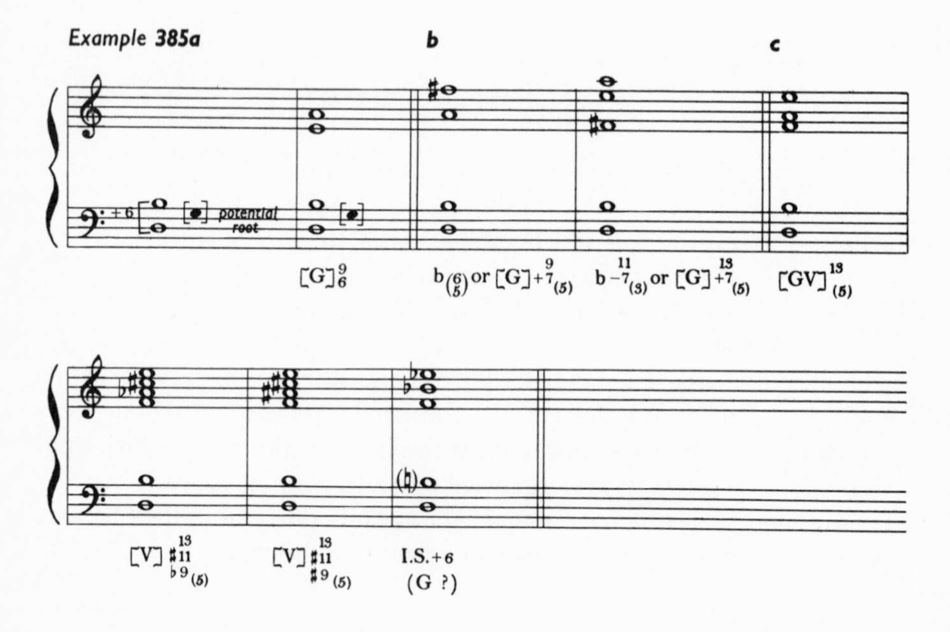

A discordant I.S. +6 is nevertheless possible. The lowest tone of the upper group is chosen by avoiding a close relationship to the root potential. See *example 386*.

Example 386

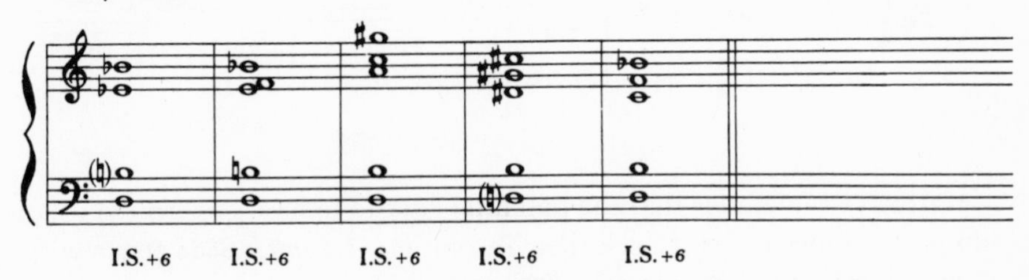

Polychords may be an unintentional result if upper triads or seventh chords are formed above either the minor or major sixth. Several are shown in *example 387*. The last chord of *example 387* illustrates the major sixth as part of a minor triad, with its dominant placed above it.

Example 387

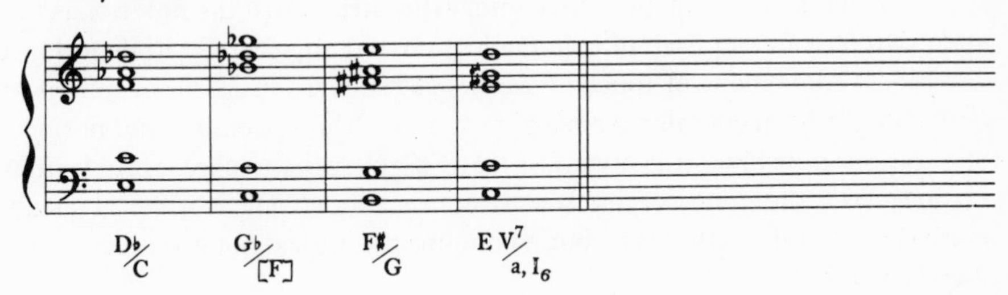

A discordant formation which is frequently used is one which places a third directly above a sixth, selecting the quality that avoids the octave formation. A minor sixth would have a minor third placed directly above it, as in *example 388a*. A wide variety of intervals may then be added to this basic quality.

Above a major sixth, a major third may be formed. This forms a minor ninth contour with the bass tone, and is a little more harsh than the preceding major seventh result. Compare *example 388b* with *example 388a*.

Example 388a **b**

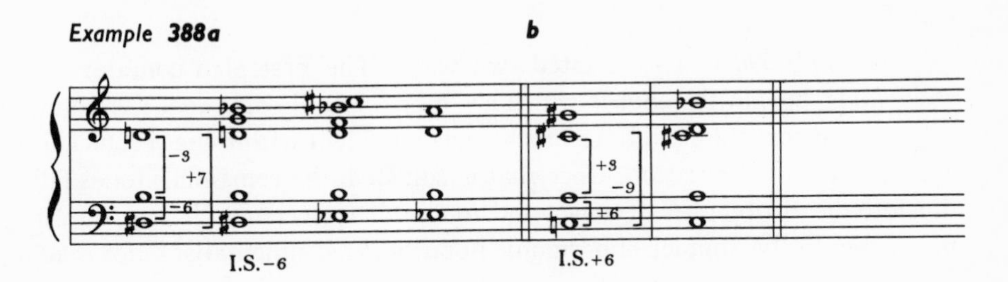

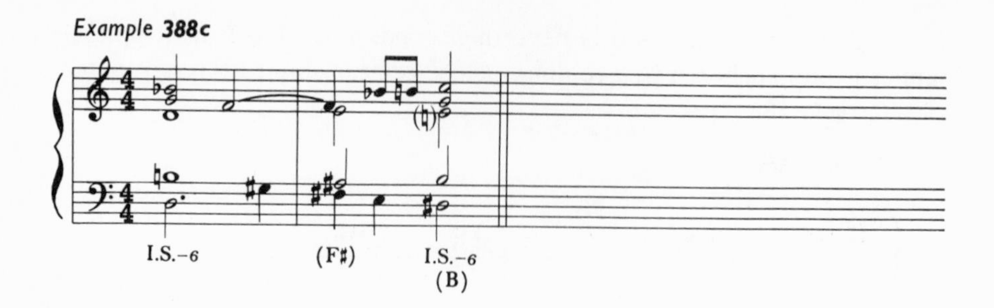

Always remember that the potential root tone may govern the relationship of the upper tones. Check their resolution. *Example 388c* starts with the second chord given in *example 388a* and illustrates the strengthening of a potential root tone through a melodic situation. The rhythmic duration of the tenor tone, B, together with the diatonic lines of both lower parts sufficiently emphasizes B as it returns in the last chord. The label I.S. –6 always bears the reference to the upper potential root tone. If the root is heard during the body of the phrase, indicate it by letter name below the I.S. designation as illustrated.

When dealing with indecisive intervallic structures, the notation is based upon two factors: an ease of communication and an accuracy in denoting the directional movement of tones. *Example 389* is written in two versions; the first *example 389a*, contains a normal notation. While listening and noting the interval relationships, it is apparent that F♯ governs the phrase. Rewritten in *example 389b*, the notation that makes F♯ visually strong is given. It is much more clumsy and unnecessary, but it contains the logical notation that supports the root tone, F♯.

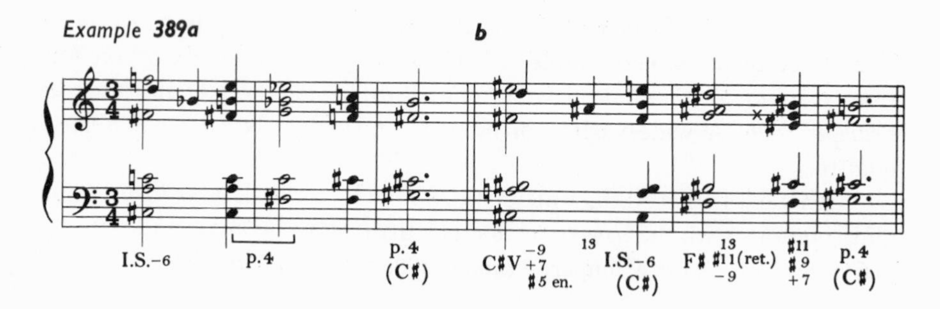

Example 390 is also notated two ways. The first plan contains fewer accidentals, but, in the chords which are more securely situated, the notation does not support the sound. The major triad, evident within the second chord, deserves a unified notation. Once that is adjusted, the remaining tones fall in line into the setting of A. If sharps and double sharps become clumsy, they may be written in the simpler enharmonic notation. Instrumentalists, not reading

the full score, prefer an uncomplicated notation. On the other hand, anyone analyzing or playing from a score prefers to see the notation that best supports what he hears.

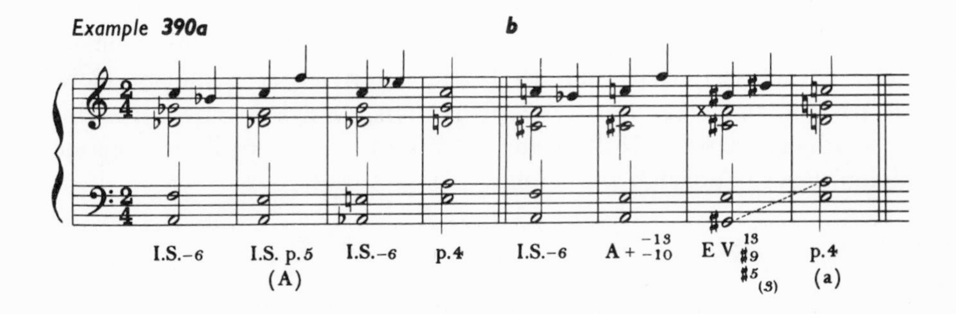

c] I.S. above thirds: Range is one of the most essential factors in evaluating harmonic structures emanating above an interval of a third, minor or major. As an interval, the major third is formed by the fourth and fifth partials of the overtone series. The major third inherits the support of the partials sounding beneath it; this includes two lower octave root tones, above which the lower tone of the major third is numerically the third re-enforcement of the fundamental root tone. With this in mind, the chords built upon major thirds are generally placed in a higher register than is necessary for the larger interval foundation. As a consequence, the tones of such a higher placed I.S. do not project the same root strength that might otherwise be felt. If the major third expands into a tenth in range, the space created between the two notes involved permits the vibrations of the lower tone to be more exposed and emit more root strength.

The I.S. formed above the major third (as well as above the minor third) is therefore very susceptible to other influences. A higher tone in the vertical structure may take the reins as a root, incorporating the lower major third into its tonal association, perhaps as an inversion. *Example 391* illustrates this occurrence, in addition to non-diatonic interval arrangements. Observe the useful fourth formations in this example.

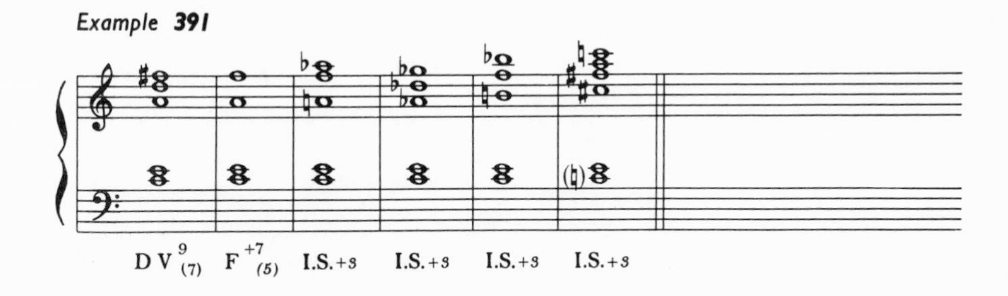

A minor third is founded on the fifth and sixth partials, neither of which is the root tone. This places the minor third into a very impartial category. It seeks to be incorporated into other tonal foundations. Of course it may be the root and third of a minor triad, but it would have to contain a strong supporting fifth or be obviously situated in a minor tonality in order to dominate within an intervallic structure as a minor third. More readily, it relates to diminished triad formations which in turn belong to a larger dominant hierarchy as part of an indeterminate root structure, or a known one heard upon resolution. *Example 392* illustrates each of the above possibilities except the diminished relationship which follows.

Example **392**

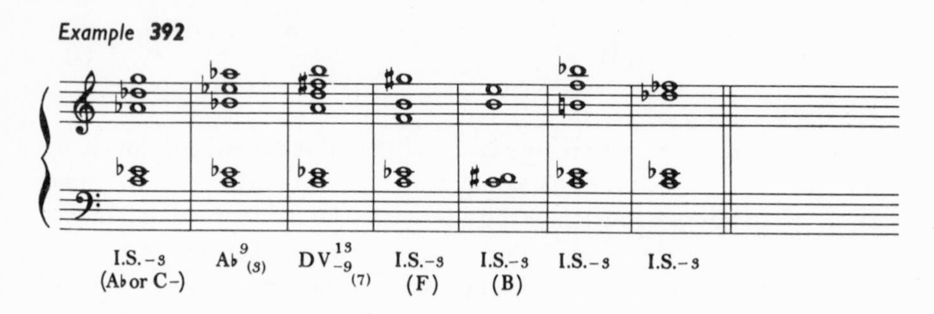

d] I.S. above a tritone interval: The intervallic structure built above a tritone interval may be the most ambiguous combination that can be formed. It need not be very harsh in its indecisive quality, but is necessarily quite active. *Example 393a* contains four of such intervallic structures, none of which, out of context, can show any root preference. As an experiment, play these structures and add a low bass tone to each. Try several for each chord. The distance between your chosen bass tone and the lowest note of the I.S. may provide a more firmly rooted chord as previously discussed.

Because the tritone implies the inclusion of two minor thirds within its frame, it frequently is used as a diminished triad above which tones of the I.S. may be added. The minor third structure, examined earlier, becomes part of the tritone relationship rather than remaining separated as a minor third. This diminished formation generally occurs in a higher register, while the tritone interval may begin quite low in the bass. See *example 393b*.

Example **393a** **b**

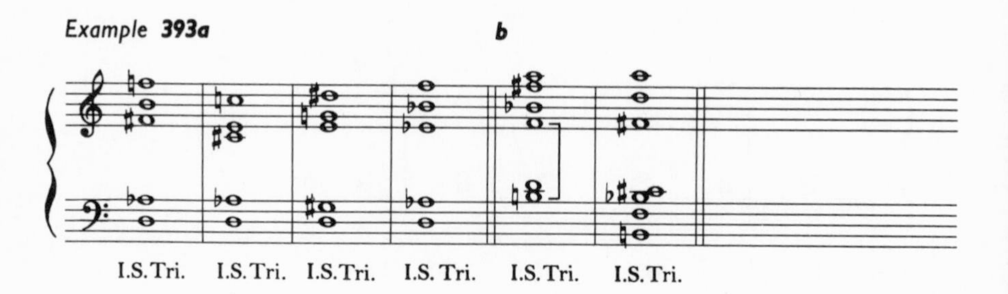

Notice the distinction between the labels I.S. Tri. and Tri. 4 (tritone fourth chord). The intervallic structure built above a tritone does not specify any organization of upper tones whereas the Tri. 4 is limited to tones comprised of vertically built fourths in which at least one interval is an augmented fourth, or tritone. The comparison between I.S. p. 4 and p. 4 (perfect fourth chord) is the same. While the latter is restricted to the perfect fourth organization, the I.S. p. 4 builds above the lowest perfect fourth interval and may contain any combination of tones. Compare *examples 394a* and *b*.

Example **394a** **b**

I.S. Tri. Tri. 4 I.S. p. 4 p. 4

e] I.S. above the sevenths: Building upon a minor seventh interval provides little opportunity to "shake" the firmness of the lower tone as root. The dominant function is hard to cancel, even with tones of the eleventh appearing directly above the basic minor seventh interval. Play the first two chords of *example 395a*. The soprano tone C♯ helps to confirm the A root in the first chord, but its omission would not upset the root strength. The second chord is clearly an intervallic structure, its upper complement of tones suggesting a D dominant minor ninth. Nevertheless, the lower seventh stands apart and emphasizes its bass tone. The third chord of *example 395a* also illustrates how the dominant quality may interject itself into a chord which appears to contain a minor third rather than a major one. The hollow space between the minor seventh actually permits the lowest tone to incorporate its overtone vibrations into the total vertical sound. The minor tenth above does not abolish the A major strength of the root tone, if aided by other tones of the harmonic series such as the ninth or thirteenth. The fourth formations, however, may inhibit the root suggestion formed by the lower seventh interval. If the fourths are superimposed immediately above the minor seventh interval, the tertiary grouping is sufficiently hampered as to negate a dominant strength. See the last five chords of *example 395a*. The designation "p. 4" represents quality and is marked below the I.S. symbol. It will be recalled that the preceding chapter discussed the possibility of an omitted tone in the fourth chord. If such an omission occurs, between bass and tenor, label the I.S. by the lowest interval and include "p. 4" below it as illustrated in the final chord of *example 395a*. Although a tritone fourth organization may also be marked when noted above the lowest interval, it is less distinct in quality, frequently blending into a dominant sound. Mark it only if enough tones spiral upward for a convincing fourth chord structure.

Example **395a**

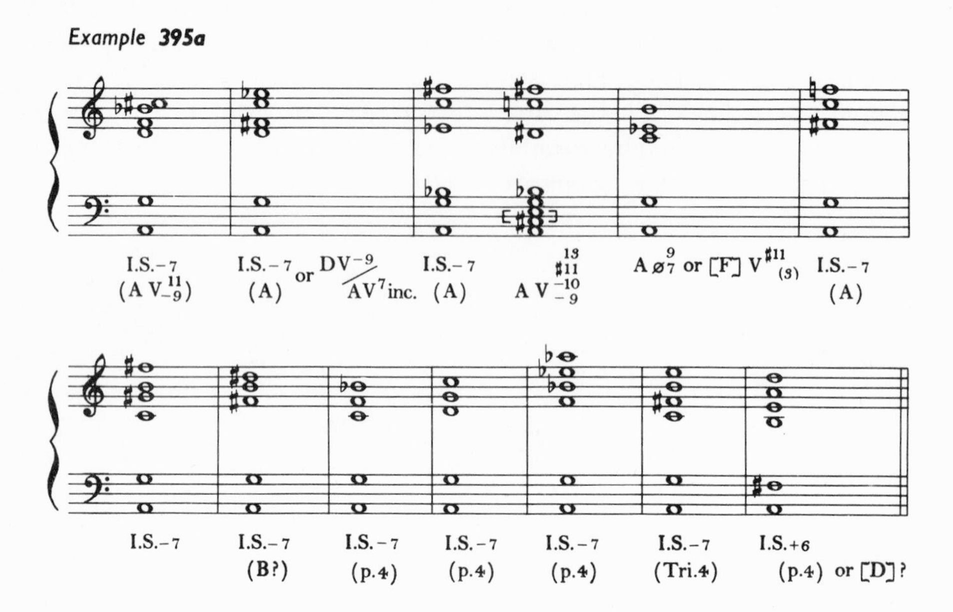

The major seventh provides an abundance of discordant intervallic structures. Discordant, but not necessarily very harsh. The space between the tones of a major seventh is wide enough so as not to cause a direct conflict. The selection of upper tones can run the gamut of interval groups. Their arrangement alone may or may not provide a root tone. See *example 395b*.

Example **395b**

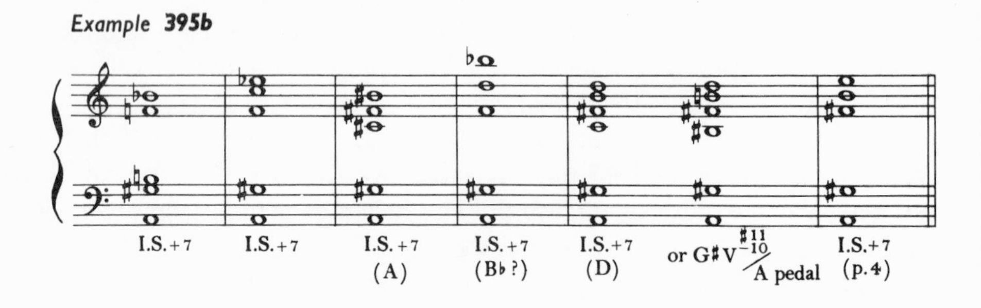

f] I.S. above seconds: By inversion, the seventh forms an adjacent interval of either a minor or major second to the lowest tone. These are best described as a cluster of two tones (or more) and serve to obscure the tonal value of the bass tones. The second itself is not important unless it represents a diatonic usage of the lowest tone as the seventh, adjacent to the root. The intervallic structure which rises above a major or minor second relies mostly upon the third note of the vertical formation for its harmonic association. This tone and the remaining upper tones generally ally themselves with a preferred tone heard from the lower group of three. The factors which indicate harmonic strength are: 1] the presence of a perfect fifth, especially when occurring as the outer interval within the three lowest tones of the I.S., 2] the suggestion of a dominant quality within any of the tones, and 3] the exposure given to certain tones by the degree of intervallic space surrounding them. Illustrating these in turn, *example 396a* shows the prominence of the perfect fifth, the cluster being adjacent to either of the tones producing the fifth. This is marked "I.S. +2, p. 5," so that the fifth is indicated as being important to the sound of the I.S. The marking for the second chord also stresses the perfect fifth and is explained fully in the following paragraphs which deal with the inner cluster.

Example 396b places the perfect fifth into an inner combination and thereby weakens its root potential (except in an obvious V^4_2 chord). Include this type of I.S. with all of the other freely formed interval combinations and mark it simply by the lowest interval, I.S. −2 or I.S. +2. All of the upper tones have equal bearing upon the lowest cluster and only as a group can they be analyzed for their harmonic association. In the last chord of *example 396b*, observe the exposure given to the upper perfect fifth. Its separation from the lower cluster makes B♭ very prominent. Indicate such potential roots by letter name below the I.S. symbol.

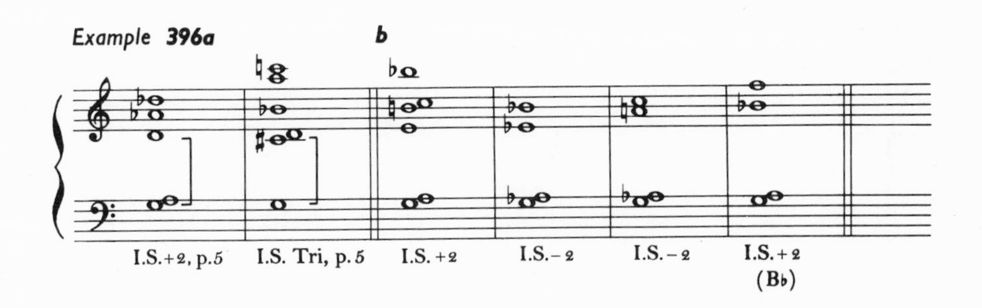

The chords of *example 396c* project a dominant influence within their make-up. The lowest interval (the minor or major second) may add a disturbing quality into the dominant sound, but generally one of the two tones will find some harmonic companions among the higher tones of the group. If this is the case, the dominant symbol together with the root tone may be included in the analysis. Remember that the movement of tones may clarify a progression and pinpoint the root tones. The enharmonic notation of the final chord of *example 396c* projects the function of two different roots, C or E. These are still intervallic structures; in fact, A♭ may also be considered as a potential root tone. The dissonant organization of intervals, such as the lower cluster, does not assume a diatonic heredity in the vertical sound, but the diatonic movement of pitch can never be completely abandoned.

Example **396c**

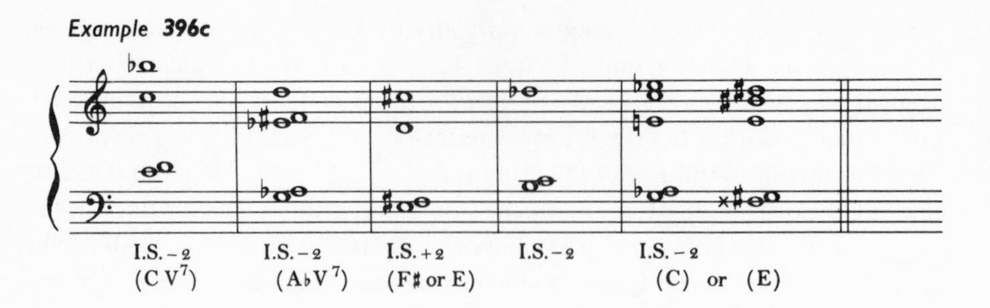

A cluster which occurs between the second and third tone of an intervallic structure, may negate the value of the interval formed by the two lowest tones, as described in the preceding paragraphs. This is due to the exposure that the upper tone maintains. It can be likened to a clamp in which the vibrations of the lower tone of the inside cluster are squelched by a more flexible and resonant upper tone. Where such a conflict occurs, the I.S. is most accurate if both tones of the cluster are represented in the symbol. Mark both intervals by their distance to the lowest tone. In this way the cluster is evident and it projects itself into the comprehension of the total harmonic sound. Play the intervallic structures in *example 396d*, listening to the dual suggestions that the inner cluster activates in the lowest tone.

Example **396d**

To summarize, do not be too hasty in applying the I.S. analysis. First check to see if the tertiary organization is implied, even if a note or two may not be "properly" located. Apply the I.S. designation only if the tertiary order doesn't fit or doesn't sound. Check the lowest two, three, or more intervals.

Remember which potential root tone the lowest intervals indicate and see if a melodic line gives it any support. A rhythmic stress given to a particular tone may provide all that is necessary for hearing a root tone. This is illustrated in *example* 396e. The rhythmic stress on F in the first measure is carried in the following dissonant chord which results in the hearing of an F root, adjacent to the seventh in the bass.

Linear tonality

Many of the indecisive intervallic structures are controlled by a melody line which has a degree of linear tonality. This over-all tonal suggestion may be present within a motive or during a phrase. It is prompted by the stronger intervals that suggest linear roots. If the harmony below the melody tones is indeterminate, the melody itself may guide the whole movement of sound. In this respect it suggests a shifting of the role of harmonic provider away from the bass and toward the melody. The bass used to control all harmonic movement, but today it may be extremely polyphonic without binding all parts into one harmonic merger. Since the ear catches the motion of the outer voices as being most prominent, it is logical that the melody can bear a harmonic responsibility if the bass becomes neutral.

In phrases where a melody is contained within a basic tonal area but is harmonized by intervallic structures which for the most part do not support it, mark the upper tonality by its letter name reference, but proceed with I.S. designations until a merger into the upper tonal association occurs. In *example* 397, the melody reflects the tonal center of A. Not until the second measure does the harmonic background truly concur.

Example 397

It may be desirable to distinguish between linear tonality and linear roots within a phrase. While linear roots are recognized within a group of two, three, or four tones of a horizontal line, and pertain to a single root suggestion; linear tonality may be made up of several linear roots and is thought of in the broad sense of tonality, not as a progression. *Example* 398 is too short to denote a tonality, but it shows the root potential provided by the upper tones (not only the melody) as it conflicts with the lower bass intervals. The upper tones revolve around E♭, the lower ones support A major. They merge through two indecisive minor third intervallic structures, and lead to a cadence on B major. The linear tonality of E♭ helps to make prominent a particular linear root, heard in the tenor line on beats two and three of the second measure. The skip of the perfect fourth creates an implied E♭ chord in the first inversion. The sound of E♭, present from the beginning, does not vanish as the chord omits the E♭ on the third beat and looks merely like a G minor-major seventh-ninth chord. It illustrates the minor third functioning as a first inversion.

Frequently, an analysis that stresses the linear concept is more appropriate than the beat by beat succession of complex intervallic structures. In *example 398*, the upper linear tonality of E♭ gains prominence as the phrase moves along. The vertical sounds provide a thick texture, rather than a harmonic tonal sense. In both of the outer voices, directional tones guide the lines toward B, the lower submediant to E♭.

Example 398

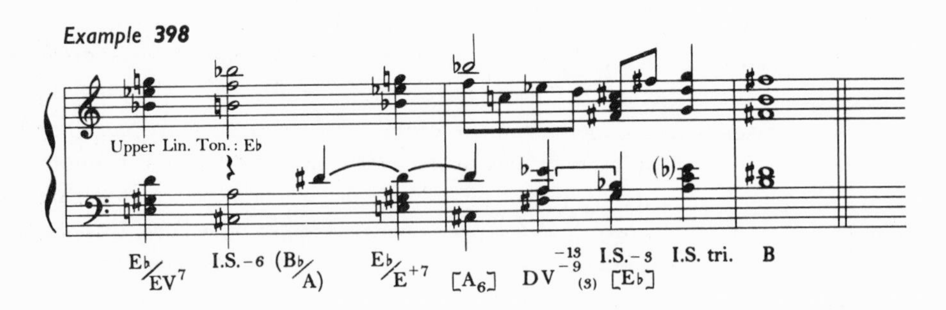

The conflict of major and minor thirds has inspired many composers by its unusual battle; few dissonances are as emphatically portrayed. (Except for clusters, more space is usually present between other double inflections. Not only that, but different interpretations can be attached to some, such as involves the perfect and diminished fifth. The latter is recognized as a raised eleventh in many instances.) The thirds on the other hand, are so close to the root that they both wish to declare their mode. (A raised ninth is only recognized above the dominant seventh complement of tones.) The harshness results when the lower use of the minor third is contradicted by an upper major third. No matter what type I.S. this may occur in, it always will sound strident, as if unfitting.

An interesting and exciting exposure of the minor and major third conflict occurs in Aaron Copland's *Piano Sonata* (1939–41). The opening phrase, quoted in *example 399* contains two particular harmonic features which deal with the third. The first is the use of cross-relation and the second, the simultaneous chordal use of the natural eleventh with the major third. In hearing this phrase, the sounds may seem quite terse and perhaps suggest an analysis of intervallic structures. The analysis given directly below the music indicates the I.S. conclusions and by observing the root potential, most of those chords become meaningful in a tertiary order. The latter is the correct conclusion, and the interval computation is a stepping-stone path which separates the immediate discordant relationship of pitches with the organized chord in which a single tone produces the conflict.

The B♭ minor key signature leaves no doubt as to tonality. It is expressed simply in a minor third interval duplicated at the octave. The cross-relation is immediately evident as the directional tone of D♭ drops to the lowest tone, D♮. The progression intentionally declares that the motive will convey the change in mode from minor, to major, and back to minor in the next chord, a tonic ninth (incomplete). This becomes a pattern in the movement, and is used with lovely lyricism in the second theme.

Suppose the second chord (of measure one) was not understood at first in its basic tonal interpretation. As an I.S. −3, it is likely to convey the third and fifth of a major triad, the root potential is B♭. There it sits in the soprano! On the other hand, suppose you juggled the given notes and produced a G♭ augmented major seventh chord. This would place the lowest note as a raised fifth, an analysis which does not convey the composer's intentions of the mixture of thirds.

The third and fourth measures also illustrate the value of thinking of chord structures from the bottom up, as collections of intervals, in the search for the root potential or the strongest interval group in the structure. The second chord in the third measure, in diatonic terms, can be either a G minor chord with both a minor ninth and minor thirteenth, but no seventh; or, it can be an E♭ triad with an eleventh added on top. It can also look like, but not sound like, an A♭ major seventh-ninth chord. The inversion in this hypothesis of the seventh and ninth in the bass, completely disproves this possibility. Nevertheless, here are three diatonic versions. The essential determination of which tone is the root, is apt to be ignored in the attempt at a tertiary organization of tones. By applying the concept that the minor third may belong in an implied major chord as its third and fifth, the root tone of E♭ is immediately understood. The

Piano Sonata. Aaron Copland

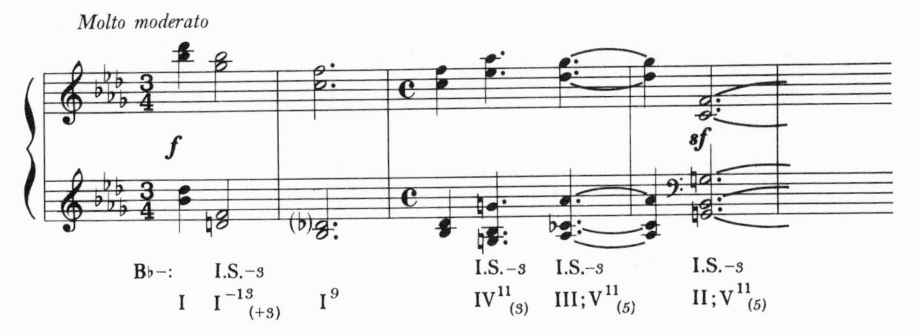

tonal feature of the deliberate stress on the natural eleventh, heard against the bass inversions of the major third, becomes clear. The following two chords utilize the same quality of sound except for a slightly different formation. This time the minor third functions as fifth and seventh of a D♭ dominant seventh chord. The natural eleventh is still in the highest part but is not in direct confrontation with the third. The root progression for these last three chords is a stepwise one, from E♭ through D♭ to C. The long directional root plan moves simply from its tonic of B♭ minor to a cadential pause on the root of C. This stark quality is used as a substitute for the dominant semi-cadence harmony of the past. Observe that the melody tone in the fourth measure is the dominant tone, and that the melody outlines the unmistakable linear tonality of B♭ minor.

Paired intervals

Intervals need not be massed in a harmonic column of tones. Any interval may be placed in a particular range, and without additional sound, may represent the total harmonic quality at that moment. This differs from two-part writing in that the latter contains motivic movement while an intervallic structure of two tones may be devoid of polyphonic interest.

This is illustrated in *example 400* together with two other aspects of intervallic treatment. Intervals may be heard as isolated units if any extremely wide range separates the conflicting pairs. Except for obvious triadic associations, a merging of tonal sounds is hampered by a gap in the middle range. This may be likened to a pedal tone situation where the range differential permits two recognized roots, that of the upper material against the rooted bass tone or tones (such as the perfect fifth ground). In non-diatonic writing, intervals of any size may be spaced at such distances that they neither merge, nor suggest their own independent root scheme. They merely denote an intervallic sound, each interval functioning separately in the wide tonal span.

Intervals moving in parallel motion constitute another form of interval design. Motion of parallel thirds or sixths in the Classical age was generally used as a passing-tone device within a known harmonic context. The Impressionistic type of parallelism expanded the passing-tone idea into passing harmonic sounds. The Modern application provides for parallel intervals which substitute for any harmonic content and also produce the sole motivic interest.

The two excerpts from Bartók, *examples 400a* and *b* illustrate the above situations. *Example 400a* is an introduction to the lyrical theme of the third movement from Music for String Instruments, Percussion and Celesta. Against a string trill cluster, parallel major seventh intervals provide all of the harmonic background. They maintain their pattern against the forthcoming melody, which is highly chromatic and can only be analyzed by its directional tones. The harmonic quality therefore arises from the parallel motion of the major seventh intervals.

Example 400b represents the goal of the phrase just described. The intervallic structure on the first beat contains only two tones, but doubled in the higher octaves. The sound is that of the tritone. Although the pitches, G♯ and D, may be interpreted as representing the tones of the dominant, Bartók at this point was more concerned with the intervallic quality than with the leading-tone characteristics of G♯.

A second tritone enters in the lower strings. Here the principle of the wide range takes effect. The treble and bass are isolated, each contributing to a quality of sound but not merging into a harmonic unit. The xylophone and timpani add to the imaginative orchestration.

Completing the measure, a brief rhythmical motive is heard in the piano. It again uses only the tritone, this time as a parallel design for emphasising the motive. Its linear shape strengthens the tone of E which functions as a dominant for the next phrase.

Motives based upon interval designs: Intervals may formulate a special design used as part of the theme's structure or even as an architectural force in shaping the form of the composition. The latter is most explicitly illustrated in the second movement of Bartók's *Concerto for Orchestra*. Pairs of instruments are used, each is given a specific interval which they play in parallel motion while stating their theme: The movement begins with two bassoons playing in parallel minor sixths. After they complete the main part of the theme, the second part is played by two oboes in parallel minor thirds. Clarinets follow playing sevenths, flutes in parallel fifths, and the first large division of the

movement closes with trumpets playing in parallel seconds. The paired instruments together with their special interval characteristics create the form for the movement.

Another type of design in which vertical intervals control the main thought in the music is one which deliberately plays with the different sizes of intervals. A design may start with a tenth and shrink to a second, or by contrast, emphasize an expanding role. If the listener's attention is made to focus upon such an intervallic scheme, then it must command the chief structural recognition for that particular phrase.

Bartók used such an intervallic design in the third movement of the *Second String Quartet*. See *example 401*. The design is one of gradual intervallic expansion, occurring in the first phrase. (Later phrases are also preoccupied with intervals, but unlike the movement from the *Concerto for Orchestra*, this movement does not shape itself upon an intervallic plan.) The opening measures are played only by two stringed instruments. After the starting

Example 401 *Second String Quartet.* **Bartók**

minor second, the second violin drops a minor third. The second measure's sequence contains a slightly larger drop of a major third. After an intervening viola and cello figure, the first motive's interval is enlarged to the descending leap of a perfect fourth. This is followed in the seventh bar by the same pattern but involving the perfect fifth interval. It is evident that the plan of widening each interval in a motivic concept supercedes that of any contrapuntal, harmonic or directional tone idea.

Linear intervals may also dominate a theme's character if a particular plan is emphasized. This is true in the principal theme of the *Fourth String Quartet* by Bartók, presented in a very polyphonic texture. The main motive appears in measure seven, having evolved gradually from the preceding intervallic fragments. It consists entirely of minor seconds. See *example* **402a**, measures seven, eleven and twelve. The contrapuntal preparation for this motive is easily seen in the first few bars; also in the canonic imitation which starts with the fifth measure and continues again in the eighth measure in its tightening motivic grasp. The minor second dominates the "theme" which is actually only the length of a motive.

Against this main idea, the cello in measures one and two also illustrates linear intervals that are chosen with an intervallic plan rather than on a harmonic or melodic basis. The starting bass tone, however, has harmonic value. The root C is announced immediately and established with many directional indications as the first section of the theme unfolds. The linear intervals which follow the first bass tone C, do so by an intervallic plan. Each interval rises by a distance of a sixth. The last of the group of five tones is the leading-tone, resolved by the first violin's answering sequence to the opening motive. The other tones of the cello part (measures one and two) do not affect a harmonic progression in any important way. Their role is one of sounding a contrary direction to the upper parts, one of supplying dissonant strength and of setting forth an intervallic structure in an arpeggio manner.

Example **402a** *Fourth String Quartet. Bartók*

The beginning of the recapitulation is quoted in *example 402b*. All motives are fully exposed. The sixths in the cello part elide vertically, maintaining their independent character against the other material. The only harmonic analysis that both the excerpts produce is in the recognition of the linear tonality of C and in the varying fluctuations of vertical tension caused by the intervals themselves.

Example **402b** *Fourth String Quartet. Bartók*

EXERCISES

A *Analysis*

1] In the excerpts quoted in *Example* **403**, distinguish between polychords, single rooted chords containing a double inflection, and intervallic structures. Vocal writing demands more care in the selection of linear intervals. Observe the smooth part-writing in this composition for mixed voices. Vertical dissonances are achieved without difficult vocal skips. (The piano accompaniment is omitted.)

Example **403a** *Tristis est anima mea. Nicolas Flagello*

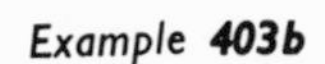
Example 403b

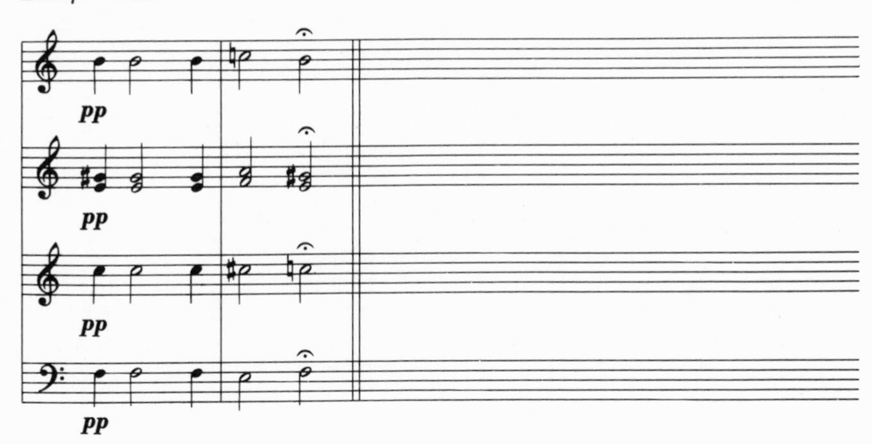
pp
pp
pp
pp

Example 403c
(Flagello)

Più lento
Sopr.
ff
Alto
Tenor
Bass.

Example 403d
(Flagello)

Lento molto
Sopr.
p
ppp
Alto
ppp
Tenor
ppp
Bass.

2] In analyzing the intervallic structures of *Example 404*, mark:
a] the tones which represent the conflict of thirds;
b] the interval of the I.S. and the letter name of the root tone, if present; and
c] any tones in the melody (beginning from measure seven) which contribute to the lower harmonic association.

Example 404 *Symphony No. 6. Wm. Schuman*

3] Analyze the intervallic designs that are part of the harmonic background, and those which govern the motivic material in *Example 405*.

Example 405a *String Quartet No. 2. Wallingford Riegger*

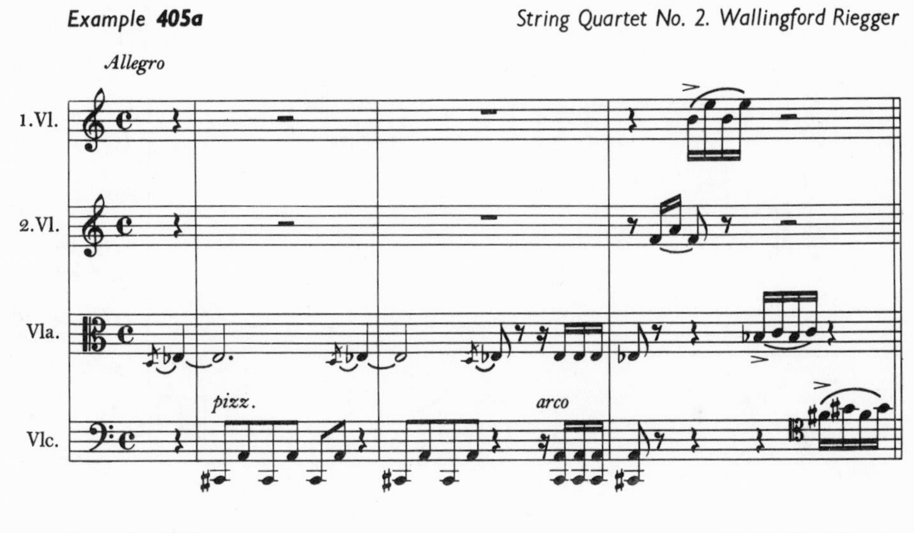

Example 405b *Wallingford Riegger*

fp
pizz.
arco
f
cresc.
p
mf
etc.

B Fill in the inner voices of *Examples* **406a**, **b**, and **c**. The I.S. indications specify a tenor note by interval but the remaining tones are left for your selection. Where a harmonic association is created, mark the letter name root below the figuration. Some chords are designated by a tertiary organization.

Example 406b
Andante
p
I.S. −3 I.S. tri. C+7 (4/2) I.S. −3 I.S. tri. I.S., p.5, −6 p.4 A V 11 (3) p.4 I.S. −7 (p.4)
I.S.+9 Tri.4 C+7 9 C V ♯11 (3) (B) I.S.+3, p.4 I.S.+7 (p.4) (E) I.S., p.4 I.S.+2−3
E −10 (3) p.4 G+7 I.S. −2 I.S., p.4, p.5 F V 9 (3)
p
a −7 9 F ♯9 (3) E V −13 −10 −9 I.S.+7 I.S., p.5 (a−)
Example 406c
Moderato
I.S. −6/+6 ·/· ·/· I.S. −6 B♭ V ♯9 f +7 −3 IS. −6 I.S. −3 I.S.+3 I.S.+6

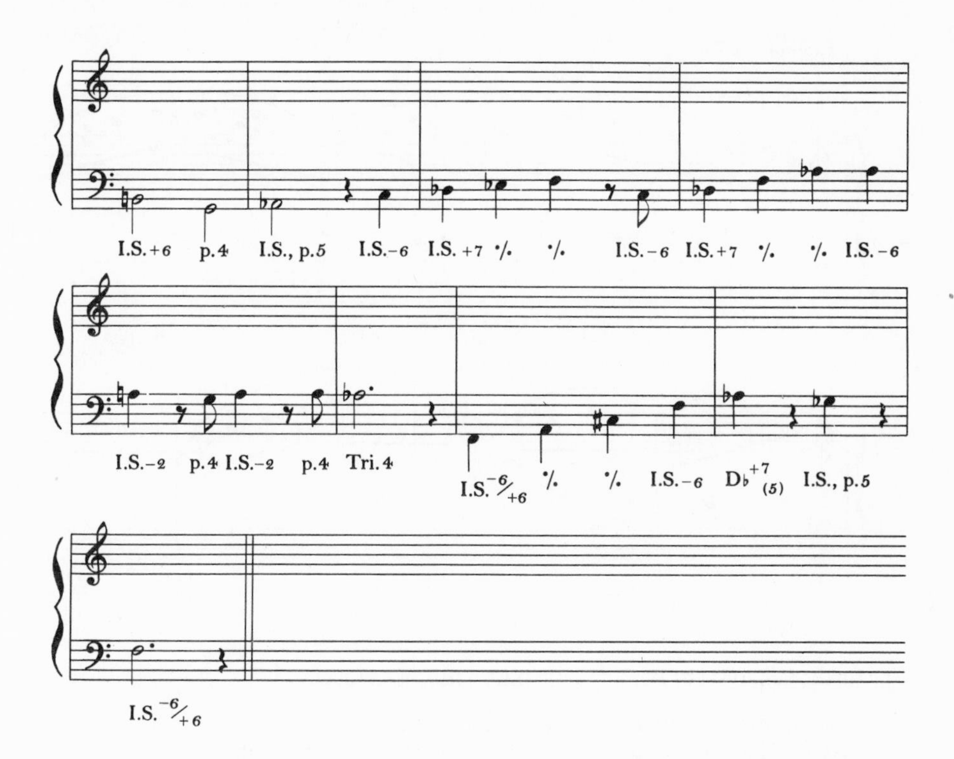

C An interval design shapes the motivic, and at times, harmonic result in *Examples 407a, b,* and *c*. Continue the given materials. Be guided by a careful application of directional tones and linear tonality. Mark the analysis after the exercise is completed.

Example **407c**

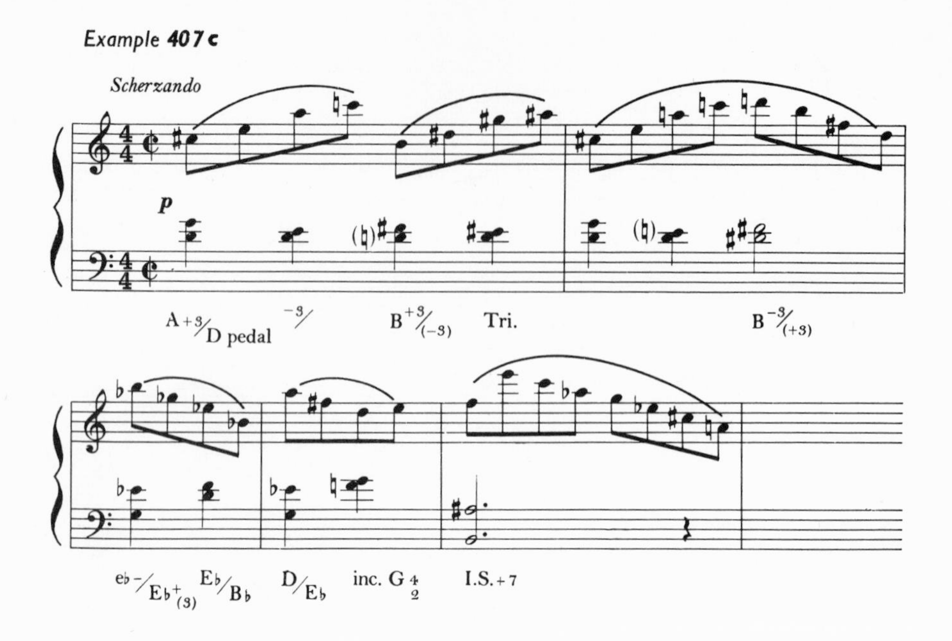

For further analysis of homophonic intervallic structures see:

Fourth String Quartet, Movement III, by Bartók
String Quartet IV, middle of Movement II, by Hindemith
Piano Fantasy, by Copland
For a linear interval design, study and listen to:
Sonata for Piano, Movement III, by Barber
Piano Sonata, Movement II, by Copland
Piano Variations, by Copland
Symphony No. IV, by William Schuman
Drei lieder, Op. 25, No. 1, by Webern

For a simple illustration of thematic material in which parallel intervals and chords encompass the whole composition, see:
Visions fugitives Nos. I, III and XV, by Prokofiev

19 The control of dissonance

Distinguishing between dissonance and discord

By definition, dissonance is a mingling of discordant sounds. Discordant sounds, however, are judged by their relationship to other sounds, and by definition cannot be determined with any precision, out of context. Musical expressions change with the passage of time. Certain intervallic combinations, dissonant in the time of Palestrina, became agreeable in the Classical age. Musical history can also show that compositions from the fourteenth century contain more "dissonance" than those of the sixteenth century, when judged by the latter standard.

Dissonance implies a sound that is unpleasing, but this reflects upon individual reactions. What may be extremely harsh for one person's taste, could be exciting and desirable to another. As a musical term, dissonance was not intended to represent an ugly sound, but rather, a sounding of tones which together do not have a close harmonic relationship, as contrasted with consonance. The following definition of "discord" is quoted from an early edition of Groves' *A Dictionary of Music and Musicians* in which the term, dissonance, is entirely omitted: "Discord is a combination of notes which produces a certain restless craving in the mind for some further combination upon which it can rest with satisfaction." Such a definition applies to all music of all ages. Every musical style has its particular discords, and a fluctuation between discords and concords must occur. Discords, therefore, have an active quality, in which the tension can be felt in greater or lesser degrees.

Melodic and Rhythmic tensions

The vertical sound alone is not the complete factor that can determine the extent of tension created in a passage. To respond to a dramatic, climactic goal in music, the tension must be built gradually, and planned to occur in a structural area appropriate to the composition as a whole. Tension is built melodically and rhythmically, then, at the point where the composer desires the ultimate amount of strain or intensity, the harmonic chord is emphasized, and thus noted for its active and perhaps dissonant make-up. But without the necessary preparation, this same chord may not engender the same degree of intensity, if isolated as a vertical structure. Review *example 28*. The release of tension is as important as its preparation. The satisfaction obtained from the change of active harmonies to the more stable chords fulfills the purpose of the entire process. If the extent of active drive was considerable, the feeling of achievement must be allowed enough time to unwind leisurely. Codettas serve this purpose. Or, the announcement of an important theme, whether previously stated or not, may provide an excellent means of expanding and retaining this sense of accomplishment. See *example 28*, measures thirty-one to thirty-four. Generally, the harmonies of such themes are stable and unhurried, contrasting with the harmonic activity which accompanies the preceding rise of tension.

In Beethoven's *Fifth Symphony*, the transition which connects the third movement with the fourth, starts upon a hushed deceptive cadence and ever so gradually builds toward the statement of the "Allegro's" principal theme. This approach contributes toward the triumphant entry of this theme, making it one of the most dramatic and exciting themes in musical literature. Beethoven put into motion all musical forces for the preparation of this brilliant "Finale." The constant pulsations of the timpani, later reinforced by the lower strings, provide the rhythmic momentum. The fragmentation of the third movement's chief motive tightens the melodic groups as it climbs in range. Harmonic tension increases as many of the ascending melodic tones do not form complete chords, but rather, intervallic dissonances which culminate in the dominant seventh chord sounding simultaneously with a sustained tonic pedal in the bassoons and in the active timpani. The resolution of this all-encompassing momentum is in the statement of the next theme. It doesn't sag, but remains alert within its own rhythmic movement and melodic dignity.

The above paragraph has described the planning and fulfillment necessary for a large climactic drive; but tension exists in varying degrees, and is part of all musical phrases. Melodic tension is felt when tones depart from the recognized tonic tone; fulfillment comes upon the tonic's return. See *example 408a*. Rhythmic tension is created by an increase of rhythmic divisions of the basic beat. One can tap with a pencil or play a drum; no pitch is necessary, see *example 408b*. Harmony is the result of several melodic parts sounding together and when these parts are coordinated to form root progressions, tension arises from two factors, namely: (1) the melodic tendencies of the individual parts continue to dictate the movement of the harmony, forming a joint melodic tension; and (2) a vertical tension may be emphasized when the parts form a discord.

Examples 408c, d, and e illustrate each of these processes within a harmonic phrase. *Example* 408c is based upon the melody of *example* 408a, and the harmony selected is deliberately devoid of a vertical discord. Upon leaving the opening tonic chord, the tenor first realizes its return in measure three. The remaining voices delay their return until measure five at the cadence. Tension toward both the I_4^6 and the dominant to tonic cadence is entirely melodic, the harmonic union of sound being drawn from the parts, and joining simultaneously in the drive toward the cadence. *Example* 408d adds a simple rhythm to the melody and its basic harmonization. By the division of the first beat of measure three into sixteenth notes, the rhythmic tension increases and culminates on the quarter note G. The preparation for this rhythmic goal was made by the eighth note divisions in the first two measures. Of special interest is the fact that neither the passing vertical discord in measure two, nor the tonic tone's arrival as a I^6_4 in measure three, supercedes the rhythmic goal on the I_6 of the third measure. An alternate melody is also shown illustrating that the rhythmic impetus may continue beyond the high G of the melodic contour, permitting the subdominant chord to be the recipient of the rhythmic movement. *Example* **408e** includes one discord and combines the elements of rhythm and melody, showing how each contributes toward the feeling of tension. The five-bar phrase, although not typical in this period, helps to evaluate the separate factors by not permitting the rhythmic symmetry of the ordinary four-bar phrase to dominate. Tension here is created in the following manner: (1) by the melodic and harmonic departure from the tonic chord; (2) the evasion from the I^6_4 into an active discord (the leading-tone seventh chord of D minor, the supertonic); (3) the rhythmic continuance of the alto line in spite of the consonant resolution to the II_6; (4) the dominant harmony with its active melodic leading-tone retains the tension until resolved at the cadence, completing the phrase. Notice the omission of the dominant seventh tone, another proof that the vertical structure, by itself, does not cause tension.

Vertical tension; discords

The beauty in music that is produced by the proper control of vertical tension was recognized by composers of all times. The suspensions of Palestrina, the pedal tones of Bach and the chromatic tones of the Classical age are all melodic features designed to create vertical tension. The resolutions of these non-harmonic tones provide a relaxation of the harmonic impetus.

A simple example of the poignancy achieved through a combination of melodic and vertical tensions is heard in the opening measures of the "Andante" movement from Bach's *Italian Concerto, example* **409**. Within this plain melodic contour, the melody rises to a peak on the subdominant harmony and on its descent, relaxes the tensions while returning momentarily to the tonic harmony in the second measure. The active leading-tone in the third measure remains unresolved for the duration of the entire bar and builds up an urgent demand for its forthcoming resolution. At this point, the tonic pedal tone, with its persistent rhythm, creates a mounting vertical discord as the upper dominant harmonies deliberately clash against the pedal tone. It must be remembered that the duration of the upper tones linger over the bass pedal forming a vertical discord notwithstanding the eighth note notation. Taking into account the leisurely pace of the harmonic movement of this introductory phrase, the

Example **409** "Italian Concerto." Bach

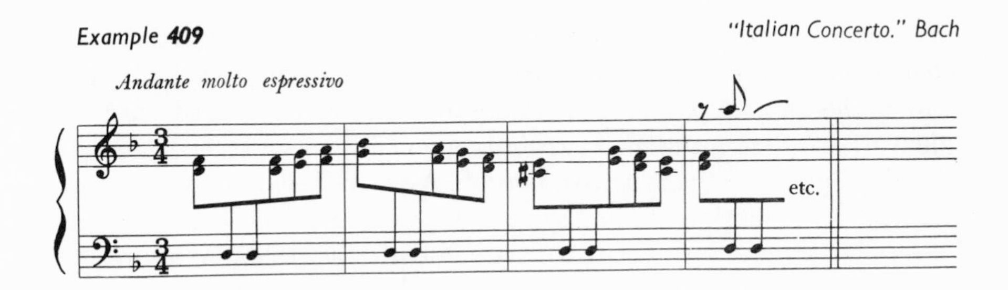

time devoted to the increase of tension is considerable. Its release, therefore, is all the more welcome.

Masterful compositions show a continuous balance between the increase and decrease of tensions. Although the fluctuation of the quality of sound is manifested in root progressions and in varying triads and seventh chords formed by the different scales, rhythmic and melodic attention must be added to this vertical sound to insure the success of a beautiful passage. In executing a harmonic exercise, complete with proper progression and voice-leading, have you ever wondered why the result may still be boring? The common four-part drills are generally devoid of the type of rhythmic interest that affects melodic movement and which focuses attention upon a select number of chords that govern the increase or decrease of tension. An exercise in which each diatonic roman numeral is preceded by an embellishing seventh chord, cannot become an artistic musical phrase, because the tensions of each embellishing chord are equal to one another, as are the resolutions formed. One phrase, therefore, is a jagged up and down experience, which can be likened to the mental picture of a saw. A boring diatonic composition may sound all right as far as chord connections are concerned, but may lack the rhythmic subtlety that enhances the differing areas of tension formed by a rhythmic movement of the harmonies involved. In a good modern piece, the astute listener will also respond to the fluctuations of harmonic intensity. If a composition seems monotonous, try to discern a level of tension and follow it in an attempt to hear a result, either up or down. Too many times, a composition lacks the necessary increase of tension (and this also applies to the most dissonant twelve-tone works), or it maintains such a barrage of intensity, that numbness sets in.

Discords must be evaluated within the scope of the harmonic intensity common to the particular style of the composition. As seen in *example* 409, Bach's use of the pedal tone provided the discord which, when analyzed together with all of the chord tones of that third measure, results in the hearing of intervals that include the tritone and the major seventh. All musical styles or periods utilize these same intervals to gain tension. As the harmonic techniques increase with musical growth, the areas of tension become more complex, with discords containing several tritones, minor seconds and their inverted uses. We do not, however, respond to this dissonance in terms of a greater tension than in the Bach, because it is all relative to the particular idiom that is exposed in the composition. This comparison is true not only between musical periods, but within the expressions of each composition. If major second clusters are idiomatic in a descriptive piece, a chord containing a minor second interval may be a focal point for the increased tension. Also, the capacity to feel tension is subjective; the range is affected by the individual's musical education and taste. The composer may manipulate changes of tension according to his inclination but these may not affect the listener in the same degree as felt by the composer.

Any guide for charting tensions is risky. As already noted, melody and rhythm are equal factors involved with the vertical discord. Nevertheless, discords can be contrasted with concords if each composition is treated within its own idiomatic context, and if some melodic license is tolerated. To the student, the value of the chart is in the discernment of different types of discords and in their discretionary use. A balance between concords and discords must take place in all compositions. A preponderance of one type of chord in a phrase would suggest a monotonous response, no matter what quality sound, consonant or dissonant, it might be.

The following guide divides the changing harmonic practices into four basic periods: the general Classical period as representing all diatonic writing; the late Romantic, which adds an expansion of harmonic material, but remains basically diatonic; the Impressionistic period; and the Modern period, encompassing both the compositions in which some diatonic elements are retained, as well as compositions written with the serial technique. Chronological dates for these periods cannot be used as composers and compositions overlap. Within the *Twenty-Four Preludes*, Opus II of Scriabin, three of the above musical periods are represented. It is also understood that musical growth builds upon the former practices, so that compositions classed as Impressionistic, will contain diatonic passages and may also dart forward and use chords more generally considered as Modern, such as the perfect-fourth chord. Within the Modern classification, it also follows that the triad belongs as rightfully to Hindemith as it does to Bach. Even the serial compositions cannot escape all former tonal hearing, as the linear writing involved may create vertical combinations which are not totally removed from earlier harmonic usage.

Because music is so flexible, and intolerant of strict laws, the following guide classifies vertical tensions into three groups: concords, discords, and in-between "dual-purpose" chords. This "gray" category symbolizes sounds which in different contexts may express a different amount of tension, thus suggesting either a concordant or discordant quality, or a degree between the two. Clarifying the use of the terms "concord" and "discord," the following approach is suggested: Discords are harmonies which require a resolution, while concords are the recipients of such motion. Definitions which attempt to specify concords or discords by strict interval distinction can only be used for limited musical periods, and in such study their understanding is most valuable, as in the knowledge of sixteenth century contrapuntal techniques. In this chart, an over-all evaluation is intended, with attention drawn toward specific intervals and their changing attitudes in the different musical styles or individual concepts.

In grouping the chords into categories of concords, discords, or dual-purpose chords, notice that some melodic association with a diatonic tonality is included. It is impossible to abandon the melodic tensions in a phrase, particularly in the Classical period, and respond only to a vertical concord or discord when analyzing the movement of tension in the complete phrase. It is with this concept that the dual-purpose listing includes the dominant triad and the tonic $^{6}_{4}$. Of course, as an isolated triad, the dominant has the same vertical make-up as any other major triad of the scale. But music is not a collection of isolated triads and when such obvious melodic tensions, as those incorporating the leading-tone or a dominant pedal, supercede the vertical tension, acknowledgement of this type of motion is warranted. In a similar respect, chords containing chromatic tones may have more discordant qualities than their diatonic counterparts. For example, the Neapolitan sixth chord, containing the chromatically lowered tones of the second and sixth degrees of a major scale, inherits a downward drive toward the cadence. Its major quality is felt quite differently from that of a dominant or tonic major triad. Nevertheless, the primary concern of this chart is to formulate a guide of vertical tensions. All melodic movement cannot be depicted, and it is here limited to the recognition of modulation and to the dominant chord, largely because of its dual role in music. When the dominant precedes the tonic chord, it creates an insistence for resolution; on the other hand, when used as a concluding chord of a phrase, as in a semi-cadence, it is the recipient of other active harmonies, and temporarily responds as a concord.

The second inversion of a tonic triad, major or minor, also is capable of a mixed evaluation. In early polyphony, the dissonant perfect fourth made it a discord, en route to the dominant triad. In the Classical usage, the tonic $^{6}_{4}$ was frequently given rhythmic stress and duration, making it a focal point of the cadence. This treatment results in a concordant quality; the satisfaction is achieved at this point of the phrase, and is merely followed by the inevitable cadence. Going beyond this cadential use, Wagner frequently placed the tonic $^{6}_{4}$ at the beginning of a phrase using it as a background for a soaring melody or *leitmotif* (see *example 28*). In the Modern period, the tonic $^{6}_{4}$ is even used as a final cadence chord. It does not give the same complete satisfaction that a root position tonic would have, but by contrasting it with the greater dissonances that precede it, the effect produced is clearly that of a concord. This is illustrated in *example* 414e together with other examples which show how this guide may be applied.

Guide of vertical tension

General Classical period:

Concords	Dual-purpose chords	Discords
a] Tonic triad b] All diatonic triads in root position and first inversion	a] Dominant triad b] Major or minor triads in the second inversion c] Diatonic minor and major seventh chords and their inversions	a] Triads containing the tritone: VII and II° and their inversions b] Seventh chords containing one tritone: V^{7}, $II^{ø7}$, V^{9} or $VII^{ø7}$ and inversions c] Seventh or ninth chords containing two tritones: VII^{o7}, V^{-9}; and inversions d] Augmented sixth chords and inversions

Late Romantic period adds:

Expansion of the diatonic and chromatic tertiary harmonic structure.

Chord members are spaced according to the normal harmonic ascendancy:

Concords	Dual-purpose chords	Discords
c] Extensions of the ninth, natural eleventh or thirteenth to minor seventh chords	d] Extensions to major seventh chords and inversions e] Minor seventh chords in which the seventh is a bass tone are frequently discordant.	e] Extensions (♯9, ♯11, 13) to dominant quality chords and inversions

Impressionistic period adds:

Chords containing clusters:

Concords	Dual-purpose chords	Discords
d] Added sixth or ninth to tonic major triads, generally forming a major second cluster	f] Minor second clusters	f] Clusters added to above discords g] Limited use of polychords, generally within dominant quality.

(The dual-purpose listings of "b," "c," and "d" are apt to represent concords in this later period.)

Modern styles add:

Intervallic Structures:

1] Complete or incomplete chords in which the chord members retain a tonal association with a root, but may be spaced without regard to the tertiary ascendancy.

Concords	Dual-purpose chords	Discords
a] Chords containing any number of added tones but selected with a greater prominence of p. 5, p. 4, third and major second interval relationships	(Continues as in above periods.)	a] Chords which through vertical placement stress the discordant intervals of of +7, −9, or −2 b] Above discordant formation plus the tritone c] Polychords including above

2] Chords built upon intervals chosen for their non-triadic associations. These chords stress the independence of all tones, rather than a grouping of chord members around a single root. They may or may not arise from the twelve-tone row.

Concords	Discords
a] Perfect-fourth chords b] Any chord containing fewer discordant intervals than present in the preceding harmony, may be felt as a concord.	a] Chords emanating from a second, fourth, tritone, sixth or major seventh, and avoiding diatonic relationships b] Two-note interval groups, in pairs or separate, if discordant and widely spaced in range, also may create maximum tension.

Not to be forgotten:

1] Melodic and rhythmic tensions are present in addition to the vertical concords and discords. Root progressions create motion intended for an eventual resolution to the tonic chord. Melodic movement: (a) has varying tensions within the diatonic scale, (b) increases tension through chromatic use, and (c) causes increased vertical discords through the simultaneous sounding of non-harmonic tones. Even a single tone can cause tension by being out of context to prior harmonies.
2] Some melodic movement combines intervals that form chordal associations. These groups are evaluated together for their vertical understanding.
3] Rhythmical motion can increase or decrease tension, regardless of the vertical sound. An accompanying range of dynamics may support either design.

Application of the guide, a graphic chart of tensions

The Classical period:

Application of this guide can be illustrated graphically. The five lines of the musical staff may represent a gradual increase of tension reading from the lowest line upward. The tonic triad is, of course, the sound around which all others revolve and will be represented below the staff appearing as a ledger line and T formation, suggesting "tonic." See graph, *example 410a*. Other root position triads are also represented by this ledger line but without the T symbol. This representation remains the same for all of the musical periods, and signifies new "tonics" in a modulation. The Classical period harmonies may then be charted in this way:

Root position chords are on the ledger line below the staff.

First inversions of major or minor triads are on the first line.

Second inversions of major or minor triads are on the first space. When hearing the cadential I^6_4, the T symbol may be added to this graph line. See the fourth and fifth measures of *example 410b*.

Diatonic minor and major seventh chords and inversions are on the second line. Tones forming the seventh are charted as such whether resulting from non-harmonic procedures (suspensions, etc.) or as direct chord members, providing they receive enough rhythmic duration to qualify as sevenths. Inversions of seventh chords need not be pictured separately.

Triads containing one tritone, II° and VII° (root position or either inversion), and the II^{ø7} are represented on the second space. The diminished quality of the supertonic triad has much more tension than its counterpart, the minor II. Its motion usually leads directly toward the dominant. The augmented triad may also be represented on this second space; an exception to the tritone qualification has to be made, but the inherent motion within the augmented triad, together with its infrequent use, makes this listing suitable. If the dominant triad becomes augmented, represent it on the third line as stated below.

The third and fourth lines represent dominant qualities and are separated into chords containing one tritone, V^7 and V^9, and those containing two tritones, VII^{o7} and V^{-9}. The added tension that the V^{-9} creates is perhaps more the result of the minor ninth interval formed with the root, than it is the cause of the second tritone. Nevertheless, both ninths (major and minor) are extensions of the dominant seventh, and the difference between the minor or major second that they form with the root, whether actual or implied (as in a VII^{o7}), is important to the vertical quality. Indicate the dominant seventh chord on the third line; the dominant ninth chord (with major ninth) on the third space; the diminished seventh chord on the fourth line; and, the dominant minor ninth chord in the space above the fourth line. Inversions are indicated in the same manner as the root position chords. The leading-tone half-diminished seventh chord functions as an implied V^9 and also uses the space above the third line. See *example 410a* and the illustration in *example 410b*.

The dominant triad (omitting the seventh or tritone interval), is also included on the third line if it is part of the perfect authentic cadence, moving directly to the tonic. This is a separate function from the half cadence which treats the dominant as a temporary chord of repose. See this graphically illustrated in *example 410b* at the final cadence.

The top line is used for the chromatic augmented sixth chords, and the inversions that their function instigates. Although it may be argued that an enharmonic dominant quality is formed, the tone tendencies that make up the augmented sixth have no relation to those of the dominant seventh. It isn't necessary to enumerate all of these differences; the most essential points involve the chromatic element in the augmented sixth chords as opposed to the diatonic derivation of the dominant seventh. This contrast, in turn, indicates the rising tendency and resolution of the tone forming the augmented sixth while the so-called enharmonic seventh has a downward resolution. The two are quite incompatible. Differences follow in the nature of the other chord members also. The leading-tone or third of the dominant seventh chord may be singled out for comment because if used as part of an augmented sixth chord in a normal Classical function, it becomes the tonic tone of the key involved. Again, the difference of function between the dominant application and that of the augmented sixth is so great (incidentally, the variation of pitch would be noted by stringed instrument performers) that this chromatic interval formation is suitably charted for maximum tension, in this period, on the fifth line of the graph.

*Example **410a***

Classical period:

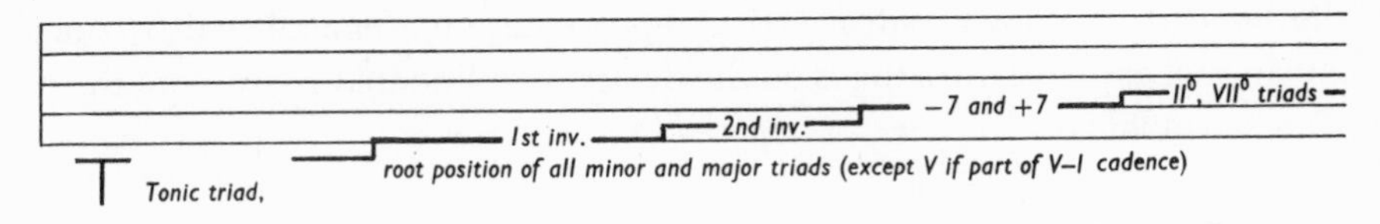

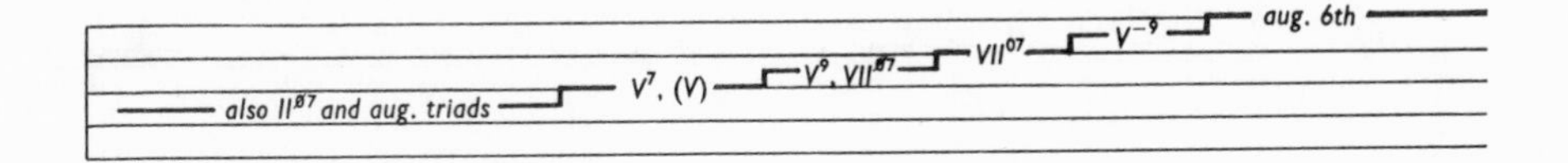

*Example **410b***

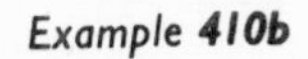

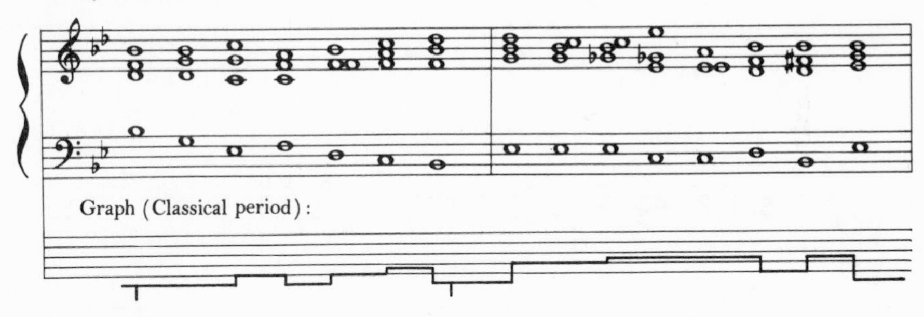

Non-harmonic tones, sounding simultaneously with chord members, create a strong discord until resolved. In this respect, melodic tensions combine with the vertical sound. In diatonic writing, the non-harmonic tone is clearly separated from the accompanying chord members, but in the Modern idiom, an ambiguity may result as the total harmonic sound incorporates many contrapuntal ideas, preventing a distinct separation of harmonic and non-harmonic tones. In charting the diatonic literature, therefore, a non-harmonic tone which through rhythmic duration and stress may sufficiently influence the vertical tension, deserves a representation on the graph. Indicate such tones with an "x" placed directly above the line or space that represents the chord quality known at the moment of resolution. See *example* 411a. If a bass tone is non-harmonic, mark the "x" below the graph line, again drawn in accordance with the quality perceived by the resolution. Do not graph unessential tones which rhythmically do not warrant a vertical representation. Remember also to include all chordal appoggiatura tones on the designated line that represents the complete harmonic quality. See *example* 411b.

Example 411a

Pedal tones (*example* 411c) supply a good amount of vertical tension. In the most familiar use, they help reduce the tension of the dominant, gradually, into the complete repose of the tonic. This pinpoints their participation primarily at the final cadence rather than at cadences within a composition. Chart all pedal tone areas with two horizontal lines, one representing the upper harmonies, perhaps changing as in *example* 411d, and the other line anchored to the starting chord that it represents. When they merge into a single response, only one line is depicted.

Rests may either be observed by a temporary cessation of the graph line, or ignored, if the harmonic continuity is apparent in spite of the visual aspect and the momentary absence of sound. Cadences are best represented by a break in the graph line, while rests within the phrase, being largely interpretive, do not halt the harmonic sound and consequently, should not be illustrated. (The next example includes both adaptations.)

The dual purpose category is not directly incorporated into the graph. The recognition that certain chords may contribute either to rise in tension, or be heard in a decreasing role is sufficient. Generally, their changeable attitude depends on a particular melodic and tonal circumstance.

Example 412, *Moment Musical* by Schubert Op. 94, No. 6, contains a representation of categories and is typical of Classical literature in so far as harmonic movement is concerned. The graph shows a constantly changing order of tensions. The manner in which the augmented sixth chords in this example are used is particularly revealing when the chart is scanned as a whole. Representing points of tension, the first use of the French sixth, measure ten, is very brief. But its tension puts the spotlight on the following triad, which is the first chromatically altered triad of the composition. Preparing for this chromatic change, the soprano tone of the augmented $\begin{smallmatrix}6\\4\\3\end{smallmatrix}$ is suspended. All of this places the emphasis on this altered mediant, as being the focal point of this part of the theme.

Immediately after the theme's cadence, in measure sixteen, a German sixth is used to begin a transitory passage into the next section. Here, the phrase opens with a startling use of active tensions. First the augmented sixth provides a diminishing tension toward a semi-cadence, but in its second occurrence, it prepares the modulation toward E major and the middle section. Both instances of the use of the augmented sixth chords have an important relationship to the composition as a whole. Observing the graph, this is made meaningful immediately in a visual manner. Naming chords is one process, but their significance within a phrase or composition must be explored if any value to their naming is to be accrued. A graph is not essential; it merely stimulates an awareness of vertical tensions. For the performer, this understanding is indispensable.

Modulation is the result of melodic movement which transfers harmonic formulas into new tonalities. In spite of the identical, vertical spacing of intervals, a modulation is related to a starting key and does not banish the stronghold that the first key establishes. Many themes modulate within their opening phrases, ending a Part 1 on a perfect authentic cadence in the dominant

Example **412** Schubert

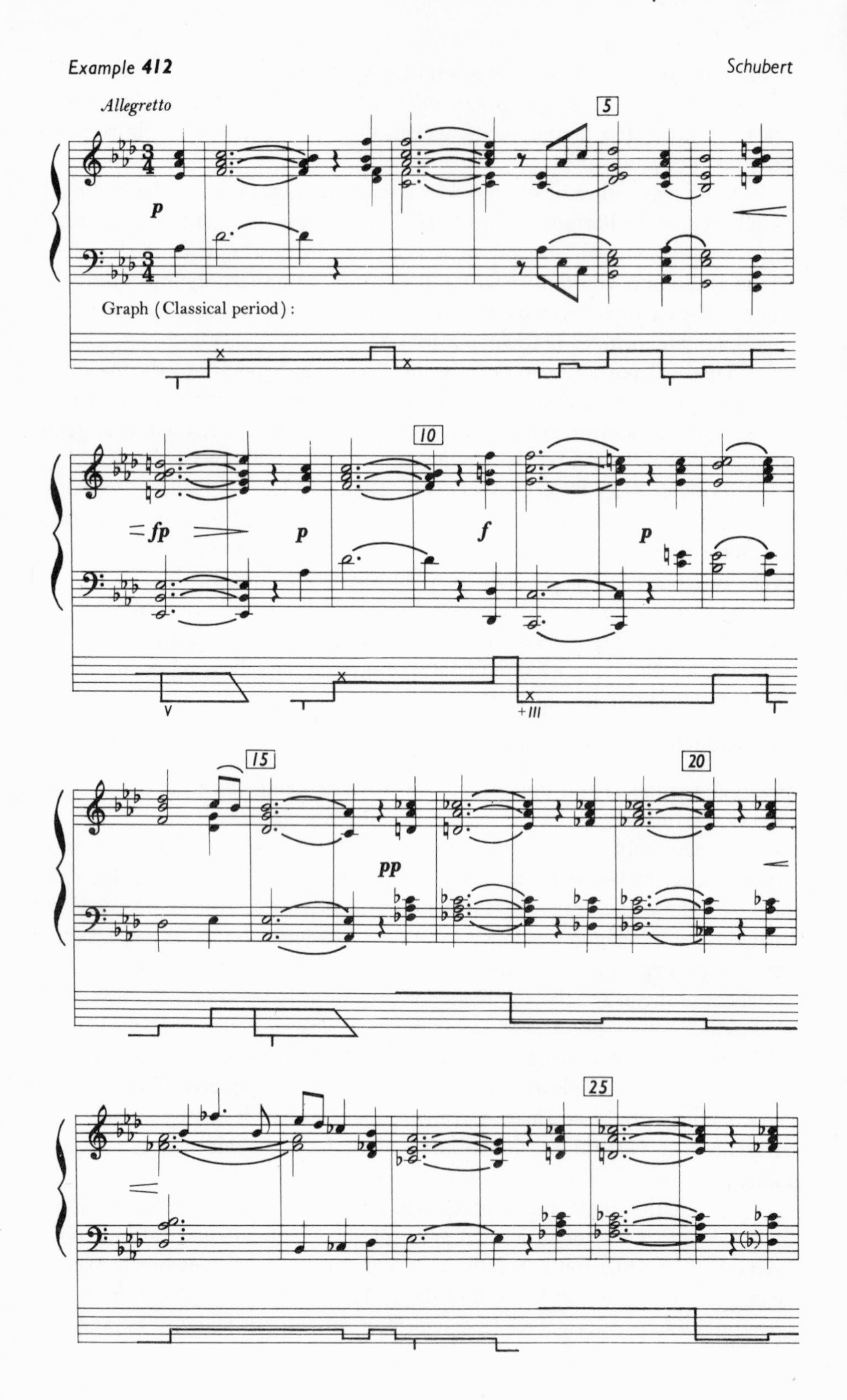

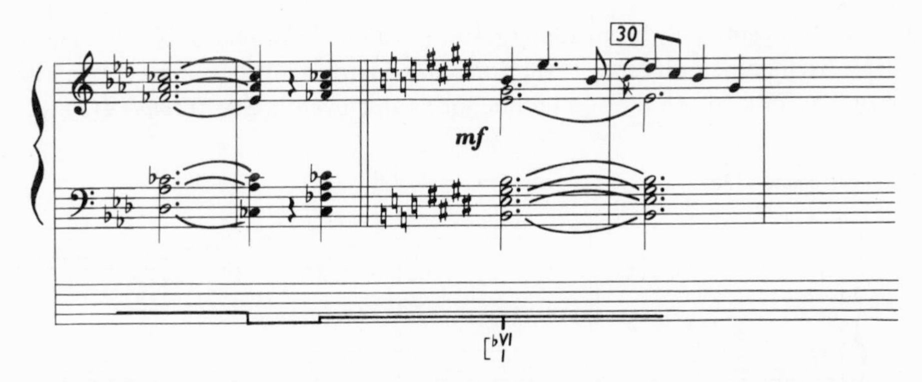

key. Vertically, it may be an exact representation of sound that later is used on the original tonic, but it can never equal the cadential satisfaction of the opening key. The first established key surrounds itself with all of the remaining diatonic and chromatic tones and permits movement in all directions limited only by the stylistic manner. Chords and harmonic sequences inherit this movement and any chart that endeavors to show vertical tensions cannot entirely omit this broad pitch movement. Include in the graph the modulation present at cadences, or in significant areas of the composition. Use the T symbol for the new tonic, but place below it the roman numeral relationship that it has with the original tonic. For example, a I^{6}_{4}–V–I cadence in the dominant key will show the roman numeral V beneath the cadential T on the chart. In this way, the essential modulating scheme is seen at a glance, together with the fluctuating tensions that may emphasize these areas. Observe the modulation as graphed at the end of *example 412*.

The late Romantic period:

Moving into the representation of the late Romantic period, nothing is changed in the order of the graph. The harmonic extensions, mostly in the nature of appoggiatura thirteenths and similar structures, are simply added to the existing seventh chord areas. A thirteenth added to a dominant minor ninth, whether conceived as a non-harmonic tone or not, will be marked in the space above the fourth line and the number 13 placed on it. See *example 413a*. The

Example 413a

natural eleventh may be an appoggiatura to a minor II^7 chord. Not having the same harmonic significance as the dominant quality additions, it may be marked either as an x, above the second line, or as an eleventh. See *example 413b*.

Example **413b**

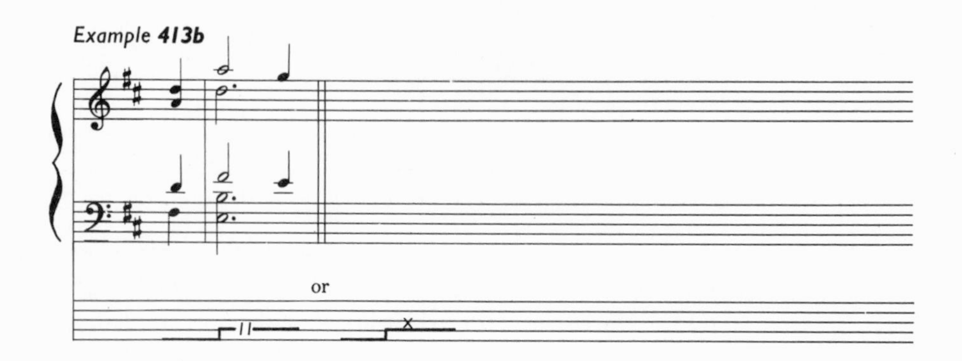

The Impressionistic period:

In charting the vertical tensions within the Impressionistic period, a regrouping of the categories is necessary if the graph is to remain within the confines of the musical staff. To accommodate the many whole-tone designs, such as incomplete tritone sounds, major-second clusters, and augmented or whole-tone dominants, the second space, just below the dominant category, is best suited for these tensions. Whole-tone structures need not be very active. Their root ambiguity provides a pleasant response and does not push toward a resolution of any particular kind. If a $V^7_{\flat 5}$–I relationship is involved within a whole-tone grouping of intervals, use the third line symbolizing the dominant function, as opposed to a vague whole-tone sound. To permit the distinction of this category, the II°, VII^o_6 and $II^{ø7}$ chords are lowered to the second line. Refer to the graph, *example 414a*. Minor and major sevenths are now separated. The minor sevenths, and their harmonic extensions (ninth, natural eleventh, etc.) are graphed on the first line and the major sevenths on the first space. This eliminates the visual portrayal of the inversions of triads, and groups the root position and both inversions on the added lower ledger line. Due to the overwhelming non-diatonic function of the harmonies in this period, this sacrifice in the chart is not harmful. Anyone who wishes to add the inversions, perhaps in some exceptionally meaningful areas, can easily do so through the standard symbols.

Lines three and four remain the same, charting the dominant qualities. Add the higher partials to the spaces, as described in connection with the late Romantic period.

The augmented sixth chords remain on the top line, but their Classical usage is infrequent, in this period. Surrounded in an idiom with much chromaticism and chordal expansions, the augmented sixths do not invoke the same active tensions that they do in the earlier periods. Although harmonic extensions of the ninth, and others, may be added to these chords, such additions are apt to cloud the main function of the augmented sixth interval and thereby weaken its distinctive quality. Except for the actual augmented sixth chords, represent higher-numbered enharmonic dominants on the appropriate space above lines three or four.

The greater tensions of polychords, and dominants with double inflections belong on the fifth line. Not used with the same degree of intensity as in the Modern period, they nevertheless were experimented with, and their dissonant results promoted a gradual connection with the sounds of early Prokofiev and Stravinsky.

Example **414a**

Impressionistic period:

Whole tone combinations
II°, VII°, II^ø7
+7 and ext.
−7 and ext.
Root, pos. 1st and 2nd inv.

V^−9 and extensions
VII°7
9, ♯11, 13
V7
including clusters
also aug. triad with +7

Polychords, double inflections, and aug. 6th chords

Clusters will be represented in the graph by the abbreviation "cl," and located on any line that denotes the chord to which the cluster is added. See *example* 414b. Isolated as a two-note group, generally present as a major second, chart this type of cluster on the second space, as derived from the whole-tone scale. See *example* 414c.

Added tones of the sixth and ninth are largely situated on the tonic chord. They do not increase tension, but rather provide a mellowing quality to concords. From an expanded dominant of six or more tones, a three note tonic resolution may sound abrupt. The added tones veil the tonic without any damage to its solidarity. They may be marked next to the T symbol as they would in the normal harmonic manner. The graph of *example* **414d** includes this at the cadence.

Parallelism, not an innovation in the Impressionistic period, but certainly an important technique which was fully explored at that time, may have many chords of an identical quality following one another. If overdone, this sameness can indeed be boring. (Review the chapter on parallelism.) Graphing a composition can be of help in making a judgement as to the wise use of parallelism in it. It must be in a minimum proportion to other fluctuating changes of tension. On the chart, draw slanting parallel lines, one for each changing chord, on the line of the harmony involved. *Example* 414e illustrates this in measures two, four, and five.

The Modern period:

The Modern period may be divided into two basic styles of composition; firstly, that which continues the growth of Impressionism and retains an overriding tonal concept, and secondly, the style of composition using a serial technique, which aims to remove the diatonic past. Serial compositions are largely contrapuntal, each voice moving quite independently. Non-serial compositions also may be highly contrapuntal, for example, the first movement of Bartók's *Music for String Instruments, Percussion and Celesta*; but harmonic areas arise from this counterpoint, building a network of focal points out of which the tonal concepts are derived. In both idioms, the vertical structures are the result of intervallic formations created by the union of moving melodic parts. Also, in both idioms, these intervallic formations may, or may not, contain a central tone as a root. It does not follow that serial compositions (discussed in detail in the next chapter) have no root possibilities, and that compositions in what today can be called the conservative Modern style, are entirely suited to a tertiary or diatonic analysis.

Intervallic structures are a vertical collection of intervals which do not rely on a root and surrounding chord members. Although they may seem to occur quite haphazardly through a melodic joining of motives (this is the favorite student excuse for a poor choice of intervals), they are actually selected with much care in terms of variety and the desired increase or decrease of tension. The function of intervals has not changed with the passage of time and musical growth. The tritone, minor second or ninth, and major seventh, have always been and still are discordant; the remaining intervals are concordant.

Intervallic structures may contain anywhere from three tones to twelve. Frequently, they may sound like incomplete chords, containing a root based on interval strength as described in the chapters on linear roots and two-part writing. It is the purpose here to help separate the concordant from the discordant intervallic structures. As seen in the dual-purpose category of the guide for vertical tensions, the major seventh may be part of either function. As a concord, it may be used as a major tonic seventh chord, I^{+7}, or occasionally on other degrees of the scale. As a discord, the major seventh interval must be exaggerated. To be more specific, in the normal diatonic ascendancy of the I^7 chord, the major seventh interval lies above a major triad. See *example 415a*. The concordant effect has been established and the seventh adds extra "color." By contrast, the omission of the middle chord members will emphasize the major seventh as it becomes the first interval placed above the lowest tone. See *example 415b*. Anything added above this major seventh will comply with this discordant setting. (Even if the chord members, the major third and perfect fifth, lie above the major seventh, the sound is more disrupting, though not necessarily discordant.) Now play *example 415c* which returns the middle chord tones and once again forms a D major seventh chord to which E♯ is related as an augmented ninth or a double inflection with the third. The interval that is exaggerated this time is the top major seventh formed by E♯ and F♯. The original major seventh, D to C♯, is in the middle and has lost much of its discordant impact. The complete chord extends the D major seventh chord and depending on context may be used in either the concord or discord classification. *Example 415d*, stripped of its inner chord members, is a discordant intervallic structure, still maintaining the root D because of the lower major third. These brief illustrations point out that incomplete chords or intervallic structures may build more tension than complete chords of many more notes.

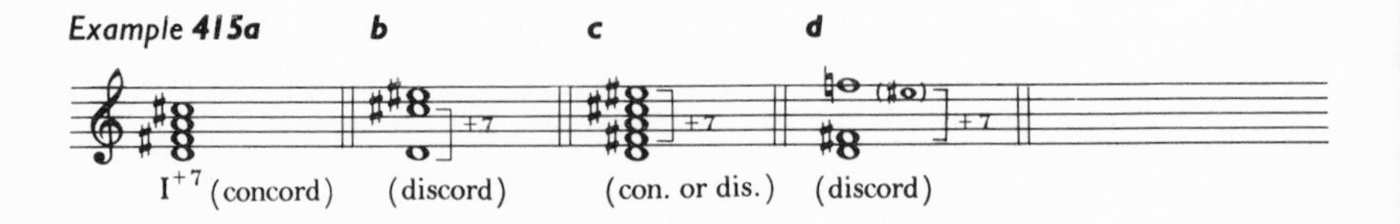

In incorporating these harmonic practices of the Modern period to the graph, three categories of intervallic structures must be added. As in the Impressionistic chart, all triads and inversions will appear on the lower ledger line. Minor seventh chords (generally completely voiced) and their extensions, are marked on the first line, and major seventh chords, in the first space. The new category, concordant intervallic structures, will occupy the second line, pushing the II°, VII°, and $II^{ø7}$ chords together with the whole-tone combinations in the second space. The dominant retains its position on the third line, but includes all extensions to the dominant major ninth on the line itself. The space above the third line will be used for marking the dominant minor ninth chords and extensions.

Occasionally, a dominant chord omits the seventh, resulting in a chord without a tritone. The ninth generally substitutes for the seventh. As long as it clearly represents dominant function, represent this chord on the third line rather than as a concordant intervallic structure on the second line.

The fourth line will represent intervallic structures, discordant, but without a tritone (major seventh, minor ninths and others). The fifth line will add to the double inflections and polychords all remaining discordant combinations which include both the tritone (one or more) and any combination of minor seconds or major sevenths. *Examples 416* to *418* illustrate the new categories.

Example **416a**

Modern period:

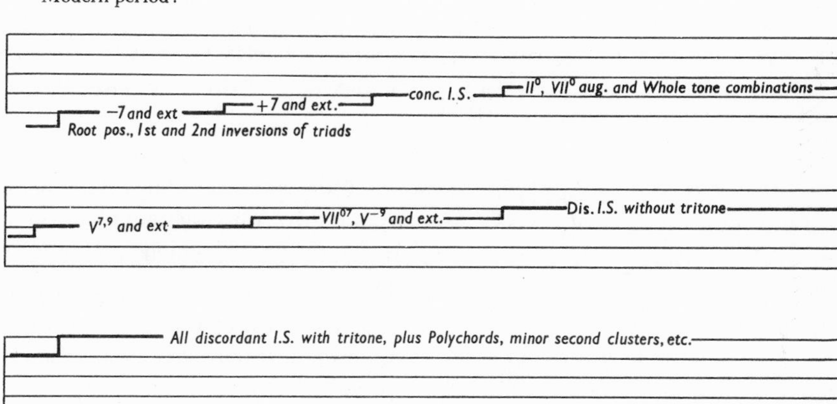

Example **416b**

Concordant Intervallic Structures, consisting primarily of +2, p.4, p.5, −7, thirds and sixths. (Indicate on second line of graph.)

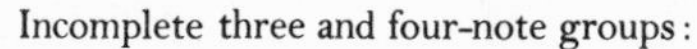

Incomplete three and four-note groups:

Perfect-fourth chords: Perfect-fifth chords:

Incomplete dominant chords are graphed on the third line, representing the dominant function:

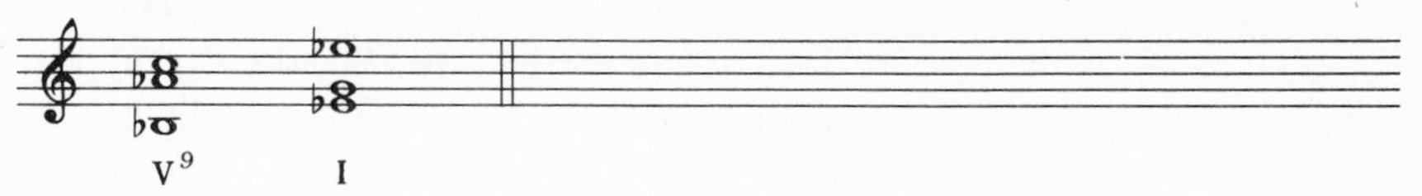

Example **417**

Discordant Intervallic Structures in which the tension is created by −2, +7, −9, but without a tritone among any of the notes. (Indicate on fourth line.)

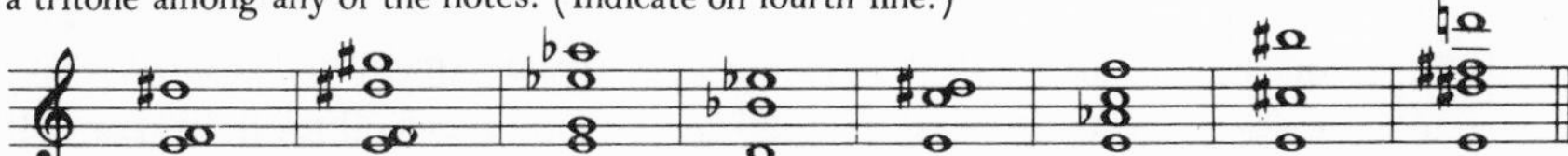

Example 418

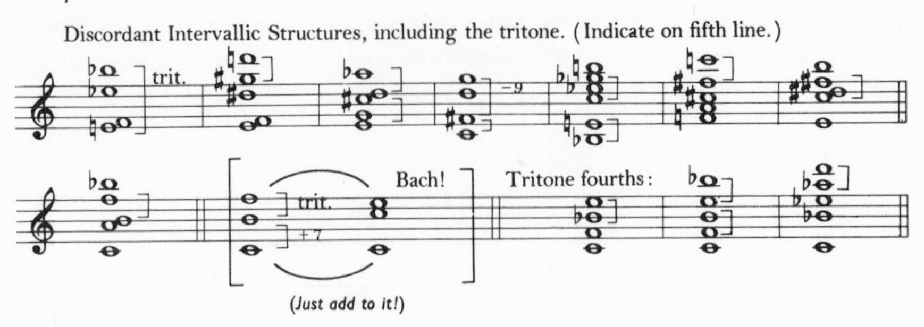

In compositions whose mien rotates only between what is charted above as lines four and five, an extra dissonant category may be added as top ledger line representing chords of seven or more tones which combine for a maximum discordant level. This added ledger line may also be used for other extreme effects, such as a climactic horizontal passage which through its linear tension is felt to supercede the preceding material. Accordingly, the space between lines four and five may be used for an I.S. which contains a tritone, but does not convey as great a dissonance as the chord which follows it. The graph is flexible and may be adapted to the individual composition.

An unpretentious waltz-like theme from Hindemith's *Second Sonata* is graphed in *example 419*. Its simplicity makes it a good choice for getting acquainted with the chart's significance. It also makes evident that even a simple theme must be carefully planned for vertical tensions, if it is to be appealing. There are no rhythmic complications, so that all tones can be studied in their total harmonic shape. Scanning the tonal movement first, the theme starts and ends in F♯, and has a free range of tones within the twelve-tone scale concept. A stepwise descending bass line governs the first half of the theme, followed by a pattern of the cycle of fifths until the cadence. As the graph indicates, the tensions are constantly varied covering a wide scope of harmonies, indicative of this period. In the second measure, the sound of an F dominant minor ninth on the first beat, shoots the tension up to the space of the V-9. It is notated enharmonically with a double inflection, but the sound speaks for itself. The tertiary ascendancy is not conflicting. It may also appear as a polychord, B over F, but here too, sound must rule over sight. Remember that polychords whose roots are a tritone apart blend together as one chord. And finally, notice too, that the chromatic motion of tones between the alto and the bass forms the augmented sixth interval, and resolves as such. This interval blends into the entire dominant function which, by the third beat, is plainly seen and resolved as a B dominant minor ninth, the double inflection representing a perfect fifth in the treble against a lowered fifth in the bass. The purpose behind the graph is to show that regardless of the method by which the measure is analyzed, the sound remains the same and may be classed by its interval make-up. The two tritones give it motion; the minor ninth is within the vertical spacing; and the B dominant quality resolves into the triad of E minor.

Measure four shows how melodic motion produces non-tertiary results. This intervallic structure exaggerates the outer minor ninth and focuses the tritone directly below the dissonant double inflection, the D♮. This jarring stress is brief, the chord moving into an active half-diminished seventh chord. This choice retains the element of motion so that in bar six a return to increased tension is effective. Here, the major seventh occurs between the lowest two voices and also forms the tritone with the melody E.

At this point, halfway through the theme, the melody forms its highest contour together with a deliberate double inflection for added dissonance. Actually, this second beat (measure six) is made up of two major sevenths, one in the treble and one in the bass. If you take these two sevenths out of context and perhaps space them farther apart in an extreme treble and bass range, and then add a double forte, "stand back" and brace yourself for this intense dissonance! In Hindemith's usage, however, this intervallic structure has an E major tonal association. The upper G♮ is not too extreme, being the enharmonic augmented ninth, but used, as notated, as a minor tenth appoggiatura to the ninth. All this, however, above the bass major seventh. The graph, nevertheless, still recognizes the discord, because it is there, whether tonally geared or not. Notice that the tritone (E and A♯) is not struck on the second beat, but its influence remains through the melodic rise of pitch.

The pictorial image of steps in the next few bars portrays the increase and decrease of tension. Observe that the graph follows the vertical sound rather than placing an emphasis on root tones which function in the dominant progression. Measure eight, for example, starts with a dominant recognition but shoots upward to represent the melody appoggiatura tone of F♮ as belonging to a discordant I.S. The line drops to the dominant placement on the third beat, to indicate a G V^{13}. Notice the omission of a tritone in this incomplete dominant. Measures nine and ten decrease the tension and provide contrast for the cadence. The root tones of the cadence are conventional, C♯ to F♯. The graphic line, however, represents the vertical sound as a discordant I.S. in preference to a dominant location. The arrangement of tones in the three-note C♯ chord is based upon a dissonant formation in order to add zest to the cadence. This is a simple theme, but one most deserving of a careful analysis.

A rhythmical influence on vertical tensions

Some rhythmic patterns group together to form a single harmonic unit within their horizontal lines. The excerpt from the opening of the second movement of Hindemith's *Third Sonata* for piano, illustrates this factor. See *example 420*. Metrically in $\frac{2}{2}$, the bass tone B♭ bounces from its fourth quarter-beat position into the chord's remaining chord tones on the following first beat. The first measure completes the tonic B♭ minor chord; the third measure completes an E♭ major, subdominant chord with the preceding bouncing B♭ suggesting a second inversion. In between, the second measure must also refer to the preceding B♭ pedal bass tone in order that the harmonic elements involved are understood. It is not a D^9, adding a thirteenth on the second half beat. Incorporating the pattern of the bass part, it is clearly an augmented B♭ chord in which the melody E♮ is a raised eleventh and the forthcoming B♮, a deliberate dissonance (double inflection), also enharmonically analyzed as a minor ninth. Both the upper melody tones resolve, as expected, from a raised tone and the enharmonically notated lowered tone. This understanding affects the graph, in that the horizontal tritone bass B♭ to melody E can be charted, resulting in the graph's rise to the top line instead of mistakenly marked as a concordant I.S. It is the repetition of this rhythmical pattern that aids our understanding of the overlapping technique of chord and bar line.

After the fifth measure, other horizontal tensions heard, are purely melodic and would be difficult to incorporate into a vertical analysis. They

belong to the study of tonal associations and movement of directional tones, which were discussed in a former chapter. The effect that certain directional tones have on tension deals with the melodic outline they create. Passages which contain a diatonic motion and then suddenly move chromatically, may increase the tension as a result of the surprising chromatic appearance. In this excerpt, B♭ minor is established as the predominating tonality. It is still present in measures five and six; the parallel fifths fitting into the descending minor scale. The last quarter beat, containing the perfect fifth C and G progresses to the chromatic B and F♯. This is an unexpected resolution of the preceding parallels. The movement involved is not manifested in that last quarter beat to the downbeat of B minor, which would be insignificant in Modern literature, but represents the entire bloc of B♭ sound progressing into a new sphere of tonality. Directional tones show the movement of B♭ to B♮ (which becomes the third of a G chord in the same seventh measure), and on to the half notes in measure eleven which stress C. The pitch direction continues to the A major cadence, the C♯ in the melody being a melodic focal point, while A in the bass, also results from the very first B♭. As the directional tones progress, mostly in this stepwise order, the tension mounts because it is felt that the music is going someplace! This is modulation expressed through the movement of certain pitches rather than as a harmonic progression.

Other horizontal indications that increase tension occur in smaller groups of tonal associations. For example, in measure eight, the stressed tone is D, and the ascending quarter beats rise through a G♯ before resolving, resulting in the outline of the tritone. This activates the measure most effectively, but to include the G♯ as a vertical addition to D would be unsuitable. The G♯ is matched with a perfect fifth, the C♯, and in that capacity, functions as a link, a passing tone, to the G ninth chord that follows. Similarly, the ascending quarter notes of measure ten outline a tritone, F to B, which also cannot be graphed vertically, but is, nevertheless, an active melodic feature that increases the satisfaction of the concordant resolution.

Cross-relations, notes that chromatically contradict each other in diatonic associations, cause tension because of their "disobedience" to the major or minor scale. In harmonic formations, these tones may be called double inflections, as occurs in the second measure where the melody B♮ is primarily a harmonic conflict. Whereas, in the ninth measure, the bass movement, G, D, E♭, may be likened to an evaded progression on the second and third quarter beats. Immediately, upon hearing the bass pitch of E♭, the melody moves through E♮ within the eighth notes. The rest below does not erase the E♭ which consequently forms the implied discordant intervals of a major seventh, and the cross-related augmented octave. This melodic choice of tones disobeys any vertical tertiary conclusion, is cross-related melodically, and yet these tensions cannot be successfully charted because of its singular, melodic, stepwise D minor appearance.

Uncharted horizontal tensions:

The fifth variation from Norman Dello Joio's *Sonata No. 3*, *example* **421**, is a fine example of subtlety amongst vertical tensions. Before attempting to decipher its harmonic background, play this excerpt several times so that the melodic tones which form the various chords gain more importance as melody tones, not just chord members. (In playing this, the right hand must skip back and forth between the upper melody and the three-note chord. The melody may also be played by a treble instrument or a third hand if help is needed for the pianist!) In listening to the harmonies, you will soon be aware of the fact

Example 421 *Sonata No 3. Norman Dello Joio*

that no tritone exists in any of the actual vertical chords. This is true of the entire variation and not limited to this excerpt. And yet, tensions do increase and decrease. Melodic motion, present in the connection of the chords and in the delicate merger of melody with harmony, supplies the shimmering rustle in an unruffled sea.

Vertically, perfect fourths and various formations derived from them, supply the misty background. Only one complete perfect fourth chord is present, located on the first beat of measure nine. Most of the fourths appear only in the right hand, as vertical formations, emanating from a bass interval of a major sixth or a minor seventh. This choice of intervallic distance clouds any diatonic reaction; a major third or a perfect fifth below a fourth formation would have certified these. Amongst the vague fourth combinations, a sprinkling of D major seventh chords give a little firmness to the harmonic setting, and at the conclusion of this variation, "D" prepares the return of the original theme, in G major.

Horizontally, the movement is highly chromatic and elusive, as if the chromatic tones are searching for their resolutions, but not reaching them. Tritones are present in the melodic movement of the chords—not always directly as in the first two measures when the lowest bass tone, A♭ moves to D, but crisscrossing between a bass tone and the following highest tone of the right hand chord. In the third measure, the bass tone G connects slantingly with the upper C♯ of the second half note chord. Against this crisscrossing, the repetitions of the top half notes E♭ and C♯ seem to seek a resolution to D. The bass tone D is a partial satisfaction, which nevertheless keeps an underlying motion going through the vertical major seventh interval. It is this type of melodic motion that is not apparent in a chart of vertical tensions, and yet is present, and our hearing is affected by it. Rather than to complicate this graph, the knowledge of horizontal melodic tensions must be remembered and recognized as a supporting factor for all vertical analysis.

The uppermost lyrical melody is interesting in that, played alone, it is completely diatonic in the key of D♭ major. In the third and fourth measures therefore, it suggests a bitonal reaction, D♭ over D. Theoretically, a triple-rooted polychord may even be analyzed in measure six (on the repeat of measure three), in so far as the highest melody now thoroughly represents D♭ while the second right hand chord is A major, over a pedal D! Let's be truthful, however, that is the eye at work—not the ear. The ear only recognizes the discords over the pedal D. The highest A♭ is also the major seventh to the A major chord, and both upper eighth notes form the diminished triad to the bass D. This results in a brief discord of the highest category on the graph. It is necessary that such eighth notes be indicated so as to more accurately represent these undulating tensions.

The dual purpose category may be applied in the last measure. The major seventh chord on B♭♭ retains much of the preceding chord's tension.

Although the graph drops to the first space, one may respond to the major seventh interval within the chord, and prefer to maintain the I.S. concept on the fourth line. Melodically, all tones resolve on the third beat.

Intervallic structures are the backbone of contrapuntal compositions. Each part moves so independently that the listener is more aware of the horizontal ideas expressed than in the harmonic result. The intervals formed by the merger of various melodies as a rule do not produce a collection of obvious blocs of chords, but instead, through the art of non-harmonic tones, they produce evasive, fluctuating interval combinations. While all of Bach's writing is harmonically rooted to diatonic traditions, the contrapuntal technique of suspensions and appoggiaturas overshadows the underlying harmony. The intervals which result from the discordant non-harmonic tones form incomplete vertical combinations, which affect the changing tensions we hear. Since each tone of the contrapuntal idea is essential, a graph must attempt to include these subtleties of the melodic writing in order to be representative. In the former examples which were charted, a simple "x" symbolized the non-harmonic tones. This is sufficient for most compositions, as it simply calls attention to the melodic factor while not interfering with the harmonic result. It is also possible to chart the entire vertical sound, by observing the actual intervals that result from the non-harmonic tones. In the realization of a figured bass, the intervals are fully noted, for example, 7–6 or $^{5-}_{4-3}$. The number 7 represents the interval of a seventh, not a seventh chord; the numbers 5 and 4 represent a simultaneous sounding of a perfect fifth, and in another voice a perfect fourth with a bass tone. This is a concordant intervallic structure, until resolved to the triad. In graphing these specific intervals, include all tones that have rhythmic significance and thereby contribute to the changing tensions. *Example 422* illustrates an excerpt from a Bach fugue, charted within the categories listed for a Modern composition. The tempo is slow, which gives the eighth note the basic pulsation, and which affects the vertical tensions. Sixteenth tones contribute only in groups of two or four, or, if struck together with another tone on a pulsated beat. The unaccented passing sixteenth moves too quickly to affect the vertical discord.

A glance at this excerpt from the twenty-fourth "Fugue" of the *Well Tempered Clavichord*, Vol. I shows the constant fluctuations of the vertical tensions. The graph speaks for itself and only a few observations may be of special interest. The first given measure prepares the entrance of the soprano voice, on the tonal answer. The harmonies fluctuate between incomplete chords and leading-tone seventh chords. Most triads contain a non-harmonic tone forming concordant intervallic structures, charted on the second line. A more discordant combination may be graphed on the fourth line. The third beat of the first measure illustrates such a dual choice. While the melodic motion is descending and the E minor chord is the resolution ot the preceding leading-tone, the suspension, in the alto, forms a ninth interval with the bass and a minor second cluster with the upper part. Assuming that the volume of the held tone is maintained, the discordant activity justifies the fourth line placement on the graph.

Having a modulating subject, the soprano answer is first harmonized by a stress on F♯ minor and then chromatically proceeds to the tonic cadence of B minor. The alto line in the second measure of this excerpt presents an interesting linear use of tension between the third and fourth beats. The rest after the lower D♯ does not completely remove the lingering pitch. If the ear

carries the D♯ through the rest, the graph shoots to the top line for a most discordant conflict, that of the natural eleventh versus the major third. However, this progression represents the merger of the IIº and the V, and may be charted either way. Notice that in the third measure, the soprano's G♯ is definitely carried through the second beat, as it completes the embellishing dominant chord. On the first beat of this measure, the tritone and major seventh are prominently emphasized. The graph line rises and then falls dramatically to spotlight the major subdominant triad. Melodic tensions now take over, as the directional tones lead to the peak on high G, against an active bass line moving in contrary motion. The goal on the fourth beat is a triad which releases some of this tension. Tonally, however, it is the submediant approached by an evaded progression and therefore continues the harmonic urgency toward the tonic cadence.

The rise toward the cadence is most exciting, as the sixteenth figure in the bass (part of the counter-subject) resolves to the cadential tone on the I_6, while all of the three upper voices suspend the entire dominant harmony, resulting in the simultaneous sounding of some extremely discordant intervals. Realizing that this graph pictures only the vertical tensions, imagine the full impact of this "Fugue" upon our hearing when all of the chromatic melodic tensions are also considered!

Contrapuntal compositions in the Modern idiom defy the separation of chord tones and non-harmonic tones except on rhythmic principles. The freedom invoked by the twelve-tone scale, whether used serially or not, produces an endless variety of vertical combinations as they are formed by the motion of the various contrapuntal lines. Who is to judge which tones, if any, were meant as chord tones by the composer, when no diatonic tradition can back up these new combinations?

In joining together several motives or contrapuntal lines, the composer is mindful of the vertical intervals and is not attempting to surround them into harmonic shapes as was done in the Classical period. In the analysis of such compositions, the intervals reveal what we hear vertically. This may be applied to the graph as was done in the Bach fugue. Bartók's first movement from *Music for String Instruments, Percussion and Celesta* is also slow, giving the eighth note the pulsating motion. See *example 423*. In this excerpt, no division of the eighths occurs, so that the graph illustrates all of the vertical combinations.

Two-voice writing requires an understanding of the intervallic tensions, but charting them is unnecessary. Factors of contrary or parallel motion, together with the melodic contour are so significant, that the vertical understanding requires only a supporting role. Nevertheless, it must support the lines well. In the first measure of the excerpt, the tritone brings in the fugal answer. (The subject may be played by transposing down a perfect fifth from the answer's starting tone of E. It merges into the illustrated $\frac{7}{8}$ measure.) Against the answer, melodic imitation rises to the D♯. The line then curves downward and releases the tension through the descending parallels. In the third measure, the contrary motion reaches its peak together with the discordant major seventh. Its immediate change of direction into another concordant parallel design, again indicates the care involved in the selection of vertical sounds. The focal point in the fourth measure is concordant this time, as the lower voice skips a perfect fourth to its highest note of the line, forming a major third with the upper melody. This concordant quality is retained until two tritones activate the end of the phrase in anticipation of the third voice.

In examining the graph of the three voice section, observe the relationship of tension with the beginnings and ends of the motivic groups. The cello now starts the subject, which consists of four small, separate motivic divisions. As the graph indicates, the tensions are contrasted between each start of the motive and its pause within the measure. The first group starts with a tritone preparation and becomes concordant on the downbeat. It concludes on the top discordant line. The second group starts simply with a minor sixth and curves into a noticeable G dominant, which cadentially progresses to C_6. This concordant response emphasizes the uppermost line which begins a small motivic group at that moment. This violin melody reaches its peak on the B♭, which first reacts to the bass tone of E♭, as an enharmonic dominant seventh, and then becomes harmonized by an F♯ major triad. Remember that rests do not immediately banish the former sound. Discordant harmonies continue from here in various degrees, until the fourth voice enters and its downbeat starts concordantly. Notice that the tones which begin the fourth cello motivic group are very discordant and that their resolution is heard at the end of the subject, on the E♮.

The different intervallic tensions that are heard at the conclusion of motives or phrases, can be compared with the Classical distinctions of cadences. Cadences in an entire composition must vary sufficiently, giving motion and continuity where needed, and pausing more readily for definitive structural areas. The same must take place in contemporary composition and the knowledge of the functions of intervallic formations is helpful in the selection of cadential material.

The need for evaluating tensions at the opening and conclusion of motives is especially applicable to compositions whose tempi are fast, or which utilize rhythmic divisions of passing tones or similar rapid melodic groups. The ear can only grasp changing tensions within a limited speed. When a pulse or beat is divided into tones whose individuality can not be fully comprehended, they become "non-essential" from a vertical, or harmonic point of view. Within these rapid groups, the tones which do stand out are the first and last tones, the tones supplying the highest and lowest peaks of the melodic contour, repeated tones, and frequently, tones left by a skip. Obviously, the most insignificant tone is the unaccented passing tone, but there are exceptions, as always!

To illustrate this point, *example* **424**, from Hindemith's second fugue in *Ludus Tonalis*, is suitable. The tempo suggested is "Gay," ♪= 200. Reactions to the hearing of this phrase in terms of vertical tension, may be noted as follows, each succeeding comment derived from further listenings:

1] A consonant start, increasing in tension toward the next phrase.

2] The $\frac{5}{8}$ meter is felt, or conducted "in one."

3] Motivic groups of two measures each occur, starting on the octave, prior to the discordant area.

4] Each motive is divided into a concordant measure followed by a discordant one, until three bars before the next phrase, where the intervals of the major seventh and minor ninth intensify the dissonance.

The graph can now pinpoint the above general statements by grouping the essential tones that contribute to the over-all quality of sound. The first note of each tenor group is depicted. It is especially significant rhythmically in that it follows a rest. In the first, third and fifth measures, it follows an octave and is shown in that manner. In the second, fourth and seventh measures, the tenor

Example **424** *Hindemith*

adds to the discordant quality that is started by the minor seventh, present in the two outer voices. The line of the graph incorporates it with the first beat because the rapid tempo does not isolate the first minor seventh in the same manner that an octave can be heard. By the same token, on the third eighth beat in the first measure, an incomplete concordant formation occurs which to the ear remains as such, even though the eye can see it merge into a first inverted D minor triad. If this last eighth note had fulfilled the starting suggestion of F major (see *example 424a*), our graph would have returned to the triad position —or may have even remained stationary as in *example 424b*. As it is, a marking of concordant harmony is sufficient. Returning to the second bar, the discordant harmony is retained, lessening only slightly as more consonant intervals appear on the fourth and fifth beats. It is important to note that the ear retains either consonant or dissonant impulses until a positive change occurs. The appearance, in this tempo of the B^6_4 on beat four is overshadowed by the previous dissonances and the following tritone. After a two-bar sequence, the tenor voice, in the fifth measure, starts the pattern on an unexpected major seventh. It jars the sustaining octave momentarily, then settles for the remaining concordant qualities. The contraction to one-bar motivic groups, together with the heightened dissonance of measure six, now propel the phrase forward. Here the major seventh is struck on the first beat; the augmented octave formed by the tenor B♮ (also the melodic peak of the inner line) and the bass B♭ is deliberately conflicting; the tenor E adds the tritone and the last eighth note is still a major seventh away from the bass and the last treble sixteenth. The line of the graph moves from the discordant I.S. without the tritone, to the top line which includes it. The final measure before the goal of C is slightly less intense due to a lowering of the pitches in the tenor line. Major sevenths and a double inflection exist between the upper two voices, but a feeling of resignation, that the maximum momentum has been achieved, is suggested by the closing in of the intervals, all heading toward C. Also indicative is the soprano repetition which compels an early resolution. Notice that this seventh measure again illustrates the graphing of only the significant qualities. Hidden amongst these dissonances is the formation of a B minor triad. It is a coincidence of counterpoint that makes it appear as a triad, not an intensional focal stronghold. It actually intensifies the dissonance of the double inflection on the third beat and resolves into the following tritone.

The difficulty in the selection of the essential intervals may vary with the composition. In general, be guided by the following steps:

1] Establish the basic pulse and relate it to the changing tensions you hear. Whole phrases may be built either on concordant harmonies or discordant ones. The change of tensions is then manifested only within large areas of sound.

2] Trace the motives and phrase lengths. Analyze first the tensions involved at the beginning and end of each group. Examine the intervening material by noting any significant contrast of tension.

3] Observe the rise and fall of the melodic contour of all parts involved. Check to see if an important goal is present and if a definite vertical discord or concord coincides with it. Do not chart a phrase unless you know what its purpose is, in the larger structure of the composition.

4] Analyze the tensions of the rhythmically stressed beats and compare them to the end of the measure. Allow the first quality you hear to remain as long as it can. Frequently, the end of a measure will clarify, rather than change the opening sound.

5] Does the horizontal sound supply more tension than the vertical sound? If so, bracket the discordant intervals and check on the "crisscrossing" of tritones or cross-relations, as described and illustrated in *example* **421**.

6] Trust your ears! Let the graph help to visually depict what you are hearing, but remember that it is not designed to incorporate everything. Use it only as a guide.

The graph cannot guarantee a successful application of harmony because it represents only the vertical conclusion. Melodic and rhythmic tensions must participate with the vertical sound for a meaningful phrase. On the other hand, the chart can be especially valuable in detecting problems associated with the movement of harmony. In today's idiom, so free in its tonal behavior, a visual aid toward a discerning selection of pitch may prove helpful. All tones in the vertical structure are examined, so that melodic considerations are not ignored in their effect on harmony. In the contemporary idiom, the distinction between the melodic and harmonic tone may be impossible to verify; in the Classical idiom, the vertical result also represents all tones, but our analytical powers permit a separation due to the understanding of harmonic tradition. After all, the progression of I–IV–V–I has been the backbone of countless phrases, and yet, the individuality of each phrase responds to the melodic writing associated with it.

If you decide that a composition does not have enough variety of tensions, you may be right! Be aware, however, that what may seem unsatisfactory to you, may not be as objectionable to someone else.

EXERCISES

A *Analysis*

Examples **425** and **426** are excerpts, particularly expressive in their varying vertical tensions. Graph the examples and include an analysis based on material from former chapters wherever suitable. Application of the guide and of the graph may be made to former examples. The following are recommended and listed according to the musical period in which they are best suited:

1] Classical period: (review graph formation on pg. 433).

Examples **6**, **17a**, **20a**, and **21**, by Brahms; try charting other Classical representations from your own collection.

2] Late Romantic period: (uses same graph as above but adds higher-numbered harmonic extensions).

Examples **28, 40, 41**, by Wagner
Examples **37** and **42**, by Chopin
Examples **85** and **86a**, by Wolf

3] Impressionistic period: (review graph on pg. 439).

Example **86b** by Wolf, chart non-harmonic tones in this excerpt.
Examples **43**, and **118**, by Vaughan Williams
Examples **44** and **119**, by Giannini
Examples **87** and **158**, by Franck
Examples **192, 199** and **202**, by Debussy
Example **157a**, by Rachmaninoff

4] Modern Period: (review graph on pg. 443).

Examples **10** and **258**, by Shostakovich
Examples **169** and **279**, by Prokofiev
Example **282**, by Hindemith
Example **403**, by Flagello
Example **404**, by Wm. Schuman
Example **425**: *Twelve Short Piano Pieces*, No. 4, by Krenek
Example **426**: *Trio for violin, violoncello and piano*; "Movement II," by Piston

Example **425** Krenek

Example **426a** Piston

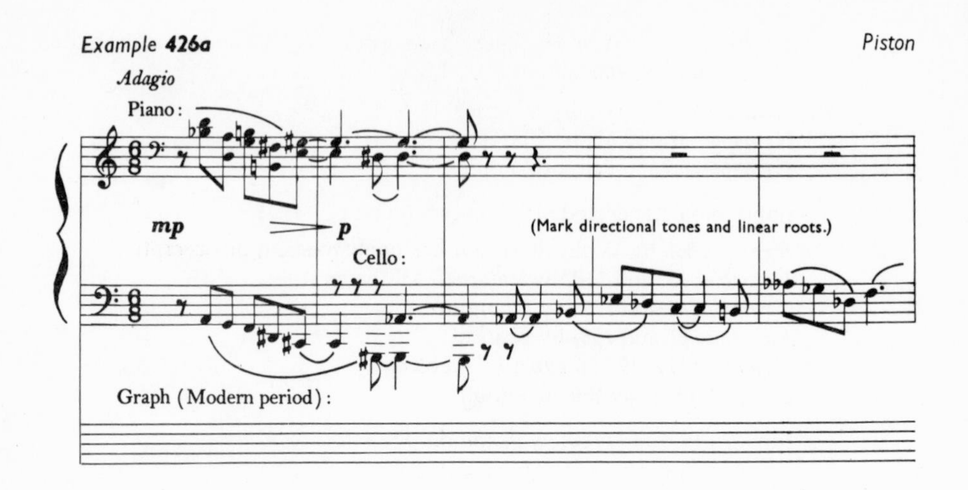

(*The sixteenth note passages are here reduced to one octave.)

B Fill in the harmonies suggested by the given figured bass. Chart your result in the graph of the Modern idiom. Remember that the intervallic structure designation does not reveal the total sound of all voices involved. You can control the amount of tension within such chords. If the chord you choose becomes a recognized seventh or ninth chord, for example, chart the sound to fit your result and change the harmonic "label" accordingly. After planning the basic chord tones, rewrite the exercise adding rhythmic and motivic interest, thereby creating a small composition. See model.

Example **427b**

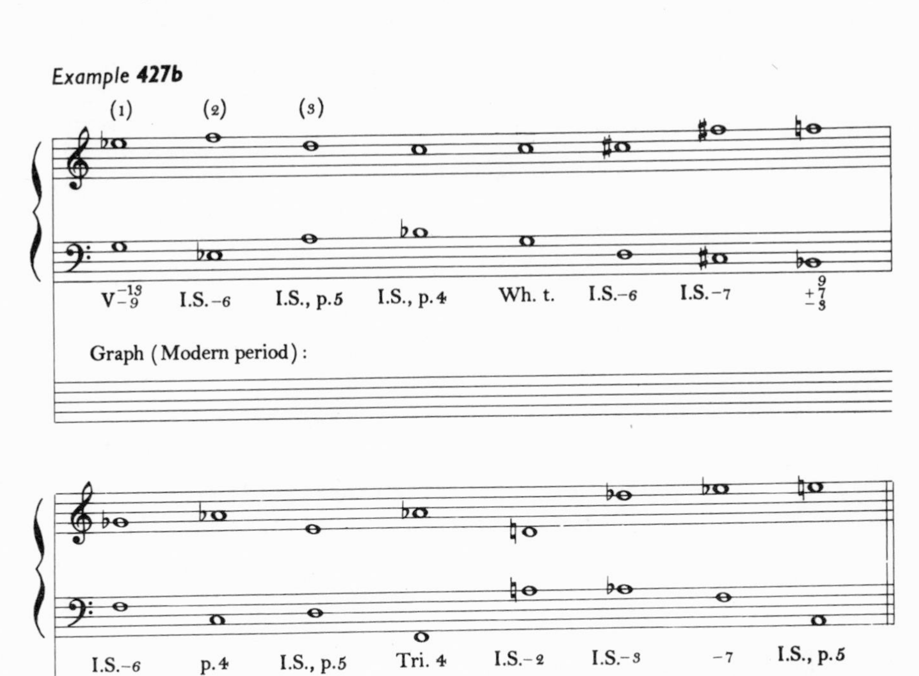

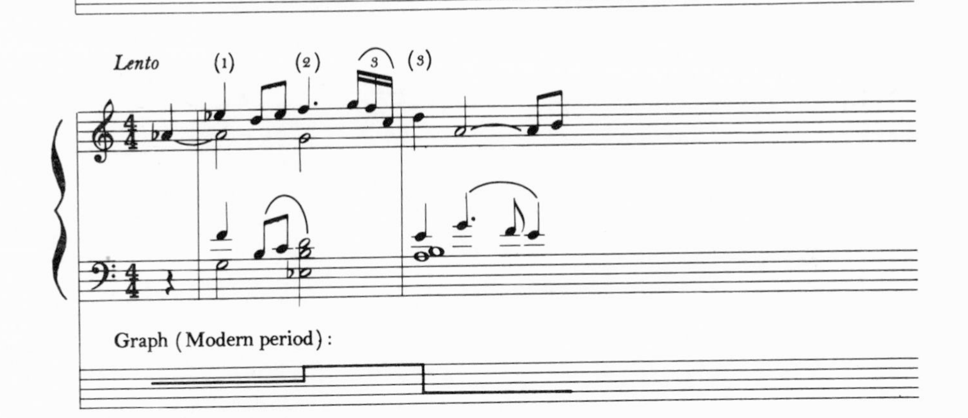

Example **427c**

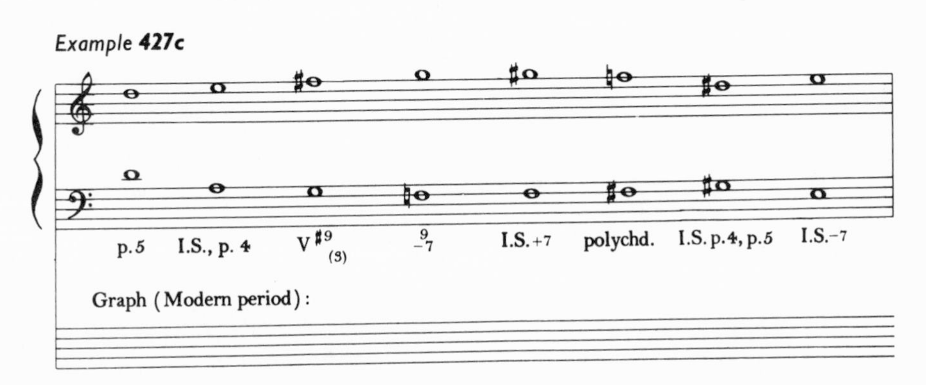

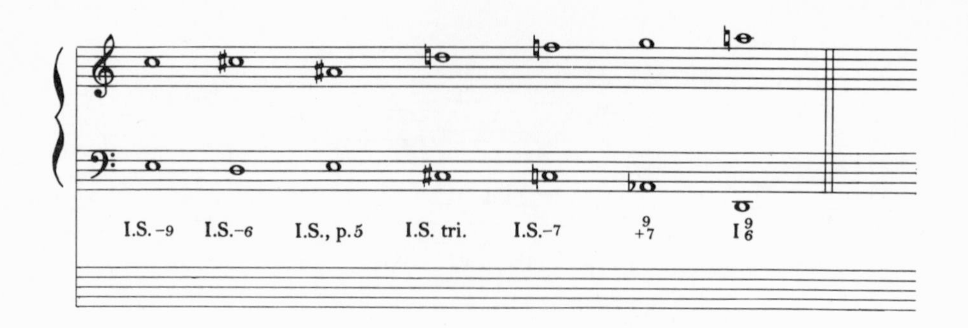

C What is wrong with the following phrases? Listen to the predominating quality of sound and choose one or two bars from each phrase that would benefit by a contrast of vertical sound. Rewrite the phrase with your correction.

Example **428c**

PART VI

The twelve-tone row

20 Its strict application

Arnold Schoenberg is credited with formulating a particular method of composing with the twelve-tone scale, a method using a twelve-tone row. It is sometimes called the twelve-tone system, but Schoenberg found dissatisfaction in that term. Today, the method is more commonly known as serialization, and compositions written upon the basis of a twelve-tone row are "serial compositions."

A background of constant musical growth led Schoenberg toward more chromaticism and more experimentation in departing from the harmonic techniques of the Romantic period. He did not suddenly "invent" the tone row as a game is invented. He was hearing and using unfamiliar patterns of sound, and sought some unity of form and procedure within which the new sounds could be contained. His creative inventiveness lay in contrapuntal channels which differed sharply from the homophonic expansion of the late Romanticists. Further growth upon triadic foundations seemed unlikely. Chromatic sounds needed a new form of expression which, for Schoenberg, lay in a style that stripped Romanticism of its harmony, but preserved its chromatic texture; a style that burst the seams of melodic thinking but did not destroy melody, and that rebelled against diatonic controls but recognized the need that all art must have a structural shape, controlled and woven out of whatever materials the artist chooses. Schoenberg relied on the tone row for this control.

His contrapuntal thinking brought about a concentration upon motives. In particular, motives linked together by an intervallic bond, the same process that Brahms used, and that takes place in all fugues. Motivic unity is not new. Where Schoenberg departed from the Classical hold on motives (Brahms also did to a lesser degree) is in the area of rhythm. Diverse rhythms accompany each reappearance of a motive. It is difficult to hear a motive's return when the rhythm disguises the intervallic bond. By the same reasoning, the lack of rhythmic repetition permits the same interval combinations to return many times without the listener being made aware of every repetition.

While working with this motivic approach. Schoenberg learned of an Austrian theorist and composer, Josef Matthias Hauer (born 1883) who was also preoccupied with a system of organization of melodic patterns. Groves' Dictionary refers to Hauer as an "originator of a system of atonal music." His system differs with Schoenberg's and it is not necessary to expound on it. What is interesting is that Hauer also took the twelve chromatic tones and placed them in fixed positions. He then divided them in half and called each group of six tones a "trope" (drawn from the early church modes). These tropes were bound together by their intervallic relationship, in a manner similar to the tone row technique that Schoenberg evolved later. In 1925, Hauer dedicated to Schoenberg his Treatise, *Vom Melos zur Pauke.* At a later date, a group of piano studies in which he used his technique, were also dedicated to Schoenberg.

The pieces which Schoenberg wrote prior to those which are serialized, stress a motivic development which is akin to the Brahmsian and Wagnerian form of motive expansion, except that it is more concentrated and more tightly held to just one or two short motives. The process of analyzing these motives is exactly the same as outlined in Chapter two. In the *Klavierstücke*, Op. 11, the first composition is made up of a six-tone motive and linked with a bass figure of five eighth notes. These can be traced throughout the composition. The rhythmic alterations are never so extreme that the ear does not catch a relationship with the original statement. The intervals involved are not always exact, as they would be in the later serial technique. Opus 11 is a testimony to the gradual evolution of the twelve-tone process. From the strong inferences contained in these early pieces, the strict technique came forth in Schoenberg's middle period, only to be gradually relieved of some of the early rigid declarations by Schoenberg himself, as well as by composers of the next generation.

The tone row consists of the twelve tones that make up the chromatic scale. They are organized into an arrangement which stresses the individuality of each tone and removes the chromatic principle of required resolution. Schoenberg called this a method of composing with twelve tones related only to each other. The row becomes the backbone of the entire composition, both in melody and harmony. This arrangement of tones, planned by the composer, is inflexible, a formula out of which motives are formed. The melody is not inflexible, but the twelve-tone row itself is fixed and remains unaltered throughout the work.

Because of this great responsibility that is given to the one particular grouping of tones, the composer selects this tone row very carefully. The organization of tones must provide a good melody, some vertical arrangements that the composer might find suitable, and above all, a flow of tones that are unrelated to each other in terms of diatonic suggestion. The row cannot contain groups of tones that would, among themselves, relate as part of a major scale. Such an obvious association of pitch would merge the tones in question into one thought, cancelling the independent stature that is desirable for each of the tones of the row.

It is within this concept that the principle of using exactly twelve tones with no repetition of pitch within the row, is proclaimed. A premature return to a particular tone might provide an auditory emphasis which could attract attention to this one tone and elevate its position into more prominence, perhaps even into a suggested key center. (That, of course, would be heresy!) Do not confuse a return to a pitch out of order in the row, with the musical repetition or immediate reiteration of pitch. When the tone row is given rhythm and musical expression, the rhythmic repetition of a single tone may take place. In fact, when two or more different forms of the row are used simultaneously, a recurring of a pitch may also take place in the phrase. But this is part of the use of a row, not the organization of the row itself. Remember that the twelve tones, placed in an arbitrary order, retain this fixed position for the duration of the composition. Mutations of melody occur with a changing selection of pitch derived from the row, but not from a changing row.

A. Construction of the row

The composer forms a twelve-tone row. It may shape into a pleasing melody or it may be planned completely theoretically, such as a row made up of twelve consecutive fourths. Since the latter design, and others similar to it have been used, composers today prefer a more individual grouping of tones, those capable of a more personal expression. Although Schoenberg did not state how the row should be laid out, or whether any diatonic features may be included, generally the following principles are considered in formulating a row:

1] Avoid a group of tones that denote a diatonic reference, such as three or more tones of an arpeggio chord, or an obvious scale association. These would not be independent but always bound together suggesting a different musical period. See *example 429a.*

2] Avoid chromatic combinations that result in the resolution of a leading-tone, *example 429b.*

3] Consider the intervals. Except in a deliberate design devoted to a particular interval, a row generally contains a balanced number of seconds, thirds, fourths or fifths, and tritones. The octave exchange is permissible for all tones, therefore seconds and sevenths are considered the same in the row, as are thirds and sixths, and perfect fifths and fourths. It is usual for the row to contain more seconds and thirds, than perfect fourths or fifths. See *example 429c.*

4] Balance of intervals is also considered in the smaller divisions that the row forms. Dividing the row in half with six tones each, or in three groups of four tones each, should result in motives of some independent interest.

5] Be sure that the last tone, or group of tones elides smoothly into the beginning part of the row.
6] Any tone may be spelled enharmonically.

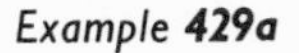

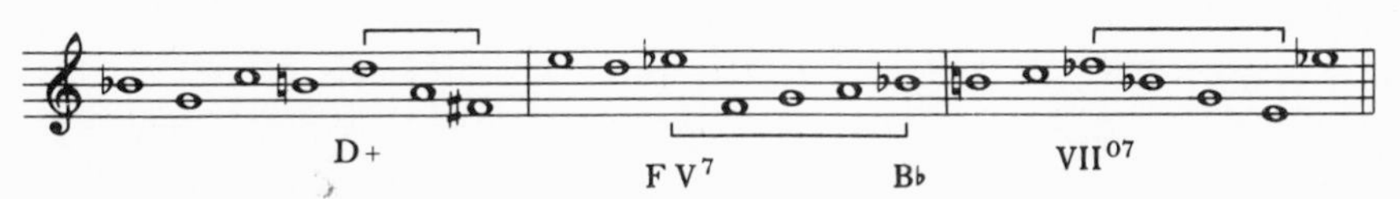

Example **429b**

Example **429c**

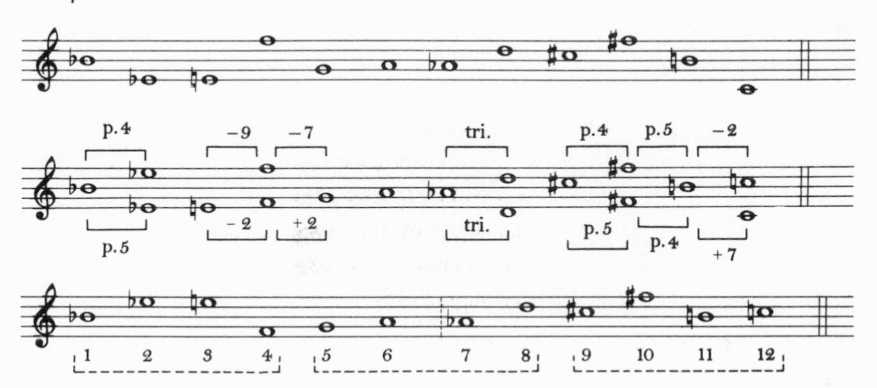

B. Implementation of the row:

1] The row has four shapes:
   a] Original form, abbreviated as "O." (See *example 430.*)
   b] Inversion, "I"
   c] Retrograde, "R"
   d] Retrograde Inversion, "R.I."

Immediately upon deciding on the twelve-tone row whether in analyzing, or composing with one, the other three forms that the row takes on are written out and numbered as in *example 430.* The intervals must remain accurate in sound, but enharmonic notation may occur. (Some theorists prefer numbering the retrograde forms from one to twelve. Composers differ in the handling of a row and it is good to remember when complex switching of plans may occur, that both numerical orders are possible.)

Example ***430***

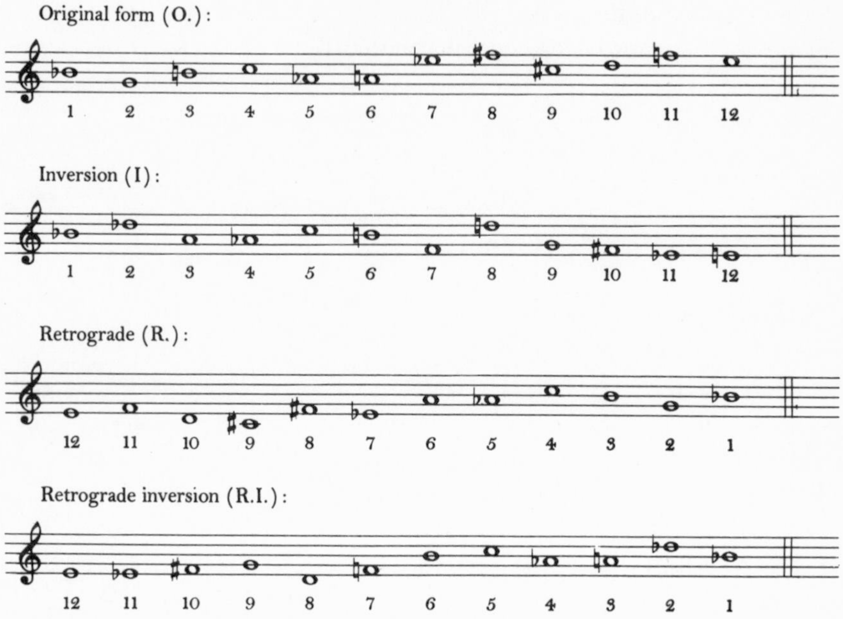

Original form (O.):

1 2 3 4 5 6 7 8 9 10 11 12

Inversion (I):

1 2 3 4 5 6 7 8 9 10 11 12

Retrograde (R.):

12 11 10 9 8 7 6 5 4 3 2 1

Retrograde inversion (R.I.):

12 11 10 9 8 7 6 5 4 3 2 1

2] Transposition. Each of the given four forms of the row may start on any of the twelve tones. This adds forty-four exactly transposed forms of the row to those given, totalling forty-eight possible pitch lines. No extraneous tones may be added to any part of the row, and no tones may be omitted.

3] Rhythmic characteristics

In giving the row a rhythmic setting, a characteristic trait developed in Schoenberg's writing and was continued by his students and other composers. Namely, the use of divided rhythms which tend to eliminate the beat and the bar line by holding tones over the expected pulse. It might be compared to an exaggerated form of syncopation except that in the latter the beat is well defined, while in many typical tone-row compositions, a beat is nullified by a large number of suspended tones. *Example* **431a** begins with a single line use of the row and contains simple illustrations of this type of divided beat. Remember that the response of this phrase is different when you hear it without observing the notation. To a performer, the pulse is there as a guide. For a listener, the second and third measures in particular, are without a "beat," the sounds occurring as if retarded rather than meticulously executed.

The row is generally stated in a straightforward manner in the first phrase. It may contain a lower voice, or any form of the row for the bass, but it should not be hidden in techniques that are later permitted during the development. It is left as a single line in *example* **431a** merely as an illustration.

Meter changes are not apt to be required in great abundance, as this type of rhythmic division smothers a bar line instead of demanding one.

4] Wide leaps are characteristic of tone row melodies, although there is nothing in the technique that insists upon them. It is more a general trait that exemplifies contemporary compositions.
5] Sharp dynamic contrasts are also characteristic of serial pieces. The short motives are brought forth in greater relief by sudden changes of dynamics. In a later expansion of serialization, rhythmic patterns and dynamics may also be organized into a series, in a manner similar to the note series. Of course, there need not be twelve dynamic levels or rhythmic designs. The composer can arrange into an order anything he considers desirable.

C. Procedures for using the forms of the row

Example 431a starts with a single line statement of the row. The example continues with illustrations of how the row and all of its ramifications can be employed. The procedures outlined at this point retain a strict approach. Some relaxation of rules will follow later.
1] The row may weave up and down fulfilling melody and bass during its accurate horizontal direction. Measures five to seven of *example 431a* illustrate this with the numbers. Notice the vertical use in the major third of the bass part. It doesn't matter which of the numbers is higher or lower.

Compared with the first phrase, it is apparent that some new motives or figures are formed by this technique. Former motives may be rhythmically modified and retained as in measures six and seven.
2] Forms of the row may overlap. The seventh measure introduces the inversion of the row in the bass. It appears just prior to the last note of the original form. It could have overlapped at any earlier point as well.

Notice the recurring pitch of D♭, enharmonic to the C♯ present on the first beat. This is permitted. In fact, the selection of which of the forty-eight varieties one might choose is frequently based on a desire to repeat a particular tone, or contrarily, to positively avoid one.
3] The row may be divided so that a latter group of "numbers" moves simultaneously with a beginning division. The divisions need not be equal. This is shown in measures seven and eight.
4] Motives and rhythmic patterns do not need to coincide with starting or ending tones of the row. The melodic figure at the end of measure eight consists of the eleventh note of the inverted form and links to a transposed beginning of another inversion. The twelfth note occurs in the bass. In a lengthier composition, new motives may appear, formed by numbers that are not in the numerical order of the row. The tones that have been "dropped" are located in an accompaniment position.
5] An elision of pitch and number frequently is used if the twelfth note is the same pitch as the first note of the next form of the series. Measure nine finishes the inverted form on E in the bass, and without repeating it, starts the retrograde inversion on the same pitch.

6] Different forms of the row may coexist as contrapuntal lines. In the ninth measure, the upper voice uses the transposed inversion against a retrograde inversion in the bass. Canonic treatment of the same series is equally useful.
7] Vertical placement of tones from the row provide the chordal punctuation. See measure eleven. Generally, the divisions are maintained, so that a chord of four tones would contain four notes of a numerical order. Other formations nevertheless do occur. The tones of all the odd numbers may be selected for one chord, and resolved into the even-numbered tones. In the chord itself, the tones need not be arranged in any particular way.
8] A horizontal melody line does not necessarily signify that only one form of the row is contained within. The tones of several rows may overlap, or cross parts, or interject their numbers into an existing form. Two forms of the series are started in measure thirteen. In the fifteenth measure, the upper part includes the tritone interval, E♭ and A, which belongs to the lower original form (transposed). This can be illustrated by a straight line which perpendicularly points to the tones which have left the initial horizontal line. As one becomes more adept at tracing the row through its maze, the numbers may be omitted and only the series need be identified, and if necessary, marked by means of such analytical lines.

The chord in the seventeenth measure numerically combines the tones of the retrograde and the retrograde inversion. Note that the lower part takes advantage of the same pitches that are necessary for the upper retrograde form.
9] The final measures of *example* **431a** also illustrate tones which are struck prematurely but retained during their expected placement. The *sforzando* bass pitch of A in measure sixteen should have occurred after the melody C, but is advanced by a sixteenth time value and retained. The same practice may be noted in the next to the last bar, when the tone C, representing number 5 of the R.I. appears simultaneously with 8 and 7 in the bass. It is then held for the approach toward the cadence. The row therefore, does not need to remain in its original horizontal layout. Consider these planned mutations as a developmental aspect of the serial writing, generally used in the body of the composition.
10] The divisions of the row may be utilized in place of the full horizontal intervallic relationship. If the triplet motive of measure two, B, C, A♭, was used by transposition so as to include and not repeat all twelve tones, this would constitute a motivic substitute for the row. See *example* **431b**. The intervals of the motive sometimes may not, of necessity, be retained precisely. The utilization of the twelve tones supercedes a particular order. In most of Schoenberg's writing, the twelve tones appear within a measure or two, numerically totalling twelve, regardless of which form of the series is involved amongst the numbers.

In these latter complex situations, it is desirable to attempt to spot certain intervallic groups that will give the clue as to the design being used. If some divisions become recognized, look for the remaining tones or look for sequential adaptations of motivic material. One aspect is certain, it is much easier to plan and work out the complicated mixtures of rows than it is to detect from the forty-eight varieties exactly what is going on!

Example 431a *Prelude, No. 2. L. Ulehla*

Example **431b**

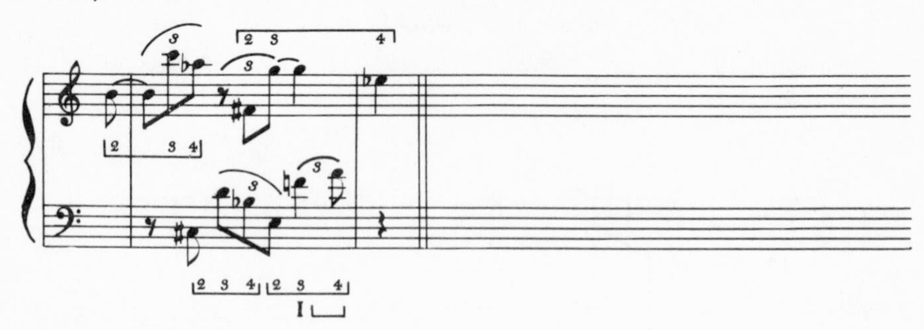

D. A lexicon of notes or music?*

So much for the numbers, and now for the music! Personal reactions to this idiom vary from intense displeasure to wondrous admiration. Music as an art must convey the composer's expressive creations. The endeavors of the composer to set forth his artistic feelings must be accepted as his personal expression. The result may then be accepted or not by the right of each listener to his own opinion. Critics of the system treat it as a game of numbers. Proponents state that the numbers are only a tool in the composer's pocket. The issue of art does not rest upon the method of creation, but upon the result. A truly inspired masterpiece will shine whether a background of organized planning was utilized or not. Planning is not restricted to an arrangement of pitch. What does matter, and what separates the artist from the novice, is that the artistic composer imposes his will upon the notes and searches for exactly that combination of sound which his inner hearing prompts him to set forth. In a system such as serialization, it is too easy to weaken and permit the tabulations to order the musical response.

Looking at *example 431a* (not a masterpiece), the techniques that have been described within the pages of this book, and which contribute toward musical results in all idioms, can be observed. Music must not be dull rhythmically, melodically, harmonically nor in its balanced use of motives, dynamics, texture and the shape or form of the whole endeavor. A composer takes on quite a responsibility, and in compositions of large proportions, the magnitude of this responsibility increases. In short pieces, the problems diminish. The structural planning is limited and designed only to convey a glimpse of one attitude, unhampered by the need of continuity for the expansion of a thought. Contrast, in the above musical areas, is not as essential. Everyone can listen to an unvaried characteristic for a minute or two. But as a composition grows, the composer's ingenuity must supply a constant source of subtle contrasts in order to keep alive a listener's attention.

With this prelude, listen to *example 431a* and evaluate its features systematically.

a] Rhythmic interest. Within the idiomatic forms mentioned earlier, there is a plan of increased activity leading first toward measure eleven, and then accelerated to the goal in measure sixteen. Longer valued rhythms help to define cadences and phrases and provide contrast following the climactic approaches.

b] Melodic interest. Follow the composition by applying the principles of directional tones. The row itself produces a network of connecting pitches. The skill is demanded in the developing passages, so that an overriding contour can be heard. Too frequently, serial compositions are examined only by what takes place in a measure, instead of the melodic shape that takes place in a phrase, and in the large contour of the whole section or piece. To illustrate only the truly significant tones that curve the entire example, the melody and bass are reduced in *example* **431c** to the important outer framework contained within this miniature piece. Observe the measure markings.

c] Motives. The rhythmic diversity of the first phrase produces three chief figures as seen in *example* **431d**. The one that contains the rhythmic impetus is Figure *b* which can be easily detected during the course of the composition. The intervals are not held to numbers 3, 4, 5 but for the most part retain a wide dissonant leap. The minor ninth outline in its original state, is substituted by a major seventh in some of the following modifications of Figure *b*. The major third is generally retained within the figure.

Figure *a* is, of course, always a part of numbers 1, 2, and 3, but only if the phrase emphasizes it does the figure come through in a meaningful response. Note that in addition to augmentation and diminution, the rhythms may be switched, permitting the dotted quarter to appear first. Some of its motivic webs are shown in *example* **431d** along with Figure *c* which is subordinate.

Example **431c**

d] Dynamics, texture, and form, all combine in this short composition. After the initial phrase which exposes all of the motivic material, a development ensues which climaxes first in measure eleven, as if closing a Part 2 with a semi-cadence. Part 3 starts with a retrograde in the melody, against the original form in the bass. The augmentation puts a spotlight on the descending minor third and it is significant in that the transposition in this third section starts on the tone of E, which is the twelfth note of the original tone row. In this way, the form moves from the last tone and leads to the first for the ending, E to B♭. This is further supported by the final selection of the series. The R.I. which moves the pitch also, from E to B♭, as symbolic of leading all to the starting pitch. The dynamics uphold the structure of the form. The texture is lyrical and transparent except for a few measures of onrushing vigor.

e] While reserving the discussion of tonality for a later topic, listen to this example from the standpoint of vertical tension. It may be charted by the graph as applied to the Modern period. A selected number of measures is graphed in *example 431e*.

E. Limitations

Consider again how much importance must be attached to the brevity of compositions similar to this one. By reviewing the analysis which was described, much was accomplished in a short space of nineteen measures. How much more could be added without resorting to changes of rhythm, texture and motive? The masterpiece goes on to achieve unity on the grand scale and must provide a drama and an excitement in its materials. The twelve-tone miniature is relieved of the need for any forthcoming contrasts. But it may combine with other equally short pieces to form a larger unit. In this case it must also show ingenuity in an imaginative succession of ideas. There is nothing in the use of a tone row that might prevent this. The limitation lies in the characteristic qualities of rhythm. It was pointed out that the beat and the bar line are frequently nullified, producing rhythmical divisions without the physical feeling of pulsations on the part of the listener. This is intriguing and may be desirable but it produces just one effect. If the pulsations are not felt, what tempo is there? What contrasts can the succeeding compositions rely on? Dynamics and texture will sustain a degree of interest, but basically, rhythm is the ingredient that has more to do in shaping the whole composition than any other factor. Our reaction to motives is through rhythm. Harmony requires a varied rhythmical execution. Therefore, if compositions abandon a rhythmic vitality for any length of time, all of the other musical qualities suffer. A common complaint, "it all sounds the same," is usually directed at twelve-tone writing when it should be aimed more specifically at the rhythmic idiom that has developed alongside the tone-row technique.

Schoenberg's *Piano Suite*, Op. 25, affords an opportunity to listen with particular attention focused upon rhythmic pulse. The set of pieces, modeled after the suites of Bach, contain a varied rhythmic and metric design, including the idiom described previously. The whole suite should be heard with an awareness as to how much time is devoted to one rhythmic plan before a contrasting strategy is employed. (An excerpt from this suite is quoted with the next topic of discussion.)

EXERCISES

A Analysis

1] *Example* 432 includes the four forms of the row in a simple straightforward manner. Mark the forms with brackets denoting each specific version.

Example 432 L. Ulehla

2a] The original form of the row employed by Ernst Krenek in this composition, *Example* 433, is given in *Example* 433a. Follow the row in its vertical use in the excerpt quoted in *Example* 433b. Include a harmonic analysis, as a review.
b] A form of the same row is used in *Example* 425, quoted for exercise drill in the control of dissonance in the preceding chapter. Review the excerpt and include the row indications.

Example **433a** Krenek

Original form:

3] Analyze motives, phrases, directional tones and some harmonic or tonal suggestions in *Example* 434, as well as the serial indications.

B 1] Write a twelve-tone row and its remaining forms, in whole tones.

2] Add rhythm to the row and connect it to the other forms of the row as a single melodic line. Give it shape via directional tones used in varying registers. The end of one form of the row need not receive a cadential pause.

C Write three exercises on the given row (*Example* 435) using the following suggested plan in each.

1] In exercise No. 1, include the following procedure:
a] Add rhythm to the row.
b] Use the retrograde form in the bass against the original form in the soprano.
c] For the second phrase, transpose the treble part, using a tritone imitation of the original row. Change the direction of the melody.

d] Against this, use an inversion in the bass starting from the first pitch of G. Include a few vertical intervals.
e] Finish with a retrograde in the treble against the original form in the bass.

2] In exercise No. 2, include the following procedure:
a] Separate the row so that some tones form a harmonic background while the remaining tones produce a motive.
b] Continue this technique using any of the forms. Attempt to increase the tension by using more tones vertically, leading toward a climax. Follow this by a decline of complex writing, so that a cadential pause results from a rhythmic slackening and a harmonic lessening of tension.

3] In exercise No. 3, fragment the row into two groups of six tones each and work with each group separately instead of utilizing all twelve tones for each form of the row. Against the fragmentation, the second part (1) may also use the same division of the row, in any manner selected, (2) may use the other half of the row, or (3) may not be involved with the fragment, but may announce the complete form of the row. The coincidence of numbers is unimportant as long as a planned design is unfolding, with a numerical logic. Remember that musical reasons should control the selection of particular tones. They, in turn, suggest a row or thematic procedure.

Example ***435***

Original form:

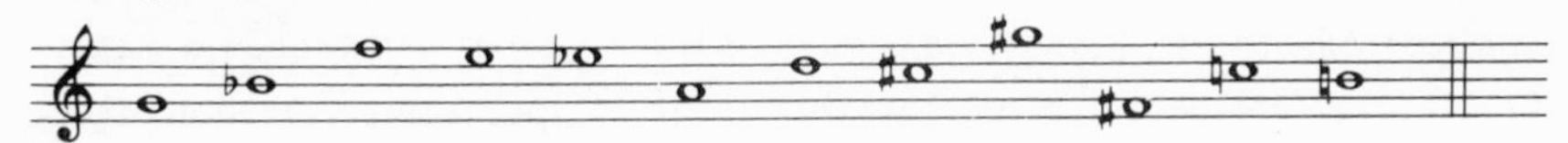

D Two-part inventions are fun to write with a tone row. Select two instruments and concentrate on rhythmic interest. Watch the directional tones and you can't go wrong!

21 Atonality

Does it exist?

Atonality is a word which today is used very freely and with so little regard for its definition. It literally means "without tonality." What it should mean is "without a diatonic concept of tonality." This change of thought might be agreeable to all, had it been part of the original association of the word. But "atonal" was and is used to represent compositions "without tonality." It is a tag that is attached to serial compositions. It is rashly applied to anything that sounds different from the familiar harmonies. In fact, it conjures a rebellious attitude on the part of many musicians because the implication in atonal is that tonality exists either in a diatonic concept or not at all.

Schoenberg strongly resented the use of the term, atonal. He offered as a substitute for atonality, "pan-tonality" suggesting a common bond or union of all tones. This is quite a contrast, a change from a negation of any merging of pitches to an incorporation of diversified tones. The real issue, nevertheless, is not in the words, but in the presence or absence of any form of tonality in compositions using the twelve-tone scale. The twelve-tone scale is inclusive of both the compositions adhering to serialization and those of an equally "dissonant" mien which do not use a tone row.

It is understandable that when the first serial compositions were heard, the sounds were so unfamiliar that tonality may honestly have disappeared. Today, we are more accustomed to advanced forms of dissonance so that it doesn't obliterate the tonal content. The dissonance, no longer a novelty, is accepted, and the large path of tonal movement is sought. Recognized as part of the contemporary picture is the fact that all twelve tones will be bustling about all of the time. Music will not turn back the clock. But neither is it established that by using the twelve-tone scale all tones emerge unrelated, and therefore produce atonality.

The twelve-tone row is constructed with the aim of composing with tones related only to one another. This, on paper, is true! In a musical phrase, all tones are not equal. The row, when placed in a musical context, is not a substitute for tonality, as has been proclaimed, but contains the nucleus of a tonal development. It is used as a theme, and its parts are subdivided into motives, similar to any Classical process. Rhythmic stresses give attention to select group of pitches. The pitch contour formed by a phrase produces some tones of prominence and others which serve in a supporting rhythmic capacity. Harmonies contain roots, without requiring a diatonic tertiary order. These are the new developments recognized today, that seemed entirely enveloped by the tone-row system several decades ago. The tonality today is not one that necessarily centers on one central tonic for the entire composition. It shifts tonal centers at will. All twelve tones may take on the equivalent role of the former tonic. But they always will assume a position that governs twelve notes, each of which may hold reign above the others at any time. Tones which start a phrase, climax the contour of a phrase, become part of a cadence; all contribute toward the movement within the phrase. They lead somewhere. The recipient of that motion has more tonal power than the insignificant motivic assortment of tones which are heard "en route." Tonality is fleeting, but it is there. It is not in the form of one key dominating all, but a transient assortment which may include all twelve tones in rotation.

What shall this form of tonality be called? At this time, no word has been coined, or approved, to adequately fill the vacancy. "Atonal" is still too convenient. It is easy to label a composition atonal and thereby eliminate any searching investigation for its tonal structure.

In the *Piano Suite*, Op. 25 by Schoenberg, which is written with the tone-row method, the last movement, the "Gigue" is interesting from two particular points of view. First, it is rhythmically strong. The pulsations are felt with an energetic power that may be likened to the Classical gigue. Secondly, the row is used with a deliberate stress for tonal supremacy. This does not mean that vertical triads are formed. It does mean that certain tones dominate others and produce a unification within the composition.

The row is given in *example 436*. Being the last movement, an initial straightforward use of the row is avoided. Each measure contains a form of the series which is marked by abbreviation, and the number 1 placed next to the starting tone for ease of identification. Measure nine contains a fragmentation of the row. Tones 3, 4, and 5 are treated motivicly and used by sequence fulfilling all twelve tones within the measure. The fragmentation started in measure five, where numerically, the inverted form for tones 3, 4 and 5 fits better than the disarranged original form. This motive culminates in the cadence in measure nine.

Every form of the series, in this first section of the "Gigue" alternates between starting on E and on B♭. These tones are not hidden, but deliberately stressed with sforzando indications. This affects tonality in that the listener is made aware of these two pitches, out of the possible twelve. Containing a tritone relationship, neither E nor B♭ can claim to rule entirely. This may account for the favoritism Schoenberg displayed toward this interval. Nevertheless, by the end of the first section, B♭ cadences securely, even with the outline of a major triad. It is not wise to say that this section was in the "key" of B♭ major. "Keys" are referred to only in the diatonic scale. What takes place here is that the tone of B♭ dominates over all twelve, and significantly, is the twelfth note of the row.

The form helps to establish what is going on. The first phrase of four bars initiates the main motive. The second phrase brings forth the triplet figure, used against Motive a. This climaxes in the ninth measure by the use of fragmentation (not removed from a Brahms technique), and a short codetta follows in a contrasting, quiet manner.

Directional tones can be studied in the second phrase. The lowest and highest tones stand out more prominently than those in between. The tones of the upper part are selected to avoid B♭ and E so that the tonal movement is toward each start of the series. Vertically, there is more dissonance at the outset of each measure (from bars five to eight), which lessens in the middle of the bar. Play it slowly. In measure five, mentally change the top E♭ to a D♯. The sound is that of a B root; the perfect fifth in the bass is loud and clear. The B is a directional tone to the following B♭. In measure six, without any enharmonic changes, an F chord is formed which leads through F♭ to the inversion starting on the bass B♭. Measures seven and eight contain tonal movement which at the end of each bar produce a cadential relationship. The descending triplet force lands in measure seven on B♮. It is mentally linked with the forthcoming E in the bass. There is no interference by the surrounding compatible intervals. The sequence in measure eight lands on F and blends with B♭.

Measure nine spotlights all of the tones that form an active, agitated, dissonant, contemporary semi-cadence! The tritones form the dissonance. The bass rises up to A♮, a leading-tone to B♭. The first tone of each upper triplet leads toward a fifth of B♭ even though it is not struck as a resolution. All together, this climactic force dramatically resolves to the hushed "tonic" note of B♭ (in measure ten).

Within this codetta, the B♭ cadence is materialized. It is shaped by the melodic contour and indicated for the performer's awareness. Measure twelve starts with a pronouncement of B♭, moves above it to add the minor third D, and F, and completes the cadence on the final tone, B♭ in the following measure.

And this is called atonal! Limitations of space prevent quoting the final cadence of the "Gigue." When listened to, its tonal properties become more and more evident. The planned directional tones move from an entire measure of repeated tones of E, to F, to an evaded cadence on a G diminished ninth chord and to a completion on B♭.

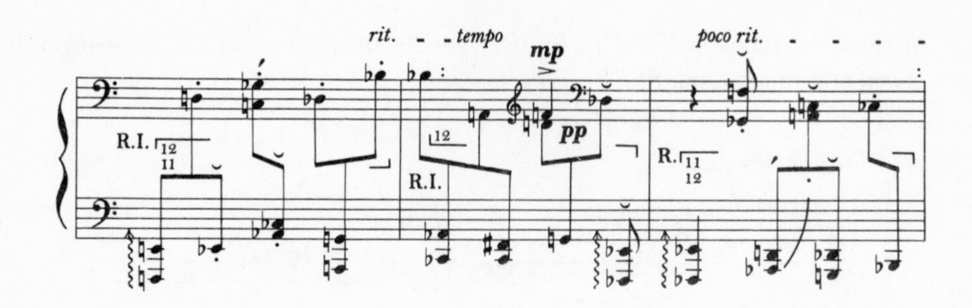

There are measures in both Classical and contemporary idioms that temporarily may show a lack of tonal direction or of a feeling of belonging to a particular tonality. A series of chromatic diminished seventh chords merged with unresolved dominants can wipe out a former key and for a while suggest a "no man's land." There is no quarrel with the fact that the contemporary composition uses more of this technique. Groups of measures and groups of phrases may be transient and may await a firmer foothold. The directional tones within such measures supply the motion that is equivalent to the chromatic chords of the nineteenth century. This motion must cease with a cadential pause (not a harmonic one necessarily), and whichever tone or group of tones receives such motion, and has a temporary settling quality, that is the one around which the others revolve. Contemporary tonality is based on a progression of sound directed by prominent tones and affected by the vertical increase or decrease of tension. One central tone may be established, governing all twelve tones inclusively, or a changing order may set up tonalities which govern sections of a composition rather than the whole.

Notation

Undoubtedly, some of the confusion regarding tonality occurred because notation reflected an arbitrary choice of tone, rather than the one which would bind tonality. It must be remembered that the aim of the tone row was to avoid a diatonic relationship. In the attempt to achieve this, an unintentional disregard for accoustical blending of tones frequently resulted.

The first two pieces of Schoenberg's *Drei Klavierstücke*, Op. 11, written prior to the tone-row method, illustrate the notational situation. Each composition is first quoted in its original notation, and is followed by an illustration of enharmonic changes that visually denote what is being heard. See *examples* **437a, b**, and *examples* **438a, b**. (The tempo is slow in both compositions.)

In the first composition, a central tonality of E is recognized, although at the outset, the selection of B is a possibility. Most chord formations are of dominant quality. The enharmonic spellings, illustrated in *example* **437b** conform to a harmonic association of tones, and provide the analysis as marked. It can be seen that there are many more accidentals placed in the original edition than are necessary. The advanced harmonic techniques that are understood today were not fully exploited at the time this composition was written. The abundance of accidentals was probably employed to avoid any question as to which tone was intended. The mixing of flats and sharps may have been meant in terms of polytonal mixtures, which today more readily surround one root or tonality.

The second composition suggests that the selection of D♭ in the melody, *example* 438a, may have been planned as an isolated polytonal motive above the rotation of F and D in the bass. The principle of linear roots could only have been in its infancy, if at all considered. Today, there is no question of the accoustical blend of tones occurring in the second measure, as supporting the root of D minor. The skip from D♭ to A♮ emerges as a C♯ to A, the dominant.

The listener is not aware of the notation, but to the performer, it may prove puzzling and misleading. The best notation is the one which provides most clarity both in terms of a tonal understanding as well as for the ease of execution. Today's performers need only the necessary sharps and flats. They do not question the note which is not prefixed by an accidental. The type of accidental which is desirable today is one which was completely unnecessary in

the diatonic structure. Namely, the tone which is given an accidental in an early part of a measure and later restated is frequently questioned. The first pitch ought to remain but with the non-diatonic melodies, there is no logical aural carry-over of the earlier pitch. Composers frequently restate such an accidental. This leads logically toward a newer method of notation which is employed by some composers, that of marking all altered tones wherever they occur. Notes left alone (except as direct repetitions), are automatically naturalized or true to their letter name.

Relaxing the "rules"

With the progress of time, the theoretic doctrines which were imposed upon a melody were gradually relaxed so as to permit a more individual creativity. The most significant advance came with the acceptance of repetition of tonal groups within the row. In the early stages of the row technique, brief neighboring tones, or trill and tremolo repetitions were permitted, as unessential ornamentation. This license was insufficient for the composer who desired a greater stability of sound. It was found that some motives preferred repetition to sequential treatment. And in harmonies, a purposeful return to a preceding chordal combination provided the extension of sound, a more climactic force for any part of the phrase. The composers imposed their will upon the tone row, but did not, in the process, entirely abandon the row's basic organization.

The repetition of motivic groups, or any small groups of consecutive horizontal "numbers" came as an inevitable by-product of certain row procedures. The need for pitch repetition was recognized even within the strict row technique. The illustrations which follow will show, by degrees, the factors which led toward more tonal stability; first through a planned selection of the forms of the series and secondly, by melodic choice within the series.

Schoenberg's *Fourth String Quartet*, Op. 37, demonstrates his selectivity of the forms of the row. The first movement is anchored in a tonality of D, which is recognized strongly at the cadence to the first section, at the final cadence of the movement, and is referred to intermittently during the body of the composition. The row, unashamedly, begins in D minor! *Example 439* reduces the quartet to three staves, suitable for playing with a solo instrument on the upper line and a piano rendition of the lower two lines. This may be reversed in the phrase starting in measure seventeen. The solo instrument may take the lowest part, as the range is still within the treble clef limit, giving the piano a coordinated rhythmic background. If possible, listen to a recording first, and then in a slower tempo, play *example 439* giving attention to all of the notes and the following analysis.

The construction of the row contains an unmistakable D minor opening. Schoenberg did not attempt to negate it, instead, used it to emphasize phrases and form. With the outline of an augmented triad in numbers 7, 8, and 9, of the row, the directional tones then lead to a perfect fourth cadence, F♯ to B.

Theme 1 is played by the first violin and consists of the twelve tones which make up the tone row. This rhythm is retained as a theme in the future references, where the form is designed specifically for such identification. The accompaniment is made up of vertical groups, organized so as to utilize the twelve tones within each measure, or fragment thereof. For example, the second measure of the theme includes numbers 4, 5, and 6, which are omitted in the accompaniment below. These accompaniment groups are not intended to produce chords in a harmonic relationship. The tonality is in the linear stress of D. It is also interesting that as the theme moves away from D, the cello line begins to favor it. This culminates in the strong placement of the D major seventh chord in measure four. This is the harmonic cadence, likened to a I^6_4, which in measure five moves by evasion to B♭. An active augmented triad in the sixth measure then pushes on toward the new phrase.

In the second phrase, the evidence of a need for pitch retention is apparent in the choice of a transposed series, an inversion starting from G. The essential tone aimed for is the long valued B in measure seven, as a continuation of the last melodic pitch of the original row. Accompanying this is a reorganization of the same tones of the eighth note figures, contained also within the preceding augmented triad. The vertical group forms an A♭ root as indicated. This chord of A♭ is used frequently as a harmonic tool, sometimes blending with a linear root of E. This occurs in measures eighteen and twenty-one. Its lowered fifth reference to D is significant.

Using the retrograde for the third phrase, the complete shape of the theme becomes clear. The rhythm of the first phrase is deliberately retained. The linear root of B is emphasized by the half notes, but the harmonic result here is not intended to denote strong roots. The force of the phrase is moving onward to the climactic cadence on D. The strength of the first violin must be heard to be believed. The perfect authentic cadence is masterfully executed by the one instrument, against an imitative response of the three quarter notes on harmonies evolved from the row.

A decision to extend the tones of the cadence occurs with the onset of the original row in measure fifteen. It functions musically as a retrograde of the cadence. A transitional phrase therefore starts with the fourth tone of the row and carries on briefly with a linear extension of the dominant A, in measure seventeen. Against this upper material, the cello brings back the same transposed inversion as used in the second phrase. The pitch of A♭ is used prominently within the phrase from measures seventeen to the first half of measure nineteen. Then through the cello F♮ and A, a suggestion of D occurs in bar twenty, in the form of its dominant. It is equivalent to a semi-cadence, used without a rhythmic pause and leading to a canonic imitation of the inverted tones of the A♭ motive. Compare measures six and twenty-one.

A decision to repeat a motive, prompted by the desire to hold the reins of tonal movement, occurs in measures eighteen and nineteen. It has particular interest in that the repeated numbers involve the last three and first three of the inverted series.

Example 439 Schoenberg

There is no shortcut to the analysis of music, serial or otherwise, if one is to separate the artistic achievement from a mathematical formula. The inspired music of Anton Webern also deserves an intensive analysis (not only the numbers). *Example 440* illustrates a blend of atonal dissonance within tonal boundaries. The second song, from *Drei Gesänge*, Op. 23, is representative of Webern. In general, there is little direct repetition of a pitch. There is much elision within the rows, that is, a single tone may serve as two numbers, each of a different form of the series. There is also a more expanded use of fragmentation of the row. A motivic group may appear isolated, without the immediate following of a horizontal succession of tones.

Listen to the entire song, if possible. Its devotion to the text is beautifully portrayed. The form divides into five short sections. The material content suggests an introduction, the main phrase, "A," a development using introductory material as a "B," a return to "A," and a codetta based on the opening. *Example 440* quotes the first two of these sections.

Before exploring the paths of the tone row, try to feel the tonal contrast between the introductory phrase, and the main theme. The first suggests a wild, boisterous vigor, and is appropriate to the poem. The second phrase removes the tension and brings forth the main motive in a tranquil setting. The dynamics, while contributing to this repose, are not the sole source. Observe the contrasting intervallic usage. The introduction emphasizes discordant intervallic structures, heard in a vertical form. This is dynamically

Example **440**

Vocal Inv. cont.
R.
R.I.
(elision)
I.
A −3 +3

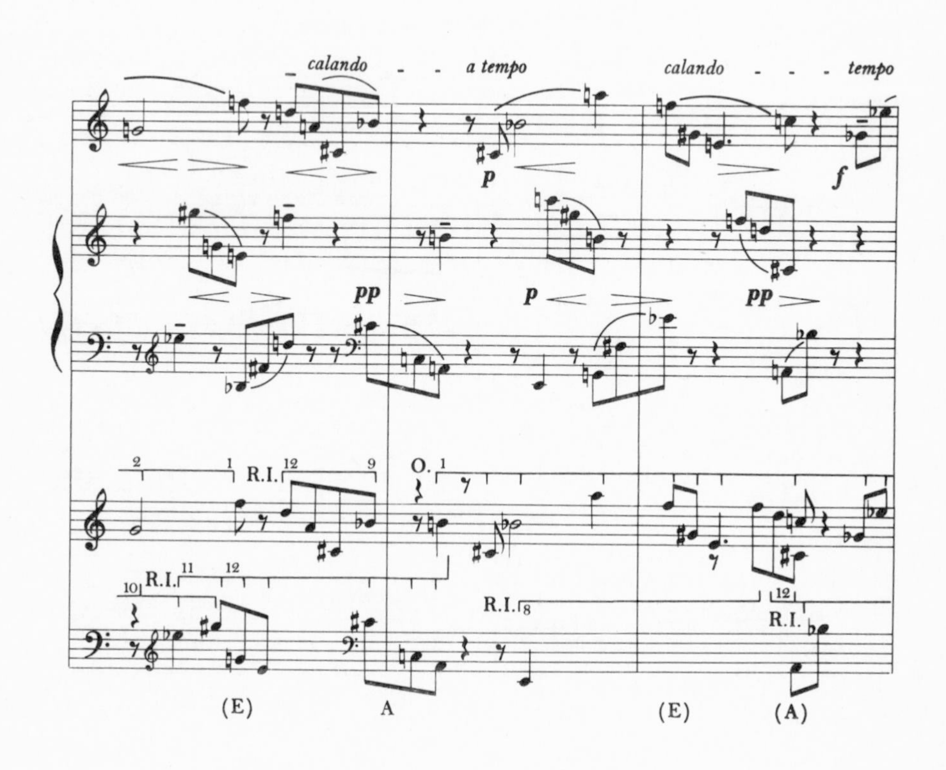
calando - - a tempo
calando - - - tempo
R.I.
O.
R.I.
R.I.
R.I.
(E)
A
(E)
(A)

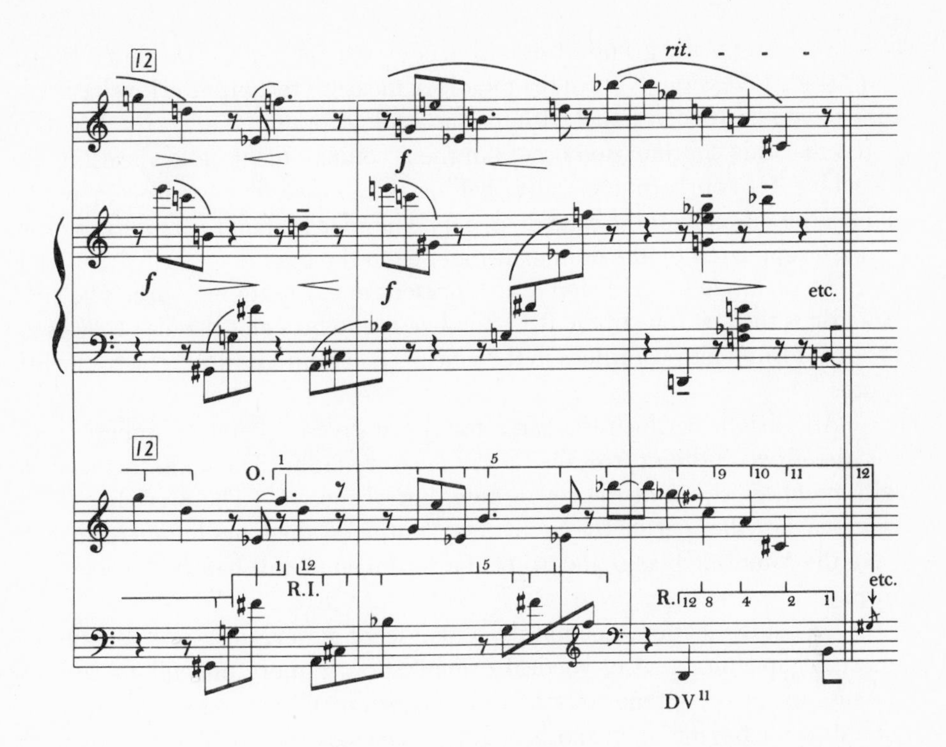

opposed to the linear weave in which the tritones are few; and the vertical co-ordination of all parts stresses a greater concordant quality.

Equally important to this restful attitude is the fact that it is rooted to tonality. The analytical reduction, together with a guide for the serial analysis, emphasizes the actual bass line so that a clearer tonal impression may be seen. The omitted tones of the treble accompaniment would not change the harmonic picture, but of course they enhance the timbre. The many returns of the root A in the bass clearly denote the tonality in which the minor and major third play an equal role. The measures in between the numerous returns to A, include the G♯ and E in various motivic groups. (Consult the original for all of these instances.) The effective increase of tension occurs toward the end of this second phrase. The root progression leads to a new chord and gives D the climactic power (measure fourteen). It is the lowest of all of the bass tones, including the rest of the song, not quoted.

The accompaniment motive which produces the root of A is most frequently drawn from numbers 2, 3 and 4 of an inverted series. But it is also located on other transposed orders, such as in the vocal line of the ninth measure, where a R.I. starts from D and supports the A root by numbers 11, 10 and 9.

An interesting fragmentation of the row appears in this instance. The *calando* group in measure nine begins the retrograde inversion but its horizontal succession is interrupted by the start of the original form. In the meantime, the descending piano group, stressing A, completes an earlier start of a different retrograde inversion. Not till the middle of measure ten with the low bass E, is the calando figure continued with the succeeding tones of that series. It will be noted that this continuation occurs in the accompaniment. The vocal line, by switching its course numerically, begins the phrase in measure ten with a duplication of pitch of the calando group. The tones retain the emphasis on A, and are supported by the dominant tone, E, in the bass.

An example of an elision is also present in the tenth measure. The right hand B♮ is the last tone of the R.I., number 1, and becomes the first tone of the original form which continues in the voice. The twelfth or first tone frequently unite.

An elision in which the same tones are given different numbers in the middle of two colliding rows occurs in measure eight. The main theme starts with numbers seven of the retrograde, untransposed. (The preceding chord contains the other part of the row.) As it continues, the tones numbered 3 and 2 have the same pitch as 9 and 10 of the accompaniment material, an inverted form.

The introduction, seemingly a tangle of notes, does not contain any unusual happenings. Any vertical organization is more difficult to decipher because the order of tones is not fixed. A chord may contain the end of a series as well as the beginning of another. The given analysis indicates the tone which starts each series.

Realizing the tonal references in the lyrical phrase, is there any particular pitch reference in the introduction that might lead to the A tonality? If a recording is not at hand, play the first two chords, followed by only the vocal line of the introduction and conclude with the three chords in measures six and seven. The directional tones point to one particular note, the leading-tone. The G♯ (notated as A♭) is the highest tone in measures two and three; in measure five, the vocal line contains it as the upper climactic pitch, and repeats it; the accompaniment ends with it in measure seven. Finally, in examining the first two chords (our analysis has progressed from the middle of the composition back to the beginning), the intervallic structure can be interpreted as containing an A root and progressing to the dominant!

Igor Stravinsky wrote *Threni*, a work for solo voices, mixed chorus and orchestra, some three decades after the start of the serial development. It is a dramatic work of large proportions which shapes its form into smaller units, but always within a grand concept of unity. It is not possible to explore a work of this magnitude within these pages. The few excerpts quoted in *example 441* will merely show a growing concept of loosening the ties of the tone row. Tonalities remain stable for longer durations. Certain tones are given prominent positions as unifying representatives of tonality. Far from being avoided, the tonal control needed particularly for a large work is emphasized. In the first movement, for example, the original form of the tone row starts so frequently on F♯ that its repetitions, which for the most part retain a vocal contour and avoid register changes, are easily identified through the hearing and do not require looking for this sense of balance.

Threni does not start with an obvious exposure of the row. It is hidden within a brief orchestral introduction. Two solo voices are then introduced against the orchestral background. They sing the retrograde forms of the row, while the text beckons all to listen to the lamentations of the Prophet Jeremiah. After an interesting *parlando* section, the tone row which is given most prominence and attention is announced by an alto bugle and solo tenor, and may be called the "original" form. It is the form that is present in the orchestral opening, although obscured by the orchestration.

Starting with this announcement of the row, *example 441a* is complete in its instrumentation. Observe (1) the frequent repetition of the figures, (2) the augmentation of the row in the tenor, incomplete until the third recurrence and (3) the tonal stability of C emphasized by the strings in the accompaniment,

chosen with a tritone relationship to F♯, the first tone of the composition, and of the row. Immediately following this excerpt, three more repetitions of the original form from F♯ are heard.

Example 441b quotes only the two vocal soloists who, as mentioned earlier, are part of the introduction and sing the retrograde forms of the row. The orchestra at this point contains four forms of the row within its own instrumentation. Play the vocal lines and notice the simplicity in the intervals. The curves of the melody are lyrically controlled without the wide leaps of an instrumental concept. From a tonal point of view, the first perfect fourth makes G♯ prominent in this phrase, and with its recurrence, holds as a linear root for five measures. Directional tones widen the melody at this point gradually leading toward F♯. The alto line supports the earlier pitch of G♯ and then follows a descending path toward the tritone pitch of C. Together, the voices weave a network of C♯, C♮, F and F♯ for a beautiful cadence.

The orchestral introduction is quoted in *example 441c*, reduced to treble and bass, but with all tones included. It has a vigor, typical of Stravinsky, in this mode of expression. It contrasts importantly with the earlier twelve-tone school in that the tones move gradually from one setting to another. All twelve tones are not massed into one or two measures as they were in the former examples of Schoenberg and Webern. The slower movement of the essential pitches allows the music to breathe and enables a composition to grow into a large structure, if desired. (For another reference, observe the slow pitch movement in the part entitled "Sensus Spei.")

The chief motive of the introduction is an eighth note leap of the minor ninth, reiterated forcefully. The F♯ to F♮ states the first two tones of the row while the only other tone involved at the very opening provides a striking dissonance in the tone of G. The brief grace note, on the bass F♯, gives a reassuring clue that the inversion of the row is begun in the bass, simultaneously with its "original" shape in the violins. The numerical progress of both series is easily traced in the reduced score, but shifts freely among the instruments of the orchestra. The sequences of the first figure are interesting in measure three, but also the prominence of the intervals of the perfect fifth deserve mention. They are marked with brackets in the example so as to show their directional pitch line. The fifths add to an openness and sparsity of pitch that is characteristic of the later idiom in Stravinsky's writing. It is a blend of a contrapuntal chamber music style with a harmonic structure that does not confuse by a multiplicity of tones but prefers a stark, bare, dissonant quality. Nevertheless, there are also moments of warmth in *Threni.* In the section entitled "Sensus Spei," the contrasts of rhythm, and of tonality lead to a middle section in which the chorus sings one of the most beautiful passages in contemporary literature. Out of context, it would not have the effect that it does in the composition. The reader is urged to listen for it, and to follow its increasing tensions toward the climax of this section. It is this type of contrast, spaced appropriately among the movements, and in this case in accordance with the text, that makes possible a unity of thought in a large composition. The serialization throughout *Threni* is in the background. In the foreground, the composer controls all of his ideas.

With composers today asserting their own individuality upon the tone row, and therefore removing some of the earlier characteristics that bore the stamp of serialization, the resulting product to the listener is not one which can be immediately defined as serial. This is largely due to an increasing number of young composers who have incorporated into their creativity all of the harmonic dissonance of the serial technique but who do not employ the actual row techniques. Today, after a hearing of his work, the composer is frequently asked if he employed a tone row. The difference between a free expression of ideas based on a tone row, and the creative approach which plans themes and motives controlled without the mathematical aspect is indiscernible in an equivalent harmonic idiom. The plans that a composer has for the development of his motives may be bound with a concept of intervallic relationship, but not necessarily in the method which prevailed and worked for Schoenberg. For example, Elliot Carter in his *String Quartet No. 2* (1959) treats each instrument with a characteristic individuality. The viola, for example, is predominantly lyrical and expressive throughout the quartet, while the second violin alternates between pizzicato and *arco* phrases as if portraying a more jovial mood. But these characteristics are also tied to a unique intervallic plan. Each instrument, almost without exception, plays only two intervals within which the motives are formed. The cello lines are restricted to the perfect fourth and minor sixth. The viola plays tritones and minor seventh intervals. The second violin part contains major thirds, major sixths and an occasional major seventh for emphasis. The first violin concentrates on minor thirds and perfect fifths. All instruments have some connecting stepwise passing tones. The material is intensely organized, not with an old plan, but with a most unusual design. It is not, however, the intervallic design that makes the music. The inspiration and creative ingenuity produce the music, the notes themselves are incidental. Each composer may have his own secret plans for selecting his notes. What matters, is whether they have expressed an artistic entity.

EXERCISES

A *Analysis*

Analyze the twelve-tone examples quoted by observing particularly the repetitions contained within the horizontal layout of the row. How does this affect the melody in terms of rhythm, tonal movement, and phrase content? Observe the manner in which a harmonic background is given to the music, also by means of a selection of pitch derived from the series.

Example 442: *Symphony No. 3*, by Wallingford Riegger
Example 443: *Three Little Pieces*, No. III, by Juli Nunlist
Example 444: *Twelve Short Piano Pieces*, No. 5, by Krenek
Example 445: *Canticum Sacrum*, Part II (Surge, aquilo), by Stravinsky

Example 442
Riegger
Allegro
Oboe
Complete
(Score
reduced)
pp
ff
pp
Fl.
rit.
Bsn.
mp
Vcl.
a tempo
Vn.
pp
Vn. II pizz.
Vla. pizz.
Vcl.
p
sfz
mf
p
Hn.
arco
p
mf
p

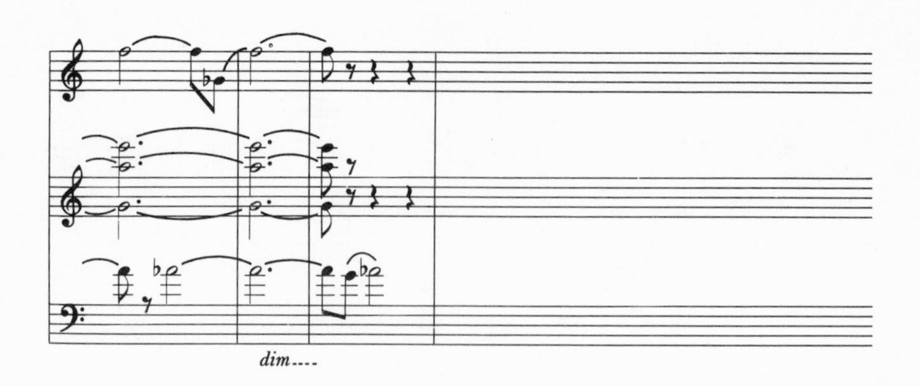

Example **443** Juli Nunlist

Example 444
Krenek
Allegro deciso
f
p
f
f
mf
p
etc.
Original form:
Krenek
Example 445
Stravinsky
♪ = 92
Tenor Solo
(text omitted)
mf
Corno Ing.
Fl.
8 Contra-bassi soli
p
Arpa

B In *Examples* **446a** and **b**, the row is stated, inclusive of repetitions within its original form. Add a second voice and expand into a short composition following *Examples* **443** and **444** as suggested models. Employ repetition for motivic, tonal, and harmonic emphasis. Do not ignore the principles of melody and of the need for variety in the vertical tensions.

C Try some three-part inventions written on your own original twelve-tone row. You may use either the strict technique as previously described, or include the less rigid controls as stated in this chapter. Concentrate on texture and dynamics for an original sound.

For further study of the row, examine all of the *Twelve Short Piano Pieces* by Ernst Krenek. Follow this by listening, and studying the completed compositions mentioned in the preceding chapters as well as the many contemporary twelve-tone compositions written by fine composers, too numerous to include in a specific reference.

22 A summary of procedures for contemporary analysis

1. Listen! Notes on paper mean nothing unless they are conveyed into actual sound. The person who is lucky enough to "hear" what he sees must consider this an added advantage but not a complete substitute for the true listening.
2. Do not scrutinize the small details before a general impression of the composition, or movement is understood. Shape the form into large divisions and gradually break each down into smaller parts. Ask yourself:

   a] Is the composer stating a theme, or motive?
   b] Is this an introductory phrase to a new part?
   c] Is this a development of former ideas?
   d] Is the tension being increased, maintained, or relaxed?
   e] Where is the goal or climax of the entire architectural structure?
   f] Is this a summary of motives as indicative of a recapitulation or coda?

3. Do not feel that a label must be attached to it in order that a form exist. Form is simply the shape in which the composer sets his ideas. It may or may not be an outgrowth of Classical forms. Every composition, regardless of idiom, must have form!
4. Choose the right type of analysis for each particular phrase or part of the composition. The analysis of predominantly homophonic passages requires more consideration of the vertical harmonies than would be necessary for a more contrapuntal composition.
5. Do not attempt to account for, or explain every note. Melodic ideas are filled with tones that contribute to an overall harmonic color but which need not be specifically identified as either chord tone or non-harmonic tone. The same reasoning applies to intervallic structures or chords containing clusters. Every note in a harmonic column does not portray an equal harmonic responsibility.
6. Do not juggle the tones. Consider the musical statement whether linear or harmonic in the exact register in which it occurs. The organization of tones

is as essential in the diatonic tertiary analysis as it is in the contemporary I.S. column.

7. Always retain a rhythmic perspective as to the value of tones.
8. Regarding tonality:
   a] Let the music first suggest a tonal anchorage, heard in particular passages, before you seek a tonal center;
   b] Tonality is flexible and need not be bound to a central tone;
   c] Linear tonality replaces the all-encompassing harmonic tonality of the former musical periods.
9. Regarding progressions:
   a] Movements of root tones replace progressions of total chords;
   b] All twelve root-tones may move independently;
   c] Relate the important tonal roots to a central one, if such exists, or to a changing, flexible design equivalent to a large-scale, modulatory root progression;
   d] Root tones are derived from linear movement as well as from vertical formations. The outer voices generally predominate in the root suggestions.

10. Be forward-looking! Accept the experimentation in the field of electronics, in improvisational composing, in the use of new instruments or in unique combinations of instruments (as is developing in the percussion section, for example), and in quarter tone ideas as well as all of the yet unexplored musical developments that will take place. It is not possible to delve into the above fields at this writing, and formulate procedures or explore methods. These techniques are now being developed and their evaluation must be left to musical history and the test of time. Progress cannot be halted, for as it moves forward it brings to new heights much of what has already been developed. By acquiring the knowledge of established Modern techniques, the educated listener will find that the new experiments in writing are not out of reach. On the other hand, it is not necessary to understand the composer's trade in order for his music to communicate an esthetic expression. What is essential is a willingness to listen. Don't bring along prejudices of a past generation to the concert hall; instead, accept the new sounds on their terms. A masterful composition will transmit some quality, whether exciting, or tender, or orchestrally colorful, or stridently bombastic. But it cannot convey any idea to ears that do not listen!

EXERCISES

A The following excerpts are selected for a review of some basic idiomatic expressions. Each example stresses a particular type of analysis but all examples require some consideration of both harmonic and polyphonic techniques. Follow the suggestions offered in the summary and apply what is fitting to each composition.

Example **447**: Fugue from *Prelude, Ostinanto and Fugue,* by Nicolas Flagello
Example **448**: *From My Diary,* No. IV, by Roger Sessions

Example **449**: *Variations on a Theme* by *Bach*; No. 5, by Ludmila Ulehla
Example **450**: *Five over Twelve*, Prelude on a Twelve-tone Row, No. 5, by Ludmila Ulehla

Example **447** — *Nicolas Flagello*

mf
mp
cresc.
meas. 50
etc.
sfz
etc.

Example 448
Roger Sessions
Allegro pesante
ff
mf
ff
mf
etc.
Example 449
Ludmila Ulehla
Tempo di Sarabande
pp molto legato
pp
ppp

Example 450 Ludmila Ulehla

f
pp
mp molto cresc.
f
ff
p
sfz
p
pp
sfz
molto crescendo
ff
meno f sfz p
pp
ff

B Harmonize the figured bass in *Examples* **451 *a*, *b*, *c*** and ***d***. Use rhythmic divisions in the upper parts. Rests may be adhered to or not depending upon the counterpoint of the other voices. Expand or retract the number of parts as is necessary. Unmarked tones may be used as passing tones or they may be harmonized by passing chords of your own choice. In addition, write your own original chord progressions. From these, many interesting compositions may grow.

Example 451c

C The melodies in *Example* 452 may be used as supplementary material for several chapters. They may be analyzed as single lines for directional pitches and linear roots. They can be adapted for two or three part writing. Harmonically, they can be used for extra drill involving a particular chord or intervallic structure. Observe the tempo in each melody. The faster pulsations require fewer harmonic changes while the slow tempi may desire an intricate harmonic blend. Add Parts Two and Three to the melodies that hopefully may inspire a development of their ideas.

Example 452a
Allegretto
Example 452b
Adagio
Example 452c
Moderato
p
pp

d
Allegro
f
mp
f
dim.
p

Acknowledgments

The author wishes to thank the many persons who have cooperated in obtaining permission from the following publishers to quote from works copyrighted by them:

Associated Music Publishers, Inc.

Hindemith, Paul: *Ludus Tonalis,* © 1943 by Schott & Co. Ltd., used by permission

Second Sonata for piano, © 1936 by B. Schott's Soehne, Mainz, renewed 1963, used by permission

Third Piano Sonata, © 1936 by B. Schott's Soehne, Mainz, renewed 1963, used by permission

Springtime from *Six Chansons,* © 1939, 1943, by Associated Music Publishers, Inc., used by permission

String Quartet No. IV, © 1924 by B. Schott's Soehne, Mainz

Ives, Charles: Concord Sonata, © 1947 by Associated Music Publishers, Inc., New York, used by permission

Piston, Walter: Trio for violin, violoncello and piano, © 1938 by Arrow Music Press, Inc. Assigned to Associated Music Publishers, Inc.

Riegger, Wallingford: String Quartet No. 2, © 1949 by Arrow Music Press, Inc. Assigned to Associated Music Publishers, Inc.

Symphony No. 3, © 1949, 1957 by Associated Music Publishers, Inc.

Tansman, Alexandre: *Suite dans le style ancien,* © 1931 by Max Eschig. Assigned to Associated Music Publishers, Inc.

Toch, Ernst: *Tanz und Spielstucke,* Op. 40 No. 13, © 1927 by B. Schott's Soehne, Mainz. Assigned to Associated Music Publishers, Inc.

Boosey and Hawkes, Inc.

Bartok, Bela: Concerto for Orchestra, © 1946 by Hawkes & Son (London) Ltd., reprinted by permission of Boosey and Hawkes, Inc.

Mikrokosmos (Vol. 6), © 1941 by Hawkes & Son (London) Ltd., reprinted by permission of Boosey and Hawkes, Inc.

Music for Strings, Percussion and Celesta, © 1937 by Universal Edition, renewed 1964. Copyright and renewal assigned to Boosey and Hawkes, Inc. for the United States, reprinted by permission of Boosey and Hawkes, Inc.

String Quartet No. 2, © 1920 by Universal Edition, renewed 1948. Copyright and renewal assigned to Boosey and Hawkes, Inc. for the United States, reprinted by permission of Boosey and Hawkes, Inc.

String Quartet No. 4, © 1929 by Universal Edition, renewed 1956. Copyright and renewal assigned to Boosey and Hawkes, Inc. for the United States, reprinted by permission of Boosey and Hawkes, Inc.

String Quartet No. 6, © 1941 by Hawkes and Son (London) Ltd., reprinted by permission of Boosey and Hawkes, Inc.

Britten, Benjamin: *Seven Sonnets of Michelangelo,* © 1943 by Boosey and Company Ltd., reprinted by permission of Boosey and Hawkes, Inc.

Copland, Aaron: Sonata for Piano, © 1942 by Boosey and Hawkes, Inc. Copyright assigned to Aaron Copland, reprinted by permission of Aaron Copland, copyright owner, and Boosey and Hawkes, Inc., sole agent

Prokofiev, Sergei: Classical Symphony, © 1926 by Edition Russe de Musique. Copyright assigned to Boosey and Hawkes, Inc., reprinted by permission.

Gavotte, Op. 32 No. 3, © by A. Gutheil. Copyright assigned to Boosey and Hawkes, Inc., reprinted by permission.

Stravinsky, Igor: *Canticum Sacrum,* © 1956 by Boosey and Hawkes, Inc., reprinted by permission

Le Sacre du printemps, © 1921 by Edition Russe de Musique. Copyright assigned to Boosey and Hawkes, Inc., reprinted by permission of Boosey and Hawkes, Inc.
Sonate pour piano, © 1925 by Edition Russe de Musique, renewed 1952. Copyright and renewal assigned to Boosey and Hawkes, Inc., reprinted by permission
Threni, © 1958 by Boosey & Co. Ltd., reprinted by permission of Boosey and Hawkes, Inc.
Vaughan Williams, Ralph: *Songs of Travel* (Part 2), © 1905 by Boosey & Co. Ltd., renewed 1933. Reprinted by permission of Boosey and Hawkes, Inc.

Carl Fischer, Inc.
Dello Joio, Norman: Sonata No. 3, © 1948 by Carl Fischer, Inc., used by permission
Shostakovich, Dmitri: *Three Fantastic Dances,* used by permission

Edward B. Marks Music Corporation.
Sessions, Roger: *From My Diary,* © 1947 by Edward B. Marks Music Corporation, used by permission

Elkan-Vogel Co., Inc.
Debussy, Claude: *Children's Corner,* Preludes Volumes I and II for piano,
Sonate pour Violon et Piano, String Quartet, reprinted by permission Durand et Cie, Paris; Elkan-Vogel Co., Inc., Philadelphia, agents for United States
Selected Songs from *Ariettes oubliées, Cinq poèmes de Baudelaire, Chansons de Bilitis, Fêtes galantes, Proses lyriques, Le son du cor s'afflige, Dans le jardin, L'echelonnement des hais,* reprinted by permission, Durand et Cie, Paris; Editions Jobert; Elkan-Vogel Co., Inc., Philadelphia, agents for United States
Nuages and *Fêtes* from *Nocturnes; Pour le piano; Prélude a L'après-midi d'un faun,* reprinted by permission Editions Jobert; Elkan-Vogel Co., Inc., Philadelphia, agents for the United States
Persichetti, Vincent: *Poems* for piano, reprinted by permission Elkan-Vogel Co., Inc., Philadelphia, copyright owners
Ravel: *Le tombeau de Couperin,* String Quartet, reprinted by permission Durand et Cie, Paris; Elkan-Vogel Co., Inc., Philadelphia, agents for United States

Franco Colombo, Inc.
Giannini, Vittorio: Songs: *Life's Span, Moonlight, Waiting,* © 1935 Franco Colombo, Inc., by permission of the publisher
Satie, Erik: *Danses de travers* from *Pièces froides,* © 1912 by Rouart LeRolle & Cie., by permission of Editions Salabert, copyright owner

General Music Publishing Co., Inc.
Flagello, Nicolas: *Fugue from Prelude, Ostinato and Fugue,* by permission, General Music Publishing Co., Inc.
Ulehla, Ludmila: *Five over Twelve, Song Without Words, Variations on a Theme by Bach,* by permission, General Music Publishing Co., Inc.

Leeds Music Company.
Kabalevsky, Dmitri: Preludes, Op. 38 Nos. 5, 6, 10, 15, 18, 21, © MCMXLVII by MCA MUSIC, a division of MCA, Inc., New York, used by permission, all rights reserved
Prokofiev, Sergei: Piano Sonatas Nos. 2, 5, 6, 7, © MCMLVII by Leeds Music Corp., New York, used by permission, all rights reserved
Symphony No. 5, © MCMXLV by MCA MUSIC, a division of MCA, Inc., New York, used by permission, all rights reserved
Rachmaninoff, Serge: Prelude Op. 32 No. 2, used by permission MCA MUSIC, a division of MCA, Inc., New York
Scriabine, Alexander: Prelude No. 21 Op. 11, used by permission of MCA MUSIC, a division of MCA, Inc., New York, all rights reserved
Shostakovich, Dmitri: Fugue No. 2 Op. 87, used by permission of MCA MUSIC, a division of MCA, Inc., New York, all rights reserved
Prelude No. 4 Op. 34, © MCMXLV by MCA MUSIC, a division of MCA, Inc., New

York, used by permission, all rights reserved
Symphony No. 5, © MCMXL by MCA MUSIC, a division of MCA, Inc., New York used by permission, all rights reserved
Symphony No. 9, MCMXLVI by MCA MUSIC, a division of MCA, Inc., New York, used by permission, all rights reserved
Symphony No. 10, © MCMLV by Le Chant Du Monde, Paris; Leeds Music Company for the entire Western Hemisphere, used by permission, all rights reserved
Three Fantastic Dances, Op. 1, © MCMXLVI by MCA MUSIC, a division of MCA, Inc., New York, used by permission, all rights reserved

Lyra Music Company.
Flagello, Nicolas: Sonata for Harp, © March 12, 1963, Lyra Music Company, 43 West 61 St., New York, used by permission

Mills Music, Inc.
Flagello, Nicolas: *Tristis est Anima Mea,* © 1962 by Mills Music, Inc., used by permission

Oxford University Press.
Vaughan Williams, Ralph: Symphony in E Minor, © in United States and all countries 1948 by Oxford University Press, London, used by permission

C.F. Peters Corporation.
Wolf, Hugo: *Spanisches Liederbuch* I, Nos. 3 and 4; *Spanisches Liederbuch* III, No. 21, with permission of the publishers, C.F. Peters Corporation, New York 10016

Theodore Presser Company.
Casella, Alfredo: Eleven Children's Pieces, No. 6, © 1921 by Associated Music Publishers, Inc., New York, renewed 1949 by Yvonne Casella, used by permission of Theodore Presser Company
Giannini, Vittorio: Prelude and Fughetta, © 1958 by Theodore Presser Company, used by permission
Poulenc, Francis: *Chansons Gaillardes* No. 1, Copyright by Heugel, 1926, used by permission of Theodore Presser Company
Schoenberg, Arnold: *Drei Klavierstücke,* Op. 11, © 1910 by Universal Edition, renewed copyright 1938 by Arnold Schoenberg, used by permission of Theodore Presser Company
Webern, Anton: *Drei Gesange,* Op. 23 No. 11, © 1936 by Universal Edition, used by permission of Theodore Presser Company

G. Schirmer, Inc.
Barber, Samuel: Capricorn Concerto for Flute, Oboe, Trumpet and Strings, © 1945 by G. Schirmer, Inc., used by permission
Second Essay for Orchestra, © 1942 by G. Schirmer, Inc., used by permission
Sonata for Piano, © 1950 by G. Schirmer, Inc., reprinted by permission
Foss, Lukas: Four Two-voiced Inventions, © 1938 by G. Schirmer, Inc., reprinted by permission
Franck, Cesar: Sonata for Violin and Piano, © 1915 by G. Schirmer, Inc., used by permission
Fuleihans, Anis: Sonata No. 1, © 1940 by G. Schirmer, Inc., reprinted by permission
Griffes, Charles: Barcarolle, Op. 6 No. 1, © 1915, 1943, by G. Schirmer, Inc., reprinted by permission
The Night Winds, Op. 5 No. 3, © 1915 by G. Schirmer, Inc., reprinted by permission
Harris, Roy: Little Suite, © 1939 by G. Schirmer, Inc., reprinted by permission
Krenek, Ernst: Twelve Short Pieces, © 1939 by G. Schirmer, Inc., used by permission
Schoenberg, Arnold: Fourth String Quartet, © 1939 by G. Schirmer, Inc., used by permission
Schuman, William: Symphony No. 6, © MCMLII by G. Schirmer, Inc., reprinted by permission
Three-Score Set, © 1943 by G. Schirmer, Inc., used by permission

Universal Edition A.G.
Schoenberg, Arnold: Piano Suite Op. 25, used by permission of Universal Edition A.G. and Mrs. Gertrud Schoenberg

Index of Musical Examples

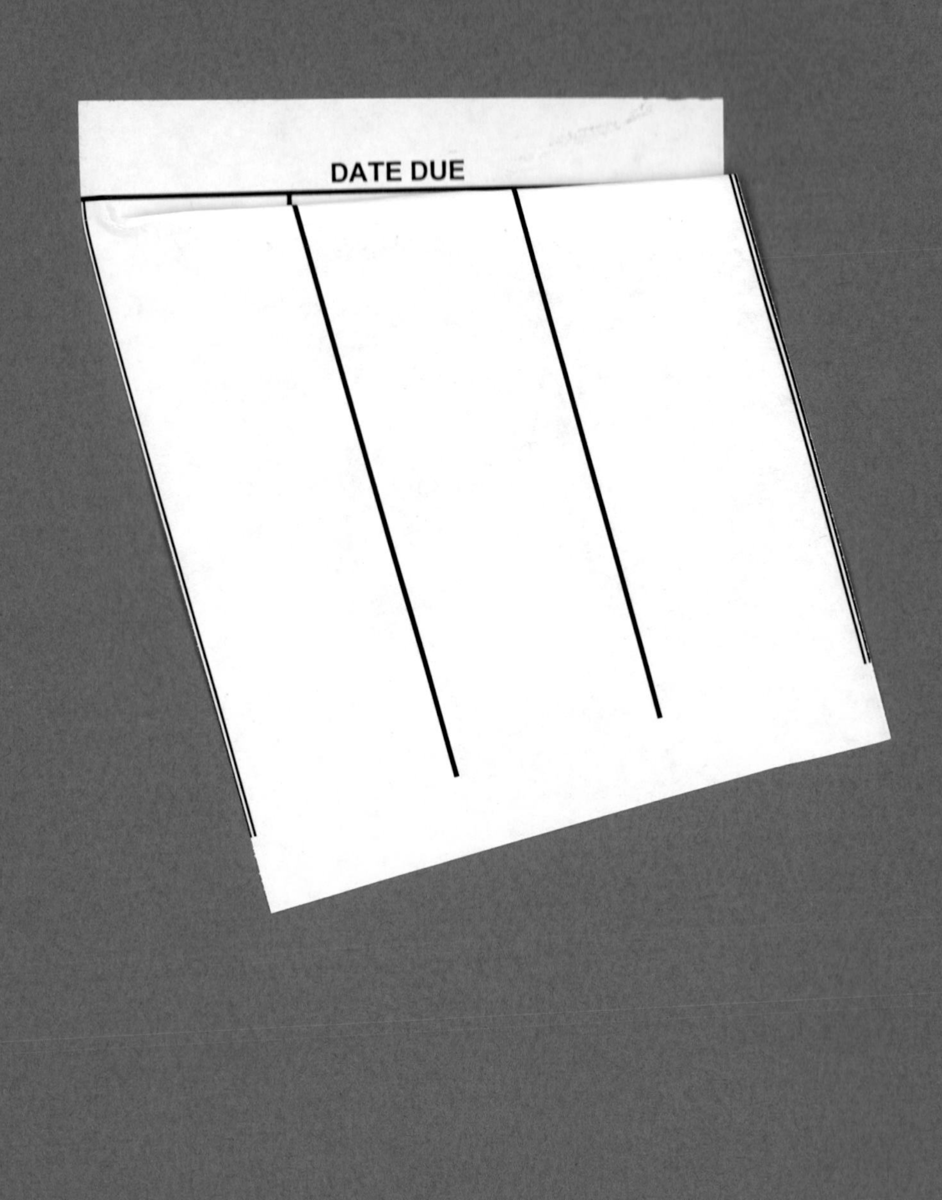
DATE DUE